T. Thomas Fortune, the Afro-American Agitator

New Perspectives on the History of the South

UNIVERSITY PRESS OF FLORIDA

Florida A&M University, Tallahassee
Florida Atlantic University, Boca Raton
Florida Gulf Coast University, Ft. Myers
Florida International University, Miami
Florida State University, Tallahassee
New College of Florida, Sarasota
University of Central Florida, Orlando
University of Florida, Gainesville
University of North Florida, Jacksonville
University of South Florida, Tampa
University of West Florida, Pensacola

T. Thomas Fortune, the Afro-American Agitator

A COLLECTION OF WRITINGS, 1880–1928

Edited by Shawn Leigh Alexander

University Press of Florida
Gainesville/Tallahassee/Tampa/Boca Raton
Pensacola/Orlando/Miami/Jacksonville/Ft. Myers/Sarasota

Copyright 2008 by Shawn Leigh Alexander
Printed in the United States of America on recycled, acid-free paper
All rights reserved

First cloth printing, 2008
First paperback printing, 2010

A record of cataloging-in-publication data is available from the
Library of Congress.
ISBN 978-0-8130-3232-0 (cloth)
ISBN 978-0-8130-3548-2 (pbk.)

The University Press of Florida is the scholarly publishing agency
for the State University System of Florida, comprising Florida
A&M University, Florida Atlantic University, Florida Gulf
Coast University, Florida International University, Florida State
University, New College of Florida, University of Central Florida,
University of Florida, University of North Florida, University of
South Florida, and University of West Florida.

University Press of Florida
15 Northwest 15th Street
Gainesville, FL 32611–2079
http://www.upf.com

For Kelly

Contents

Acknowledgments ix
Introduction: T. Thomas Fortune the Afro-American Agitator xi
Brief Chronology of Fortune's Life xxxix
Prescript: "Our Fortune" xlii

Part 1. Politics, Economics, and Education 1

1. Who Will Own the Soil of the South in the Future (1883) 3
2. Status of the Race (1883) 6
3. The Civil Rights Decision (1883) 15
4. Between Two Fires (1883) 18
5. A New Party/But It Will Be! (1884) 24
6. The Negro in Politics (1886) 27
7. Negrowump (1886) 74
8. The Kind of Education the Afro-American Most Needs (1898) 85
9. The Negro's Place in American Life at the Present Day (1903) 92
10. The Voteless Citizen (1904) 103

Part 2. Civil Rights and Race Leadership 113

11. The Virtue of Agitation (1883) 115
12. Civil Rights and Social Privileges (1886) 118
13. Afro-American League Convention Speech (1890) 134
14. Are We Brave Men or Cowards? (1894) 153
15. Mob Law in the South (1897) 158
16. Immorality of Southern Suffrage Legislation (1898) 165
17. False Theory of Education Cause of Race Demoralization (1904) 171
18. Failure of the Afro-American People to Organize (1906) 180
19. The Breath of Agitation Is Life (1914) 184
20. The Quick and the Dead (1916) 192
21. A Man without a Country (1926) 201
22. Segregation and Neighborhood Agreements (1926) 203

Part 3. Race and the Color Line 207

23. John Brown and Nat. Turner (1889) 209
24. The Color Line (1883) 212

25. The Afro-American (1890) 215
26. Whose Problem Is This? (1894) 221
27. The Latest Color Line (1897) 230
28. Race Absorption (1901) 237
29. Who Are We? Afro-Americans, Colored People or Negroes? (1906) 248
30. We Must Make Literature to Make Public Opinion (1924) 253
31. Separate the Douglass and Lincoln Birthdays (1928) 255

Part 4. Africa, Emigration, and Colonialism 257

32. The World in Africa (1885) 259
33. An African Empire (1887) 261
34. Will the Afro-Americans Return to Africa? (1892) 264
35. The Nationalization of Africa (1895) 271

Postscript 281
Selected Bibliography of Fortune's Writings 283
Selected Bibliography for Further Reading 287
Index 291

Acknowledgments

In the process of anthologizing T. Thomas Fortune's work, I have accrued a number of debts. My thanks to Ernest Allen Jr. and John H. Bracey Jr. for encouraging me to collect Fortune's writings in the first place and for their sage advice and counsel along the way. I would also like to thank my professors and colleagues over the years at the University of Massachusetts. Reading, researching, and writing about African American history is a labor of love that became so much easier when I entered the W.E.B. Du Bois Department of Afro-American Studies at the University of Massachusetts in the fall of 1998. My six years in the department were enlightening and inspiring. The faculty, including Esther M. A. Terry, Ernest Allen Jr., John H. Bracey Jr., Steve Tracy, Manisha Sinha, James Smethurst, Michael Thelwell, William Strickland, and Robert Paul Wolff, have all been supportive of my work and have been willing to have conversations with me on any subject of black history and literature at the drop of a hat. It was truly a mentoring environment.

An ever-growing circle of vigorous intellectuals has inspired me to become a better scholar and writer through their conversations and examples. I would particularly like to thank David W. Blight for his assistance and conversations throughout the years. I wish also to thank those who have lent their support and advice about T. Thomas Fortune over the course of my work on this anthology. I want especially to thank Fitzhugh Brundage, James Danky, Mark Elliott, Jeffery B. Ferguson, Glenda Gilmore, Eddie S. Glaude Jr., David A. Goldberg, Darlene Clark Hine, John Higginson, Jonathon Holloway, Fred Morton, David Roediger, John David Smith, and David W. Wills.

My editors at the University Press of Florida, Jacqueline Kinghorn Brown and Eli Bortz and his assistant, Heather Romans, have provided careful guidance through the entire process of preparing this anthology. I thank them for their assistance and patience. I would also like to thank Meredith Morris-Babb for her early support for the project, and Derek Krissoff, who is no longer with the Press, for his early support and assistance. In addition I thank early readers of the anthology, who gave equal doses of criticism and encouragement.

The bulk of the revisions for this anthology were completed while I was a Cassius Marcellus Clay Post-Doctoral Fellow in the Department of History at Yale University. I would like to thank the Clay family for their generous financial support that aided me in researching and compiling this collection. I am also very grateful to the Department of History's faculty and staff for their support. In addition I thank the staff and associates of the Gilder Lehrman Center for the Study of Slavery, Resistance, and Abolition for supporting and offering critical insight on my scholarship during my time at Yale.

My debt of gratitude also goes to my extended family, the Alexanders, Campbells, and Farrells, for their support and faith over the years. The most important acknowledgment, however, goes to Kelly, my lovely wife: whatever I do is made possible by you. I would like to thank you for the steadfast support, sustaining love, and *patience* you have given me over the years. I also thank you for your willingness to "look this over one more time." Your readings and critiques of this anthology and anything I write improve my work beyond imagination. I thank you for everything. With much love, this book is for you.

T. Thomas Fortune the Afro-American Agitator: A Collection of Writings, 1880–1928

Introduction
The Negro wants to have engraved on his heart, "I will not retreat, I will not yield, I will be heard."

The radical journalist Timothy Thomas Fortune was one of the leading voices of black America from 1880 to 1928, a period of American history marked by tremendous growth and expansion for the nation as a whole. For African Americans, though, it was an era marked by the necessity to turn inward in response to the continued erosion of their rights, privileges, and opportunities, as well as the escalation of lynchings and mob violence.[1] Though recognized by his peers as an individual of great influence and intellect, historians have often neglected T. Thomas Fortune's importance during the period in favor of individuals such as Ida B. Wells-Barnett, Booker T. Washington, Marcus Garvey, and W.E.B. Du Bois.

In his seminal work *Negro Thought in America, 1880–1915: Racial Ideologies in the Age of Booker T. Washington*, August Meier created interest in Fortune and his efforts with his discussion of Fortune's importance as editor, thinker, and ear for Booker T. Washington; but the Wizard of Tuskegee overshadowed his confidant in Meier's overall analysis.[2] Following Meier's lead, Fortune biographer Emma Lou Thornbrough produced a significant work, *T. Thomas Fortune: Militant Journalist*, charting the editor's eventful life, but she too concluded that Washington was the dominant figure in the relationship between the two leaders. Moreover, she seldom highlighted Fortune's intellectual thought and only dealt superficially with the ideological questions that faced Fortune and his peers.[3] One consequence of the influence of these two important works has been that many historians accepted these portrayals of the editor without examining his writings directly and missed the strength that Fortune's peers recognized.

In 1907, when Fortune stepped down from the editorship of the *New York Age*, John Mitchell Jr., editor of the *Richmond Planet* and lifelong friend of Fortune, declared that "one sturdy, patriotic warrior has left us and the entire race should be in tears."[4] Fortune had spent his life fighting for the rights of African Americans, intellectually, politically, financially, and personally. He called out to the race in 1884, declaring, "Our rights, our liberties, must be forced from the States, the counties, the municipalities. . . . Will you do it! Dare you do it!"[5] Fortune dared. Throughout his years as a journalist, he demonstrated by action and through his editorial page that he had the courage to speak whenever his rights or the rights of the race were abridged. He called for race pride, created civil rights organizations, supported industrial and higher education, and spoke out on nearly every issue important to the race throughout his forty-seven-year career. His language was sharp and cutting and his invectives dipped in gall. This collection of writings, the first of its kind, will place Fortune back among his contemporaries as an individual who had a conscious commitment to the best interests of his race.

T. Thomas Fortune was born on October 3, 1856, in Marianna, Jackson County, Florida, one of seven children born to Sarah Jane and Emanuel Fortune. Fortune's parents were slaves of one Ely P. Moore—Sarah Jane was a child of a Seminole Indian and an African American woman of mixed ancestry, while Emanuel was the son of an Irishman, Timothy Fortune, and an African American woman who claimed Anglo-Saxon and Spanish Indian descent as well.[6] After Emancipation, Emanuel took the family name and began working as a shoemaker and tanner and was soon swept into Reconstruction politics.

Emanuel Fortune, like many of his peers, was terrorized for his political activity. During the Ku Klux Klan hearings he testified before the Congressional Committee that he had heard an "indirect expression made by the crackers" that "those damned politicians should be got rid of." He also recalled that he once spoke of John Brown at a political rally and had a pistol pulled on him by a member of the audience.[7]

During the Reconstruction years, young Timothy Fortune witnessed the frustrations of his father and others in the community as they struggled for their rights as citizens. Years later, in his autobiography, serialized in the *Norfolk Journal and Guide* and the *Philadelphia Tribune*, Fortune explained, "There is no condition one can live in which strains the nerves and confuses thought more than a lawless one; a condition in which a person knows that his life is at the mercy of any assassin who can catch him off his guard, . . ." His family, and southern blacks in general, asserted Fortune, "lived in that sort of condition all through the Reconstruction period, when none could call his life his own, and fear and demoralization dominated the lives of all men."[8]

Throughout this period, according to Fortune, "sharp shooters sneaked" around his house every night. But his father, "a dead shot," had built a "trap door under the bed on the first floor" with "a small arsenal in reach" and was prepared to defend his family and home if anyone approached the house.[9] After three individuals were killed for their political activity, however, Emanuel believed the costs had become too high and moved his family from Marianna to Jacksonville in 1869.[10]

During this time, Fortune also began his formal education when he enrolled in a Freedmen's Bureau school in Marianna, where, by his own account, he caught "the book learning fever."[11] A few years later, when his family moved to Jacksonville, he enrolled briefly at the Stanton School. Fortune later attended Howard University in Washington, D.C., for approximately two school terms between 1876 and 1878.[12]

Even more significant than this formal education was the practical education he received working as a printer's assistant for a number of newspapers. He practically grew up in newspaper offices, working at an early age for the *Marianna Courier* and later for the *Tallahassee Sentinel*, the *Jacksonville Courier*, and the *Jacksonville Daily-Times Union*. It was with these papers that Fortune found his love for journalism, educated himself in the ways of the newspaper business, and strengthened his reading and writing skills. Acknowledging the importance of this practical education, Fortune later noted that the "old printing offices were wonderful schools. In them, Horace Greeley and Frederick Douglass learned more than in schools. . . . Mr. Lincoln was educated in the same way. And what Americans made a more valuable contribution to the history of their times than Greeley, Douglass, and Lincoln?" The young Timothy Fortune understood by these examples of "representative" Americans, black and white, that journalism was a vocation that would allow him to have a voice in the nation and advocate for the causes to which he was committed.[13]

While attending Howard University, Fortune began working for the *People's Advocate*, run by John Wesley Cromwell, a graduate of the law department of Howard University and the first African American lawyer to appear before the Interstate Commerce Commission.[14] During his tenure at the *Advocate*, Fortune's intellectual and social horizons were significantly expanded. A great deal of his growth came from his associations with the African American intellectual community identified with the paper as well as with other individuals living and working in Washington. While associated with the *Advocate*, Fortune met and worked with individuals such as Frederick Douglass, Alexander Crummell, Richard T. Greener, George H.

White, William D. Crum, John C. Dancy, Hugh M. Browne, Jesse Lawson, John Edward Bruce, and William Calvin Chase. Although their support for Fortune's social and political positions may have ebbed and flowed over the years, a number of these individuals remained his friends and allies throughout their lifetime. It was also during his time in Washington that Fortune married Carrie C. Smiley, of Jacksonville, Florida. Shortly after their wedding, on February 22, 1877, the two left the city to return to Florida, where Fortune taught in the Florida school system.[15]

After two years of undertaking the "distasteful work of school teaching," the Fortunes moved from Florida to New York City, where T. Thomas hoped to return to journalism.[16] Upon their arrival Fortune took a position with a white paper, the *Weekly Witness*. During the day he worked for the *Witness* and at night he began collaborating with two friends, George W. Parker and Walter J. Sampson, on Parker's journal the *Rumor*. In 1880, less than one year after arriving in the city, Fortune became the editor of the black weekly and transformed it from a weekly tabloid into a more serious journal. Fortune sought to create a "journal to contend for the just rights of his race," explained William Simmons in his biography of Fortune in *Men of Mark*. Fortune "maintained that for a paper to be a power for good among his people, it must be fearless in tone, that its editor should not fail to speak his just convictions, and that he should hold himself aloof from parties and maintain his position untrammeled by parties and party bosses." With this in mind Fortune and his partners turned the *Rumor* into a formidable race paper, which later became the *New York Globe* in 1881.[17]

The *Globe*'s militant and uncompromising position on civil rights was evident in its early editorials. The paper was founded in an era when the social and political revolution of Reconstruction was going backward. From the editorial page Fortune called upon the black community to respond to the declining conditions. In early 1883, Fortune asked his readers, "When murder, usurpation, intimidation, and systematic wrong are practised in upon the violation of law; when the Negro who steals from society what society steals from him under the specious cover of invidious law is hung upon the nearest oak tree, and the white villain who shoots a Negro without provocation is not so much as arrested—when society tolerates such an abnormal state of things, what will the harvest be?" Fortune answered that violence may be the only logical response and that "the people of the United States will find all too soon that they are playing on the top of a volcano which is liable to erupt at any moment."[18]

Later in the same year, Fortune declared, "There is but one way to put a period to the force and violence of a Bourbon—use more force and violence than he uses. As he believes in brute force, he respects it, even when it is used by those he hates and stabs in the dark. . . . Let the colored man stand his ground. There is far more honor in dying like a free man than living like a slave."[19]

Although he advocated the use of violence in self-defense, Fortune also called on the federal government to protect the African American citizen against white violence and the disintegration of rights guaranteed by the Reconstruction amendments. As he explained, "We fully understand the law of the United States—we know that it has the power to make citizens, and we know that it has no power to protect them. . . . That is, we have had, since the close of the war, every possible species of rebellion, usurpation, violence and down-right anarchy in some states, but the federal government has at no time interfered effectually in the interest of good government." He maintained that "this is a government of the people—not white or black people but of the people. It is against this very arrogance that we protest. In a commonwealth of equals such as ours claims to be, no race, class or party has the right to claim to be the 'governing class.'" Until that goal was reached, Fortune argued, the nation would remain contentious.[20]

In such a situation, Fortune urged his readers to stand firm and protest. In an article "The Virtue of Agitation," he declared: "We believe in dissatisfaction; we believe in the manifold virtues of agitation." He urged the community to stand up and be counted, proclaiming that "mental inertia" and "tame submission" was death. African Americans, according to Fortune, needed to understand that "agitation, constant protesting, always standing up to be counted, to be heard, or to be knocked down" was the spirit that "breeds respect and dulls the edge of tyranny."[21]

Following the Supreme Court's decision in the *Civil Rights Cases* of 1883, when the Court declared the Civil Rights Act of 1875 unconstitutional, Fortune used the pages of the *Globe* to express the feeling of betrayal harbored by the African American community. "The colored people in the United States feel today as if they have been baptized in ice water," Fortune exclaimed. Over the next few weeks he continued to articulate disappointment with the state of affairs of the nation and began expressing his desire for the black community to begin moving toward more political independence.

According to Fortune, "The [Republican] party has lived out its usefulness, because it has betrayed the people and joined the hands of the greedy cormorants of society." The editor remarked that in order to enjoy a temporary triumph by placing "a prating, vainglorious, nerveless (wo)man in the

White House" in 1876, the Republican Party had sacrificed the black vote. It should therefore no longer garner the support of the community until it demonstrated that it was willing to stand up for black rights. If the party could not reform, according to Fortune, "it must go."[22]

Fortune's outspoken ideas concerning American politics, the race issue, and the necessity for the African American community's political independence were formed during the early years on the *Globe* and wove a continuous thread throughout his journalistic career. During the same period, the twenty-eight-year-old editor was asked to write a book on the relationship of politics to landownership and labor issues for a series entitled *American Questions*. The book, his first and only book-length study, *Black and White: Land, Labor and Politics in the South*, published in 1884, presented his radical political and social ideas with perspicuity and candor.[23] The work contains a vigorous denunciation of racism as well as an optimistic contention that the black and white class struggle would end oppression in America.

In a period in which industrial slavery and sharecropping had replaced chattel slavery, Fortune believed that black and white laborers throughout the nation had to recognize "that they have *a common cause, a common humanity and a common enemy*."[24] The work also promoted Fortune's idea of political independence: "The hour has come when thoughtful colored men should cease to put their faith upon broken straws; when they should cease to be the willing tools of a treacherous and corrupt policy."[25] He declared, "Let there be no aim of *solidifying* the colored vote.... When colored voters differ among themselves and are found on both sides of local political contests, they will begin to find themselves of some political importance; their votes will be sought, cast, and counted."[26]

He observed that the white South, having asserted its "superiority in the matters of assassination and robbery," had "settled down upon a barrel of dynamite, as [it] did in the days of slavery, and will await the explosion with the same fatuity and self-satisfaction true of him in other days."[27]

Fortune also challenged the nation to institute a more effective educational system. He advocated industrial education, but he understood the importance of higher education as well. Using words that anticipated those of Booker T. Washington, Fortune wrote: "I do not inveigh against higher education; I simply maintain that the sort of education the colored people of the South stand most in need of is *elementary and industrial*. They should be instructed for the work to be done."[28]

Finally, in *Black and White* Fortune argued that the lack of land ownership was a key factor in the failure of blacks as a race to prosper and develop in the South. Much of this analysis demonstrated Fortune's familiarity with social thinkers such as Karl Marx and Henry George; his work has been lauded by many scholars as the first serious economic study of the race issue and one not surpassed until W.E.B. Du Bois' *Black Reconstruction* some fifty years later.[29]

Shortly after the publication of *Black and White*, the *Globe* ceased publication due to financial difficulties. Two weeks later the *New York Freeman* came on the scene, with Fortune as the sole editor and proprietor. With the *Freeman* the editor continued his "battle for justice and fair play for the race."[30] In fact, it was with the *Freeman* that Fortune really blossomed into a leading African American journalist. As the only editor and proprietor of the newspaper, Fortune was free to express his strong positions and unorthodox political views, including support for race pride, black political and economic power, black self-reliance, and political and civil agitation, and for maintaining an independent position in national politics.[31]

During this period, among other issues Fortune also began to argue for reparations for the crimes of whites against Africans. "Whites," he said, "are responsible to the African people of this country for the principal and compound interest" on the wages of each slave.[32] Fortune later would commend the argument of Eugene M. Camp, who also advocated the necessity of reparations, but he urged Camp to appeal to his race and ask them to ante up.[33] Fortune knew, however, that this would be like getting blood from a stone as white Americans would continue to "refuse to refund what they have stolen from" Africa and Africans over the course of two-hundred and fifty years of bondage.[34]

While editing the *Freeman*, Fortune also began writing editorials for the former assistant editor of Horace Greeley's *New York Tribune* and former assistant secretary of war Charles A. Dana's *New York Sun*, one of the leading white newspapers of the country. The editor also began working on a large pamphlet, *The Negro in Politics*, in which he continued to strengthen his case for political independence. In the pamphlet he again assailed the Republican Party for its position on the race issue. As he had done numerous times, Fortune declared that the African American community did not owe the Republican Party any favors. The "truth of history compels the statement," the editor argued, "that the great Emancipator was more of a politician than an Abolitionist; that he freed the slave by proclamation more as a war measure than from motives of love for the slave; that he did not believe that the slave could be made a citizen but should rather be colonized," and, Fortune declared, "had he not been martyrized by a skulking assassin, the treatment of questions affecting us would have been vastly less favorable to us than they have been."[35]

Moreover, Fortune argued, the "party of great moral ideas" had turned a blind eye to the bloodshed from 1865 to 1876 by the midnight riders and skulking assassins. This was unforgivable to the fiery editor, and worse was that not "*one* black leader, *one colored leader* . . . had the manhood, the honest loyalty to race" or "the courage" to speak out against the crime.[36] And now leaders such as Frederick Douglass continued to cast their lot with the party. "Enough!" Fortune argued. Douglass was a wise man but "in no sense a prophet."[37] Fortune urged the African American community to look out for itself first. "Throw away sentimentality in politics," he urged, and act on the motto "Race first; then party."[38] In Fortune's estimation, too many black leaders had sold out the race and themselves in the quest for power. As he explained, "Instead of loving the race, . . . each one of us seeks to get as far away from his African origin as circumstances will permit."[39] And in doing so, black leaders swallow "without a grimace every insult to their manhood or their rights which pseudo friends and avowed enemies have heaped upon them."[40] "You do not need" maintained Fortune, "to be a Democrat or a Republican to force from politicians your honest rights: *You simply need to be men*, conscious of your power."[41]

This political motto was pushed forth in 1887 when the fiery editor called for the creation of a national civil rights organization, the National Afro-American League. He had first raised the issue in early 1884 following the infamous Supreme Court decision on civil rights and the Danville, Virginia, riot of the previous year. With such backward steps taking place, the editor called for an organization that would stand as an "uncompromising defense of the race with which we are identified." "Let us agitate! *agitate!* AGITATE! until the protest shall wake the nation from its indifference," Fortune declared. "You must fight your own battles," he urged. "You must come together. Brave men, men of brains—these must come to the front, and laying aside all selfish and personal aims labor for the upbuilding of the race and the full concession to us of each and every right guaranteed to us by the Constitution of the United States. And the masses must sustain such men."[42]

The idea did not gain much momentum, but after three years of continued deterioration of black America's political and social position in America, Fortune again believed it was necessary to create a civil rights organization to speak for the race.[43] His proposals demanded that unity, cooperation, and organized effort through the apparatus of the Afro-American League become the hallmark of the race's protest against the injustices of the day. "Let the whole race be moved by one impulse," Fortune exclaimed. "Let us make the echoes of our indignant protests ring throughout the world, until injustice shall hide its head in confusion and dismay."[44]

The response of the black community and press to Fortune's call for the creation of a united organization was predominantly favorable. The young Booker T. Washington expressed his enthusiasm when he wrote, "Push the battle to the gate. Let there be no hold-up until a League shall be found in every village." John Mitchell Jr. was also among the many who responded favorably. From his paper he called for black America to "follow words with action.... Let the cry for organization go forth until the country is girdled with organizations of colored men who will be able to demand recognition and force the respect due the law by all men." Mitchell was so encouraged by the prospects of the league idea that he created the first state league in Richmond, Virginia, on June 22, 1887.[45]

That same year Fortune stepped down from editorship of the *Freeman* and handed over the reins to his brother Emanuel and friend and business partner Jerome B. Peterson. The reason for this move was for the financially deficient *Freeman* to gain some much needed political subsidies. This could not happen with its independent editor at the helm. After changing its name to the *Age* and declaring its support for the Republican Party, the newspaper's new editors were able to find funds to cover its operational expenses. At this time, Fortune continued to write signed columns for the *Age*, and became a regular columnist for Dana's *Sun*. It was also around this time that Fortune made the acquaintance of Booker T. Washington. Over the next twenty years the two formed a close but often stormy friendship that lasted until the sale of the *Age* to Washington in 1907. As Fortune explained in 1899, and would reiterate in 1916 in his essay "The Quick and the Dead," he and Washington shared "basic views in the race question":

> He [Washington] is naturally conservative in his views on all questions, while I am naturally radical.
> He speaks always from the point of view of a leader who lives and labors in the South, and who believes that in order to gain one point in manhood development something can well be yielded upon another, and that we are to depend mostly upon education, property and character to pave our way to success; while I speak from the standpoint of

a man who lives and labors in the North, and who does not believe in sacrificing anything that justly belongs to the race of manhood or constitutional rights.[46]

Although the two leaders differed in temperament and methods, they admired one another and found it advantageous to develop a close relationship over the years. In Washington Fortune saw an individual who could connect to the people and the nation in ways he could not. Following his 1895 Atlanta address, Fortune wrote to the principal and said, "It looks like you are our Douglass and I am glad for it. . . . You are the best equipped of the lot of us to be the single figure ahead of the procession. *We must have a head*, and it ought to be in the South."[47]

Over the next twelve years, Fortune aided Washington in attaining his position of leadership. Fortune was a consultant to Washington on a number of issues and was employed as a ghostwriter, often without pay, for many speeches as well as for articles and books credited to Washington, including *A New Negro for a New Century* and *The Negro in Business*. Fortune also devoted much of his time to promoting and working for race organizations in which both individuals were interested, such as the National Negro Business League, the Negro Press Association, and the Afro-American Council. At the same time, Washington was subsidizing the *Age* and often covertly bankrolling the "radical" actions of Fortune, including the activity of the Afro-American Council.[48]

In the late 1880s and early 1890s, Fortune became a leading promoter of the term "Afro-American" as the racial designation for blacks in the United States. The moniker the community would use had become a hotly debated issue in the late-nineteenth and early-twentieth centuries as individuals advocated for the terms "Negro," "Colored," and "Afro-American." Fortune placed himself at the center of much of the debate. He tried, unsuccessfully, to convince Booker T. Washington to use "Afro-American," asking him shortly after his Atlanta Exposition address if he could not see his "way to use the term Afro-American when speaking of the race as a whole."[49] Washington, however, like a number of individuals, including W.E.B. Du Bois, Alexander Crummell, and John E. Bruce, preferred the term "Negro," with a capital "N".[50] Fortune did not, however, believe that the term Negro would ever be given dignity, and, as he explained to Washington in 1895, "We are not all black and colored and yellow, but we are all Afro-American."[51]

In an article published in the *Arena* in 1890, responding to Alabama senator John T. Morgan's claim that the term Afro-American was used for mulattoes in an attempt to gain access into the white families of the nation, Fortune argued that the term was "the most comprehensive and dignified term in sight to cover all the shades of color produced by the anxiety of the white men in the South to 'secure their incorporation' without marriage into the black families of the country!"[52] Years later, in 1906, Fortune argued against Atlanta University professor J.W.E. Bowen's assertion that "Afro-American" was the "least sensible" term to use as a race designation. Fortune argued, "We are African in origin and American in birth . . . therefore by logic of it Afro-Americans."[53] Shortly after the printed debate with Bowen, Fortune spoke before the National Negro Business League and argued:

> You can take your choice of names, BUT I AM AN "AFRO-AMERICAN." All the white newspapers of this country regard you as "negroes" and write Negro with a little "n.". . . They regard you as a common noun. . . . Now I get around that undesirable title by adopting "AFRO-AMERICAN," which calls for the use of two big capital "A's." (Laughter and applause.) I AM A PROPER NOUN, NOT A COMMON NOUN![54]

For about twenty-years Fortune was the chief advocate of the term, attempting to persuade leaders of the race that it was the appropriate racial designation.[55]

Connected to his advocacy for the term "Afro-American," Fortune was invariably a *race man*, promoting race pride and race unity and solidarity. Fortune's pamphlet *Negro in Politics* was essentially a plea to place race before party, where the editor called on the community to have "loyalty to race." Throughout his writings there were often "race pride" statements and arguments put forth for the race to have loyalty and pride. One strong example was in 1899, when Fortune got into a debate with Frederick Douglass Jr. over the race's responsibility in erecting a monument in honor of John Brown. Fortune instead called on the community to honor Nat Turner's memory. As he explained, "Nat. Turner was a black hero. . . . White men care nothing for his memory. We should cherish it." Moreover, Fortune argued, "It is quite remarkable that whenever colored men move that somebody's memory be perpetuated, that somebody's memory is always a white man's."[56] In a follow-up editorial, Fortune retorted, "What we protest against is Negro worship of white men and the memory of white men, to the utter exclusion of colored men equally patriotic and self-sacrificing. It is the absence of race pride and race unity which makes the white man despise black men all the world over."[57]

Demonstrating his race pride further, in 1896, in response to an *Atlanta Constitution* article claiming he had no African blood, the fiery editor retorted, "Just what I am I have never undertaken to determine, but I do not think that I should allow the effort to rob me of the portion of African blood that I possess to pass unchallenged. I want all the blood that rightfully belongs to me."[58]

Although Fortune was a strong advocate of race pride, at times he also advanced the seemingly contradictory idea that miscegenation and intermarriage were the answer to racial problems in the United States. Fortune was not alone in his advocacy of amalgamation, but it did put him in direct opposition with a number of race leaders, including John E. Bruce, Alexander Crummell, W.E.B. Du Bois, and Booker T. Washington.[59]

Fortune made his most definitive and comprehensive statement on racial amalgamation in an article published in the *New York Herald* and *Los Angeles Times* in 1893 and republished, in slightly varying form, in the *AME Church Review* as "Race Absorption" in 1901.[60] Fortune, like Frederick Douglass before him and Charles Chesnutt after, viewed amalgamation and the ultimate loss of racial distinctiveness as the *summum bonum*.[61] Such an argument is in direct conflict with that of Du Bois in his "The Conservation of Races" address before the American Negro Academy in 1897.[62] Both Du Bois and Fortune argued that African Americans were American by birth, in language, political ideas, and religion, but for Du Bois it ended there. Black America's Americanism went no further than that they were "Negroes, members of a vast historic race" and that distinctiveness had to be fostered and celebrated.[63]

Fortune also recognized the historic connections with the "African fatherland," but for him that connection was becoming weaker and Afro-Americans were becoming more fully absorbed into an American race. He argued that, "as far as the Afro-American is concerned, all the other distinct race elements of our citizenship have to confront the same destiny. They are doomed to extinction as race forces and to absorption into the body of the American people." Although this prospect was "repulsive," according to Fortune there was no other option in American society. "If there is a race element in the population incapable of being absorbed," he argued, "that element has no place whatever in American life, and will always be regarded as a national menace. We may desire race homogeneity as a matter of sentiment or pride of race," he asserted, but "a minority race in instant contact with a majority race will be either absorbed or exterminated."[64] Finally, he argued that "absorption has proceeded so far in this country that the Negroid type has been very nearly destroyed. . . . We have a new type in the Afro-American race. It will not revert to the Negroid type, because it has no chance to do so, while the forces of absorption are in operation in every corner of the Republic, whether we like it or not."[65]

Despite Fortune's belief that amalgamation was one of the solutions to the race problem, he never wavered in his struggle for African American civil and political rights, either by action or through the pen, on the editorial page or through his use of moral suasion. Along with his promotion of the term Afro-American and his discussion of race absorption, in the latter part of the nineteenth and the early years of the twentieth centuries, Fortune also became one of the leading voices calling for racial equality. In February 1889, nearly a year and a half after he left, Fortune returned to the editorship of the *Age*. His presence was immediately felt as the paper once again became independent in the political arena, and his sharp tones on race and political issues were noticed and welcomed on the editorial page.

Shortly after his return, he began calling for a national convention of the Afro-American Leagues. Over the past couple of years the organization had been slowly developing on the local and state levels, and he believed the time had come to convene on the national stage. In January 1890, 141 delegates from twenty-three states assembled in Chicago to create the first national civil rights organization. Fortune, the temporary chairman, gave a strong address and immediately set the mood of the event by declaring that the delegation was in Chicago "as representatives of 8,000,000 freemen, who know our rights and have the courage to defend them. We have met here to-day to emphasize the fact that the past condition of dependence and helplessness upon men who have used us for selfish and unholy purposes, who have murdered and robbed and outraged us must be reversed." He believed that the delegates before him represented a group of new abolitionists, and he congratulated them for having been aroused from "the lethargy of the past." The radical editor then set a militant tone for the convention and the league itself when he declared that blacks ought not stand idly by as they were stripped of their rights. They must "fight fire with fire. . . . It is time to face the enemy and fight inch by inch for every right [that the white man] denies us." Fortune was elected secretary of the new organization, and Joseph C. Price, president of Livingston College in North Carolina, was elected president. The following year, Fortune was voted president at the second annual meeting, held in Knoxville, Tennessee.[66]

Over the three years of its existence, the Afro-American League challenged attempts to segregate schools in Ohio, discrimination in insurance rates in New York, and separate coach laws in Tennessee. The organization also tested discrimination in restaurants with T. Thomas Fortune's case against the Trainor Hotel, which became a kind of embarrassing cause célèbre for the movement due to Fortune's reported fondness for drink. Despite small instances of success, however, the national organization folded in the early months of 1893. Fortune cited lack of funds and lack of support by the masses as the reason for the quick demise of the group. Less than a year after proclaiming the organization defunct, he attempted to rekindle the League's flame around the antilynching activities of Ida B. Wells, whom Fortune had employed and supported after she left the South. This was to no avail, however, and ultimately the organization quietly faded away on the national scene.[67]

The League idea, however, did not die, and the organization continued to function on the local and state levels. In the spring of 1898, Alexander Walters, a bishop in the AME Zion church and continuing supporter of the Afro-American League idea, appealed to Fortune to call a meeting of like-minded individuals who understood the necessity of reviving the national civil rights organization. In September, two years after the Supreme Court, in *Plessy v. Ferguson*, approved the "separate but equal" doctrine, and the year the Court upheld Mississippi's disfranchisement legislation in *Williams v. Mississippi*, this desire became a reality. The Afro-American League was reborn on the national level as the Afro-American Council under the leadership of Bishop Alexander Walters, with Fortune as the chairman of the executive committee.[68]

The Council's history is much richer than scholars have argued in the past. Although internal divisions, many of which were brought forth by Washington's involvement, hampered the organization, the group did manage to agitate consistently for the rights of black Americans—often with the secret funding of Washington himself. The activities of the Afro-American Council and those of its predecessor, the Afro-American League, represent an important chapter in African American social and political thought. In a period increasingly dominated by the ideas of industrial education and accommodation, the League and the Council represented the persistence of a protest tradition. The group's platform emphasizing civil rights and suffrage, along with the promotion of racial solidarity, economic nationalism, and self-help, was an attempt to merge together in one organization many of the political ideologies that dominated and divided black intellectual thought at the time. The activities of the two groups, between 1890 and 1910, and the organizations that developed in their wake represent one example of the African American community's various organizational responses to the growing Jim Crow system. More importantly, the activities of the League and Council demonstrate that agitation existed in the "age of accommodation" and prefigured many activities and the style that the National Association for the Advancement of Colored People developed over the twentieth century, especially its "go into the courts and fight it out" mentality.[69]

Fortune was elected president of the Council in 1902, a position he held until 1904, when he left due to a failed fund-raising tour and disillusionment that the masses would ever support the civil rights organization.[70] What was most frustrating for Fortune, however, was the failure of the leaders of the race to actually support one another in their efforts. According to the seasoned activist, the greatest shortcoming of the race was their failure to set aside their egos and learn to follow someone else, everyone was clamoring to be *the* leader, *the* voice of the race. As Fortune explained in an article in the *Colored American Magazine* shortly after his resignation from the Council, the race was suffering from a deadly disease: "We have a condition in which every man feels that he is as good and knows as much as his neighbor, and refuses to follow if not allowed to lead. Demoralization, therefore, paralyzes the thought and action of the race. That is the situation to-day."[71] After resigning his presidency, Fortune continued to work with the organization intermittently, but he never again held a position of leadership.

During his involvement with the Afro-American League and the Council, T. Thomas Fortune took his promotion of agitation beyond the pages of his newspapers and speeches. In the late 1880s the editor fought to integrate schools in New York City and Brooklyn. And in 1891, Fortune won a verdict in his suit against the Trainor Hotel for refusing him service. After the ruling, saloons in the New York region agreed to serve African Americans but would break the glass mug as soon as a black patron had finished his drink. Fortune reacted by entering establishments accompanied by at least ten individuals and would wait until the glasses were broken to order another round—the saloons soon stopped the practice. He was also known to protest, with the flash of a firearm, the practice of overcharging blacks for a nickel glass of beer. In addition, the Afro-American agitator was arrested on a number of occasions throughout his life for challenging discrimination, including among others, in 1897 when he protested his inability to purchase theater tickets in New York City.[72]

Throughout his stint with the Council, Fortune also worked quite closely with Booker T. Washington on the legal cases of the organization, such as suffrage test cases in Louisiana in 1898 and in Alabama in 1903 and 1904.[73]

Additionally, Fortune worked with Washington on the creation of the National Business League, an idea that developed out of the Council's Business Bureau, headed at the time by W.E.B. Du Bois. The editor also supported Washington's views in the pages of the *Age* and wrote occasional speeches and essays for the Tuskegee president. In 1903, despite Fortune's attacks on President Roosevelt's racial politics and appointments, Washington aided him in securing an appointment as special immigrant agent of the Treasury Department. In this position Fortune traveled to the Philippines to study trade conditions.[74]

After the turn of the century, Fortune and the Wizard of Tuskegee began quarreling more frequently over political issues. The two had always agreed that Fortune's editorial page was the place for him to express his views, and oftentimes Fortune's words were coming into conflict with Washington's. Moreover, Washington was increasingly frustrated with the editor's personal habits—Fortune's alcoholism was taking control over his life in the new century, and his financial unreliability was becoming excessive. In 1907 Washington gained financial control of the *Age*, one of the many papers he subsidized, and Fortune was removed as editor. Later that year Fortune suffered a nervous breakdown from which he never really recovered.[75]

After the *Age*, Fortune continued working in the world of journalism and often used his pen to agitate for the social and political rights of African Americans as well as to offer comments on the cultural, economic, social, and political development of the race. He kept writing for the *New York Sun* until 1914, when he moved to Washington, D.C., to establish the short-lived *Washington Sun*. During the first two decades of the twentieth century, he also published in a number of black and white journals, magazines, and newspapers, including, among others, *AME Church Review*, *Colored American Magazine*, *Wichita Searchlight*, *Independent*, and *Favorite Magazine*. In 1909 Fortune once again started his own paper, the *Yonkers Standard*; after its failure, he became the editor for the *Colored American Review* for its final issues. He also assumed the position of associate editor for the *Philadelphia Tribune*, and shortly after that he became affiliated with the *Amsterdam News*. After his move to the District of Columbia and the failure of his *Sun*, he began writing for the *Norfolk Journal and Guide*, and later became a contributing editor for the paper in 1922, a position that he held until his death in 1928. Finally, in 1905 Fortune published a volume of poetry, *Dreams of Life: Miscellaneous Poems*, a collection of published and unpublished poems that he had written over the past twenty-odd years. Among the verses included in the volume were a poem written in honor of the Seminoles called "Fah, Fah," and a moving, long poem for his brother Emanuel. Although his poetry never matched his prose, literary critic and historian Joan R. Sherman notes, "His poetry offers fascinating glimpses of Fortune's ideals and aspirations, of his self-image and his sentimental nature."[76]

During the 1920s Fortune moved back to the New York City region. While maintaining his connection with the *Journal and Guide*, he began writing pieces for the *Inter-State Tattler* and the *Baltimore Afro-American*. In 1923, while he continued to write for various newspapers, Fortune began devoting most of his time to the task of editing the *Negro World*, the organ of Marcus Garvey's Universal Negro Improvement Association.

It may seem odd for some that Fortune, who became involved with Garvey and Garveyism after the UNIA leader was convicted of mail fraud, associated himself with Garvey and his separatist movement. Fortune had many times opposed the emigration rhetoric of Henry McNeal Turner, believing that "the African here is an American by birth, education, and religious belief. He takes only an American's interest in Africa and what goes on there."[77]

Despite his comments, however, Fortune was far from indifferent to Africa. In the 1880s Fortune reacted to the growth of colonization and firmly stood against the actions of the European powers. After England invaded the Sudan, the editor retorted, "England has no business in the Soudan [Sudan] and she will receive no more than her just deserts if every army she sends there is cut to mince meat by the El Mahdi."[78] As European activity on the continent increased, the editor continued to sympathize with those fighting the invaders and predicted redemption in the end. "Bloodshed and usurpations, the rum jug and the Bible—these will be the program of the white race in Africa, for, perhaps, a hundred years," claimed Fortune.

> But, in the course of time, the people will become educated not only in the grasping and cruel nature of the white man, but in the knowledge of their power, their priority ownership in the soil, and the desperation which tyranny and greed ever fail to breed for their own destruction. Out of the convulsions which are sure to come an African Confederation, not unlike that of Germany, will certainly be evolved.... So out of toil and privation and long agony good will will eventually come to the swarthy millions of our father land.[79]

Such sentiment as well as his earlier proclamations of race pride, self-reliance, self-help, and race solidarity certainly aligned him with Garvey's positions. Moreover, Fortune would have agreed with the immediate goals of Garvey and the UNIA. As Garvey explained, "We are organized for the absolute purposes of bettering our condition, industrially, commercially, socially, religiously, and politically . . . to lift ourselves and to demand respect of all humanity."[80]

Thus, in Garvey, Fortune saw many of the principles that he had espoused for a lifetime in action and on his editorial pages. Possibly most important for Fortune was the support, at least in sentiment if not financially, that he witnessed the UNIA receiving. As he explained in an editorial in the *Norfolk Journal and Guide* after Garvey was convicted of mail fraud, "Marcus Garvey is down and out, but he taught us that mass organization of African people is possible because he accomplished it."[81]

In Garvey, Fortune may have seen the black Charles Parnell, the Irish firebrand and leader of the Irish National League, whom he had called for from the pages of the *Globe*, *Freeman*, and *Age*, the leader he desired to push his Afro-American League off the mountaintops and into the valleys. "What was the dramatic element" lacking from the NAACP and the Urban League, "as it was also in the National Afro-American League, the forerunner of them all," asked Fortune from the editorial page of the *Negro World*. "The lacking dramatic element," he wrote, "was the direct and insistent appeal of Mr. Garvey to the race, nationality and self-interest of the Negro people—the conservation of their social, civic and economic values, with the redemption of Africa from the white rule and exploitation and the building of an African State by the Negroes for the Negro in Africa."[82]

Fortune therefore attached himself to the "dramatic" leader he had been searching for, and from the editorial page of Garvey's *Negro World*, the Afro-American agitator continued to push the messages that he had been promoting for forty-two years. He advocated political independence, he spoke out against racial violence, and he argued for race pride. Most important, he maintained that the race had to agitate for their rights, wherever they lived. In a column written in 1926, he warned his readers that, while "nationalization in Africa is the main objective," "in reaching it we cannot sacrifice our social, civil and economic values in the countries where we have been scattered as British subjects, French subjects, and the like, and as citizens of the United States, without privileges and immunities specifically guaranteed by the Federal Constitution, and which no State may 'deny or abridge.'"[83] Two years later he would tell the readers of the *Negro World*, "There are so many privileges and immunities denied us as citizens, . . . that we would be discouraged at the prospect of the long fight we have before us." But Fortune assured the readers that history was on their side, and if they refused to fail and were willing to fight for what was rightfully theirs, they would succeed. "I feel that way about it now at the age of seventy-five [sic] as I did at the age of twenty-one," he proclaimed. "I want all the young and the old people of race to feel about it in the same way."[84]

A short time after this editorial, in early 1928, due to illness, Fortune left the staff of the *Negro World*, moving from his home in Newark, New Jersey, to Philadelphia, to live under the care of his son, Dr. Frederick W. Fortune. On Saturday, June 2, 1928, T. Thomas Fortune died in St. Marks Hospital in Philadelphia. In its obituary of Fortune, the *Amsterdam News* assessed Fortune's life in the following manner:

> New York has lost the greatest Negro leader it ever had. The Negroes of this city, though few of them realize it, owe a large part of their privileges and personal security to T. Thomas Fortune. Never thinking of himself, never counting the cost or the danger, he fought unceasingly. . . . His leadership was brilliant, fearless, aggressive and incorruptible. He never fawned or flattered, never bent his knee for expediency, never sold himself or his people . . . he was always a sincere friend or a sincere enemy.[85]

The following week Kelly Miller, dean of Howard University, published an article in the same paper, "The Passing of T. Thomas Fortune," where he argued that "after all is said and done, Timothy Thomas Fortune represents the best developed journalist that the Negro race has produced in the Western world. His pen knew but one theme—the right of man. His editorials were accepted throughout the journalistic world as the voice of the Negro."[86]

Upon his death, Fortune was clearly recognized as the dean of African American journalism and as a man who knew his rights and had the courage to defend them in print and action. He was a man who followed his own convictions throughout his life. In 1883, following the Supreme Court's ruling on the civil rights cases, he urged his readers to "stand their ground on this civil rights business." From the pages of the *Globe*, he declared, "Let colored men assert their rights, and if they have to die in defending them, or bankrupt themselves, better a dead man or a pauper who dared to assert his manhood," he reasoned, "than a living slink who prized his miserable life and money above the right to live as a man."[87] Throughout his life Fortune stayed the course. He deserves to be placed upon any cenotaph of race leaders.

This volume invites readers to discover, or rediscover, T. Thomas Fortune through his own writings. It contains thirty-five documents, the majority of which have not been reprinted since their initial publication. *Black and White*, Fortune's only book-length study, is not included due to space constraints and the fact that, unlike the majority of the other selections, it has been reprinted in recent years. Included in the volume, however, are a number of editorials and essays that demonstrate many of the same themes Fortune would further explore in the pages of *Black and White*. Also included, reprinted for the first time, is Fortune's insightful pamphlet *The Negro in Politics*. This powerful pamphlet, combined with the thirty-four essays, articles, and editorials written by Fortune from 1880 to his death in 1928, demonstrates the breadth, militancy, and originality of his writings.

In assembling this collection I have selected representative samples that not only capture the voice and rhetoric of T. Thomas Fortune but also provide a rich record of the hopes and dreams, struggles, and frustrations of the fiery editor and the African American community in general as they sought to defend themselves against the nation's backpedaling from the promises of the Reconstruction era and the onset of the Jim Crow system. I have reproduced these writings as they appeared in original form, retaining the original spelling, grammar, capitalization, and punctuation. It is my hope that this collection will resurrect and honor the work of the Afro-American agitator T. Thomas Fortune as well as spur new engagements, and offer a more nuanced view of the role of agitation in the "age of accommodation."

Notes

1. For the epigraph, see "Crisis for the Negro Race," *New York Times*, June 4, 1900. The *Times* quotes Fortune as using the term "Negro"; more than likely, he used the term "Afro-American." In the quote, Fortune is evoking the memory of William Lloyd Garrison, who stated in the first issue of the *Liberator* that "I am in earnest—I will not equivocate—I will not excuse—I will not retreat a single inch—AND I WILL BE HEARD." See *Liberator*, January 1, 1831. For more on the period, see August Meier, *Negro Thought in America, 1880–1915: Racial Ideologies in the Age of Booker T. Washington* (Ann Arbor: University of Michigan Press, 1963); Robert L. Factor, *The Black Response to America: Men, Ideals, and Organization, from Frederick Douglass to the NAACP* (Reading, Mass.: Addison-Wesley, 1970); Emma Lou Thornbrough, *T. Thomas Fortune: Militant Journalist* (Chicago: University of Chicago Press, 1972); Leon F. Litwack, *Trouble in Mind: Black Southerners in the Age of Jim Crow* (New York: Alfred A. Knopf, 1998); C. Vann Woodward, *The Strange Career of Jim Crow* (New York: Oxford University Press, 1966); Edward L. Ayers, *The Promise of the New South: Life after Reconstruction* (New York: Oxford University Press, 1992); Michael Perman, *Struggle for Mastery: Disfranchisement in the South,*

1888–1908 (Chapel Hill: University of North Carolina Press, 2001); and Shawn Leigh Alexander, "'We Know Our Rights and Have the Courage to Defend Them': Agitation in the Age of Accommodation, 1883–1909" (Ph.D. diss., University of Massachusetts–Amherst, 2004).

2. Meier, *Negro Thought in America*.
3. Thornbrough, *T. Thomas Fortune*.
4. *New York Age*, October 31, 1907.
5. *New York Freeman*, December 6, 1884 (emphasis in original).
6. *Atlanta Constitution*, December 17, 1896; *Norfolk Journal and Guide*, July 16, 1927; Thornbrough, *T. Thomas Fortune*, 3–4. In his autobiography, serialized in the *Norfolk Journal and Guide*, Fortune states that his great-grandmother "claimed Jewish descent as well." See *Norfolk Journal and Guide*, July 16, 1927.
7. Joint Select Committee to Inquire into the Condition of Affairs in the Late Insurrectionary, *Report of the Joint Select Committee to Inquire into the Condition of Affairs in the Late Insurrectionary States: Made to the Two Houses of Congress February 19, 1872*, vol. 13 (Washington, D.C.: U.S. Government, 1872). Emanuel Fortune's testimony is in 13:94–101. See also Allen W. Trelease, *White Terror: The Ku Klux Klan Conspiracy and Southern Reconstruction* (Baton Rouge: Louisiana State University Press, 1995); and Thornbrough, *T. Thomas Fortune*, 11–19.
8. *Norfolk Journal and Guide*, October 1, 1927. See also Thornbrough, *T. Thomas Fortune*, 18–19.
9. *Norfolk Journal and Guide*, September 3 and October 1, 1927.
10. *Norfolk Journal and Guide*, October 1, 1927. See also Emanuel Fortune's testimony in *Report of the Joint Select Committee*, 13:94. For more on Florida during the period of Reconstruction and beyond, see Paul Ortiz, *Emancipation Betrayed: The Hidden History of Black Organizing and White Violence in Florida from Reconstruction to the Bloody Election of 1920* (Berkeley: University of California Press, 2005). Fortune explained in his memoir that his mother had been a victim of the Ku Klux Klan brutalities, but he did not give any details. See *Norfolk Journal and Guide*, October 22, 1927. One of the individuals killed was Calvin Rogers, and Fortune later wrote a poem about him and his fight; see "Bartow Black," *AME Church Review* 3 (1886): 158–59. For details on Rogers' death, see *Report of the Joint Select Committee*, 13:94, 192.
11. *Norfolk Journal and Guide*, July 23, 1927.
12. Ibid.; Thornbrough, *T. Thomas Fortune*, 24–28.
13. *Norfolk Journal and Guide*, July 23, 1927, and September 10, 1927. See also Thornbrough, *T. Thomas Fortune*, 19–24.
14. Cromwell was also a prominent member of the Bethel Historical and Literary Association and was secretary and a founding member of the American Negro Academy. For more on Cromwell, see I. Garland Penn, *The Afro-American Press and Its Editors* (1891; repr., New York: Arno Press, 1969); Jacqueline M. Moore, *Leading the Race: The Transformation of the Black Elite in the Nation's Capital, 1880–1920* (Charlottesville: University Press of Virginia, 1999); Elizabeth McHenry, *Forgotten Readers: Recovering the Lost History of African-American Literary Societies* (Durham, N.C.: Duke University Press, 2002); Adelaide M. Cromwell, *Unveiled Voices, Unvarnished Memories: The Crom-*

well *Family in Slavery and Segregation, 1692-1972* (Columbia: University of Missouri Press, 2006); and Alfred A. Moss, *The American Negro Academy: Voice of the Talented Tenth* (Baton Rouge: Louisiana State University Press, 1981).

15. Thornbrough, *T. Thomas Fortune*, 24-32.

16. *Norfolk Journal and Guide*, December 3, 1927.

17. Ibid.; William J. Simmons, *Men of Mark; Eminent, Progressive, and Rising* (1887; repr., New York: Arno Press, 1968), 786; Penn, *Afro-American Press*, 133-38; Thornbrough, *T. Thomas Fortune*, 35-67.

18. *New York Globe*, January 13, 1883.

19. Ibid., November 10, 1883.

20. Ibid., February 17, 1883.

21. Ibid., August 18, 1883 (chap. 11 in this volume). See also Thornbrough, *T. Thomas Fortune*, 35-67.

22. *New York Globe*, October 20 and October 27, 1883 (chaps. 3 and 4 in this volume).

23. Timothy Thomas Fortune, *Black and White; Land, Labor, and Politics in the South* (1884; repr., New York: Arno Press, 1968). For reviews of *Black and White*, see the *Nation*, November 27, 1884; *Washington Grit*, September 20, 1884; *Dial*, December 1884; the *Critic*, February 14, 1884; and T. McCants Stewart, "Black and White Reviewed," *AME Church Review* 1 (January 1885): 189-99.

24. Fortune, *Black and White*, 242 (emphasis in original).

25. Ibid., 127.

26. Ibid., 129-30 (emphasis in original).

27. Ibid., 240.

28. Ibid., 81-82 (emphasis in original). Industrial education was strongly advocated in the 1880s for both African Americans and white Americans. Fortune's ideas were greatly influenced by his friend T. McCants Stewart, who had traveled to Liberia and conducted a study of industrial education in Liberia as well as at Hampton Institute in the United States. See T. McCants Stewart, *Liberia: The Americo-African Republic* (New York: Edward C. Jenkins' Sons, 1886). See also Louis R. Harlan, *Separate and Unequal: Public School Campaigns and Racism in the Southern Seaboard States, 1901-1915* (New York: Atheneum, 1969); James D. Anderson, *The Education of Blacks in the South, 1860-1935* (Chapel Hill: University of North Carolina Press, 1988); and Thornbrough, *T. Thomas Fortune*, 74-76. For further discussion of Fortune's position on education, see T. Thomas Fortune, "The Kind of Education the Afro-American Most Needs," *Southern Workman* 27, no. 1 (1898): 4-6 (chap. 8 in this volume); Fortune, "Industrial Education; Will It Solve the Negro Problem," *Colored American Magazine* 7, no. 1 (1904): 13, 15-17; and Fortune, "The College Bred Negro," *Boston Transcript*, May 8, 1900.

29. For more on Fortune's *Black and White*, see Thornbrough, *T. Thomas Fortune*, 69-78; Jean M. Allman and David R. Roediger, "The Early Editorial Career of Timothy Thomas Fortune: Class, Nationalism and Consciousness of Africa," *Afro-Americans in New York Life and History* 6 (July 1982): 39-52 [55]; Jean M. Allman and David R. Roediger, "Black Nationalism and Class Consciousness: T. Thomas Fortune and the *New York Freeman*," *New Left* 3 (Fall 1978): 2-9; and Meier, *Negro Thought in America*. For more

on Fortune's thoughts on Marx and general socialist writings at the time, see *New York Freeman,* February 14, 1885.

30. *New York Freeman,* November 23, 1884.

31. For more on Fortune's editorial career, especially during the years of the *Freeman,* see Thornbrough, *T. Thomas Fortune,* 79–104; Donald E. Drake, "Militancy in Fortune's New York Age," *Journal of Negro History* 55 (October 1970): 307–22; Allman and Roediger, "Black Nationalism," 2–9; and Joan R. Sherman, *Invisible Poets; Afro-Americans of the Nineteenth Century* (Urbana: University of Illinois Press), 144–45.

32. T. Thomas Fortune, "Civil Rights and Social Privileges," *AME Church Review* 2, no. 3 (1886): 119–31.

33. Eugene Marchel Camp, "Our African Contingent," *Forum* 1, no. 6 (1886): 562–71; *New York Freeman,* July 31, 1886.

34. *New York Freeman,* July 31, 1886.

35. Fortune, *The Negro in Politics: Some Pertinent Reflections on the Past and Present Political Status of the Afro-American, Together with a Cursory Investigation into the Motives Which Actuate Partisan Organizations* (New York: Ogilvie and Rowntree, 1886), 15–16. See also Thornbrough, *T. Thomas Fortune,* 96–97, 89. Fortune often harangued the Republican Party and Abraham Lincoln. See, for example, the *New York Globe,* March 17, August 18, October 20 and 27, 1883; *New York Times,* March 14, 1883; *Black and White;* and *Negro World,* February 14, 1925, and September 3, 1927.

36. Fortune, *The Negro in Politics,* 21–26, 24–25.

37. Ibid., 29.

38. Ibid., 58–59, 38.

39. Ibid., 34.

40. Ibid., 60.

41. Ibid., 58.

42. *Hartford Telegram,* reprinted in *New York Globe,* January 19, 1884 (emphasis in original); *New York Freeman,* December 6, 1884. See also Factor, *Black Response to America,* 117–20; Thornbrough, *T. Thomas Fortune,* 106; Meier, *Negro Thought in America;* and Alexander, "We Know Our Rights."

43. For general information about the period, see Rayford Whittingham Logan, *The Betrayal of the Negro: From Rutherford B. Hayes to Woodrow Wilson* (1965; repr., New York: Da Capo Press, 1997); Meier, *Negro Thought in America;* Litwack, *Trouble in Mind;* Factor, *Black Response to America;* Wilson J. Moses, *The Golden Age of Black Nationalism, 1850–1925* (Hampden, Conn.: Archon Books, 1978); Kevin K. Gaines, *Uplifting the Race: Black Leadership, Politics, and Culture in the Twentieth Century* (Chapel Hill: University of North Carolina Press, 1996); Ayers, *Promise of New South;* and Woodward, *Strange Career of Jim Crow.*

44. *New York Freeman,* June 18, 1887. See also Thornbrough, *T. Thomas Fortune;* and Alexander, "We Know Our Rights."

45. *New York Freeman,* June 18, July 9, and September 17, 1887; Thornbrough, *T. Thomas Fortune,* 108; see also Louis R. Harlan et al., *The Booker T. Washington Papers,* 14 vols. (Urbana: University of Illinois Press, 1972–1989), 2:357.

46. *Boston Globe,* January 14, 1899.

47. T. Thomas Fortune to Booker T. Washington, September 26, 1895, *Booker T. Washington Papers*, 4:31 (emphasis in original).

48. Booker T. Washington, N. B. Wood, and Fannie Barrier Williams. *A New Negro for a New Century: An Accurate Up-To-Date Record of the Upward Struggles of the Negro Race* (Chicago: American Publishing House, 1900), Booker T. Washington, *The Negro in Business* (Boston: Hertel, Jenkins, 1907). For more on Fortune and Washington's relationship, see Thornbrough, *T. Thomas Fortune*; Louis R. Harlan, *Booker T. Washington: The Making of a Black Leader, 1856-1901* (New York: Oxford University Press, 1972); Louis R. Harlan, *Booker T. Washington: The Wizard of Tuskegee, 1901-1915* (New York: Oxford University Press, 1983); Meier, *Negro Thought in America*; and Alexander, "We Know Our Rights."

49. T. Thomas Fortune to Booker T. Washington, September 26, 1895, *Booker T. Washington Papers*, 4:31.

50. Alexander Crummell, John Edward Bruce, Booker T. Washington, and W.E.B. Du Bois preferred the term "Negro." Crummell considered the term "Afro-American" "a bastard, milk and water term," and John E. Bruce thought that "Afro-American" and "colored" were terms used by those who were "neither fish, nor fowl, nor good red herring" and any other term than Negro was an effort by "hybrids" to distinguish themselves from others within the race. As the twentieth century progressed, most used "Negro" as long as it was capitalized, "a proper noun" and not a "common noun," as Fortune would argue. Both Du Bois and Washington subscribed to this logic. For Fortune's thoughts on the name debate, see T. Thomas Fortune, "The Latest Color Line," *Liberia Bulletin*, no. 11 (1897): 60-65; "Afro-American or Negro?" *Outlook* 62, no. 6 (1899): 359; "The Afro-American," *Arena* 3, no. 6 (1889): 115-18; "Race Designation," *Appeal* 1906, 2; and "Who Are We: 'Afro-Americans, Colored People, or Negroes?'" *Voice of the Negro* 3, no. 3 (1906): 194-98. For a discussion of the debate over the use of the terms, see, among others, Robert Terrell to John E. Bruce, September 29, 1896, and Alexander Crummell to John E. Bruce, March 22, 1898, *John E. Bruce Papers*, Schomburg Center for Research in Black Culture of the New York Public Library; Booker T. Washington to Hamilton Holt, May 31, 1907, *Booker T. Washington Papers*, Schomburg Center for Research in Black Culture of the New York Public Library; Alexander Walters, *My Life and Work* (New York: Fleming H. Revell, 1917), 200-201; Arius, "The Race Designation: Shall It Be 'Negro' or 'Colored'?" *New York Globe*, December 1, 1883; E. J. Waring, "The Term Afro-American: The Author of the Term States the Grounds of His Authorship," *New York Age*, January 2, 1892; "What's in a Name?" *AME Church Review* 14, no. 3 (1898): 380-81; "Afro-American," St. Paul *Appeal*, May 16, 1891; "A Minuscule," *AME Church Review* 21, no. 2 (1904): 126-40; "Shall Negro Begin with a Capital 'N'?" *AME Church Review* 21, no. 2 (1904): 192-94; "By What Name Shall We Be Called," *Southwestern Christian Advocate*, April 13, 1905; John Daniels, "Afro-American or Negro?" *New York Age*, October 5, 1905; John E. Bruce, "'Negro,' 'Colored,' or 'Afro-American,'" and "Who Are We," in *The Selected Writings of John Edward Bruce: Militant Black Journalist*, ed. Peter Gilbert (New York: Arno Press, 1971), 50-52, 106-8; J.W.E. Bowen, "Who Are We? Africans, Afro-Americans, Colored People, Negroes or American Negroes?" *Voice of the Negro* 3 (1906): 31-36; J.W.E. Bowen, "Mr. Fortune on 'Who Are We'?" *Voice of the Negro* 3 (1906):

215; Henry B. Blackwell, "Colored People Not Negroes," *Colored American Magazine* 15, no. 2 (1909): 110-11; "What Is the Proper Name for the Black Man in America?" *New York Tribune*, June 10, 1906; and "Editorial: Naming the Race," *Alexander's Magazine* 2, no. 2 (1906): 17-18. See also Willard B. Gatewood Jr., *Aristocrats of Color: The Black Elite, 1880-1920* (Bloomington: Indiana University Press, 1990); Glenda Elizabeth Gilmore, *Gender and Jim Crow: Women and the Politics of White Supremacy in North Carolina, 1896-1920* (Chapel Hill: University of North Carolina Press, 1996), 15; Litwack, *Trouble in Mind*, 458-63. For a discussion of the earlier debate on race designation, see Ernest Allen Jr., "Afro-American Identity: Reflections on the Pre-Civil War Era," *Contributions in Black Studies*, no. 7 (1985): 45-93; and Patrick Rael, *Black Identity and Black Protest in the Antebellum North* (Chapel Hill: University of North Carolina Press, 2002).

51. T. Thomas Fortune to Booker T. Washington, September 26, 1895, *Booker T. Washington Papers*, 4:31. Fortune did, however, emphatically attach himself to the race. After the *Atlanta Constitution* published an article claiming that he had no "African blood," Fortune wrote to the paper declaring himself a member of the race and stating, "I want all the blood that rightly belongs to me." See "T. Thomas Fortune: Philanthropist and Man of Genius; Who Is Laboring for the Negro's Advancement," *Atlanta Constitution*, September 27, 1896; and T. Thomas Fortune, "Fortune Has African Blood," *Atlanta Constitution*, December 17, 1896.

52. T. Thomas Fortune, "Afro-American," *Arena* 3 (December 1890), 115-18 (chap. 25 in this volume). For Morgan's article, see John T. Morgan, "The Race Question in the United States," *Arena* 10 (1890): 395-98.

53. J.W.E. Bowen, "Who Are We?" *Voice of the Negro* 3 (January 1906): 32; Fortune, "Who Are We?" *Voice of the Negro* 3 (March 1906): 197-98 (chap. 29 in this volume); J.W.E. Bowen, "Mr. Fortune on 'Who Are We?'" *Voice of the Negro* 3 (1906): 215.

54. National Negro Business League, *Report of the Seventh Annual Convention* (Boston: Charles Alexander Book and Job Printer, 1906), 156.

55. Thornbrough, *T. Thomas Fortune*, 131-35.

56. *New York Age*, January 12, 1889 (chap. 23 in this volume).

57. *New York Age*, January 29, 1889 (chap. 23 in this volume).

58. *Atlanta Constitution*, December 17, 1896. Fortune is responding to the article "T. Thomas Fortune: Philanthropist and Man of Genius," which had appeared in the *Atlanta Constitution* on September 27.

59. See Meier, *Negro Thought in America*; Thornbrough, *T. Thomas Fortune*; Harlan, *Making of a Black Leader*; Wilson Jeremiah Moses, *Alexander Crummell: A Study of Civilization and Discontent* (New York: Oxford University Press, 1989); Ralph L. Crowder, *John Edward Bruce: Politician, Journalist, and Self-Trained Historian of the African Diaspora* (New York: New York University Press, 2004); and David Levering Lewis, *W.E.B. Du Bois: Biography of a Race, 1868-1919* (New York: Henry Holt, 1993).

60. *New York Herald*, July 9, 1893; *Los Angeles Times*, July 16, 1893; T. Thomas Fortune, "Race Absorption," *AME Church Review* 18, no. 1 (1901): 54-66 (chap. 28 in this volume).

61. Frederick Douglass, "The Color Line," *North American Review* 132, no. 6 (1886): 567-77; Douglass, "The Future of the Colored Race," *North American Review* 141, no. 5

(1886): 437–40; Charles W. Chesnutt, "The Future American," *Boston Transcript*, August 18, August 25, and September 1, 1900.

62. W.E.B. Du Bois, *The Conservation of Races*, American Negro Academy Occasional Papers, no. 2 (Washington, D.C.: American Negro Academy, 1897). See also Lewis, *Biography of a Race*.

63. Du Bois, "The Conservation of Races."

64. Fortune, "Race Absorption," 65.

65. Ibid.

66. *Official Compilation of Proceedings of the Afro-American League National Convention, January 15, 16, 17, 1890* (Chicago: J. C. Battles and R. B. Cabbell, 1890), 8, 12 (chap. 13 in this volume). See also Alexander, "We Know Our Rights"; and Thornbrough, *T. Thomas Fortune*, 105–35.

67. See Alexander, "We Know Our Rights." For information on Wells, see Ida B. Wells-Barnett, *Crusade for Justice: The Autobiography of Ida B. Wells*, ed. Alfreda M. Duster (Chicago: University of Chicago Press, 1970); Ida B. Wells-Barnett, *Southern Horrors and Other Writings: The Anti-Lynching Campaign of Ida B. Wells, 1892–1900*, ed. Jacqueline Jones Royster (Boston: Bedford Books, 1997); Linda O. McMurry, *To Keep the Waters Troubled: The Life of Ida B. Wells* (New York: Oxford University Press, 1998); and Patricia A. Schechter, *Ida B. Wells-Barnett and American Reform, 1880–1930* (Chapel Hill: University of North Carolina Press, 2001).

68. Alexander, "We Know Our Rights." For information on the period, see Meier, *Negro Thought in America*; and Logan, *Betrayal of the Negro*. For the two cases, see *Plessy v. Ferguson*, 163 U.S. 537 (1896) and *Williams v. Mississippi*, 170 U.S. 213 (1898).

69. Alexander, "We Know Our Rights."

70. T. Thomas Fortune, "The Quick and the Dead," *AME Church Review* 32, no. 4 (1916): 247–52 (chap. 20 in this volume).

71. T. Thomas Fortune, "False Theory of Education Cause of Race Demoralization," *Colored American Magazine* 7, no. 7 (1904): 473–78 (chap. 17 in this volume).

72. Thornbrough, *T. Thomas Fortune*; Alexander, "We Know Our Rights"; *New York Amsterdam News*, June 6, 1928; and *New York Sun*, November 1, 1897.

73. See Shawn Leigh Alexander, "The Afro-American Council and Its Challenge of Louisiana's Grandfather Clause," in *Radicalism in the South since Reconstruction*, ed. Chris Green, Rachel Rubin, and James Smethurst, 13–38 (New York: Palgrave, 2006). See also Thornbrough, *T. Thomas Fortune*; Alexander, "We Know Our Rights"; Meier, *Negro Thought in America*; Louis R. Harlan, *Making of a Black Leader*; and Harlan, *Wizard of Tuskegee*.

74. See Thornbrough, *T. Thomas Fortune*; Alexander, "We Know Our Rights"; Meier, *Negro Thought in America*; Louis R. Harlan, *Making of a Black Leader*; and Harlan, *Wizard of Tuskegee*. For details on Fortune's trip to the Philippines, see T. Thomas Fortune, "The Filipino [Part I]," *Voice of the Negro* 1 (March 1904): 93–99; "The Filipino [Part II]," *Voice of the Negro* 1 (May 1904): 199–203; and "The Filipino—across Luzon [Part III]," *Voice of the Negro* 1 (June 1904): 240–46. See also Thornbrough, *T. Thomas Fortune*.

75. Thornbrough, *T. Thomas Fortune*, 177–321. See also Harlan, *Making of a Black Leader*; Harlan, *Wizard of Tuskegee*; Louis R. Harlan, "Booker T. Washington and the

Voice of the Negro, 1904-1907," *Journal of Southern History* 45, no. 1 (1979): 45-62; Meier, *Negro Thought in America*; August Meier, "Booker T. Washington and the Negro Press: With Special Reference to the Colored American Magazine," *Journal of Negro History* 38, no. 1 (1953): 67-90.

76. Sherman, *Invisible Poets*, 150.

77. Fortune, "Race Absorption," 61-62 (chap. 28 in this volume). For more on his attacks on the emigration and colonization plans of individuals such as Turner, see Fortune, "Will the Afro-American Return to Africa?" *AME Church Review* 8, no. 4 (1892): 387-91 (chap. 34 in this volume). See also Fortune, "The Latest Color Line," *Liberia Bulletin*, no. 11 (1897): 60-65 (chap. 27 in this volume); *New York Age*, January 4, 11, and 18, 1890; *New York Sun*, April 5 and August 30, 1896; and *Boston Transcript*, May 10, 1900.

78. *New York Freeman*, February 14, 1885 (chap. 32 in this volume).

79. *New York Freeman*, January 18, 1887 (chap. 33 in this volume).

80. Marcus Garvey, *Philosophy and Opinions of Marcus Garvey*, ed. Amy Jacques Garvey (New York: Atheneum, 1992).

81. *Norfolk Journal and Guide*, June 30, 1923.

82. *Negro World*, July 3, 1927.

83. Ibid., July 3, 1926.

84. Ibid., February 11, 1928.

85. New York *Amsterdam News*, June 6, 1928. For more eulogies of Fortune, see obituaries in *Negro World*, June 16, 1928; *New York Age*, June 9, 1928; *Philadelphia Tribune*, June 7, 1928; and *Pittsburgh Courier*, June 9, 1928.

86. New York *Amsterdam News*, June 13, 1928.

87. *New York Globe*, December 20, 1883.

Brief Chronology of T. Thomas Fortune's Life

1856
Born October 3 in Marianna, Jackson County, Florida
1869
Fortune family moves from Marianna to Jacksonville, Florida
1876
Fortune enrolls at Howard University in Washington, D.C.
Begins working for John W. Cromwell's *People's Advocate* in Washington, D.C.
1877
Marries Carrie C. Smiley
1878
Fortune and Carrie move back to Florida, where he teaches school for a brief period
Carrie gives birth to a son (name unknown) who dies as an infant
1879
Moves to New York City, where he begins working for the *Weekly Witness* and also collaborates with George W. Parker and Walter J. Sampson on *Rumor*
1881
Starts the *New York Globe* with George W. Parker and Walter J. Sampson
1883
The *Globe* claims six thousand subscribers
Carrie gives birth to a girl, Jessie
1884
Publishes *Black and White: Land, Labor and Politics in the South*
Fortune and his partners cease publication of the *Globe*
In December, after the demise of the *Globe*, Fortune starts the *Freeman*. The editor also begins writing editorials for Charles Dana's *New York Sun*
Carrie gives birth to a second son, Stewart
1886
Publishes pamphlet *Negro in Politics*
1887
Calls for the creation of a national civil rights organization, the National Afro-American League

Steps down from editorship of the *Freeman*. Paper is renamed the *Age*, under Fortune's brother Emanuel and Jerome B. Peterson. Fortune increases his writings in the *Sun* and publishes weekly columns in the *Age*

1888

Son Stewart dies from pneumonia, contracted during the blizzard of 1888

1889

Returns to editorship of the *Age* after the death of his brother Emanuel, who contracted pneumonia during the blizzard of 1888

1890

Formulates the Afro-American League in Chicago. Fortune elected chairman of the executive committee

Institutes discrimination suit against the Trainor Hotel

1891

Elected president of the Afro-American League

Carrie gives birth to their fourth child and third son, Frederick

Fortune and lawyer T. McCants Stewart win case against the Trainor Hotel

1893

Announces demise of the Afro-American League on the national level

1894

Supports Ida B. Wells' development of antilynching activities. Tries to reorganize the Afro-American League around Wells' activities

New York Court of Appeals upholds Fortune's victory against the Trainor Hotel

1898

Fortune and others reorganize the Afro-American League as the Afro-American Council. Elected chairman of its executive committee

1900

Supports Booker T. Washington in the creation of the National Negro Business League

1902

Becomes president of the Afro-American Council

Appointed special envoy to the Pacific for Theodore Roosevelt's administration

1904

Steps down from the presidency of the Afro-American Council

Begins aiding Fred Moore in editing the *Colored American Magazine* and writing an editorial column, "The Way of the World"

1905

Publishes a volume of poetry, *Dreams of Life: Miscellaneous Poems*

1906
Ceases his partnership with the *Colored American Magazine*
Fortune and Carrie separate
1907
Fortune loses control of the *Age*. Has a nervous breakdown
1910
Becomes a regular contributor to the *Philadelphia Tribune* and the *Amsterdam News*
1914
Moves to Washington, D.C., and begins publishing the short-lived *Washington Sun*
1915
Moves to Indianapolis to join the *Indianapolis Ledger*
By the end of the year, after the *Ledger* ceases publication, Fortune moves back east
1916
Becomes editor of the *Colored American Review*
1919
Begins publishing editorials for the *Norfolk Journal and Guide*
1920
Becomes contributing editor of the *Inter-State Tattler*
1923
Becomes editor of Marcus Garvey's *Negro World*
1928
Dies June 2 in Philadelphia, under the care of his son Dr. Frederick Fortune

Prescript

Our Fortune

Great warrior, seared and battle scarred
By conflicts rife, prolonged and hard,
    Why sheathe thy sword?
But now we hear the distant peal,
And see the awful flash of steel
    Of servile hordes.
Emboldened by the painful pause,
Of thy great work in freedom's cause;
    For thee they feared.
In thee they saw a master mind,
Too brave to cringe and stand behind
    A hireling herd.
When yellow journals' torrid breath,
Surcharged the sulphurous air with death,
    We did not fear.
We could exclaim, although the blast
The old ship threatened shroud and mast:
    "Fortune is there!"
A helmsman seasoned, true as steel,
Who never quakes in woe or weal;
    We'll not despair!
Blow wind, let waves leap mountain high;
    High;
Let lightnings flash athwart the sky;
    "Fortune is there!"
The Saxon had no task to lead
His own; in duty bound to heed
    His stern commands
To rise, and in one solid band,
Unite to keep their native land
    In Saxon hands.

'Twas thine the work to educate,
And lift thine own from low estate—
    From bondage free.
Fetters of unbelief to break,
Race pride and courage to awake,
    Thy worth to see.
The NEW YORK AGE from age to age
Must live; a legacy each page.
Although thy magic pen may rust,
The hand which grasped it turn to dust,
Thy heroic service, manner, bold,
In grateful hearts shall ne'er grow old.
A crown of glory be thy need.
With Dana, Godwin, Greeley, Reed,
Thy name upon the deathless scroll
    Must live till ages cease to roll.

"Jack Thorne," Brooklyn, November 6, 1907, *New York Age*, November 7, 1907

PART 1

Politics, Economics, and Education

In Freedom's Cause

> In Freedom's Cause—who dies in vain?
> Let cowards wear the slaver's chain!
> First know your rights, then let him die
> Who dares those rights to you deny,
>   There is no law, but law of right!
>   All other law is made
>   By brutal conquest, selfish might,
>   The masses to degrade.
> Let Freemen face their brutal foes,
> Where'er the tyrants deal the blows,
>   And pause not in the fray
>   Till they have won the day!
> And some must die; but others free
>   Will live to reap the victory!

New York Age, January 5, 1889

1

Who Will Own the Soil of the South in the Future

In an editorial entitled "Who Will Own the Soil of the South in the Future," published in both the *Christian Recorder* and the *Globe*, Fortune sets forth a position on landownership that he would further develop in *Black and White*. Heavily influenced by the ideas of Henry George and other agrarian radicals, Fortune believed that there needed to be a fundamental change in the ownership of land. In this editorial, he demonstrates his frustration with the monopoly of landownership and his belief that land was the common property of the people and should be available to those who cultivate the soil. Although he does not call for the complete abolition of private property in land, as he would in *Black and White*, one can see the germination of Fortune's idea more than a year before the publication of his larger study.

Who Will Own the Soil of the South in the Future—*New York Globe*, **April 28, 1883**

In the discussion of the labor problem in the South, the writers on the question have a delightful way of drawing conclusions that is really amusing. All of them speak of whites as the landowners and employers of labor—likely to remain such—and of the blacks as the laboring class—likely to remain such. Now, nothing could be more illusory than this cranksided picture, which nine white men in ten think not only just but likely to remain so. But there is another side to the picture—a black side, if you will.

Absolute individual ownership in the soil, while it may be, and I think is, wrong in principle, is recognized in law as just and consistent, and any man, whatever be his color, has the right to the exclusion of all others. It has been admitted time and again that the blacks are pre-eminently the farm laborers of the South; that to all intents and purposes they have practically a monopoly of this extensive and rich branch of industry. It is susceptible of demonstration that this class of our population are investing largely in land, that they are doing this more and more as the years come and go; and the possibilities are that, with vastly diffused intelligence and advanced notions of the value and necessity of wealth, the power and immunity which accrue from ownership of the soil, this class, pre-eminently agriculturally disposed, will invest yet more extensively in the soil of the South—that they will not remain always the hewers of wood and drawers of water. Any conclusion based upon the future of the South in which the colored man is put down as the perpetual foot-ball of other men, whose only essential difference is a white skin, is false in conception and will confound the vanity and the hope wrapped up in it.

The colored man is a factor in the South whose present worth has been willfully and maliciously ignored and whose future worth it is not easy to estimate. Henry George[1] got confused just here when he deduced (in his book "Progress and Poverty") that the whites would find free black labor cheaper in the end than was slave labor. He premised, of course, that the whites would always control the soil, hence his false deduction. He who owns the soil owns him who works on it. But where all have an equal chance to buy as well as to work, the laborer will eventually become the employer; this more especially where such laborer enjoys practically a monopoly of the labor market, as is the case in the South. Looking at it from this standpoint, and recognizing the fact that it is natural for man to assert his mastery over his time and the produce of his labor wherever and whenever possible, it is an open question who will own the bulk of the soil of the South a century hence. I know of a half dozen colored men in Florida whose aggregated acres foot up to two thousand; the colored men of Georgia must control some five thousand to eight thousand acres, if newspapers statements are correct; and the same is true all through the South. The tendency among Southern colored men is to own the land they till. The more intelligence they have the more the tendency develops. And it is natural.

Professor Gilliam's scare-crow article in the *Popular Science Monthly*[2] while full of imposing absurdities, yet contains many truths whose possible verification nauseates the stomachs of that class of American numbskulls who hope and pray that the colored man will find in the same sort of freedom other people grow fat on, the elements of stagnation, disintegration and death. I believe in an intense practical manhood. A few years ago we were forced to wear a chain, to come at another man's command. We had no other incentive to labor than the lash, no other reward for labor than a bare subsistence. How is it to-day? The boundless field of labor and the market rate of wages are spread before us. We have the same opportunity to labor, to save and acquire land and money that others have. Are we less susceptible to the allurements of these inducements than other men? I think not. I think that the mental, the same as physical make-up of the race is the same as the intolerable, the arrogant and the pretentious white fellow who claims a monopoly of all the virtues of the head and the heart.

I believe that absolute individual ownership in the soil is contrary to the intentions of Providence; I believe that one man has as much right in the soil as another; I believe that land should be as much the common property as air and water; I believe that crime and pauperism spring from the system by which one can claim an absolute ownership in what nature intended should be common property. But these views are contrary to the established order of things. Our sociology upholds ownership, absolute and inalienable, in the soil, and as all wealth springs from this source, and as wealth is the demarcation line which defines man's position in the social scale, we do wisely to adjust ourselves to the order of things which governs us if we do not govern them. Then let every colored man get as much land as he can and let him keep as much of it as he can.

Notes

1. Henry George (1839–1897) was a political economist who proposed the "single tax" on land. He is the author of the influential *Progress and Poverty* (1879) and *Social Problems* (1886).

2. E. W. Gilliam, "African in the United States," *Popular Science Monthly* 22 (February 1883): 433–44. Gilliam furthered his argument a year later in "The African Problem," *North American Review* 139 (November 1884): 414–30.

2

Status of the Race

On September 17, 1883, Fortune was called before Senator Henry W. Blair's Committee on Education and Labor to present his facts and opinions on the "status of the race." In his testimony one can find many of the themes that he would develop further in *Black and White*, especially on education and the status of the African American laborer. Fortune, like a number of the other African American witnesses, took the opportunity to protest discrimination in public facilities and other wrongs suffered by the black population in the South. Fortune, in particular, seized the opportunity to expose the wrongs of the growing convict lease program.

Status of the Race —*New York Globe*, September 22, 1883; *Report of the Committee of the Senate upon the Relations between Labor and Capital* (Washington, D.C., 1885), 2:522–29

I have been requested by your Honorable Committee [the Education and Labor Committee] to submit the following paper on the status of the Negro population of the United States.

According to the census of 1880 there were in the country 6,580,793 people of African parentage. In 1790, according to the first census, there were only 757,208. The increase of population from 1850 to 1860 under the slave regime, was 22.1 per cent; from 1870 to 1880, 34.8. The increase is and will continue to be healthy in the state of freedom, since human effort and propagation have their greatest expansion in a state of freedom from all tyranny and narrowness. If we were freer our growth and expansion would be far greater. As it is we are fettered by the State and repressed by individuals and corporations, we are not free as other men to come and go to make and spend, to enjoy the protection of the law or to share, in short, in all the rights and immunities of Government. Like the Irish subjects of Great Britain, we have received everything from our country but justice—that she has always and still denies to us in equal degree with others of our fellow-citizens.

This vast body of our population has, since the foundation of our Republic, been a subject of the gravest moment—having put brother against brother and father against son in the home, in the halls of legislation and on the field of battle. But in all the conflict the Negro has never received full justice at the hands of the Government—or Federal or State—and he does not receive it to-day in any portion of the vast territory of this country.

At the close of the Great Rebellion the Negro population of the country was thrown upon its own resources, as it were; made men and citizens at one stroke of the pen; poor, ignorant beyond measure, cowed and debauched by the foul iniquity of slavery, and surrounded by a hostile public sentiment, which vented itself in all sorts of intolerance—in assassination, intimidation and open robbery. Assassination for political causes has ceased, because no longer necessary, but intimidation and robbery remain. So that the Negro population of the South is to-day, as it was thirty years ago, a disturbing element, requiring a wise statesmanship to properly adjust it. But instead of attempting honestly to adjust it, the people of the country constantly talk of eliminating the problem from political discussion and consideration—as if it were possible to heal a cancer by leaving it severely alone.

The greatest misfortune which the Government of the United States placed upon us up to the close of the war was the almost universal illiteracy of the masses—illiteracy which was designed and made irrevocable by most stringent of statutory enactments. Our intellectual and material poverty, absolute bankruptcy, were caused by the government, which closed the book of knowledge and denied us the common right to accumulate. We are not responsible even to-day for the wide spread poverty which obtains among us. We have not yet facilities and aptitude to amass vast fortunes by speculation and peculation, but we are learning to emulate the virtuous example of our white fellow citizens in this regard.

Considering honestly our beginning the following facts are of interest. From the Bureau of Statistics we find that the enrollment of colored youths, as far as reported by State School officers, for the year 1880, was 784,709. Per cent of the colored youth of school age enrolled, about 48. Colored school teachers in the United States,—males, 10,520; females, 5,314; total, 15,834. Normal schools for colored youth, 44; teachers in these, 227; pupils, 7,408. High schools, or academic, for them 36; teachers in them, 120; pupils, 5,327. Universities and colleges for the race 15; teachers in them, 119; students, 1,717. Schools of Theology for them, 22; teachers, in them, 65; pupils reported, 880. Schools of Law, 3; teachers in these schools, 10; pupils in the same, 33. Schools of Medicine, 2, with 17 teachers and 87 pupils.

According to the census of 1880 there was in the South a total school population of 5,426,890—3,758,480 were white and 1,668,410 were colored; enrolled, white, 2,013,684; colored, 685,942. The total appropriation for school purposes by these States is set down at $12,181,602—being the beggarly pittance of $2.26 per capita. Only 31 per cent of white and 26 per cent of the colored children of Louisiana avail themselves of the public school advantages, while the State appropriates the munificent sum of $529,065 for educational purposes, being $1.94 per capita. Florida, with a school population of 82,606, appropriates only $134,880 for school population of 38,800, appropriates $368,343, and 61 per cent of the white and 73 per cent of the colored school population are enrolled, the per capita being $9.49. In the District of Columbia 5.7 per cent of the school population cannot read and 18.8 per cent cannot write, while in Florida 38 per cent cannot read and 43.4 per cent cannot write. These facts are suggestive. Aside from the vastly inadequate work being done in the South by States, it should not be omitted here that Northern churches and organizations and individuals contribute quite as much annually to the education of the Freedmen as the States, but the contributions from these sources are uncertain and fluctuating. Yet after all that is done is considered, it must be conceded that ignorance is growing in the South as rank as the grasses that choke her cotton and corn. Whether it be the poverty of the States or disinclination of the people to tax themselves for the rooting out of illiteracy and the vices it breeds, I am not prepared to say; but that the evil is vast and menacing all must concede.

The rural journals of the South, which are usually ignorant of the first principles of political economy, object to popular education on the ground that the blacks pay no taxes, supremely oblivious that the laboring classes of every country always create capital and pay in rental the taxes of the land owner, who has no more inherent right in ownership of the soil then the laborer. What the State refuses to pay for education it gladly pays for penitentiaries, preferring a pound of remedy to an ounce of cure.

It must not be forgotten that the teachers employed in the South labor under many and serious disadvantages which react with fearful effect upon the pupils. Because of the miserly compensation and the shortness of the school term together with the social ostracisms of the South, competent teachers cannot and are not always secured. The school term in the South does not average more than 4 months for colored schools, and I doubt much if the salary will average thirty dollars per month—subject to further reduction on school warrants by scalpers and others. At least this was my unfortunate experience in Florida as a teacher. And then these school teachers are subject to all sorts of persecutions from school superintendents and trustees and the braggarts of the town. The position of a colored school teacher in the South is not a desirable one from any standpoint. Before I would teach again in the South I would drive a dray on the public streets.

I do not believe in centralization of Government. I know the evils which come upon the people by merging into the hands of the few men who must of necessity administer Government more power than they should have. And yet I am thoroughly convinced that the education of the people is a legitimate function of Government and is not in any sense a feature of centralization, but is eminently a feature of self preservation. We make lavish appropriations for harbors, forts, the navy and the army for the common defense, but illiteracy is a more insidious foe from within than any that can or will assail us from without.

I would advocate the creation of a Bureau of Education, with four commissioners, one for each section, and I would advocate an annual appropriation of $25,000,000 to $30,000,000, to be applied according to the ratio of illiteracy. It could be applied through the superintendents of Education of the several States, subject to the approval of the commissioner or commissioners, or by some other method more effective and satisfactory.

The desire of the colored people of the South to take advantage of educational opportunities is too well known and too conclusively demonstrated to require more than passing notice.

It may be pertinent to say here that there are in this country 7,646 colored ministers of all denominations and a church membership of nearly 2,000,000 souls.

It is often charged that the race is lazy, but I think the charge absurd. If it is lazy now what must it have been under the system of slavery? It is undeniable that the Negroes of Georgia own 680,000 acres of land, cut up into small farms, and in the cotton States they own and cultivate 2,680,000 acres. Dr. Alexander Crummell,[1] in his thoughtful reply to the misrepresentations of Dr. Tucker[2] of Mississippi, says, basing his estimate on the 680,000 acres owned by us in the State of Georgia, "Let us put the figure as low as 400,000 acres for each [meaning Southern] State—for the purchase of farm lands has been a passion everywhere with the freedmen—this 400,000 acres multiplied into 14, i. e. the number of chief Southern States, shows an aggregate of 5,600,000 acres of land, the acquisition of the black race in less than twenty years." Again, we find, that the Freedman's Bank, which was opened in 1865 and closed in 1874, had no less than 61,000 black depositors, the sum total of whose deposits was $56,000,000. Again, from 1857 to 1861, under slave labor, there were produced 18,230,738 bales of cotton; from 1878 to 1882, 27,667,367 bales—being a balance in favor or free labor of 9,436,639 bales. A still more striking illustration is given in the case of the State of South Carolina. In 1849 and 1859 she raised 654,313 bales of cotton with slave labor; in 1879 and 1882, under free labor, she raised 1,153,306—a difference in favor of free labor of 498,993 bales; in 1859 her wheat crop was 1,285,631 bushels, in 1882, 2,973,600—a difference in favor of free labor of 1,687,969 bushels; in 1859, her oat crop was 936,974 bushels, in 1882, 8,094,600—a difference in favor of free labor of 7,057,626 bushels. Speaking of the marvelous and satisfactory figures, the Boston *Herald* of a recent date says: "Free labor, protected in its rights, improved transportation, better fertilization and culture, and the sub-division of the lands, are at the bottom of this wonderful growth."

I have no doubt that if comparisons were made as to the production of other States, like favorable results could be shown. And still there are men who seriously allege that the Negro is lazy. I am free to admit that a large percentum of the Negroes squander much time in fishing and hunting and loafing, still the great mass of the people are honest, steady laborers. They must of necessity be, else how account for the steady increase of production in the South?

Now, in view of these facts it will naturally be asked why the Negro population continues poor and ignorant. The answer is a direct refutation of the statement made to your Honorable Committee on Thursday last by Mr. John C. Calhoun[3] as to the rate of wages and the manner they are paid in the South. The average rate of wages received by a farm laborer in the South is fifty cents, out of which the laborer must feed and clothe his family. He seldom has any rent to pay and he seldom ever sees a cent of money. He is paid in "orders" on some storekeeper friendly to the planter. The laborer cannot negotiate these precarious "orders" at any other than the store indicated. Hence the system of fraud is connived at and practiced to the utter demoralization and impoverishment of the ignorant, helpless laborer. This system of "orders" has reached perfection by the mutual understanding which has grown up between the planter and the storekeeper.

I remember an instance which strikingly illustrates the pernicious features of the system. At a place on the Suwannee River in Florida, there is a large sawmill, owned by a gentleman who also operates a large farm. This man owns the entire town and all the land for miles around. He owns the only store but one in forty miles of the place and will not allow any one else to sell anything. He pays his employees in "orders" on his store; and so expensive is it to live at that place that I knew men who on falling out with the proprietor were compelled to walk away from town because they had been unable to save money to ride. The planters and storekeepers understand their mutual interests so thoroughly that few colored laborers on farms ever get their hands on a dollar bill. I attended a panoramic exhibition at the little colored church at this place once, when the bookkeeper of the firm stood at the door and "passed in" all those who desired, noting the name of each in a little book. When they all passed in he gave the showman an "order" for his money and told him to call at the office the following day and collect, which was done. This sort of things breeds improvidence, but not thriftlessness, because to be improvident, the "orders" must be obtainable and they are only obtainable when the work has been performed.

The system of share labor is equally unsatisfactory to the laborer. He is compelled to give a lien on his unplanted or unharvested crop to be able to run his farm, and his account at the store at the end of the year usually brings him in debt. My father once kept an account in the literal sense, that is to say, he kept an account of the things he "took up" at the store as well as the storekeeper. When the accounts were footed up at the end of the year the thing became serious. The storekeeper had one hundred and fifty dollars more against my father than appeared on the latter's book. Of course there was a wide difference of opinion, but my father settled the account according to his book, and told the merchant he was at liberty to sue for the remainder. But the merchant failed to do it, and his books will show a shortage of $150 to-day, if he has not balanced the account to profit and loss. But, of course, the mass of colored men who farm on shares or labor by the year, and keep an account do not, because they cannot, keep a record of every purchase; and it is by this means that they are swindled and kept forever in debt. I have known honest but ignorant colored men who have lost large farms magnificently accounted by such thievery. The black farmers, and those in other occupations at the South, are robbed year after year by the simplest sort of devices; and the very men who rob them are the loudest in complaint that the Negroes are lazy and improvident. For my part, I am surprised that a large number of them does not go fishing, hunting and loafing.

The artisan and common laborers in the cities of the South fare better, but the wages they receive would be spurned by the white artisans and day laborers of any Northern or Western city. Masons and carpenters average, not $2.50 to $5, as stated by Mr. Calhoun, but $1.50 to $3. Other laborers receive from 75 cents to $1.25 per diem.

The statement has been made to your Honorable Committee that a better feeling between blacks and whites is becoming more and more apparent, but I doubt it. There is an undercurrent of restlessness in the South which the newspapers and reform politicians attempt to smother, but nothing can smother it. The longer the blacks enjoy the state of freedom, the more education and property they acquire, the more restless they become; so that I am free to admit that this startling conclusion arrived at by Prof. Gilliam in a recent article in the *Popular Science Monthly*,[4] will, in the main, be largely verified within the time specified by him. The man who thinks the blacks of the South will always patiently endure the wrongs heaped upon them; misapprehends that human nature which is the same in the Spartan Helot, the Russian serf, and the Irish peasant.

The penitentiary system of the South—with its famous chaingang and convict features—is not equalled in inhumanity, cruelty, and deliberate fraud to any other institution outside of Russian Siberia.[5] Even the Charleston *News and Courier* and the Savannah *Morning News*—papers which no man will claim are over sensitive as to how much a Negro suffers—have declared the convict lease system of Alabama, Georgia, and South Carolina a disgrace to civilization. When such papers as these cry out "Horror! Horror!" it is high time for less hidebound papers to look into the matter. The penitentiaries of the South are full of honest men; as well as thieves, for the law of the South has been purposely framed to convict the Negro, guilty or not guilty. These men are sentenced to long terms of imprisonment upon charges and evidence which would not be entertained for a moment in any court of law north of Mason and Dixon's Line, the object being to terrorize the blacks and furnish victims for contractors, who purchase the labor of these wretches from the State for a song. Of course, this one-sided administration of justice demoralizes the ignorant blacks, as it is intended to do. The white man who shoots a Negro always goes free, while the Negro who steals a hog is sent to the chaingang for ten years. During the past month I noticed three instances of the acquittal of white murderers of colored men.

Colored men are, generally speaking, denied the common rights to serve on jury in the South. Hence they never expect justice, and they always receive the full extent of punishment cunningly devised to reach their case. They hold no offices by appointment under the State Governments, and, because of intimidation and violence and fraud, they hold very few through the suffrage of their fellow-citizens. Their educational interests suffer in consequence. Respectable colored men refuse to travel in the South, because corporations sell them $25 worth of accommodations and force them to accept $10 worth. When they can, they refuse to be thus outrageously robbed. They cannot receive shelter and food in hotels and inns, and places of amusement and culture are barred against them. All these wrongs retard the progress of the race, and make the suggestion of amicable relations ridiculous, not to say absurd. The condition of affairs in the South is volcanic in the extreme, and they become more so year after year, not less because of the apparent calm.

I think that the establishment of postal banks would benefit the poor class of people all over the country, and especially in the South. These banks would be scattered far and wide, and the positively known reliability of the Government would secure at once confidence and conduce to economy and comparative independence among the laboring poor.

I think that National aid to education would be a National blessing.

I think that the Government should refund to the freedmen the $4,000,000, worth of interest, out of which they were robbed by the Freedman's Bank harpies.

I think that it would be advantageous to my race if Congress would pass a bill introduced by Congressman Phelps[6] of Connecticut, creating a commission to thoroughly investigate the condition of affairs in the South, with special reference to the condition of the colored people. I think the report of such commission would open the eyes of the country. The people who do not want any outside interference into the affairs of the South are the ones who have usurped authority and who tyrannically use it; hence the urgency of the necessity for honest investigation.

Notes

1. Alexander Crummell (1819–1898) was an African American Episcopalian priest, missionary, scholar, and educator. He spent twenty years in Liberia as a missionary and educator and promoted the Christianization and civilization of Africa. In 1873, Crummell returned to the United States and founded and served as pastor of St. Luke's Episcopalian Church in Washington, D.C. He later taught at Howard University (1895–97) and founded the American Negro Academy in 1897. For more information on Crummell, see Wilson Jeremiah Moses, *Alexander Crummell: A Study of Civilization and Discontent* (New York: Oxford University Press, 1989). Fortune is referring to Crummell's pamphlet, *A Defense of the Negro Race in America from the Assaults and Charges of Rev. J. L. Tucker, D. D., of Jackson, Mississippi* (Washington, D.C., 1883). The pamphlet was republished in Alexander Crummell, *Africa and America* (Springfield, Mass., 1891), 83–125.

2. Joseph Louis Tucker (1842–1906), a white clergyman of Jackson, Mississippi, read a paper at the Protestant Episcopal Church Congress, "On the Race Relations of the Church to the Colored Race."

3. This John C. Calhoun was the grandson of former South Carolina senator and proslavery advocate John C. Calhoun (1782–1850).

4. E. W. Gilliam, "African in the United States," *Popular Science Monthly* 22 (February 1883): 433–44. Gilliam furthered his argument a year later; see Gilliam, "The African Problem," *North American Review* 139 (November 1884): 414–30.

5. Fortune wrote a strong editorial against the convict lease program a few months after this testimony. See *New York Globe*, February 2, 1884.

6. James Phelps (1822–1900) was a Democratic congressman from Connecticut from 1875 to 1883.

3

The Civil Rights Decision

On October 16, 1883, the Supreme Court ruled the Civil Rights Act of 1875 unconstitutional. Although the Act was never fully enforced, it protected all Americans, regardless of race, in their access to public accommodations and facilities such as restaurants, theaters, and trains and other public transportation and protected their right to serve on juries.

Fortune's first editorial on the subject captures the feeling of much of the African American community, whom he claimed felt as though they "had been baptized in ice water" and told they were "aliens in their own land." The editorial also represents the beginning of Fortune's frustration with the political choices of the African American community and his push for independent politics.

The Civil Rights Decision —*New York Globe,* October 20, 1883

The colored people of the United States feel to-day as if they had been baptized in ice water. From Maine to Florida they are earnestly discussing the decision of the Supreme Court declaring the Civil Rights law to be unconstitutional. Public meetings are being projected far and wide to give expression to the common feeling of disappointment and apprehension for the future.

The Republican party has carried the war into Africa, and Africa is accordingly stirred to its centre.

We need not at this time review the legal aspects of the law or decision. In times past we have done so.

It was only a few months ago that the Supreme Court declared that the Ku Klux law was unconstitutional[1]—that the United States was powerless to protect its citizens in the enjoyment of life, liberty, and the pursuit of happiness. What sort of Government is that which openly declares it has no power to protect its citizens from ruffianism, intimidation and murder!

Is such a Government worthy the respect and loyalty of honest men? It certainly does not enjoy our respect and our loyalty to it is the cheapest possession we have.

Having declared that colored men have no protection from the government in their political rights, the Supreme Court now declares that we have no civil rights—declares that railroad corporations are free to force us into smoking cars or cattle cars; that hotel keepers are free to make us walk the streets at night; that theatre managers can refuse us admittance to their exhibitions for the amusement of the public—it has reaffirmed the infamous decision of the infamous Chief Justice Taney that a "black man has no rights that a white man is bound to respect."[2]

We look facts squarely in the face; we are not given to dodging and hedging—we believe in striking squarely from the shoulder. Then, what is the position in which the Supreme Court has left us? Simply this—we have the ballot without any law to protect us in the enjoyment of it; we are declared to be created equal, and entitled to certain rights, among them life, liberty and the pursuit of happiness, but there is no law to protect us in the enjoyment of them. We are aliens in our native land; we are denied the equal measure of protection which flows from citizenship, and which is denied to no other class of American citizens—denied to us because the position we hold to the American people is a decidedly new and peculiar one. The colored people have been told emphatically that they have the ballot, and if they cannot use it, it can't be helped. We are placed at the mercy of lawless ruffian; we are declared to be the victims of infamous injustice without redress; we are told that we can expect nothing from the United States government, which we have always regarded as the football of the States—an expensive thing that could just as well be lopped off as not.

The Republican party has certainly tried the faith of the colored man. It has gradually stripped him of all the rights which had been given to him for his valor in the field and his patriotism in time of peace. We maintain that the Republican party has made an infamous use of the power which our votes aided to bestow upon it; we maintain that it has betrayed us at every point, and that it stands to-day denuded of its successful hypocrisy, a mean, cunning, treacherous organization.

We should not misinterpret the signs of the times; we should not be deceived by men and parties; we should not hide it from ourselves that there are huge breakers ahead. The Democratic party is a fraud—a narrow-minded, corrupt, bloody fraud; the Republican party had grown to be little better. We do not any longer know where to put our hands upon it; we are no longer able to say whether it is a friend or foe.

We are disgusted with the Democratic party.

Our faith in the Republican party hangs upon the frailest thread.

The Government of the United States is the puppet of the States—a thing without power to protect the citizens of its own creation.

Notes

1. In 1883 the Supreme Court ruled the Ku Klux Klan Act of 1871 unconstitutional. Although the Act was not rigorously enforced, it allowed the government to act against terrorist organizations. See *Civil Rights Cases*, 109 U.S. 3 (1883).

2. Roger B. Taney (1777–1864) was chief justice of the U.S. Supreme Court from 1836 to 1864. He authored the majority decision in *Dred Scott v. Sandford*, 60 U.S. 393 (1856). For more information on the *Dred Scott* decision, see Paul Finkelman, ed., *Dred Scott v. Sandford: A Brief History with Documents* (Boston: Bedford Books, 1997).

4

Between Two Fires

In his "Between Two Fires" editorial, Fortune continued his assault on the Supreme Court decision in the *Civil Rights Cases* and his assertion that it was time for the African American community to demand that the Republican Party reform itself if it sought to continue to receive the black vote. Moreover, the piece demonstrates the harsh editorial pen of the twenty-seven-year-old Fortune as he attacked the "Republican" who wrote a letter to the *Evening Post* blaming the African American community for their situation, as well as his strong words against General Ulysses S. Grant and Rutherford B. Hayes, the latter of whom he referred to as "a prating, vainglorious; nerveless (wo)man."

Between Two Fires —*New York Globe,* October 27, 1883

The Supreme Court has rendered us this service in declaring the Civil Rights law unconstitutional,[1] that our friends have spoken out boldly, while our enemies—and they are legion!—have improved the occasion to open up the vials of their wrath. To our friends we are profoundly grateful, and to our enemies we are prepared to say we return them scorn for scorn, contempt for contempt, and defiance for defiance. We are not to be browbeaten into servile compliance by adverse decisions on our common and inalienable rights as men and citizens, nor are we to be awed into submission and complacent acquiescence by the malignant exultation of our foes. We are men; we are citizens. We have right and justice on our side. Upon a platform so catholic as this we can afford to entrust our cause to the sober better sense of the American people—that people who know how loyal we were to the Union in the darkest hour of our National existence and how devoted we have been to principle in all the time since we have been clothed in the comely habiliments of citizenship.

The man who dares to charge that we have ever been disloyal to the Union is either a knave or a blatant ignoramus; the man who dares to charge that we have ever been false to principle knows full well that he is a low-lived vagabond who sacrifices truth and fair play upon the altar of infamous prejudice and inflated self importance.

We do not ask the American government or people for charity—we leave that boon to be conferred upon aliens fleeing from the tyranny of European governments; we do not ask any special favor from the American government or people—we leave that to be conferred upon the cringing, skulking bruisers who assassinate and rob in the broad glare of noonday. But we do demand that impartial justice which is the standard of reciprocity between equals. We are not Chinese peons, knocking at the door of Congress for the privilege of sharing in the putative liberties of this hidebound government, with a mob of Sands Lot vermin dogging our heels; not at all! We are free men; we are American citizens; we are equal before the law as the whitest man that was ever bleached by the snows of Caucasus, and we demand that that equality shall have ample and unequivocal and impartial hearing before the laws of the land and the august bar of public opinion.

The honor of citizenship was not conferred upon us because men loved us; it was conferred upon us because our conduct in the war, when men's nerves and souls were tried, earned it; and with the history of our valor on the field before his eyes, the man who says we are cowards is himself a coward and a malignant detractor.

A correspondent in the *Evening Post* of this city hisses the following poison to ease his troubled, sordid soul.

> SIR: The Civil Rights Bill decision comes as a just retribution to the colored people for their infamous conduct in assisting the Southern Democrats by their votes to commit that gigantic crime, the repudiation of the Southern State bonds.
>
> I hold some of the bonds repudiated by the State of South Carolina on the 22d of December, 1873. That repudiation act was passed by a legislature largely composed of colored members, and which had a Republican majority. The State sold these bonds in the New York market for 60 to 85 cents on the dollar. That money was spent in South

Carolina, the colored man getting a large benefit from it in schools, etc.; yet they helped to repudiate these bonds without any shame or conscience whatever.

The repudiation broke the strength of the Republican party of South Carolina. From that day it was a doomed and guilty thing; and when the Democrats got control they hastened to deprive the colored man of his civil rights very effectually by the bull-dozing process. For years the Negro has had no civil rights in South Carolina that a Democrat was bound to respect.

Did the colored man then fight for his rights? Not a bit of it. He tamely submitted; and his submission showed his inferiority to the white man.

Mr. Greener[2] says that they will now fight for their rights. It remains to be seen if they will. They have no fairer field than in South Carolina, where they out-number their white oppressors two to one. Yet it is precisely in that State that they have shown the most cowardly submission. They certainly must work out their own salvation; for if they expect the people of the North to fight their battles for them they can wait until doomsday, for it will not be done. Republican sympathy they may get, but I do not believe that the Republican party will go any further than sympathy.

New York, October 16.

A Republican.

The correspondent, who is a typical Yankee, would weigh in the same scales dollars and cents and human rights. His cowardice shows itself in a meaningless pseudonym, and his narrowness of vision cannot reason upon the fall of government upon other than Shylock[3] causes; it is the pound of flesh that he wants. He fails to take into consideration that the men who engineered the repudiation measures in the South Carolina legislature were Northern harpies who posed as the reflex Republican sentiment of the North—men fertile in every expedient for self-aggrandizement, utterly unscrupulous of the means employed. Where did these Republican leaders of the South come from? The North, of course! Where did they go when thievery had produced violence and assassination which ran them out of the South? To the North, of course! And to-day, the same villains who robbed the *Post*'s correspondent are living in luxury in New York and the North, while the poor black man remains in the South to shoulder the odium. Had the colored men of the South been wise they would have secured their share of the plunder.

We do not countenance robbery and murder, but where under the sun can you find a more unscrupulous thief than the white man? Does he not live by robbery? What is Wall street but a den of genteel sharpers? The white merchants, speculators and farmers of the country—do not they live by gouging their neighbors? If the correspondent of the *Post* would admit the truth he would say that he has been robbed of more money in Wall street than he lost by the repudiation act of 1873, which was conceived and engineered by Northern carpet-bag adventurers.

The statement that the repudiation of the State bonds of South Carolina "broke the strength of the Republican party" in that State is a malicious lie! It was the infamous treachery of General Grant's[4] administration and his Republican Congress, which permitted lawlessness to run riot at Hamburgh and Ellenton,[5] which broke the strength of the party in South Carolina! It was the infamous barter and treachery of the Electoral commission, headed by the same Chief Justice Waite[6] who declared the ku klux law and the Civil Rights law unconstitutional—Chief Justice appointed by President Grant—and the effeminate, the puerile, the nerveless policy pursued by Mr. R. B. Hayes,[7] the precocious President from Ohio, which broke the strength of the Republican party of South Carolina. The maintenance of any other ground for the usurpation of the government of South Carolina is a deliberate prevarication of fact and a bold and unscrupulous attempt to shift responsibility.

"Did the colored man then fight for his rights? Not a bit of it. He tamely submitted; and his submission showed his inferiority to the white man!" The colored man did not fight for his rights then because it was the duty of the Government to fight for him. What is government instituted among men for if not to protect them in their constitutional rights—in the enjoyment of life, liberty and the pursuit of happiness? Is government an ornament? Is citizenship a useless appendage? Is it to be expected that the citizen pay taxes for the maintenance of police for the conservation of law and order and in addition buy a gun and make himself a policeman to protect his person and property for the lawlessness of reckless cutthroats? The hot headed lunatic who writes to the *Post* thinks so; the Judge of the Supreme Court declare, in substance, that each citizen is a law unto himself, and that if he would enjoy the benefits of citizenship he must become an outlaw. We are twitted for not taking the Irish dagger in our hand, for not placing the Russian dynamite under the state house,—we are twitted by a so-called "Republican"—God forgive the sacrilege!

As far as the editor of this paper is concerned, he believes in using every argument which men employ to force respect of their rights, and he would take arms this moment, if it were necessary, to assert his rights to think, to speak and to vote. When the law refuses to protect him he would protect himself, and the cowardly correspondent of the *Post* can very easily test the sincerity of the statement, if he will put himself to the trouble. We do not stand alone. There are black men all over the country who would die before they would submit to the least abridgment of their common rights. And South Carolina, the hot bed of nullification, rebellion and usurpation, may yet have to answer for the wrongs she heaps upon her colored population.

We propose to work out our own salvation; and, although we have in times past fought the battles of the North, we do not expect the North to fight our battles for us. There are good men in the North, men who have been friendly to us in sunshine and storm, and we can still rely upon their friendship. They recognize our loyalty to the treacherous Republican party; and they appreciate our services and loyalty. It is the loyalty of this class that we can rely upon when the storm breaks. They are men who recognize that manhood is the stamp of universal brotherhood, and who rate no men or race as inferior stock because slavery and oppression have done their utmost to bankrupt them of every attribute of manhood.

Sympathy of the Republican party indeed! The correspondent of the *Post* shows how supremely ignorant he is of the history of his country; he shows that he is ignorant of the fact that his own party has been enabled to rob the country for the last twelve years through and by our ballots. We do not ask the corrupt Republican party for its sympathy; we spurn it with loathing and contempt! Sympathy indeed! Who asks the Republican party for sympathy? Have we, do we ask for it? We ask for justice, simple justice!

In 1876, in order to enjoy a temporary triumph, in order to place a prating, vainglorious, nerveless (wo)man in the White House, the Republican party sacrificed the black vote of the South, and it has reaped disaster and infamy ever since. It cut itself loose from the issues upon which the war was fought and won; it threw the black vote overboard, and it has not enjoyed one single triumph since, and it never will again, unless it takes up the thread of its political vitality where it left off in 1876. Without our vote the Republican party is doomed. It is doomed to disruption, because it has sacrificed principle on the alter of expediency, because it has called in the assistance of the Devil to fight the battles of the Lord. And now it talks about giving us sympathy! It may keep its sympathy; we want none of it. The party has lived out its usefulness, because it has betrayed the people and joined hands with the greedy cormorants of society—because it has grown wealthy and arrogant and indifferent. The people demand that it reform itself—or it must go!

Notes

1. On October 16, 1883, the Supreme Court ruled the Civil Rights Act of 1875 unconstitutional. Although the Act was never fully enforced, it protected all Americans, regardless of race, in their access to public accommodations and facilities such as restaurants, theaters, and trains and other public transportation, and protected the right to serve on juries. See *Civil Rights Cases*, 109 U.S. 3 (1883).

2. Richard T. Greener (1844–1922), first African American to graduate from Harvard University (1870). Greener later taught at the University of South Carolina and Howard University before becoming U.S. consul and diplomat to India and Russia. For more on Richard T. Greener, see Michael Robert Mounter, "Richard Theodore Greener: The Idealist, Statesman, Scholar, and South Carolinian" (Ph.D. diss., University of South Carolina, 2002).

3. The merciless usurer in Shakespeare's *The Merchant of Venice*.

4. Ulysses S. Grant (1822–1885), Union army general and U.S. president from 1869 to 1877. Fortune published his poem "General Grant—the Dying Chief" in the *New York Freeman*, April 11, 1885. The poem contains the stanza, "The glorious patriot chief we love / Is summoned to the Courts Above! / The God of Hosts, the God of Power, /Strikes down the tall, the massive tower; /Bids the stout heart that made us free / Pass into immortality."

5. On the centennial celebration of the Declaration of Independence, six members of a black militia were murdered in Hamburgh, South Carolina. The U.S. House of Representatives discussed the massacre, and its deliberations were published as a pamphlet. See *A Centennial Fourth of July Democratic Celebration. The Massacre of Six Colored Citizens of the United States at Hamburgh, S.C., on July 4, 1876. Debate on the Hamburgh Massacre, in the U.S. House of Representatives, July 15th and 18th, 1876* (Washington, D.C., 1876). On September 20, 1876, racial violence stemming from an incident on September 15 in Silverton, South Carolina, spread to Ellenton, South Carolina. Before federal troops restored order, more than one hundred African Americans lost their lives in the rioting in and around Ellenton.

6. Morrison R. Waite (1816–1888) was nominated by President Grant in 1874 as chief justice of the U.S. Supreme Court.

7. Rutherford B. Hayes (1822–1893) served as U.S. president from 1877 to 1881. The certification of his election was preceded by the Compromise of 1877, which led to the withdrawal of federal troops from the occupied southern states, Florida, Louisiana, and South Carolina.

5

A New Party/But It Will Be!

In "A New Party" and "But It Will Be!"—editorials written while finishing *Black and White*—Fortune demonstrates his growing belief that the conditions of workers, black and white, are the same and, consequently, so is their cause. He calls for workers "of the South, the North and the West" to create "a solid front to the masterful forces which press them down." "Opposition to this unification," he argues, "is suicidal."

Equally important, Fortune attempts to demonstrate that the same economic forces that are shaping the lives of white workers, here and abroad, are also affecting the lives of the African Americans. Because of this, according to Fortune, blacks should have an equal place in the struggle for economic justice. These are themes that he would further develop in the latter half of *Black and White*.

A New Party —*New York Globe*, April 5, 1884

A new party of living principles appears to be the greatest need of the times. The Republican party may be styled a party of "organized hypocrisy and plunder," while the Democratic party may be styled a party of "organized ignorance and brigandage." Neither of these parties cares a tinker snap for the poor man. They are run in the interest of capital, monopoly and repression. A new party, opposed to these methods has just been organized in this city under the name of the "Liberty League."

This latest organization is intended to focalize the "new political forces," forces easier to speak of in a general way than to specifically define. No one denies the crying necessity of a new party. There are "new forces" in our politics which cry aloud for organized action and agitation. The oppression by the moneyed power of the masses; the denial of rights which lie at the roots of our institutions; the venality of legislators, and the pliability of the interpreters of the laws—all these things imperatively show the necessity of organized resistance.

The time is fast approaching when something must be done to stay the onward march of organized robbery and general misgovernment, or we will fall into the horrors of irretrievable ruin and misery which afflict the people of the old world.

The colored people of the United States have a peculiar interest in the creation of a new party which shall champion the equal rights of all—in the granting of more of the immunities of civil government, and in the easement of the enormous burdens placed upon labor by onerous taxation and unjust laws enacted in the special interest of capital, to defraud labor of its just portion of its production wealth. The future warfare in this country will be based upon resistance to further encroachments upon the rights of the people by the landed aristocracy and money sharks to whom the servants of the people have granted unjust enfranchises.

The laboring men of the South, the North and the West have a common cause and they will yet present a solid front to the masterful forces which press them down, will yet stand in solid array against the men who revel in luxury while labor, the wealth creating power, shivers in the March winds and dies by the wayside. The inequalities which are fast becoming more marked between the dweller in the hovel and the dweller in the palace, must produce here the same appealing distress that curses every country on the continent of Europe, and the same desperate struggle will follow. Indeed we stand in the midst of such distress. Wisdom, therefore, would dictate the early inauguration of systematic and intelligent resistance.

Then, let the people organize, for by organization alone wrong and oppression thrive.

But It Will Be!—*New York Globe*, April 12, 1884

The Charleston (S.C.) *News and Courier* says:

> "THE GLOBE believes that the South will yet melt her disintegrated elements into an harmonious, loyal and prosperous people. Of course it is the business of THE GLOBE to talk in that strain, but as a matter of fact there would be 'no hope' for the South if there was such amalgamation as is described. It would drag down the whites to the level

of the worst of the blacks, and make the South a new St. Domingo. It will not be."

Upon the statement of the *News*, we base the inference that the South will always remain solidly white and solidly black; that injustice will always dictate the administration of justice; that the suffrage will always remain an engine to oppress the black and the white laborer; that Bourbon politics will always dominate in the South, and that race discords will lengthen out to infinity.

We repudiate in their entirety the assumptions of the *News*; we repudiate them because they are at variance with the theories of our government, with sound logic, and with the signs of the time.

American progress is essentially iconoclastic. It takes peculiar delight in knocking down idols which stand in its pathway to a fuller emancipation of the masses from the oppression of the many and the exaltation of the few. The Southern problem is not peculiar, only in the differences of race, which really is no peculiarity. We have the same problem in the North—the German, the Irish and other races contending for the mastery at the polls and for an equal distribution of the production of wealth.

The *News* should not oppose itself to the natural, the inevitable adjustment of conditions in the South. As the slave power fell by its own inherent weakness and by refusing to make advantageous compromise, so opposition to the advancement of the people will but accelerate its progress to a final and satisfactory adjustment.

There should be no such conflict of mutual interests as the *News* advocates by insinuation. The people of the South are one people, living under like conditions, with the identical interests. They must unite their forces; they will unite their forces. The opposition to this unification is suicidal, and we are surprised that intelligent men should declare "it will not be." On the contrary; it will be!

6

The Negro in Politics

Fortune's 1886 pamphlet *The Negro in Politics* is a strong condemnation of the Republican Party and a grand promotion of his "Race first; then party" philosophy. He assailed Frederick Douglass and others who called for sentimental support of the Republican Party. He demanded that African Americans stop following leaders like Douglass, who "have swallowed without a grimace every insult to their manhood." Where is your race pride, he asked his readers. "Instead of loving the race," he insisted, "each one of us seeks to get as far away from his African origin as circumstances will permit." Fortune called for the intelligent use of the ballot for the race. The ballot is a weapon, and Fortune demanded that the community use it as such. "The man who possesses the ballot and cringes and fawns upon his equals and spends his days in begging for what is legally his, is a coward who disgraces the dignity of his sovereignty," he declared.

The Negro in Politics: Some Pertinent Reflections on the Past and Present Political Status of the Afro-American, Together with a Cursory Investigation into the Motives Which Actuate Partisan Organizations **(New York: Ogilvie and Rowntree, 1886)**

I. Introductory

There are many aspects of the colored man's status in the American body politic which will bear the crucible of confidential exposition and discussion.[1] I think we have attained to that position of importance in American politics which warrants a thorough understanding, not only of the manifold obligations which citizenship has imposed upon us, but of the peculiar policy which the race has pursued for the past twenty years. I have not hesitated in years past to expose the absurdity of that policy to enforce respect for our manhood, or to secure to us the measure of right and justice which belongs to us because of our citizenship. Laws amount to nothing if they are not backed up by public opinion; and in the absence of such public opinion the manifest interest of aggrieved classes is to labor to create it.

There was a time, not long ago, when the race was utterly helpless; when it possessed no inherent power; when it was bound hand and foot, soul and body; when it could not resist tyranny or protest against cruelty and villainy; when it was the unresisting victim not only of individual cormorants but the laws of the land, State and Federal. In this helpless state of vassalage and servitude,—wherein manhood was crushed out and the irrepressible tendency of reason to assert its divine presence was scrupulously guarded and suppressed,—nobody expected that we would do more than bend to the yoke, as a race, accept the hard conditions imposed upon us cheerfully, and to expect that the years as they came and went would bring to us, or to our wives and children, no change for the better. The world was not, therefore, surprised that brave and generous men outside the race should step forward to contend for the right because it was right. The "wee sma' voice" of Benjamin Lundy[2] swelled into a clamor when William Lloyd Garrison,[3] with his uncompromising determination, joined him in his labors; and when the impassioned and intrepid Wendell Phillips[4] and the profound and tenacious Charles Sumner,[5] together with their earnest and courageous coadjutors in the good cause, had cast sufficient bread upon the waters, it was natural that the Puritanic John Brown[6] should strike the blow at Harper's Ferry which vibrated through four years of sanguinary war, and culminated at Appomattox Court House in the complete rout of the odious, hydra-headed slave power.

While from the nature of our situation it was necessary for the proper conduct of the agitation for our manumission that it should be conducted by such favored men as are here mentioned, it should be remembered to the eternal credit of the race that it was not silent and inactive during that agitation. It produced courageous men like Denmark Vesey[7] and Nathaniel Turner[8] who crystallized their discontent into armed resistance and died rather than breathe the fetid atmosphere of unjust and cruel servitude. No monument marks their resting place, to blazon forth the glory of their ingrained manhood and courage; not that they do not eminently deserve such mark of a race's grateful and proud remembrance, but because the race is sadly lacking in the quality of *esprit de corps* and proper race pride; because it is still permeated with the virus of jealousy, envy and discord—produced by the odious condition of slavery; because men of the race are still unwilling to concede that there is or can be anything higher, nobler, grander than that which emanates from their own dwarfed and biasly developed individuality; because each man of us, however ignorant and impecunious, deems himself the peer of the greatest intellects the race has produced, and spurns to follow, though himself utterly powerless to lead. This phenomenal idiosyncrasy would appear supremely ludicrous to well informed men, if no disastrous and deterrent consequences attended its impudent exhibition and brazen practice. Besides these courageous men whose humble resting place is marked by no marble shaft, we produced during the period of Anti-Slavery agitation men of soul-stirring eloquence and erudition. Among these I may mention with pride and pleasure Frederick Douglass, Samuel Ringgold Ward, Remond, McCune Smith, Henry Highland Garnet, Wm. Wells Brown, Robert Purvis,[9] and others—men whose eloquent voices and tireless pens pleaded, in season and out, for their brethren groaning in foul bondage. They did magnificent work in arousing the public conscience and forming public opinion; but they were essentially followers, not leaders in the great movement. They could not have been otherwise, under the circumstances although many of them possessed in large measure the prime elements of successful leadership. The temper of American sentiment was not such as to admit of colored leadership in the anti-slavery conflict; and, strange as it may seem, the temper of crafty politicians has been such since our manumission and enfranchisement as to crush out, with the earnest co-operation of our deluded race, every man who has had the capacity, the courage and the opportunity to lift up his voice against a second, and almost as odious, enslavement as the first.

From having been liberated from the thraldom of chattel servitude, enforced by law and custom, the race has for years bent the knee to as crafty and selfish a set of men as have ever in the history of the world played upon the gross ignorance and childish credulity of a race or class—a set of men who have made no promise to the hope that they have not broken to the expectations; who have played fast and loose with the confidence of the race in the halls of legislation, in executive chambers and in courts of justice; and, while posing as the party of great moral ideas, have managed to alienate to private persons and corporations a vast territory out of which could easily be carved a magnificent empire, and created, together with the development of vast corporate and protected interests, a class of millionaire sharks who are potential enough to shape the policy of government and to influence even the court of final resort in its interpretation of the Constitution and the law. *Falsus in uno, falsus in omnibus,* they have managed by loud protestations of good will and unselfish devotion, to fill the eyes of the race with cayenne pepper, to make it feel that it was the idol of the household, when in fact it was simply a football and laughing stock, used to advance the fortunes, pecuniary and other, of men whose first principle of public conduct was self interest. This may be evaded; it cannot be denied. The dupes of party or the paid hirelings may attempt to show the contrary, but the fact remains, and cannot be rubbed out.

My advent into the field of journalism, when a mere youth, four years ago, was marked by an emphatic protest against the existing political vassalage of the race, from which it derived neither honor nor the respect of mankind, and which has in every instance been requited with contempt and neglect by the sharpers and jugglers who have gained most by it. Time and again have I asked, What have we gained by our political vassalage? and, no man has been found who has been able to answer the question to the satisfaction of candid men. They have been as dumb as oysters as to the main charge here made, because the facts were against them. Leaders and people have remained ignominiously silent upon the purely argumentative side of the issue, and have spoken and written only to show what was done for the race by the Abolitionist sentiment before the war, or the honest sentiment of the Union after the collapse of the odious slave power—all which the Republican party and its deluded or subsidized henchmen have arrogated as the peculiar beneficence of the party of "great moral ideas;" when the fact is that what has been conferred upon us by the politicians was forced from them by the public opinion of the country. It is peculiarly the nature of the politician that he stands always with his "itching palm" extended, ready to "bend the supple hinges of the knee that thrift may follow fawning." Public sentiment is his master, and he cringes to his master more abjectly, more servilely, than ever did the helpless black slave of the South. He studies the political horizon of public opinion with as much assiduity and scrupulousness as ever did mariner turn, tempest tossed on the angry waves of the Atlantic, to the North Star.

The history of the race since 1865 should teach us that there is no more tricky and slimy thing in the catalogue of duplicity and cowardice than the average politician; and yet we are supremely ignorant in this matter, and hasten, with a glibness, the outgrowth of ignorance, to brand as a traitor any man of us who has the intelligence and the courage to protest against the broken promises, the sugar-coated capsules, of political mountebanks.

Nor are the ignorant, the vicious, or the well-meaning of the race chargeable alone with this blindness to the innate depravity of the average politician. The so-called leaders of the race—the men who have come down to us with settled, non-progressive ideas, from the antislavery conflict, and men thrown up on the waves of Reconstruction politics, who have been fed stingily of the leavings of the crib of public patronage—these men, who are regarded as the leaders of the race, have swallowed without a grimace every insult to their manhood or their rights which pseudo friends and avowed enemies have heaped upon them. The slaves of one set of sharpers, and browbeaten, shot, and roundly abused by another, they have accepted the situation with a resignation really laughable and to some extent inexplicable—on other hypothesis than that they hoped, often not in vain, that the cunning hand that had the dispensation of public patronage would dole out a bone to them. And if there is anything more to be contemned and despised than the average politician, it is the class of persons who represent a race or cause upon purely selfish grounds—who are ever ready to use voice or pen to extenuate or apologize for the too manifest injustice of the masters they serve for a few pennies or a "little brief authority."[10]

It was the curse of the Irish cause up to the time that Charles Stewart Parnell[11] assumed the leadership of the Irish Parliamentary party that the British government could always silence with honors or filthy lucre the leaders put forth by that people to battle for their rights. The incorruptible integrity of the Parnell party of to-day has created more respect for the Irish people in all parts of the world, and forced more justice from the reluctant grasp of Great Britain, than had been true, since the time of Oliver Cromwell.[12] The British government has been taught by the Parnell party that what is required of it is, *not sinecures and bribes for individual Irish spokesmen, but justice for the entire Irish people.* Hence the magnificent triumphs which have crowned the patriotic leadership of the Irish Parliamentary party; hence the still greater triumphs which are still a possibility in the immediate future.

Have we ever produced a man in any way comparable to Charles Stewart Parnell? Have we a man to-day in any respect his peer? Yes, in intellect; but in nothing else. The intense love of race, and the readiness at all times to sacrifice personal ambition or aggrandizement for the good of the race, so many examples of which have been given to the world by the Irish people, are almost wholly wanting among us. Instead of loving the race, instead of recognizing that individuals are nothing, each one of us seeks to get as far away from his African origin as circumstances will admit. The majority of us no sooner mount to giddy heights on the shoulders of the race than we desert the cause and live henceforth oblivious, apparently, that the struggling mass needs brains and wealth and leadership to master the situation in which it finds itself.

We are lacking in true dignity; true manhood; true courage. And, being so woefully deficient in these grand fundamental qualities, as a race, we make haste to discredit them when they appear in isolated individual instances among us, and brand all such as run counter to our projects, who dare to think and act contrary to the rule we have laid down for our own guidance, as hirelings or knaves, or both.

I give every man credit for honesty and capacity until he demonstrates that he is depraved and superficial. The men who stand out as the representatives of the race in this country, and have done so since the war, have fought, when they did fight, the battles of party, and not of race. To them, it was party first, last, and all the time. The manipulations of the ward heelers in caucus, or the bigger fish in conventions, have always been accepted by them as being as binding as the laws of the Medes and Persians. They have resolutely shut their eyes to the patent fact that the policy and the *personnel* of parties have undergone, in the last two decades, an almost entire metamorphosis; and that, as far as the race, or the rights of the race, are concerned, neither party cares a snap of the finger for them. They still swing on to the tail end of the political kite; still dream that Sumner and Phillips are their champions; deluded themselves into the laughable belief that they are a great power in the consideration of parties, when, as a fact, their voting strength has, very largely, been neutralized since 1876 by the very party they serve with such blind zeal and devotion.

I propose in the following pages to speak my mind freely on the present political status of the race. I shall spare neither friend nor foe when he stands in the way of the race, because I shall unburden my mind not as a Republican or a Democrat, but as a colored man, who firmly believes that parties are the creatures of circumstance, and that they cease to be a golden calf when they deviate from the paths of virtue, honor and consistency.

So many men of the race have imputed to me selfish purposes in the views I have from time to time advanced, and others have taken so much pains to charge me with youth and inexperience, and with unpardonable impudence in placing my views in opposition to those entertained by older and wiser soldiers than I claim to be, that, singular as it may appear, I am persuaded all the more to continue to oppose my views to theirs, to arraign parties and men, when they prove recreant or malicious, and to still maintain the unselfish purposes which have always been my inspiration in contending for the right. I firmly believe, and have long advanced the belief, that the policy we have pursued was delusive—wholly inadequate to secure to the race the enjoyment of the measure of right and justice, to compass which support is usually given to parties; and so believing, I would prefer to stand up and be counted alone than to stand up and be counted with a million in the wrong.

That so many men in all parts of the country are coming to see the matter as I see it is substantial evidence that the period of sentimental politics is gradually drawing to a close, and that the period of practical common sense politics is upon us.

II. Attitude Of The Politicians

When the Abolition sentiment of the country had forced the question of African slavery squarely to the front as the one absorbing issue; when the American people had resolved that chattel slavery was a foul and loathsome fester in the body of the Republic, contrary to the instincts of humanity and the laws of God; when clearly there could be no evasion of the matter, the politicians took hold of it, pro and con, in earnest, and became more righteous in their advocacy or denunciation than the good people who had through years of toil and discouragements, rotten eggs and anathemas, fought the good fight, because it was good. The politicians saw that there was "something in it," and they made haste to out Herod Herod in taking position in the line of preference and promotion. It was a grand scramble in 1856 when the Whig, the Free Soil, the Loco Foco,[13] and all the other parties, guided by their High Priests, marshalled under the banners of the Republican and Democratic parties. Then the men and the women who had forced the question upon the country were crushed to the wall, and the politicians came to the front, henceforth to do the bidding of the people and to claim all the glory of the crusade and the victories won by the people. Many a gallant self-seeker was ground to powder in jumping from one side of the question to the other, because it was not an easy matter to tell just which one of the many gales of public clamor would carry the politician safely into the haven of honor and emolument. Daniel Webster[14] and Henry Clay[15] were among the horribly bruised and mangled unfortunates who were caught between the upper and nether stones of public opinion of the times. Wendell Phillips has painted for us in the following the blighted hopes of three men who were tossed upon the billows of uncertainty in the eventful reorganization of parties consequent upon the introduction into practical politics of the slave question. The picture is full of pathetic interest. Mr. Phillips wrote:

"The white race of Massachusetts was as true as this to the Negro in 1821, when Shaw, of Lanesboro, and Mason, of Boston, two of the most prominent, promising, and rising politicians of Massachusetts, voted for the Missouri Compromise and betrayed freedom. Though afterwards some Tories hid Shaw in the council and bore with him in the legislature, he was politically dead. It was like reducing Sherman to the ranks. Whatever he touched he killed. The State remembered ever after to forget them. They were never counted thenceforth in the census of the common-wealth. Politically, they were more thoroughly dead than the mummies of the time of Cheops.[16] About these, idle science sometimes busies herself. But no one was ever idle enough in Massachusetts to ask whether or where Mason and Shaw were buried. In this generation it would be hard to find a man able to swear that either of them ever existed. No man ever dared to whisper that Massachusetts was cruel or revengeful. Like some half forgotten tragedy, the tradition lingered among the arches of caucuses and conventions; and no Massachusetts man ever repeated the offense until he had given up all hope of Massachusetts votes. When, on the 7th of March 1850, Webster, for the first time since 1821, dared to put his foot down in the fatal tracks Mason and Shaw had left, he had first counted the cost. He knew he was bartering the certainty of Massachusetts approval for the chance of South Carolina's vote, Repudiated by Massachusetts—sent to that same living tomb which she builded for Shaw and Mason—and heated by the South, the broken-hearted traitor crept home to die at Marshfield. Thenceforth Northern men took warning. Negroes! I point you to the example. Be just as exacting, just as relentless."

But the politicians got their bearings after awhile. Like bloodhounds, they are not long to be baffled when the scent is fresh and the game valuable. And then came that long period of anxious hope and despondency, during which a tremendous war was waged to the bloody end, the perpetuation of the union of the States assured, and the slave manumitted. The years from 1861 to 1865 were full of stirring events, which reconstructed in large measure the frame work of our government.

But during all this time the black man was regarded as a passive or acquiescent factor in the great tumult over him and about him; in so far forth indeed that the politicians were not disposed to permit him to bear arms in defense of the Union, and only conceded this privilege when the life of the Nation hung between the doubtful hazard of success and the dreadful sword of Damocles. The greatest politician produced during the last half century, then President of the United States, wrote these words, which were the sentiments of all or most of the politicians who had grappled the slave question:

> "My paramount object in this struggle is to save the Union, and is not either to save or destroy slavery. If I could save the Union without freeing *any* slave, I would do it; and if I could do it by freeing all the slaves, I would do it; and if I could save it by freeing some and leaving others alone, I would also do that."*

Surely the language here quoted is plain enough to be understood; certainly no man will be found to contest Mr. Lincoln's right to speak for the politicians and the "party of great moral ideas" of his time because he was the authorized representative and spokesman of each one of them. There is not a shadow of obfuscation here as to the attitude of the politicians on the slave question. There came a time when Mr. Lincoln saw that he could free all the slaves and save the Union at the same time; and he had the courage to issue the Emancipation Proclamation and leave the saving of Union to God and the Union soldiers under General Grant. The colored people of this country go wild over the name of Abraham Lincoln; I reverence it myself; but the truth of history compels the statement that the great Emancipator was more of a politician than an Abolitionist; that he freed the slave by proclamation more as a war measure than from motives of love for the slave;† that he did not believe that the slave could be made a citizen but should rather be colonized; and I firmly believe that, had he not been martyrized by a skulking assassin, the treatment of questions affecting us would have been vastly less favorable to us than they have been. Yet, I would not be understood as assuming that Mr. Lincoln sympathized with slavery *per se*, or with the slave power. On the contrary he was bitterly opposed to both these gigantic monsters; but he would put a period to their insufferable existence or the extension of their power within constitutional limitations. As President, every step he took was gauged by constitutional power; nor could the persistent advice of Senator Sumner and his co-adjutors, the deluge of anti-

---

* President Lincoln's letter to Horace Greeley, dated August 22, 1862.

† In his inaugural address, Mr. Lincoln said: I have no purpose, *directly or indirectly,* to intefere with the institution of slavery in the states where it exists. I believe I have no lawful right to do so, *and I have no inclination to do so."* And, speaking as if to the people of the South: "You can have no conflict, without being yourselves the aggressors: we are not enemies, but friends."

slavery petitions and delegations, nor the jibes of Horace Greeley[17] force him from what he regarded as his constitutional entrenchments. It required the deafness and insolence of the slave power and the frightful exigencies of the Union Cause to compel him to issue the Emancipation Proclamation.

I revere the memory of Abraham Lincoln as much as any other patriotic American. I believe he came forth, at the proper time, thoroughly prepared, to do a certain work; and then, when he had completed that work, he was translated to receive the just reward of the good and faithful servant. I desire simply in the reference here made to him and his policy to emphasize notorious facts of history which may have escaped the attention of the race, thereby making them to feel and act as if they had been in 1861 the especial proteges of politicians, any more than they were in 1876, or are now; to illustrate the patent fact, to which we seem stone blind, that politicians are simply the servants of public opinion, and do more or do less in a given line of policy only as long as they are encouraged by popular plaudits and substantial support to do so. Instead of looking at the matter from the Utopian standpoint of eternal gratitude, swayed by a sentimentalism, of which politicians have made greedy capital upon which to mount to power and affluence, we should eschew nonsense in politics and proceed to use the franchise as the weapon of protection it was intended originally; use it as the Irish, the German and other classes use it.

I have referred in the course of this discussion to "Sentimental Politics." I would not be misunderstood in the use of this terminology. What I would convey is, that the anti-slavery agitation was based largely upon abstract moral right, without special reference to the Afro-American's capacity to enjoy intelligently the prerogatives of freedom and citizenship. These latter were remote questions, to be left for arbitrament to the future, and they were so left. The purpose of anti-slavery agitation was to place before the American people the moral putrescence and the gross civil iniquity of chattel slavery. During the progress of the agitation other ideas obtruded themselves, or were obtruded, upon the country; so that the question became like floating atoms, and the colored man was invested with a vagueness not warranted by his very common identity with average humanity, subjected to similar straits. The sentiment outside of politics—the period before the public mind was educated up to giving coherence and system to the theories of the agitators—is what I mean by "Sentimental Politics." When the politicians took up the question—gingerly, albeit—in earnest, at the dictation of their masters, the people, it was removed from the sphere of incoherence, of moral rectitude; and was henceforward used as a leverage by politicians to advance selfish individual and partisan ends. In short the colored man became the *pons assinorum* of Republican politicians in their transit from mediocrity and obscurity to fortune and fame. The chasm between the noble, humane, and minutely defined attitude of Garrison and Gerrit Smith[18] and the vacillation in the policy of the politicians headed by President Lincoln will at once be apparent; while the tremendous hiatus which divides the Sumner and Seward stamp of Republican and advocates of justice and fair play for the colored man from such purely mercenary Republican adventures as Mr. James G. Blaine, late Republican candidate for President, and John Sargent Wise, late Republican candidate for Governor of Virginia can be likened to nothing outside of the yawning gulf with which John Milton has divided Heaven from Sheol—if I may use a refinement of a very harsh word supplied us by the genius, modesty, and delicate sense of the humorous, of the latest revisers of the Scriptures.

During all this time—covered by the period of the anti-slavery agitation (from 1815 to 1861) and the period of political badinage and uncertainty (from 1861 to 1865)—the colored man was practically, a silent spectator, with very little voice and participation the great matters in which he was so nearly concerned. He was as so much clay in the hands of the potters, largely the sphinx of the whole situation—the object around which philanthropic sentiment weaved its sweetest and holiest wreathes and partisan fury lashed itself into the agonies of sanguinary warfare.

In the war between the States, it is true, his sympathies were entirely on the side of the Union as opposed to the Confederate States government; and, when the time came, when he was called upon to assist in preserving to posterity The Sisterhood of States, he responded nobly and grandly, as he had done in other years, in the Great Revolution and in 1812.

The American Government has never yet in the hour of peril appealed in vain to its colored population and it never will. And this fact, if no other reason were forthcoming, should be amply sufficient to incline the American people to grant the race that unqualified measure of civil liberty and justice, in the absence of which freedom and citizenship are a burden and farce.

But the period of sentimental politics soon passed away, and the period of practical politics came with the termination of the War of the Rebellion and the manumission of the slave, other and grave questions developed to try the patience and wisdom of the country, and to demonstrate again for the benefit of mankind that the politicians of Greece and those of America have a common origin and similarity of method in working out their destiny of selfish greed and personal ambition.

III. Practical Politics (1865 to 1876)

When the war was at last fought to the finish, and the noble Lincoln assassinated, the country found that instead of having been solved, the questions affecting the colored man were really just becoming very intricate and interesting. The war was over; the colored man was no longer a slave, but the conquered South and the emancipated slave remained. What was to be done with these twin troublesome children of the government? That was the puzzling question.

I never go to my library but that my eyes fall upon the thirteen bulky volumes of Congressional reports of "The Ku-Klux Conspiracy," and, as often as I gaze upon those bulky volumes, a cold chill creeps over me.[19] They teach some truths recorded no where else in the wide range of modern literature; they teach some lessons not found chronicled elsewhere outside the caricatures of the dabblers in fiction and romance.

Those volumes teach us (1) that the Republican politicians, in setting the questions growing out of the war, affecting the colored man, proceeded upon theories nowhere to be found in the annals of dealing with vanquished foe and an enfranchised class, and that, as a matter of course, terrible and bloody failure was the sequence; they teach us (2) that the colored man was utterly unprepared to exercise discreetly and wisely the franchise which had been given him as a reward for the assistance he had rendered in preserving the Union, and that in the hands of white sharpers he was as helpless as ever he had been in the hands of the slave driver; and they teach us (3) that one hundred years of self-government, with thousand years of Christian civilization to draw upon, had not tempered or uprooted the savage instincts of cruelty and barbarism in the white man. He was still the savage, transmuted and transplanted, who had fled before the invading armies of Julius Caesar in Britain.

It has become fashionable to speak of the Reconstruction governments of the South as "Negro governments," and to refer to the period during which they flourished as "period of Negro domination"—the period to which the whites of the South are now wont to refer, whenever the question of the colored man's rights under the Constitution are matters of controversy or arbitration, with a shrug and a shudder. The impartiality of history will correct these selfish, malicious and unjust characterizations. There were no "Negro governments," there was no "Negro domination," at any time in American history. There was a period when certain States—which should have been remanded to a territorial form of government after the war—were ruled from Washington through special agents and envoys, who were voted into office by colored voters, just as the colored slave had put money in the purse of the slave-holder at his stern command, during the existence of chattel slavery. It was only a change of masters. The one had used the lash and the brutal power of ownership; the other had appealed to the hopes and fears of the man. In either case he was no more than a tool, worked for all he was worth by the National Republican party through such soporific agencies as Stearns and Conover of Florida; Spencer of Alabama; Franklin J. Moses of South Carolina; Wm. Pitt Kellogg and Governor Warmouth of Louisiana; Governor Ames of Mississippi; Powell Clayton of Arkansas,[20] and men of their class—a class of men who abused the confidence reposed in them by the unsuspecting colored people for the vile purpose of plunder and selfish advancement; and who—when by their gross mismanagement of authority and shameful plunder, they had made the South bankrupt in purse, a squeezed lemon, and a hell for colored people—quietly sneaked away to hide in other scenes their infamy and live in ease upon the proceeds of their thievery, leaving the poor colored man to bear the burden of contempt and ill-usage and to pay in burdensome taxation the onus of the debts contacted, from the scanty proceeds of his daily toil in the corn and cotton-field—that is, such debts as have not been repudiated by the "Holier-than-Thou" white people of the South. Where are they now, the carpet-bag carrion crows? What care they for the people they robbed or the people whose confidence they so infamously abused? Go seek them, he who would drag them again to the public gaze, scattered through the North and West unhonored, unknown, unsought—so many Benedict Arnolds in the sea of population!—except ex-Governor Moses, whose propensity to thieve proved so strong, from the practice had in South Carolina, that he has constantly been an occupant of some northern penitentiary the last few years, and at the present time he is serving a term in a penitentiary in Massachusetts. Pity it is, that more birds of his feather were not similarly accommodated in the penal institutions of the country. Justice would thereby be somewhat appeased, and the righteous edge of the lance of invective somewhat blunted. May the God of eternal justice and righteousness mete out to the rascals, in the day of reckoning, reward commensurate with the enormity of their rascality.

It was the National Republican party, through its carpet bag agents, which ruled and plundered the South under the Reconstruction governments, not the colored people; and any inference or characterization not in harmony with this plain historical fact is a malicious and uncalled for prevarication, which does infinite injustice to a class of persons who have always been "more sinned against than sinning."[21]

Very true, there were in every one of the legislatures of Reconstruction governments large numbers of colored men, Senators and Representatives; but in every instance these men were counseled and led by their white compeers. How could it have been otherwise under the circumstances? In what crucible of experience, what academy of learning, what school of ethics had those colored legislators, weighted down with the burden of august authority, mastered the intricate science of government and moral purpose? Were they not fresh from the hands of a master who had drilled the intellect down to the level of brute instinct? Certainly. And yet some of those men were capable and honest and remained uncontaminated by the fetid atmosphere they breathed. But the majority of them were not so fortunate. They succumbed to the pernicious teachings and the corrupt practice of their white associates and masters. That they erred no man will gainsay; that they estimated the magnitude and far reaching influence of the offense committed by their connivance it would be unjust to infer or to insinuate. I know full well it is a time-honored maxim of the common law that ignorance is no excuse for crime; but the enlightened sentiment of mankind has decreed that in passing sentence upon the guilty his ignorance and his motive shall weigh in palliation of his offense.

If, however, there were no other offset to the corruption and ignorance of the carpet-bag governments, the intemperate violence and bloodshed practiced by the whites would serve as one. There never was a time in modern civilizations when wholesale corruption and bloody violence kept closer or more confidential association.

There came a time when this unnatural alliance could no longer be maintained; when corruption was stopped because there was nothing more to steal and blood ceased to flow because violence had in a measure satiated its lust and exhausted its victims. And, then, after one last grand masterstroke of villainy and perfidy, the alliance was dissolved, and the bloated and characterless carpet-bagger went out of the halls of legislation and Executive Chambers, back into the obscurity from which he had emerged; the Negro, who had been flattered with a few offices and perforated with bullets occasionally, went back to the fields, the machine shops and domestic service, from which he had been dragged by an abnormal condition of affairs; and the restless, tireless, blood-thirsty Ku-klux and White Liner was again in the saddle of power. It was a sad, a melancholy crumbling of air-castles—built by the politicians on the sand of politics. And the poor black man, as in the first occupancy of the air-castles, was the poorest of this odd, this unnatural trinity. The carpet-baggers bequeathed him as a crushing legacy all the vices of their example and precept—they had no virtues to bequeath. Of course the *"last grand masterstroke of villainy and perfidy"* here referred to was the shameful bargain, the open sale and purchase, by which the State governments of Florida, South Carolina and Louisiana were given to the Bourbons of those States in return for their electoral votes, which were counted for Rutherford B. Hayes, the Republican candidate for President. The confiding colored voters of those states—men who had sacrificed everything, even precious life itself, for the Republican party—were basely deserted by their pseudo friends in the hour of trial. I brand this treachery as the very basest in the annals of perfidy, and I appeal to the Tribunal of Eternal Justice for its exact counterpart. Principle was abandoned; honor was thrown to the winds; and loyal men and true—men who had never proved recreant in duty to the party of great moral ideas, who had stood immovable through evil report as well as good—were turned over, bound and gagged, to the men who had fought four years in open rebellion to destroy the Union of the States, and who had fought from 1865 to 1876—not in brave, open and manly combat, but as midnight riders and skulking assassins—to abrogate and make of none effect the Constitutional Amendments—which the blacks of this country had earned by 200 years of unrequited toil, by honorable service in the first two wars with Great Britain, and by furnishing 200,000 valiant troops to the Union Cause in the Great Rebellion.

Cite me *one* black leader, *one colored* leader, who has had the manhood, the honest loyalty to race, the courage, to characterize in fitting terms this most phenomenal, extra-ordinary and unparalleled crime and perfidy. Why were they silent? Why are they silent? I am too generous to charge them with craven fear that the honest sentiment of the country would not have applauded their righteous indignation! I would hang my head in shame and confusion to insinuate that this silence was due to selfish hopes of personal advancement! If this be true, to what are we to attribute the silence of the spokesmen of the race in this vital matter, and their constant efforts to curry favor and personal advancement by such silence?

I do not write in the heat of passion, or of disappointment, or from a sense of vanity, or in derogation of any man's honor, loyalty, or self-respect. I write in cold blood in the interest of the black millions of this country who have been slaughtered by pretended friends, whose perfidy has been passed over in silence, or apologized for, by the men whose bounded duty it was to maintain the interests and the honor of the race. In the face of their past acceptance of such things, in the face of their present attitude of apology and extenuation of the faults of the party and its leaders, which have profited so long by our ballot, or by making issues of our misfortunes, I ask in sober earnestness, Is such a state of things to continue? Are we to continue to follow men who have, in the main, demonstrated capacity in only *one* element of leadership—the element of self-preservation? In the name of the young men of the race, men born or educated since the war, men who have grown up under new and more favoring conditions,—in the name of the aggressive and self-respecting men of the race, I protest against a leadership predicated upon selfish purpose and craven fear.

The policy which led up to the outrageous condition of affairs in 1876 was strictly in keeping with that grand masterstroke of political infamy. Absolute in the power of every branch of the government controlling a majority of the State governments, with the honest sentiment of the country backing them up, the Republican politicians would have us believe they were powerless to stay the hand of lawless cut-throats—who defied in the full glare of day the august authority of the law, both Federal and State!—killing innocent men in cold blood, outraging defenseless women, and blocking the pathway to the ballot box with murderous weapons! Are we to accept this plea of the Baby act? I do not accept it. It was a vile surrender of principle; an infamous abandonment of loyal allies; and is in no sense to be condoned or forgotten.

What did the party gain by its open barter and sale in 1876? It gained Rutherford B. Hayes; it gained scorn and contempt for abandoning the vital principle which had made it invincible; it gained discredit with the honest voters of the country which entailed upon it a succession of defeats, up to the present time, in nearly every State which cast its electoral vote for General Grant in 1868 and 1872—and the debt is not yet cancelled. The colored people of this country are just beginning to understand the policy pursued for so long by the politicians of the Republican party.

IV. The Political Situation Since 1876

Mr. Frederick Douglass is in many respects the most striking character the race has produced in this country. By his eloquence, learning and courage in a time that tried men's souls, and in a period when colored men of parts were extremely rare, he managed to secure a position among men of thought and activity which he has conferred vast prestige upon the race at large and upon himself in equal degree. The race at large is proud of Mr. Douglass, and nonetheless so that he has said and done some things which were not easily to be swallowed and far less easily to be digested.

Mr. Douglass is regarded by the country at large as the ripest thinker of the race, and we are free to subscribe our assent to this judgment, in a measurable degree. There was time when he stood among us without a peer as orator, thinker and writer; but the car of progress and favoring conditions have so multiplied our orators and thinkers and writers that he is sapient indeed who can point out the one man of us who towers above all the others as pre-eminent in these three departments of human excellence. As an orator he must long stand without a peer; as a thinker, he will long be rated among the best; as a writer he has for years had competitors with whom he must divide the honors. I have no doubt that he is gratified that the race has produced men within the past two decades to share the heavy burden of honors he was once compelled to bear alone; for even glory, like most other things, needs companionship to be fully appreciated and enjoyed.

There has not been a time since the war when the race was not ruled almost entirely by sentimental politics,—weighted down with a sense of infinite obligation to somebody for the God-given right to be free and the Constitutional right to vote—or, oftener, to be shot in attempting to vote. Mr. Douglass has been credited with a sentiment which may be regarded as the alpha and omega of sentimental politics, when he declared that "the Republican party is the ship; all else is the ocean." Nine-tenths of the colored people of the United States accepted this Utopian deliverance as law and gospel, at the time it was spoken; not five-tenths of them believe it now. Why? Because events have disabled the Republican ship and the colored people have not been engulphed in the ocean waves. It takes a reasonable amount of substantial evidence, after a decent lapse of time, to bolster up a statement based purely upon imagination and fear. But in this instance, the march of events has demonstrated that while Mr. Douglass may be a wise man he is in no sense a prophet. It is no discredit to his intelligence and patriotism, however, that events have failed to give him the measure of confirmation he might have expected or hoped for, because all down the ages men,—from fear or vain-glory or selfish purpose,—have constantly shot at the sun and hit a stump. It is well to aim high if you strike low.

But Mr. Douglass was not alone in the sweeping statement he made, as to the attitude of parties towards us. He had a majority of the thinkers of the race, and nearly the entire masses, on his side. They all felt that their rights in a broad sense and their selfish purposes in a narrow sense depended entirely upon the success of this party and the failure of that. They had been educated in a school of experience where this species of economic philosophy was the first and last thing taught. The human mind is capable of receiving any doctrine, however absurd, if properly manipulated within certain periods and under certain conditions. Thus the accident of habitat operates directly upon religious beliefs, and the intense republican born in the United States may have been a most obsequious tool of kingcraft born within the dominions of the Czar of Russia.

We have been free more than two decades. During that time we have assisted by our votes to create four Republican Administrations, and gave what assistance we could to the creation of the fifth. But the Nemesis of Fate was against us; and James G. Blaine[22] went down in the storm he had impudently and rashly lashed into fury. During those two decades we were taught to look to Washington as the seat of supreme power and the repository of the loaves and fishes of patronage. During that period the thirteenth, fourteenth and fifteenth amendments to the Federal Constitution were proposed by Congress, adopted by the States and approved by the President; and the Ku-Klux law and the Civil rights law were passed to give force and effect to the new amendments—to secure to the new citizen all the rights which properly attach to citizens, without reference to color or previous condition of servitude. During the period five of the States, lately in rebellion, were controlled by white sharpers, backed by black votes and by the authority of the Federal Government. The part we played in the Reconstruction era was supremely disastrous to us and to the States under our control, or the control of the sharpers who ruled by sufferance of our votes. With a million men armed with the ballot we produced no man whose name will be remembered by the next generation; for already the names of Dunn, Ransier, Revels, Long,[23] and others are only remembered because they came over as a legacy to the party which had sacrificed their constituency on the altar of selfishness, expediency and base ingratitude, and could not consistently and decently throw them overboard. But this was at last accomplished; for a leader without a constituency, like the leaders of the Reconstruction period who appeared at the last Republican convention at Chicago, command neither the respect nor the confidence of politicians, who traffic first, last and all the time in votes. They know nothing of, they care nothing about, *sentiment*; and their great moral ideas dissolve into thin air the moment they find you are a mendicant—seeking your just rights or a divide of the loaves and fishes of place. *You can't throw dust in a politician's eyes; you can't impair the brassy sheen of his monumental cheek; you can't touch his vanity or his influence, unless you have votes to deliver.* The Republican politicians used our votes and flattered self-esteem just so long as our votes held out; when we no longer had votes with which to help them to win victories, they made issues of our misfortunes, not to assist us, but to boost their fast waning power. It is for us to decide whether this selfish policy shall be continued.

The Republican Party has steadily declined in power since 1876—since it sacrificed principle to perpetuate its control of the Federal power and patronage. At each election since that date its majorities in all the States have either stood still or fallen away. This result is a very natural one. The party came to the front in 1856 as a party of great moral ideas; principal among those ideas was the one that right was right, whether it was within or without the purview of the Federal Constitution. This idea did not gain a firm footing until the war had progressed very far towards a termination; but under the leadership of Mr. Sumner, Mr. Chase,[24] and others it became the leading article of Republican faith, and the politicians, large and small, as a matter of fact, adopted it, and by the vehemence and vociferation of their advocacy of it soon cajoled themselves and the people into the belief that they, the politicians, were not only the champions but the originators of it. So successful were the politicians, up to 1876,—by patting the colored man on the back and doling out to him in isolated instances a small office,—in spreading abroad the error that they were and always had been the peculiar friends of the poor colored man, that the poor colored man, with a unanimity most astonishing came to the conclusion that he owed the politicians a *debt of gratitude which could only be liquidated by eternal loyalty and abject subserviency to the politicians.*

This class of sharpers were not only surprised by this unexpected view of the case, but, as soon as the novelty of its absurdity passed away, proceeded to impress it upon the colored people that the idea of *eternal gratitude* did not originate out of the ignorance and inexperience of the race, but was really based in the most obvious and incontestable facts. And, like Shylock, the politicians have insisted, and do now insist, upon exacting the pound of flesh.

If the politicians were the only parties to combat in this matter the victory would be speedy and complete. So firmly rooted is the idea, however, that the man who would combat it finds determined opposition, not only from the politicians, but from the race at large and the men who stand out as their leaders. It is not easy to combat error when it is so firmly intrenched behind selfish greed and dense ignorance. And men in every age, from Socrates and Tiberius and Caius Gracchus[25] to Toussaint L'Ouverture[26] and John Brown, have, in espousing opinions in advance of their times, fallen martyrs to, or been maligned and traduced by, the rampant spirit of selfishness, fanaticism, and intolerance, which handicap progress in every age. But the just cause must prevail; truth will be vindicated; and equity and righteousness be exalted: so with the rights of the black man; and that though he oppose to them his own ignorance and fears and, apparently, selfish advantage, or be they opposed by men who profit by the misfortune of their fellows or are actuated by the small prejudices or false convictions which are outgrowth, purely, of education and environment. Revolutions never go backwards, although they may, seemingly, pause for a time in their onward progress to the sublimation of human excellence and universal justice and harmony.

We have made marvellous advancement in educational, moral, and material concerns. We have stood still in nothing but matters political. In these, instead of having gone forward we have apparently gone backward. This may not be literally true, yet it is largely true, especially in the South. In that section the civil rights we enjoyed by law and popular sufferance during the Reconstruction period have been swept away by a retrogression to its former state of the public mind or by State and corporate action; and the Supreme Court of the United States, composed of a majority of Republican judges, has affirmed that the States severally have absolute jurisdiction in all such matters of internal and municipal regulation; the unrestricted exercise of the ballot,—placed in our hands by the provisions of the fifteenth amendment to the Constitution, and exercised by us during the period of Reconstruction,—has been abridged, neutralized, or denied in nearly every State south of Mason's and Dixon's line, by the violence of lawless individuals, with the unblushing connivance of the authority of the States; and their conjoint infamy in this matter has been countenanced as perfectly legal or permissible by every Republican President from General Grant (1868), to Mr. Arthur (1885); and no Republican President, even when open rebellion and anarchy prevailed, has ever outlawed by Proclamation such State, and enforced such Proclamation by the strong arm of the military power of the Government; while no Republican Congress ever did more than "investigate" and "report" to Congress upon the crying disorders prevailing from 1866 to 1876 in every one of the States lately in secession. On the contrary, a Commission created by a Republican Senate and a Democratic House of Representatives, by a vote of eight to seven, recognized this lawlessness and usurpation as excusable (in 1876), in the count by which Mr. Hayes was made President, and the State Governments of Florida, South Carolina and Louisiana were handed over to the Democratic party; and that, too, when it is notorious matter of history that the Republican candidates of those States led their Democratic opponents both as to the State and electoral ticket.* This violence and unblushing usurpation of government was further affirmed to be excusable and legal by the, Supreme Court, composed of preponderating majority of Republican justices, in passing upon the constitutionality of the Ku-Klux law, where it was affirmed, in the face of the fourteenth amendment to the Constitution† that the Federal Government had no jurisdiction in such matters as denial of the rights of life, property or the exercise of the suffrage within the jurisdiction of States. This, in short, is the *reductio ad absurdum* of the matter by the Supreme Court.

These are some of the counts in the indictment which I bring against the Republican jugglers of the past two decades, which lead me to declare that while we have gained substantial advantage in every other avenue of progress, we have lost, instead of gained, anything in politics.[27] No colored man in the South will fail to perceive the force of this observation. The question very naturally and properly presents itself: "Why is this so?" The answer may appear difficult to some, but to me it has for years been as plain as the glorious sunlight of Heaven. "Why is this so?" Because in all matters of a political nature we have confided implicitly in the leadership of white men, whose

---

* The vote for Presidential electors in the three States was as follows:

	Hayes (Rep).	Tilden (Dem).
Florida	23,849	22,923
Louisiana	75,135	70,636
South Carolina	91,870	90,906

The vote on the candidates for Governors of those States was as follows:

	Rep.	Democratic	Rep. maj.
Florida	23,666	23,208	458
Louisiana	74,624	71,198	3,426
South Carolina	86,504	83,071	3,433

The figures in the Presidential count I take from Appleton's Encyclopedia; in, the Gubernatorial count from the "Tribune Almanac" for 1877.

It will be readily seen by a comparison of the tables here given that there was no way by which the Republican Presidential electors could have been elected and the Governors defeated. And yet the politicians made the ends meet,—accepted the Presidential vote as cast by the people and reconstructed the vote for State officers to suit themselves and the Democratic part of the three States.

† No State shall make or enforce any law which shall abridge the privileges or immunities of citizens of the United States; nor shall any State deprive any person of life, liberty, or property, without due process of law, nor deny to any person its jurisdiction the equal protection of the laws—*Section One.*

main purpose was, not to see justice done us, but to secure all the notoriety and emolument for themselves our votes gave them opportunity to scoop in. They have never bothered themselves about the colored man's rights; they have in every instance feathered their own nests, made hay while the sun was shining. While the colored man was hurrahing himself into a state of frenzy and getting shot on all sides for his sentimental loyalty, the politicians were smiling in their sleeves at his supreme ignorance and gullibility and piling up the dollars their to account—by bankrupting States and taking bribes from railroad and other corporate swindlers and land grabbers, and dividing the proceeds of other schemes of a selfish nature. These are frozen facts, substantiated by the records of States and Congress since the war.

We have built up church organizations with more than 2,000,000 communicants, with learned bishops by the score and zealous, capable preachers by the thousands; we have built and maintain, on our own account, more than a dozen colleges for the higher education of our youth; we have honeycombed the southland with capable, earnest, self-respecting pedagogues and pedagoguesses; have built and now conduct mercantile, newspaper and banking enterprises, on a small scale admittedly; we have secured landed interests in every State and territory in the Union, and in some States own magnificent farms, "with cattle on a thousand hills,"[28] to use a nice figure of speech; we have developed a beautiful home life in a very large measure, where affluence, refinement, and virtue make the hearth stone "a thing of beauty and a joy forever"[29]—all these things have we accomplished, by the kindly assistance of the wealth, philanthropy and toleration of some and the earnest, persistent and malicious opposition of others;—all these things, and more, have we accomplished, by the innate genius, stickability and manhood of the race, in a collective as well as individual capacity, and thereby wrung from the reluctant lips of avowed enemies golden opinions. This much has been accomplished through the leadership of the colored preachers, teachers and toilers of the race, laboring for the upbuilding of the race; and no colored man can be found to deny the fact or to traduce and anathematize the noble colored men and women of the race who have gone forward in accomplishing the pleasing result! We have spurned the white man's selfish leadership or interference in these matters; we have fallen back upon our own genius and manhood, and the results—*speak for themselves!*

But when it comes to politics; when it comes to an issue as to who shall control our ballot; when it reduces itself to who shall say what measure of right and justice the colored man should have, how he should secure it, and in what manner, then the race quakes like Mount Ætna when Jupiter turns over, and rushes pell-mell into the arms of some white ward heeler or National white tricksters, trimmer or demagogue to shield it from the wrath impending—or, oftener, apprehended to be impending! Result: the white representative grows fat and sleek, makes grandiloquent spread-eagle orations on the hustings and in the halls of legislation; "investigates" "outrages" and "reports" to Congress; waves the "Bloody Shirt" to fire the enthusiasm of the liberty-loving men of the Nation, and—*leaves the colored man practically without protection in State or Federal courts!* This has been the "old, old story" for twenty years! To me, it is a sickening, a disgusting state of things, and I protest against it with all the manhood and intelligence of my nature, and shall not cease to so protest until the matter is righted.

I was born in Florida in 1856. I was just old enough in the period of Reconstruction to observe the course of things without thoroughly understanding them. My father, E. Fortune, Sr., was a prominent figure in the politics of those times.[30] He was a member of the Constitution Convention of Florida and a member from Jackson County of the first three or four sessions of the Legislature under the Reconstruction regime. I am in position to know that he came out of that cesspool of duplicity, cunning and corruption an honest man, wiser than when he went into it. And he now enjoys the confidence and respect of the best people of his State. By the influence he possessed I was made a page boy in the Senate when I was quite a lad. In this position I became acquainted with the mercenary character of the men who ruled the State, deceived the colored people, and at last sold them out to the enemy for a paltry mess of pottage;—the Stearnses, the Conovers, the Dennises, the McLinses,[31] and others, who are eternally damned to posterity. The carpet-bagger* of Florida was typical of his species—oily, mercenary, hypo-critical, cowardly—and, yet, the colored people of my State firmly believed that the sun of splendor, glory and purity rose and went down in these fellows. Where are they to-day? Nearly all of them have the mark of Cain stamped upon their foreheads; few of them can look an honest man in the face without flinching. And these were the men, in every Southern State, in whom the colored people reposed the priceless gem of their most unqualified confidence. Did not this class of men receive their orders directly from the National Republican party? Were they not the

---

* Some of the carpet-bagger politicians of Florida, whom I knew personally, were earnest, capable, honest men. Among these I might name Congressman Wm. J. Purman, Charles M. Hamilton, Judge Locke, John Q. Dickinson (who was assassinated by the cut-throats of Jackson County), Hon. J. C. Greeley, and a few others.

trusted leaders in that section of the dominant party? Certainly they were. No honest man will impeach the veracity of the statement.

There came a time, not many years ago, when I went to Washington, not as an office-seeker, but as a young man to attend school at Howard University. Here my good fortune followed me, and I was in the best of positions to study the carpet-bagger at the very seat of government. What a spectacle he was! A gambler, a drunkard, a libertine, whose vote was always up to be knocked down to the highest bidder! I have seen them at the gaming table; I have seen them reeling in the streets, drunk to imbecility; I have seen them sneak into the Theatre Comique and into C street houses of gilded infamy! And these men represented the black millions of the South! And I know that no colored Senator or Representative in Congress could reach the high functionaries of the Republican party unless he sneaked through the misused influence of one of these white things to whom the black millions had delegated all the political power they had to bestow. Let any man, friend or foe, name me one of those men who has left any but an ignominious impress upon the legislation of those times! Name for me one of those men who demonstrated ability and integrity, in Congress or out of it, which would secure for him a confidential position in any mercantile house of New York. And the black Senators Congressmen and State Legislators of those times— name me one of them who resented this infamous leadership! Name me one of them who produced works which will preserve his name and memory to the next generation of colored men. Why is this true? Simply because the black henchmen could not rise superior to the white men of mediocre abilities and mercenary dispositions whom the leaders of the party commanded them to fall down and worship. They were joined to a putrid corpse, and they could neither get away from it nor rise above it. The white rascals used them to gain power and wealth, the same as they used the masses of the race; and although they lived in an atmosphere permeated with wholesale plunder,—which bankrupted States, counties and municipalities,—not one of them possessed sufficient shrewdness to secure enough of the plunder to buy more than a bottle of rum or a plug of tobacco; therefore while they bear the opprobrious imputations of being corrupt, they have nothing to show for this unenviable reputation. We would gladly impute to their honesty the phenomenal impecuniousness with which they emerged from the Bacchanalian revel of corruption, but we have nothing but our love of race upon which to base so generous an inference.

These are plain facts, which no man can deny. I do not parade them here for any other purpose than all the more forcibly to impress it upon the race that this species of policy on the one hand and leadership on the other can secure for us neither the measure of right and justice which our ballot should exact for us nor the respect of mankind. The truth should be told only for the purpose of correcting error; because none but a malicious and callous iconoclast could find any pleasure in tearing down the sacred altars of a people simply for the fun of the thing. It was only a few weeks since, in the city of Washington, that a gentleman said to me, "Fortune, you are wrong; the people are against you; facts are against you; the condition and the attitude of parties make impossible the theories you preach; *and you are too young in years and the affairs of men to place yourself in opposition to the acknowledged leaders and thinkers of the race.*" Without stopping then and there to show him the fallacy and folly of his reasoning, I came home to New York and began this pamphlet on "The Negro in Politics." In the midst of my newspaper work, after the labor of the day, I here find time to combat error, to assail perfidy, and to justify my position of "*Race first; then party.*"

V. Present Attitude of Parties

When it can be successfully shown, as I have done, that the Republican party has systematically used the colored voter for its selfish purposes, and that it has, at no time in its checquered history, scrupled to sacrifice his person or his dearest interests in its pursuit after success, is it not matter of astonishment that no colored man of parts should have placed the facts squarely before the people, backed up by a manly protest? I think so. It is not so strange that the masses of the race should feel that they are weighted down with a debt of eternal gratitude to the politicians, because superficial indications have led them to conclude that they owe the politicians everything; nor is it strange that they should look suspiciously upon a colored John crying in the wilderness. We do not usually go to laymen for learned discourses on the mysteries and beauties of theology; we leave these things to the Doctors of Divinity, who spend their days in the contemplation and exposition of mysteries to which there can be no earthly solution but which it pleases the Doctors of Divinity to seek tirelessly to solve. We naturally expect them to be learned in things unknowable and to inform the ignorance of the rest of mankind in these matters. We do not go to a grocer for an opinion on a point of law; civilization has evolved a horde of sharks for this business; nor do we go to the average citizen for a lesson in the very intricate subject of social science; but we do expect that the men who are fitted by education and pursuits to be learned in this matter will instruct the people in them. I am not, therefore, surprised at the strong partisan spirit, and the widespread ignorance, which prevail among the colored people of this country as to the attitude of party towards them, and the purely selfish motives which always inspire and actuate the cunning manipulators of party. Where ignorance prevails we expect to find intolerance, bigotry and fanaticism,—not only in matters religious but political as well. It has been true in all ages of the past, and, I expect, will be true in all ages of the future. But there can never be any excuse or plausible explanation for the exhibition of intolerance, bigotry and fanaticism on the part of intelligent men; and when we find such fostering the delusions of the masses and catering to those who profit most by those delusions, we are constrained to interpret their conduct upon the grounds of fear, of superficial education or of selfish and, therefore, ignoble purposes.

We want men of intelligence, discretion and courage; men who have the manhood to contend for the just rights of the race without fear or favor; men who will permit no considerations of a personal nature to stand between them and the cause of the people. Have we produced such men? Have we such men among us now? If so, I do not know them; I have not heard of them: and I believe I know personally or by reputation every colored man in the United States who is worth knowing.*

On the contrary we produced and we have now, no one man in active politics who is not the tool or the echo of some white man; who regulates his acts or his utterances to the sneezing of white politicians, who have money or influence to barter for such acts or utterances. Bound to the party machine, inspired by the hope of personal advancement or emolument, or swayed by craven fear; our men hold their breath when the magnates of party crack the whip, and not one dares to question the methods of a nomination or the character of a nominee. The party may have proved itself treacherous as in the Presidential matter of 1876, or in the interpretation of the Constitution in the Civil Rights and Ku-klux laws; or the candidate may be corrupt and

---

* The only colored men who, in the past ten years, have vigorously protested against the policy of the Republican party towards the race are, prominently, Lawyer Edwin G. Walker and James M. Trotter of Massachusetts; Geo. T Downing of Rhode Island; James C. Matthews of New York; Robert Purvis, William Still and Lawyer James D. Lewis of Pennsylvania; R. D. Beckley of Virinia; Peter Clark of Ohio; Lawyer F. L. Barnett; Editor A. F. and Rev. C. S. Smith of Illinois. Hon. P. B. S. Pinchback of Louisina was always restive under carpet-bag dictation, and bolted party nominations several times. Lawyer L. A. Martinet, while editor of the *Louisiana Standard,* supported Gray (Democrat) against Kellogg (Republican) for Congress in the last election. Mr. Downing has been among the most tireless of Independent colored men.

vicious, as in the case of Mr. James G. Blaine, by the showing of evidence in his own handwriting, or he may be a political adventurer and blackguard like John Sargent Wise;[32] it does not matter about such things, these are of no moment—*the Republican party can do no wrong, its leaders are the salt of the earth and cannot putrefy!* It is almost a waste of time and intelligence to combat this sort of nonsense, this sort of ignorance, this sort of pigheadedness.

When a black man steps to the front and challenges the equity and the logic upon which we predicate our partisan fealty; when he produces facts and figures to fortify the position he takes, what is the fate to which he is subjected? Leaders and people rise up as one man to crush him out and to damn him as a traitor or a crank! Is it not true?

I have been called a Democrat a thousand times, have been anathematized by leaders and people as a traitor and denounced as a vainglorious self-seeker. Why is this? Simply because I have refused to be dictated to, when the rights of the race were in question, by the white men who manipulate our votes for their own benefit—and that though the command came from James G. Blaine or William Mahone.[33] My experience has been identical with that of every colored man who in the past decade has stepped aside from the beaten track of party subserviency and dared to question party methods and policy and the character and antecedents of men placed in nomination by the Republican party.

But there are, happily, abundant signs that the iron-clad political thought of the race is softening, and that the long and profitable disposition of our voting strength and intelligence by the politicians is becoming to be better understood and therefore discredited. When men begin to doubt old beliefs are in danger; when they begin to think error must yield; when leadership and policy are questioned,—especially when these have been deceptively and treacherously practiced,—new leadership and policy are things of immediate possibility. Every political move within the past decade has had a direct tendency to make the race think, to make it restless, to make it inquisitive; so that to-day it is on the tip-toe of expectation.

What is the present attitude of parties towards us?

We have shown that the politicians since 1865 have used the race simply to further their own ambitious and selfish schemes; we have shown that the only substantial things we have gained are the three amendments to the Federal Constitution—amendments which were conceded to us more in deference to the progressive tendencies of the age, more as a liquidation of the service rendered to the Union by the 200,000 black troops, than from any love the politicians bore us; we have shown that all of the measures passed by Congress, based upon the three amendments, intended to secure to us the ample measure of right and justice guaranteed by the Constitution, were so emasculated in the passage by tricky politicians that when subjected to the crucial test of Supreme Court interpretation, they were declared to be so much waste paper, without force or binding effect,—all this have we shown, demonstrating by logical premise and conclusion that while in every instance where we had relied upon race genius and leadership we had gained substantial, tangible and obvious results, while in every instance where we had relied upon the leadership of white men we had gained absolutely nothing but sneers of contempt and bullets of vengeance. I think the showing should make us thoughtful, should make us seriously reflect upon the wisdom of our past political conduct and leadership, and to decide if our future shall be but a repetition of that of the past.

When Mr. Blaine and Mr. Logan[34] were placed in nomination by the Republican party for the positions of President and Vice-President many thoughtful colored men were seriously disposed to question the soundness of the nominations, not so much in the case of General Logan as in that of Mr. Blaine. This politician had seriously impaired his standing with the race because of the tricky position he had taken in Congress on questions affecting the race, and especially in the matter of the Force Bill, which he had openly opposed. And when the Democratic party placed in nomination Governor Grover Cleveland, of New York, and Hon. Thomas A. Hendricks,[35] of Indiana, when the two tickets were squarely in the field, there were not wanting colored men in various parts of the country who perceived that the Republican party had seriously blundered, and who were disposed to accept Mr. Cleveland as the better and safer man of the two. But this disposition produced such a howl of infuriation and indignation from the race and its leaders that the venturesome colored would-be bolters bottled up their honest purposes and supported the Republican ticket or registered their protest by a silent vote. Men owe a great deal of deference to the opinions of their fellows, and the average colored man owes more to the immediate opinion of his race than other classes of our fellow citizens. The colored man has been educated in a school where political servility was the test not only of matriculation but of standing, and to prove deficient in this matter subjected him to the derision and contempt of those with whom his lot was cast; then, too, poverty has such a strong hold upon us that few of our men were in position to pursue a course of political independence. So it came to pass that, although the candidate placed in nomination for President by the

Republican party was known to be an extremely tricky politician, who had used his public offices to the detriment of the interest of the general public and for his own enrichment; that he had deserted the race in a matter of legislation vital to the interests of the race, for the obvious purpose of currying favor with the South; that he was the especial favorite of land swindlers, corporation tricksters, and individual adventurers greedy to enrich themselves at the public expense, and that to the influence of these disreputable elements, more than to any others, he owed the honor of the nomination, which should never have, been given him; in spite of these facts, forcibly put and generally known at the time, not one leading colored man in all the Union felt the ground beneath him sufficiently firm to squarely and manfully place himself in opposition to the Republican nominees. Such a step would have been suicidal. If they did not support Mr. Blaine, they sulked in their boots sucked their thumbs, and permitted the political revolution to transpire without rendering it any such support as would give the race any other than a personal claim upon the successful party.

What was Mr. Blaine's policy towards us? In his letter accepting the nomination he was at unnecessary pains to speak of the South and the political condition obtaining there in terms, altogether ignoring the colored people, and flattering to the pride and abnormal vanity of the whites of that section, who were virtually the only electors of the South. In doing this, and leaving it to General Logan to tickle the vanity of the colored people and to appeal to that sentiment in the North and West which was true and faithful to the purer and loftier principles of Republican policy, Mr. Blaine showed himself the oily politician all men knew him to be. He was after votes. He had hopes, so boundless was his conceit, that his jingoism would enable him to carry at least two of the Southern States. In fact he was reasonably certain that West Virginia and Tennessee would give him their electoral votes. Had he been a wise man, a less egotistic man, he would not so have misjudged Southern white, human nature. Daniel Webster[36] before him had made a similar mistake.

Mr. Blaine packed the National Republican Headquarters in New York with a set of men without fame reputation before he unearthed them, and who, since the issues of the election, have relapsed into the oblivion out of which he dragged them. These men were simply the echoes, the factotums of Mr. Blaine. They were selected to bob up or bob down at Mr. Blaine's nod. I know from personal knowledge that these men were in full accord with Mr. Blaine's policy of "taffy and plenty of it" for the South. The colored man stood no show at the National Republican Headquarters. A policy was initiated and systematically pursued, at the instance of Mr. Blaine and in accord with the sentiment of his managers, by which the colored men were utterly ignored in every respect; and I have yet to hear of *one* colored man who was treated fairly by the Committee.

At the Republican Headquarters colored men were not expected to make themselves at home. While there was a bureau in the Headquarters, with a suave "Man Friday" at its head, to attend to every class of people and to cater to every species of interest and sentiment, the only colored men employed there were two flunkies. These are frozen facts. If they be not true Hon. Frederick Douglass, Hon. John Mercer Langston;[37] Hon. Blanche K. Bruce;[38] Hon. John R. Lynch;[39] Prof. Richard Theodore Greener,[40] and others, are in position, armed with the necessary personal experience and intelligence, to disprove them. These men, who are learned and reputable, finished scholars and polished orators, who had been loyal to the Republican party, some of them when Mr. Blaine was sticking type in a Maine printing office—were they, the acknowledged political High Priests of the race—were they called upon to inform the ignorance of the Committee on questions affecting the colored vote? Were their services solicited and utilized by the Committee, as the services or other men were, to advocate Republican doctrines either for the benefit of colored audiences or white ones? I know that Mr. Douglass and Mr. Lynch and Professor Greener made a few speeches to the colored voters of Indiana and Ohio, but they, I am persuaded; felt the humiliation of the position in which the Committee cheerfully placed them, and were extremely pleased when the labor assigned them was finished. They knew they were being used by designing men, but the habit of obedience was so ground into their natures that they could not say "No!" when the master commanded. I do not censure them; we were all in the same boat, and were compelled by force of habit and the commands of the white politicians, enforced by the masses of the colored voters, "to dance to the music like little men"—very small men! I simply refer to the matter here to show the race, and the leaders also, the very false and ludicrous position which we occupy in politics, and how utterly impossible it will be for us to gain anything substantial in politics by the maintenance of such false and ludicrous position in the future. If we had gained anything in the North or in the South by the policy we have pursued I would not murmur; but I have shown that we have gained nothing—absolutely nothing.

At one period in the progress of the Blaine campaign the establishment of a branch of the committee in the South was seriously debated; circulars to that effect were widely circulated, and some city in Tennessee hit upon as the base of operations. About this time Mr. Blaine started on his Western tour of exhibition and salamming. Presidential candidates never resort to this trickery except when their prospects are cloudy. Mr. Blaine's prospects were cloudy the moment he was nominated, and remained so until he was defeated at the polls. They were never cloudier, in any stage of his career, than they are to-day.

When Mr. Blaine reached Fort Wayne, Indiana, on his tour of exhibition and salamming, news reached him that West Virginia, on which he had placed his heart, had cast its vote for the Democratic candidate. Mr. Blaine immediately lost his temper, and the speech he delivered at that point was full of rage defiance and denunciation of the South. Place the blood-and-thunder sentences of this speech by the side of the caramels-and-soda water sentences in his letter of acceptance and the tricky nature of this bilious politician is made facetiously apparent. The South was denounced in round numbers, and the idea of a headquarters in Tennessee was dropped as if it had been a hot potato.

Mr. Blaine was beaten at the polls in November. No candidate ever died harder than he. When the news of his defeat reached him at his Augusta (Maine) home the politician was thoroughly unnerved. A large number of his townsmen gathered in front of his home, on the night of November 18, 1884. It was a dolorous occasion—for Mr. Blaine. He made a speech. His speech has furnished the text for all the Republican speeches made since, and a few Republican conventions have embodied the germinal idea in their platforms. The colored people are interested only in the "Blaine Idea" of "Politics in the South" and "Political Equality a Necessity," and they are interested in these because Blaineism and republicanism have come to be interchangeable terms. I give Mr. Blaine's idea of "Politics in the South," after his defeat, as outlined in his Augusta speech:

> Few persons in the North realize how completely the chiefs of the Rebellion wield the political power which has triumphed in the late election. It is a portentous fact that the Democratic Senators who come from the States of the late Confederacy all—and I mean all without a single exception—personally participated in the rebellion against the National Government. It is a still more significant fact that in those States no man who was loyal to the Union, no matter how strong a Democrat he may be to-day, has the slightest chance of political promotion.
>
> The one great avenue to honor in that section is the record of zeal-

ous service in the war against the Government. It is certainly as astounding fact that the section in which friendship for the Union in the day of its trial and agony is still a political disqualification, should be called now to rule over the Union.

All this takes place during the lifetime of the generation that fought the war and elevated into practical command of the American Government the identical men who organized for its destruction and plunged us into the bloodiest contest of modern times. I have spoken of the South as placed by the late election in possession of the Government, and I mean all that my words imply. The South furnished nearly three-fourths of the electoral votes that defeated the Republican Party, and they will step to the command of the Democrats as unchallenged and as unrestrained as they held the same position for thirty years before the Civil War.

Perfectly true; but if the, Republican Party had done its duty from 1868 to 1876, when lawlessness walked abroad in the South, with Federal troops scattered all over that section; had Republican Congresses done more than "investigate" and "report" to Congress upon the slaughter of black men at Hamburg and Ellenton and all over the South, by which entire States were usurped; had the Republican party stood by the black man of the South in 1876; had the Republican party done its duty by the colored Republicans of the South Mr. Blaine's yell of despair and rage would never have been uttered. Such pusillanimous inventions as the Republican party practiced towards the colored people of this country always return to plague their inventors. Politicians of Mr. Blaine's calibre now know this to their sorrow. The Republican politicians, by their base treachery, have made the colored people of the South suffer untold tortures; it is no more than just that the Republican politicians should be made to suffer some—that they may feel how the shoe pinches, you know.

But the passage Mr. Blaine's Augusta speech referring to "Political Equality" is one of the most startling things ever spoken by any politician who has been supported to a man, almost, by a class. He said:

> Gentlemen, there cannot be political inequality among the citizens of a Free Republic; there cannot be a minority of white men in the South ruling a majority of white men in the North. Patriotism, self-respect, pride, protection for person and safety for country all cry out against it. The very thought of it stirs the blood of men who inherit equality from the Pilgrims, who first stood on Plymouth Rock, and from

liberty-loving patriots who came to the Delaware with William Penn. It becomes the primal question of American manhood. It demands a hearing and a settlement, and that settlement will indicate the equality of American citizens in all personal and civil rights. It will, at least, establish the equality of white men under the National Government, and will give to the Northern men who fought to preserve the Union, as large a voice in its Government as may be exercised by the Southern man, who fought to destroy the Union.

I do not need to dwell upon this cold-blooded proposition that if colored men are not allowed to vote the Republican ticket they should be disfranchised. Mr. Blaine's idea was recently incorporated into the fifth article of the platform of the Republican party of New York State, adopted at Saratoga, September 22, 1885. The article reads as follows:

> "That while we cordially endorse the dying sentiments of the great soldier and citizen, Ulysses S. Grant, in favor of harmony and good feeling between the North and the South, we insist that an end shall be put to the criminal evasion of the guarantees of equal civil and political rights promised by the Constitution to every freeman. The right of suffrage must be maintained free and untrammelled, *and if that right is unlawfully denied to any part of the people of any State, its representation in Congress and the Electoral College should be reduced.*"

This is reducing Mr. Blaine's theories to a very comprehensive and tangible basis. I have reasonable grounds for believing that the next National Republican Convention will incorporate in its platform some such proposition as that adopted by the Republican Party of New York State. It will be very likely to do so if the Blaine craze lasts until the convention meets. I think the Republican Party has already committed itself to the issue.

It will be interesting to see where the colored vote will stand when the Republican politicians shall make an issue of the proposition that "If the black man be not permitted to vote the Republican ticket shall be disfranchised." Will the colored voters support the G.O.P. on an issue of that kind? From the showing I have made in the progress of subject, I am led to believe that a great many would support the Republican ticket, simply because it was the Republican ticket, if the Republican question at issue was, *"All colored men found living after the passage of this law shall be hanged."* The matter of our party fealty really reduces itself to this absurdity. Indeed, the matter presented itself to colored voters in this light on a small scale in the recent contest in Virginia, where John Sargent Wise, the brazen Republican candidate for Governor, used the following language, in addressing three thousand colored electors at Norfolk, October 23, 1885, as reported in the New York *Herald*:

> "The fight in Ohio was made against Foraker[41] on the ground that he (Foraker) opposed mixed marriages and mixed schools. Mr. Wise stated that he opposed both. In regard to inviting Negroes to his kitchen, he said there were distinctions in social life. It always was so and always will be so. Simply because he knew a man in business it did not follow that he must invite him to his house. Every man selects his own friends for his social circle. 'If I were to put on my swallowtail coat, with my card case in hand and call upon you, said he to his colored auditors, 'you would pay me to leave you.' God made white men white and black men black, and He knew what He was doing when He did it, and he did not intend that they should mix together socially. God did not make mulattoes. If He had wanted them He would have used very different material for making them.'"

This was the creature who had the impudence to expect to be elected Governor of Virginia by colored votes! This is the miserable creature who received at least 100,000 of the 120,000 colored votes of Virginia! Further than this: The colored voters of that State were especially indignant that some ninety-five colored men should have met at Lynchburg and denounced in fitting terms this political trickster. Three of the five colored newspapers published in Virginia gave this man their hearty support. After he was defeated, one of these papers, the *Virginia Critic*, published at Staunton, in its issue of Saturday, November 14, gave us this picture of the sort of thing the Mahone Republican machine really was:

> "We desire to say that Virginia's 121,000 black voters were entirely ignored. The State Executive Committee is composed of white men who cut and dried the late canvass, not placing a colored man on the list as State canvasser. Out of 100 counties not a colored man graced a chair as chairman, and not a candidate for the Legislature wore a black skin; if he did he was a white man. They placed a candidate in the field totally repugnant to the colored voters and he was beaten, and if placed in the field again he would suffer another defeat two-fold worse than the former. The black sons of the Old Dominion weren't blindfolded like the black sons of the Buckeye State. The counties composing the

"famous" Black Bell where the colored vote is largely in majority, that has been the backbone of the Republican party in the State and which has been carried by Mahone ever since 1879, gave large Democratic majorities. The Democrats elected 14 members to the Legislature from counties where the colored population is largely in majority, and one or two Senators."

Colored voters, how does this strike you! The National Republican party endorsed the Mahone machine, and sent him large sums of money and some of its best speakers to help pull Mahone and his candidate out of the mire!

Colored men of the United States look upon the Republican, party of to-day as it is,—James G. Blaine at one end preaching that the Negro must be disfranchised if he be not permitted to vote Republican jugglers into office, and John S. Wise at the other preaching that "God made white men white men and black men black, and He knew what He was doing when he did it, and He did not intend that they should mix together socially," and that so far as mixed schools and mixed marriages were concerned, he was opposed to both! *This is the Republican party as it is!* I submit that we should inspect the thing at close quarters and see how we like it.

VI. Cleveland Democracy

I make no plea for the Democratic party. It is a familiar acquaintance of the colored people of the United States; but I am free to say that, as a party of opposition, it has been up to quite recently, consistent in its opposition to our exercise of the functions of citizenship. The elevation of Mr. Cleveland has, we must all agree, had a marvelous influence for good on the policy of the Democratic party towards us. He has placed the Democratic party in advance of itself, and it cannot go backwards if it would. It must continue to grow more broad, liberal and tolerant in matters affecting us. For this we have to thank President Cleveland.

An editorial article which I wrote on "Mr. Cleveland and the Colored People" appears in the *New York Freeman* of October 17, 1885, and as it expresses my views on the policy pursued by President Cleveland, I insert it here:

"Our article of September 12, on the appointment of Hon. Moses A. Hopkins[42] to the Liberian Mission has drawn forth much criticism from colored and white sources. The colored papers have been unable to see why we should praise Mr. Cleveland for the measure of recognition he has given the race. We do not blame them for their inability to see why we have "rendered unto Caesar the things that are Caesar's." When you are supremely ignorant of what belongs to Caesar how can you render unto him what belongs to him? Not every man who wraps about his person the mantle of an editor, or preacher, or teacher, or mentor at large of the race, is prepared either by education or native abilities to play other than a subordinate or very ridiculous part in the role he has assumed. But the braying of an ass will always proclaim his proper place in the animal family, however completely he may cover himself with a lion's skin.

"We do not set ourselves up as an apologist for the Democratic party; but we trust we have sufficient magnanimity to recognize any advance which that party may make towards us, and render unto the Chief Magistrate of our common country—who is as much, in a broad sense, the President of one partisan one race, as he is of another—the measure of praise, commendation and thanks which his conduct of the public business and his attitude towards the race may warrant.

A correspondent of the *Maryland Director* takes us severely to task for our editorial of September 12. The *Director* occupies a very modest niche in journalism and its correspondent, we judge, occupies a much more modest niche in the domain of intelligent controversy. We notice these twin modest roses here simply because they voice the opinions and feelings of a very large percentage of the race.

"What," asks this correspondent, "has Mr. Cleveland done that the *Freeman* should accord him praise? Was it not his duty to give to colored men the appointments he has given?" We have little heart to stoop to answer such puerile nonsense such appalling ignorance of politics, and—of the history of the past thirty years. But these same questions are asked, we doubt not, by hundreds of colored men all over the Union, and this fact must in a measure dignify our notice of the matter. We reply to the questions in their order.

(I) Why does the *Freeman* accord President Cleveland praise? Because Mr. Cleveland came to the Presidency, the first Democrat since Buchanan's term expired in 1861, under very trying circumstances. The black man had been liberated during this period from slavery by the chances of war and enfranchised because, in our Republic, freedom and citizenship are the inevitable complement of each other. The attitude of the Democratic party towards the colored people had for years been one of repression and oppression, so that such long-headed thinkers of the race as Mr. Douglass had come to regard the Republican party "as the ship and all else as the ocean." It would be highly interesting to know if Mr. Douglass still entertains this Utopian opinion. When the Democratic Party triumphed, when the Plumed Knight sank beneath the political waters he had so lashed into fury, when Mr. Cleveland was sworn in as President of the United States, the colored people all held their breath in anxious expectation. Then came delegation upon delegation to the White House, and Mr. Cleveland took special pains to impress upon each one of them that in so far as he had power the right of the colored man should be respected. Has he kept his word? Let us see.

When Meade, the Copiah County Bulldozer, was appointed to be postmaster at Hazelhurst, Miss., the President promptly revoked the appointment when Meade's record was placed before him. This was a direct warning to all the cut-throats in the South that the Democratic President did not tolerate their bloody practices and had no honors to bestow upon them.

When the Signal Service officer at Pensacola, Florida asked for an assistant the War Department sent him the first man on the list. This man, Wm. Hallett Greene, of New York, happened to be colored. The signal officer at Pensacola refused to receive the colored man assigned him. He was thereupon commanded to report to Washington to explain his conduct. Being unable to do this he was reduced to the rank and pay of a private soldier.

When a new fledged graduate of the West Point Military "Charity Concern" was assigned to a colored regiment, and protested against the assignment on account of the color of the regiment, the Democratic Administration told the fastidious lieutenant that there was no difference recognizable at the War Department in the army based on color, and that he must report for duty as assigned, or get out. And he reported.

(2) "Was it not the duty of the President to give colored men the appointments he has given?" The question is supremely ridiculous. It is a firmly rooted precedent in parties, coming down to us from antiquity and crystallized into an invariable custom, that the transfer of power from one party to another presupposes a redistribution of such offices of the government as in their nature in any way tend to give shape, or assist in giving shape, to the policy of the party dominant for the time being. This view of the matter was severely emphasized by the Republican party during its twenty-three years of power, during which time

the Democrats were rigidly ruled out of all participation in conducting the affairs of the government.

When Mr. Cleveland was sworn in as President he found a multitude of colored men in office. These colored men had been born and nurtured in the creed of Republican politics. They had always been Republicans. They had done all they could to elect Blaine. They had been extremely severe upon all colored men who dared to criticise or to bolt the party they idolized and which had fed to them the crumbs from the table of public patronage. There was not, on an average, one good, square colored Democrat in every State in the Union. Had Mr. Cleveland followed established precedent he would have bounced every one of these colored officeholders. Has he done this? Let us see.

Of three diplomatic positions allotted to us by the Republican Party, two have been filled by colored men, viz.: The Haytian Mission, by Dr. J.E.W. Thompson,[43] of New York, vice Hon. John Mercer Langston, resigned; the Liberian Mission, by Rev. Moses A. Hopkins, of North Carolina, vice John H. Smythe, superseded; Hon. H. C. C. Astwood, appointed Consul to Santo Domingo by President Arthur, still holds over.

Of the five positions of importance held by us in the District of Columbia, Hon. B. K. Bruce has been superseded by Gen. W. S. Rosecrans, a white Union soldier; Hon. Frederick Douglass, as Recorder of Deeds, John F. Cook, Collector of Taxes, George F. T. Cook, as Superintendent of Colored Schools, and Dr. Charles B. Purvis, as Surgeon of the Freedman's Hospital, hold over seven months after Mr. Cleveland has been installed as President.

Of the upward of one thousand colored employees in the departments at Washington when the Democrat's came into power not one per cent of them has been removed.

Of the upward of two thousand colored men who hold minor positions throughout the country not two per cent of them has been removed. We saw, for example, two colored letter carriers serving under a Democratic postmaster of Lynchburg, Va.

We have attempted to show why we think well of President Cleveland. We think we show good reasons for such partiality as we have indulged.

In concluding this article I said what I still desire to emphasize:

"We do not edit THE FREEMAN in the interest of the Republican party, or of the Democratic Party, but in the interest of the race; and in dealing with the questions affecting us we propose to be fair to all men and all parties. We want the race to exercise a broader toleration in all things, and not to think that because a man does not see as they see, speak as they speak and act as they act, he is either a knave, a traitor, an ignoramus, a coward, or a crank.

We are here to fight for the rights of the race, and we propose to fight, be the enemy parties, or individuals, or intolerant members of the race. We feel that we are honest; we believe we understand the condition of the race, we think we comprehend the motives which actuate parties; these being true, we shall fight it out on the lines we laid down five years ago, when we began to edit the *New York Globe* of sacred and revered memory."

I might add, by way of parenthesis, that no Republican newspaper, speaker or henchman, has attempted to explain or deny the facts here set forth. I regard their discretion as the efflorescence of wisdom. Not so can I commend them for persistently recurring to the condition of the colored people of the Southern States in the interest of "a fair vote and an honest count"—the making of issues of our misfortunes for the purpose of advancing the fortunes of their party, without any intention of ameliorating our condition by congressional or other legislation. For have not Republican Congresses enacted class laws,—thoroughly emasculated, which a Republican Supreme Court has more than once declared to be without warranty in the Federal Constitution, therefore void and without binding effect upon the States? Certainly. And these politicians know, and we are learning to know, that if they should wave the so-called "Bloody Shirt" from now until doomsday, "investigate" and "report" outrages to Congress every hour, and pass civil rights and Ku-klux laws by the ton, these things could have no more effect upon the administration and course of justice in any Southern State than upon the administration and course of justice in Ireland or Dahomey. The politicians know this thoroughly, and they do but practice upon our ignorance and fears when they appear year in and year out upon the "stumps" and in their platforms waving the "Bloody Shirt," the emblem of their fatuity, and helplessness, and utter hypocrisy. Do you doubt the truth of this statement after reading the record of Republican crawfishing in the preceding chapters of this sketch? Note the insincerity of these politicians in this matter of making issues of our misfortunes in the case of Senator John Sherman and Governor elect J. B. Foraker, who, having vociferously orated for weeks in Ohio and New York, during the canvas ended November 3, 1885, when called upon by General Mahone to come into Virginia and help him pull through his putrescent candidate, John Sargent Wise—did they wave the Bloody Shirt in the face of the F. F. Vs?[44] Not a whit of it! When they got into Virginia, they talked tariff, and such truck. If they were sincere in this matter, if they desired to do more than make issue of it for partisan advantage, why, when the opportunity came to them in Virginia—why did they not "beard the lion in his den, the Douglass in his hall?" I leave it to the Cincinnati *Commercial Gazette*, the New York *Tribune*, and other such partisan spread-eagles, to give the phenomenon "a local habitation and a name." No; one such rebuke as President Cleveland gave the cut-throat blood-suckers of Copiah County when one of them slipped into the postmastership at Hazelhurst, Miss., is worth all the "waving" and "investigating" Mr. Sherman and coadjutors can give us.

These matters must be settled in the States. The Supreme Court has told us so in language not to be misunderstood. It is for the race to work out a status for itself in the States. The Republican politicians of the North cannot be of any service to them. Consequently they should cease to dream of any assistance from without and proceed to deal with the matter, on their own account, from within. "Can't do it?" Do you reply. Then you might as well sink down by the wayside and be trampled to death by the mob; because a man or a race which does not possess sufficient courage and intelligence to fight its own battles will be the football of every upstart in search of fun.

VII. Conclusion

We have the ballot. It is, in a republic, a free man's shield and buckler. It is given to him for his protection; it is given to him as a protection against the designs of corrupt and treacherous persons, individually or collectively; and it is expected that he will use the ballot for his protection and the protection of the general interest. The man who possesses the ballot is a sovereign in his own right, the peer in all civil matters of the highest as well as the lowest of his fellow-citizens. The man who possesses the ballot and cringes and fawns upon his equals and spends his days in begging for what is legally his, is a coward who disgraces the dignity of his sovereignty. You do not need to be a Democrat or a Republican to force from politicians your honest rights: *You simply need to be men*, conscious of your power. Thus armed, Republican tricksters, Democratic jugglers, and Copiah County and Danville mobocrats would no more dare to outrage you than they would the Irish or German sentiment, or the moneyed and corporate interests of this Country.

You can't do this by following white political upstarts in their wild goose chase after power and wealth; you can't do this by rushing pell-mell in one direction at the crack of the whip in the hands of James G. Blaine or Samuel J. Tilden,[45] or any other white politician. You can only do this by acting as men; by having thorough organization and competent leadership, and by using these to advance men in Federal or Municipal affairs, North or South, who recognize your worth and voting strength, and are willing to give you absolute justice in return for your support. This is the only road to success. It is the common highway to civil equality and justice. Have your own organizations; have your own leaders; distribute yourselves into all parties; trust only such men as trust you; mercilessly destroy any man who dares to insult your manhood. Throw away sentimentality in politics; throw away nonsense. These can win you nothing but contempt and neglect. The times change and men and parties change with them. We must not stand still; we must grow, constantly. We should learn that, in politics as in business, value is only given for value received; and that as in the one case, so in the other, the sharpest, keenest, subtlest forces will win. There is no sentiment in the transaction. It is a pure matter of business every time. You must be cool, cold, frigid and wide awake to win.

We oppose the Democratic party and support the Republican party as if there were any difference in their aims and purposes, at bottom; when the fact of the matter is each of them is a machine, worked by shrewd manipulators for their own personal advantage, without any regard whatever for the interest of the "dear public." It is on both sides a grand scramble for a chance to get the spoils of place; an opportunity to come in on the "ground floor" in the sequestration of the public domain to railroad corporations and syndicates and dividing the proceeds; in sharing the, profits of placing the National bonds, granting charters to National banks, and protecting the manufactures of the country which long ago ceased to be infantile. In this grand scramble, "the under dog in the fight"—the colored man robbed of his Constitutional prerogatives, the laboring class robbed of a just proportion of the proceeds of their toil, the poor Indian fleeced of everything—what time or inclination have the politicians to think of these—further than to use them to advance their selfish purpose? If you cannot make the politician see that by ignoring your honest claims you will take money out of his pocket and remand him to the rank and file, by casting your vote against him, he will pass you by "as the idle wind which he regards not." We cannot run away from this first law of successful politics. We have had the matter forced upon us for twenty years, and it is about time that we began to understand its iron-clad nature and application.

There is no other race beneath the sun of Heaven which would be satisfied with the contemptible status we occupy in the politics of the country without showing signs of restlessness and discontent. I never met a white Republican in the North or South who did not talk and act as if I belonged to him and his party, body and soul, simply because my face was colored; and just in proportion as this spirit has obtruded itself upon me have I felt indignant and disgusted and rebellious.

I think far more of Benjamin F. Butler,[46] who, as a Democratic Governor of Massachusetts, elevates a respectable colored lawyer to the position of a District Judge, than I do of Governor Robinson,[47] a Republican, twice elected, who has kept no promise he made to the colored electors of Massachusetts; nor is my regard for Governor Butler diminished by the fact that the colored Judge is a narrow-minded, unreasoning partisan, who did not disdain to take honor and emolument from the hands of a man and a party he despised. General Butler has always known how to heap coals of fire on the heads of his enemies, and he did this effectively when he forced the nomination as Judge of this colored lawyer upon the Republican Legislature of Massachusetts for confirmation. It was a bitter pill. They have not followed the example set them by the Democratic Governor, but if the colored electors of Massachusetts knew how to make their ballots speak in the language which always makes politicians wince, they could make their fellow Republicans toe the mark. They can do it; they have the power. Will they do it?

The same is true of Mayor King of Philadelphia,[48] a Democrat who because of the support of a large number of colored voters, placed a considerable number of colored men on the police force, and in other places under the municipal government. When Mayor King was up for a re-election the colored voters failed to sustain him. The Republican candidate carried the election. Has this politician followed the example set him by Mayor King? Not at all. He has not appointed one colored man to the police force; on the contrary, I am told, he has diminished the number bequeathed him by Mayor King.

In the late municipal election in Baltimore, it is reported that 4,000 colored voters refused to vote the Republican machine ticket. If this be true, it remains to be seen how the new Democratic Mayor will conduct himself towards the colored people. It would be hard for him to treat them with more contempt and indifference than the Republican machine has treated them in the past.

In the late election in Virginia it is stated that a great many colored men supported Fitz Hugh Lee[49] in preference to John Sargent Wise for Governor. The policy pursued by Governor Lee will be watched with interest.

There are everywhere signs that the colored voters are losing confidence in the politicians and are relying more and more upon their own discretion and leadership. I would encourage this disposition, not in the interest of any party or set of cunning politicians, but because I feel that the race should use judgment in political matters; firmly insisting, in every instance where they give support, upon proper concession of right and justice, and upon proper respect of the honest manhood of the race. Parties are nothing but the instruments of tyranny when they degenerate into machines, when they cease to represent progressive justice. It is for the people to see to it that parties conserve the public interest, or submit to defeat and humiliation. It behooves us to consult our own interest in the future. It is pure nonsense to expect others to perform this duty for us.

THE END

Notes

1. The core of Fortune's argument for political independence was strongly argued in an address entitled "Colored Men of America!" published within the first month of the *Freeman*. The piece was an attempt to wake up the African American community after Grover Cleveland's 1884 election. See the *Freeman*, December 6, 1884. Fortune also put forth his argument of political independence in his book *Black and White; Land, Labor, and Politics in the South* (1884; repr., Chicago: Johnson, 1970).

2. Benjamin Lundy (1789–1839), Quaker abolitionist and editor of the abolitionist newspaper *Genius of Universal Emancipation*. For more on Lundy, see Merton L. Dillon, *Benjamin Lundy and the Struggle for Negro Freedom* (Urbana: University of Illinois Press, 1966).

3. William Lloyd Garrison (1805–1879), abolitionist, editor of the *Liberator*, and founding member of the American Anti-Slavery Society in 1833. For more on Garrison, see Archibald H. Grimké, *William Lloyd Garrison: The Abolitionist* (New York: Funk and Wagnalls, 1891); Henry Mayer, *All on Fire: William Lloyd Garrison and the Abolition of Slavery* (New York: St. Martin's Press, 1998); James Brewer Stewart, *William Lloyd Garrison and the Challenge of Emancipation* (Arlington Heights, Ill.: H. Davidson, 1992); and William E. Cain, ed., *William Lloyd Garrison and the Fight against Slavery* (Boston: Bedford Books, 1995).

4. Wendell Phillips (1811–1884) was a distinguished abolitionist and antislavery orator. Fortune wrote a moving obituary of Phillips; see *New York Globe*, February 9, 1884. For more on Phillips, see James Brewer Stewart, *Wendell Phillips, Liberty's Hero* (Baton Rouge: Louisiana State University Press, 1986).

5. Charles Sumner (1811–1874) was a senator from Massachusetts who was a vocal

antislavery advocate and a leader of the Radical Republicans during the Civil War and Reconstruction. Fortune gave a strong address in memory of Charles Sumner, in which he also promoted the need for the creation of a civil rights organization. See *Hartford Telegram*, January 11, 1884; and *New York Globe*, January 19, 1884. For more on Sumner, see David H. Donald, *Charles Sumner and the Coming of the Civil War* (New York: Knopf, 1960); and Manisha Sinha, "The Caning of Charles Sumner: Slavery, Race, and Ideology in the Age of the Civil War," *Journal of the Early Republic* 23 (2003): 233–62.

6. John Brown (1800–1859) was a radical abolitionist who led twenty-one followers in an attack on the federal arsenal in Harper's Ferry, Virginia, on October 16, 1859, with the intention of liberating and arming slaves. For more on Brown, see W.E.B. Du Bois, *John Brown: A Biography*, ed. John David Smith (1909; repr., Armonk, N.Y.: M. E. Sharpe, 1997); Benjamin Quarles, *Blacks on John Brown* (Urbana: University of Illinois Press, 1972); John Stauffer, *The Black Hearts of Men: Radical Abolitionists and the Transformation of Race* (Cambridge: Harvard University Press, 2002); and David S. Reynolds, *John Brown, Abolitionist: The Man Who Killed Slavery, Sparked the Civil War, and Seeded Civil Rights* (New York: Alfred A. Knopf, 2005). Fortune wrote a poem about Brown while visiting Kansas and published it in the *Age* in 1907. See "With John Brown in Kansas," *New York Age*, September 19, 1907.

7. Denmark Vesey (1767–1822) was a freed African slave who conspired to lead a slave revolt in Charleston, South Carolina, in 1822. For a biography of Vesey, see Douglas R. Egerton, *He Shall Go Out Free: The Lives of Denmark Vesey* (Madison, Wisc.: Madison House, 1999). For a discussion of the Vesey conspiracy, see Michael P. Johnson, "Denmark Vesey and His Co-Conspirators," *William and Mary Quarterly* 58(2001): 915–76. See also the articles that respond to Johnson's piece: "The Making of a Slave Conspiracy, Part Two," *William and Mary Quarterly* 59(2002): 135–202. For general information on slave revolts in America, see Herbert Aptheker, *American Negro Slave Revolts* (New York: International Publishers, 1983).

8. Nat Turner (1800–1831) was an enslaved African who led a slave rebellion in Southampton County, Virginia, in 1831. For information on Turner, see Scot French, *The Rebellious Slave: Nat Turner in American Memory* (Boston: Houghton Mifflin, 2004). For general information on slave revolts in America, see Aptheker, *American Negro Slave Revolts*. Fortune published a poem honoring Turner in 1884, "Nat Turner," *AME Church Review* 1 (October 1884): 101, and "Nat Turner," *Globe* October 18, 1884.

9. Frederick Douglass (1818–1895); Samuel Ringgold Ward (1817–1866); Charles Lenox Remond (1810–1878); John McCune Smith (1813–1865); Henry Highland Garnet (1815–1882); William Wells Brown (1815–1884); Robert Purvis (1810–1898). For a good summary of the activities of black abolitionists, see Benjamin Quarles, *Black Abolitionists* (New York: Oxford University Press, 1969).

10. William Shakespeare (1564–1616), *Measure for Measure*.

11. Charles Stewart Parnell (1846–1891) was an Irish politician who promoted the idea of home rule for Ireland. Parnell's thoughts greatly influenced Fortune, and his Irish National Land League was the inspiration for Fortune's Afro-American League.

12. Oliver Cromwell (1599–1658) was an English military leader and politician and English head of state from 1653 to 1658.

13. Loco Foco was a name given to a group of Democrats who broke from the party in New York in 1835.

14. Daniel Webster (1782–1852) was a politician who was elected to the U.S. House of Representatives and Senate from New Hampshire and Massachusetts.

15. Henry Clay (1777–1852) was a senator and representative from Kentucky. He became known as the Great Compromiser for his ability to find compromise between the North and the South on the issue of slavery, especially in 1820 and 1850.

16. Cheops was the second king of the Fourth Egyptian Dynasty (2551–2528 B.C.).

17. Horace Greeley (1811–1872) was the founder and editor of the *New York Tribune*. See Robert Chadwell Williams, *Horace Greeley: Champion of American Freedom* (New York: New York University Press, 2006).

18. Gerrit Smith (1797–1884) was an abolitionist who befriended and supported John Brown. For more on Smith, see Stauffer, *Black Hearts*.

19. Joint Select Committee to Inquire into the Condition of Affairs in the Late Insurrectionary, *Report of the Joint Select Committee to Inquire into the Condition of Affairs in the Late Insurrectionary States: Made to the Two Houses of Congress February 19, 1872*, vol. 13 (Washington, D.C.: U.S. Government, 1872). It should be noted that Fortune's father, Emanuel Fortune Sr., gave testimony for the inquiry. See also Allen W. Trelease, *White Terror: The Ku Klux Klan Conspiracy and Southern Reconstruction* (Baton Rouge: Louisiana State University Press, 1995).

20. Republican politicians and carpetbaggers: Marcellus L. Stearns (1839–1891), Simon Barclay Conover (1840–1908), George E. Spencer (1836–1893), Franklin J. Moses Jr. (1838–1906), William Pitt Kellogg (1830–1918), Henry Clay Warmouth (1842–1931), and Powell Clayton (1833–1914).

21. William Shakespeare (1564–1616), *King Lear*.

22. James G. Blaine (1830–1893) was a Republican politician from Maine who ran for president in 1884 and lost to Democrat Grover Cleveland.

23. Oscar Dunn (ca. 1820–1871) was elected lieutenant governor of Louisiana in 1868; Alonzo J. Ransier (1834–1882) was elected lieutenant governor of South Carolina in 1870 and served as representative in Congress from 1873 to 1875; Hiram R. Revels (1822–1901) was the first African American to serve in the Senate, representing Mississippi from 1870 to 1871; and Jefferson Franklin Long (1836–1901) served as a Georgia representative from 1870 to 1871.

24. Salmon Chase (1808–1873) was a Republican politician who was a member of Abraham Lincoln's Cabinet and was appointed by Lincoln as chief justice of the U.S. Supreme Court in 1864. For more on Chase, see Doris Kearns Goodwin, *Team of Rivals: The Political Genius of Abraham Lincoln* (New York: Simon and Schuster, 2005).

25. Tiberius Gracchus (163–132 B.C.) and Caius Gracchus (154–121 B.C.) were brothers and Roman politicians.

26. Toussaint L'Ouverture (1743–1803) was a leader of the Haitian revolution. For more on L'Ouverture and the Haitian revolution, see C.L.R. James, *The Black Jacobins; Toussaint L'Ouverture and the San Domingo Revolution* (New York: Vintage Books, 1963); and Laurent Dubois, *Avengers of the New World: The Story of the Haitian Revolution* (Cambridge, Mass.: Belknap Press of Harvard University Press, 2004).

27. See also Bess Beatty, *A Revolution Gone Backward: Black Response to National Politics, 1876–1896* (New York: Greenwood Press, 1987).

28. Psalm 50:10.

29. John Keats (1795–1821), "Endymion."

30. For more on Florida during Reconstruction and its aftermath, see Paul Ortiz, *Emancipation Betrayed: The Hidden History of Black Organizing and White Violence in Florida from Reconstruction to the Bloody Election of 1920* (Berkeley: University of California Press, 2005).

31. Marcellus Lovejoy Stearns (1839–1891), Simon Barclay Conover (1840–1908).

32. John Sergeant Wise (1846–1913) was a Confederate lieutenant and later Virginia representative as a Readjuster.

33. William Mahone (1826–1895) was a former Confederate soldier and Readjuster politician in Virginia.

34. John A. Logan (1826–1886) was a major general in the Union army, and ran as James G. Blaine's vice presidential nominee in 1884.

35. Thomas A. Hendricks (1819–1885) was elected the twenty-first vice president of the United States as Grover Cleveland's running mate in 1884.

36. Daniel Webster (1782–1852) was a senator from Massachusetts and prominent Whig politician.

37. John Mercer Langston (1829–1897) was an educator, politician, and civil rights activist. In 1864 Langston was elected president of the National Equal Rights League, which campaigned for black suffrage. He later served as the dean of Howard University's law department and was appointed U.S. minister to Haiti in 1877. In 1888 he ran for Congress in Virginia and won his seat after a year-and-a-half battle, serving only for six months. For more information on Langston, see William Cheek and Aimee Lee Cheek, *John Mercer Langston and the Fight for Black Freedom, 1829–65* (Urbana: University of Illinois Press, 1989). The Cheeks' book only covers Langston's career up to the end of the Civil War; see William Cheek's dissertation for details on Langston's post–Civil War career. William Francis Cheek, "Forgotten Prophet: The Life of John Mercer Langston" (Ph.D. diss., University of Virginia, 1961).

38. Blanche Kelso Bruce (1841–1898) was an ex-slave elected to the Senate from Mississippi; he served from 1875 to 1881. For more on Bruce, see Lawrence Otis Graham, *The Senator and the Socialite: The True Story of America's First Black Dynasty* (New York: HarperCollins, 2006).

39. John R. Lynch (1847–1939) was a politician and civil rights activist who was the first African American Speaker of the House of Mississippi (1869–1873) and represented Mississippi in the U.S. Congress from 1873 to 1877. For more on Lynch, see John R. Lynch, *Facts of Reconstruction* (New York: Neale, 1913).

40. Richard T. Greener (1844–1922) was the first African American to graduate from Harvard University (1870). Greener later taught at the University of South Carolina and Howard University before becoming U.S. consul and diplomat to India and Russia. For more on Greener, see chapter 4, note 2.

41. Joseph B. Foraker (1846–1917) was an Ohio governor and senator.

42. Moses A. Hopkins (1846-1886) was a North Carolina African American who was appointed minister of Liberia in 1885.

43. John Edward West Thompson (1855-1918) served as minister to Haiti from 1885 to 1889; John Mercer Langston (1829-1897) served as minister to Haiti from 1877 to 1885; Moses A. Hopkins (1846-1886) served as minister to Liberia from 1885 to 1886; John H. Smythe (1844-1908) served as minister to Liberia from 1878-1881; H.C.C. Astwood served as U.S. consul in San Domingo.

44. First Families of Virginia.

45. Samuel J. Tilden (1814-1886) was the Democratic candidate for president in the disputed election of 1876. Tilden lost to Republican candidate Rutherford B. Hayes.

46. Benjamin F. Butler (1818-1893) was a Massachusetts politician who was a member of the House of Representatives and later governor of the state. During the Civil War his administration occupied Union-controlled New Orleans.

47. George Dexter Robinson (1834-1896) was a Massachusetts politician who defeated Benjamin F. Butler for governor in 1884 and served in that position from 1884 to 1887.

48. Samuel George King (1816-1899) served as mayor of Philadelphia from 1881 to 1884. He was defeated by William Burns Smith.

49. Fitzhugh Lee (1835-1905) was a Confederate general who was elected governor of Virginia in 1886.

7

Negrowump

In his important address for the twenty-third anniversary of the Emancipation Proclamation, Fortune took the opportunity to continue his push for independence in politics and for his "Race first" philosophy. Given in Oswego, New York, on August 6, 1886, Fortune lambasted the audience and the race as a whole for the lack of "race pride and confidence." In Republican and Frederick Douglass territory of New York, he called on the race to stand up and demand their rights and to act no longer as slaves to one political party or the political machine. He said, "You are simply a political cipher in the South and a voting machine in the North; and your Douglasses.... and the rest have no more influence on the politics of the country nor the policies of the parties than so many Aunt Dinahs." Fortune called on the community to declare themselves Negrowumps and act behind his motto of "Race first; then party."

Negrowump: 23rd Anniversary of the Emancipation Proclamation, Oswego, N.Y. —*New York Freeman,* August 14, 1886

Mr. Chairman and Fellow-Citizens: In the enjoyment of that perfect freedom to which every child of God is entitled, we meet here to-day in the richest and grandest Commonwealth of the American sisterhood of States to commemorate the twenty-third anniversary of our liberation from the thraldom of chattel slavery. We meet here to-day as coequal citizens before the law of fifty millions of people who dwell beneath the silken folds of the star spangled banner, and who comprise one of the freest, richest and most progressive confraternities of mankind which ever resolved themselves into "Government of the people, by the people and for the people." We meet here to-day to attest to our fellow-citizens of all races and nationalities that, while we revel in the glories of the promised land, where unto we were lead by the anti-slavery hosts, we are yet not unmindful that for thrice forty years we wandered in a howling wilderness of unutterable darkness and desolation. We meet here to-day to keep fresh in our minds and the minds of our children the wrongs which have been righted, and to insist upon a full concession of all rights still denied us as coequal members of State or of Federal Government. In returning in this manner thanks to the God of nations for the measure of right and justice conceded to us, and in demanding the full payment stipulated in the bond of sovereign manhood and citizenship, we do but exercise that magnificent prerogative which our forefathers wrested from the avarice and cunning of British tyrants more than a hundred years ago.

Fellow-citizens, we do wisely to assemble ourselves in this manner once a year. We do wisely to thus come together that we may review the past and the present and to philosophize upon the future. We do wisely to thus meet in vast concourse that we may rejoice in the conscious might of numerical strength and to renew those tender sympathies of race which pulsate the hearts of all who feel a pride in the ethnological divisions into which God has divided the children of Adam. Therefore, fellow-citizens, if the periodical commemoration of the emancipation of the race shall serve the purposes here indicated, we do well to perpetuate it. We have yet many things to demonstrate which only love of race, race pride, race unity, time, perseverance and manly courage, guided by judicious leadership, can make a living, a blessing reality. It might not be inappropriate to remark here that in times past we have had no race pride, no race confidence, no race leadership. We have simply followed where other men were pleased to lead us,—whether in the long chase of unrequited toil, in the furious charge of battle, or as voting machines to advance the fortunes of parties or of men. In all, we have bent our backs to the cruel lash, bared our breasts to the fury of shell and canister, and sacrificed our civil rights upon the spurious altar of unreasoning and misguided gratitude for favors received. But we have come into a new manhood, and have learned what our rights are and are learning how to demand them as brave men and as sovereign citizens. Occasions like unto this should teach us lessons which shall serve to advance us in the scale of honest manhood and good citizenship, and I believe they serve that purpose.

...Fellow citizens: I come now to a discussion of our political status. We number 7,000,000 of the 53,000,000 of our population. The popular Presidential vote in 1876 was 8,319,760; in 1880, 9,218,161; 1884, 10,054,706. It is safe to say that we cast, or should have cast, one-seventh of this popular vote;

if so we find that we controlled in the Presidential election of 1884, 1,436,100 votes. The Democratic candidate was elected on a plurality of 23,005.

What do these figures teach? They teach that, in 1884, we could have turned the scales against the Democratic candidate and still have had 1,413,095 votes to spare; they teach that we have a tremendous power which we do not know how to use; they teach that having numerical strength enough to defeat any Presidential candidate placed in the field, we have not political sagacity to compel the Democrats of the South to give us justice in the making or the enforcing of the laws, or to compel the Republicans of the North and the West to treat us other than babies,—to be spanked at pleasure and to be denied a seat at the banquet of victory and to have no pie whatever.

With a million and a half of votes to back us up, we have been shot down like dogs at Danville and Carrollton, and no notice had been taken of the matter; with one million and half of votes, our greyhaired Bishops and defenseless women have been thrown off public conveyances, and the Supreme Court of the land has declared that the aggrieved had no redress, save at the hands of the soulless corporations and their hirelings who perpetuated the outrages! With one million and a half of votes, all, or nearly all, allies of the Republican party in 1884, not one colored man in all the Union was deemed worthy to occupy any position of confidence at the National Republican Headquarters in New York; no colored man whatever was treated as a representative of this vast vote; not one colored man enjoyed the confidence of the Blaine managers. I tell you to-day, fellow-citizens, that if you will give me the control of 436,100 of the 1,436,100 colored votes in this country, to be used to enforce the just rights of the race, I would make any party who dared outrage those rights eat the dust of bitter defeat; I would make any corporation, enriched by conference of its franchise from the whole people, which should dare to violate the contract entered into by the sale of a ticket, and which should dare to outrage by violent ejectment from its cars any citizen who had paid for their privilege—give me one half million votes, and I would make such corporation whistle for its franchise!

But what has been the result to us of our voting? We elected Grant in 1872; we elected Hayes in 1876; we elected Garfield in 1880; and we did all in our power to elect Blaine in 1886,—Blaine, who has always catered to the South; Blaine, who defeated the Force Bill; Blaine, who declared just after his defeat that if the colored voters of the South were not allowed to vote the Republican ticket they should be disfranchised for the purpose of establishing at least the equality of white men under the Constitution. Show me one principle of human rights the race has won by its solid support of Hayes, of Garfield, or of Blaine, and I will show you a stream running up the sides of a mountain or a politician who is not as slippery as an eel. What was the ballot given us for? To continue this party or that party in power, or to subserve the common rights conferred upon us by the 13th, 14th and 15th Amendments? Do you suppose that the Republican party or the Democratic party has any time to waste on voters who do not know what their rights are, or how to vote to secure those rights? What do you care for parties further than they serve as a medium through which to secure those just rights to which you are entitled under the Federal Constitution and the Constitution of the several States? Some of our ablest men talk and act as if parties made men, instead of men making parties. Why, Fellow-citizens, to paraphrase a beautiful conceit in Tennyson's[1] "In Memoriam:"

Parties may come, parties may go,
But men go on forever.

For five years I have edited a newspaper in New York City. During all that time I have consistently battled for the common rights of the race as against the common and the usurped rights of politicians. During that time blood-and-murder Democrats have called me a fire-eating Republican sore head, and knuckle-close Republican machinists have called me a Democrat, and the hireling of Democrats. When rogues so far disagree an honest man should have no trouble in getting his just deserts. If you should ask me if I were a Republican, I should answer you, "No!" If you should ask me if I were a Democrat, I should answer you, "No!" If you should ask me, "what are you anyhow?" I should tell you that I am a Negrowump! A Negrowump![2] And I say to you, as I have said in my paper for five years, "If this be treason, make the most of it!"[3]

Mr. Frederick Douglass is, in many respects, the most remarkable man the race has produced in this country. He has received at the hands of the American people more honor, and when he speaks it is to a larger audience than any other colored man can hope to reach. I am proud of the friendship of this distinguished member of the race, and I sincerely regret that he has become so thoroughly saturated with partisan politics as to have ceased to be almost in anything a Negrowump. This is all the more remarkable since Mr. Douglass was a Negrowump since before the Republican party was born in 1856. When Mr. Douglass, Gerrit Smith, Wm. Lloyd Garrison, Lucretia Mott, Wendell Phillips, Sojourner Truth,[4] and a host of others were standing up manfully battling for Negro manhood, there was not yet any Republican party.⁵ Indeed the anti-slavery issue had not then reached the importance of engaging the active support of politicians. On the contrary, Henry Clay⁶ and Daniel Webster⁷ were splitting hairs in Congress to appease by cowardly compromises the rampant spirit of slavery to prevent the extension, not to abolish, the infamy; Charles Sumner⁸ was getting his head crushed by Preston Brooks⁹ in the Senate of the United States, and John Brown was getting hung at Harper's Ferry,¹⁰ for protesting against the iniquity of slavery, and Abraham Lincoln was sparring with Stephen A. Douglas¹¹ in Illinois without once placing himself squarely on record as in favor of the abolition of slavery.¹²

No, there was no Republican party when Mr. Douglass and the army of noble men and women were being rotten egged for creating issues which culminated in the birth of the Republican party and the precipitation of the Civil War. There was nothing in the Republican platform upon which Abraham Lincoln was elected President which aimed at any more radical measure than confining slavery within the territory then cover by it. When the Southern slave holders precipitated the Civil War by firing upon Fort Sumter the Democrats of the North, Democrats like Benjamin F. Butler,¹³ rushed in to defend the Union, and without seeming to do so, became members of the Republican party. Indeed, as many men went into the war for the Union who had been life-long Democrats, as men who belonged to the Republican and other parties. These Democrats,—fully one-half the men who opposed secession to the end,—these Northern Democrats, came out of the war as good Democrats as they went into it. They did as much to make possible this twenty-third anniversary of emancipation as their Republican brethren in arms. No one knows this more thoroughly than Mr. Douglass. The men who controlled the Republican party and the advocates of abolition were very distinct from the beginning. Had the white men been able to subdue the South without the assistance of colored men; had the Southern Confederacy listened to the repeated overtures of President Lincoln, it is very doubtful if I should be speaking to you to-day. Mr. Douglass knows all this better than I do. He knows how hard he and his anti-slavery associates had to plead for every concession to freedom from the politicians for the war period; he knows that when black men were being shot down in cold blood and swung up to the limbs of trees throughout all the South, no Republican Congress ever did more than resolve and investigate the matter,¹⁴ and that when terror reigned in Florida, South Carolina, Louisiana and Mississippi, no Republican President, from Grant to Arthur, ever declared those States in rebellion, and put such down with the strong arm of the Federal authority. Then came the cowardly treachery of 1876, when the Electoral Commission, composed of seven Democrats and eight Republicans, declared that Hayes and Wheeler had been elected President and Vice-President of the United States by the Electoral votes of Florida, South Carolina, and Louisiana, but the Republican candidates for Governor and legislators had not been elected, and that, too, when it was clearly demonstrated that the vote on the State ticket was larger, or as great, as that on the Electoral tickets. Then came the decision of a Supreme Court overwhelmingly Republican that the Ku-Klux law was null and void and unconstitutional. We had hardly recovered from the shock of this tremendous and monstrous construction of the Constitution when the same Supreme Court declared null and void and unconstitutional the Civil Rights bill.[15] All this Mr. Douglass knows as well as you and I do!

And, yet, Frederick Douglass, who was a Negrowump before the Republican party was born and before I was born, can so far forget, as to say, speaking, as it were, for the entire race in this country, in his Emancipation oration, at Washington, last April, the 17th, that

> No man can serve two masters in politics any more than in religion. If there is one position in life more despicable in the eyes of man, and more condemned by nature than another, it is that of neutrality. Besides, if there is one thing more impossible than another, it is a position of perfect neutrality in politics. Our friends, Fortune, Downing,[16] and others, flatter themselves that they have reached this perfection, but they are utterly mistaken. No man can read their utterances without seeing their animus of hate to the Republican party, and their preference for the Democratic party.[17]

Fellow-citizens: I can proudly say here to-day, what I said hundreds of times before, that I have not spared the Republican party when it has been recreant to its promises to the race. I have never given it a lashing which it did not deserve, and which was not fortified with facts based upon its treachery to the race which no man could deny or explain away. And it can not be shown that I ever minced my English in denouncing Democratic opposition to our rights, or in holding up to the scorn and reprobation of mankind the lawlessness of those Southern men who have made their section a reproach and a by-word among the nations of the earth. I have not coined my cheek to gain the cheap favor of the politicians of either party. When the rights of the race have been trampled under foot, I have not paused to see who the offender was; I have simply resented the injury by telling the truth. I do not expect men who have grown gray in the service of this party or that to go after any new policy which I may advance; I do not expect them to see things as I see them. But I do but echo the sentiment of a vast army when I say that the younger and more progressive men of the race are weary of having a million votes sacrificed annually upon the altar of gratitude, to give more power and emolument to an army of men who neither respect us for the sacrifices made nor reward us for the valuable services rendered. We want value received for all we deliver, and, what is more to the point, we are determined to have it. We have not deserted any party; the party deserted us; we have not played fast and loose with the politicians; they have played fast and loose with us. We are sick of the farce, and we propose to work a change, and we do not much care who is offended because we demand what is our own and will not be satisfied with anything short of that.

Fellow citizens: In the South, where the vast majority of our brethren reside, and must always reside, we exercise almost little influence upon the affairs of States as if no Fifteenth Amendment to the Constitution armed us with the ballot; we have no more voice there in the making and the enforcing of the laws than aliens have; we are taxed without representation; and denied, in many instances, trial by jury; we are robbed of our honest wages by cunningly devised laws made in the interest of the planters, and we are fined and sentenced to long term of imprisonment for trivial offenses for the sole purpose of supplying the camps of prison labor contractors with healthy, able bodied men; we are denied all the conveniences and comforts of travel and accommodation, and can find redress in neither State nor Federal courts. Our offenses against law and order are adjudicated by mobs, and sentence executed by masked outlaws. This is, virtually, the state of affairs in the South, although all seems calm and serene on the surface. It was true under Hayes and Garfield and Arthur, who were Republican in their politics, and it is true under Cleveland, who was elected as a Democrat, but who has shown that he is as broad on questions affecting us as any of the Presidents before named.

I have not drawn upon my imagination in the picture I present to you of the condition in the South; neither have I drawn upon the doctored reports as they appear from day to day in the white papers of the North and the South. On the contrary, I base my deductions upon statements as they appear week after week in the one hundred and more colored papers scattered all over the land. They tell the truth, because the man struck is the man who yells. I say here to-day that the mightiest champion the race has at this hour is these same one hundred colored papers which the race refuses adequately to support. It is therefore your duty to sustain these struggling newspapers. If you have not subscribed for one in the past, if you do not subscribe for one now, go and do so! It is a duty you owe to yourself, to your children, and to the race at large!

I have drawn for you a picture of the condition of the race as it obtains in the South. What is the condition in the North and the West? There are some thirty thousand colored voters in New York State. What good have these votes ever accomplished for you? What measure of respect have they gained for you from your fellow-citizens? Point me one colored man in New York State whose influence is worth a snap of the finger with either a Republican or a Democratic politician. You are simply a political cipher in the South and a voting machine in the North; and your Douglasses, Lynches, Bruces, Langstons[18] and the rest have no more influence on the politics of the country nor the policies of parties than so many Aunt Dinahs. The million and a half voters they represent have no more potentiality then they have! Why is this true? I repeat, why is this true? It is because this million and a half of voters are Republicans and not Negrowumps; because they habitually overlook their own interests in conserving the interests of white politicians who profit by your loyalty and treat you with contempt after the election is won.

And now, Fellow-Citizens, I have detained you long enough, but on an anniversary of this nature it is well to talk plainly to each other; it is well sometimes to call things by their proper names. I don't believe in whitewash.

But I should be unjust to you and to myself, if I should omit on this occasion to say a few words concerning the accession of the distinguished New Yorker who now presides over the destinies of this great nation as its Chief Executive. Before the Democratic party came into control of the Government a great many colored people felt that great danger to their rights would result from that accession, but all these fears were allayed by the patriotic utterances of President Cleveland, even before he took the oath of office, and he has constantly shown by word and deed since his inauguration that he recognizes that we are in the broadest sense his fellow-citizens and that we are entitled to representation under the Government even under a Democratic Administration. He is a broad minded, liberal man of the people, who believes and acts upon the conviction that public office is a public trust. He has given to colored citizens of New York State two offices of great consequence,—the Haytian mission and the Recordership of Deeds of the District of Columbia,—nor does his rejection by a Republican Senate detract anything from the good intentions of the President. I have no doubt you are, as I am, proud and grateful, not only for the honor thus done us, but for the establishment of the precedent that a Democratic President can appoint colored men to as high and important offices as a Republican President. The precedent is worth more to us than we may now think, as time will demonstrate.

In conclusion, Fellow-Citizens, let me again say, we do well to keep green the memory of this day; we do well to thus assemble once a year that we may review the past, dwell upon the condition of the present and speculate upon the future; we do well in this manner to come together that we may feel the great encouragement there is in numerical strength. Let us feel encouraged; let us rely more upon ourselves and less upon others; let us look more and more to our own leadership and less and less to the leadership of those who love us only for what they can make out of us; and thus helping ourselves, be assured that we shall enjoy more and more the esteem and confidence of our fellow-citizens, and receive at last "the well done, thou good and faithful servant,"[19] of Him who makes even the wrath of man to serve Him.

Notes

1. Alfred, Lord Tennyson (1809–1892), "In Memoriam."

2. For more on Negrowump politics, see Bess Beatty, *A Revolution Gone Backward*. Fortune published Gus Bert's "A Song of the Negrowump" in the *Freeman*: "The Negrowump is a lively bug . . . / He fights always an honest fight / For race—not party shams. . ." *New York Freeman*, April 23, 1887.

3. Patrick Henry (1736–1799) was the colonial orator and statesman who declared, "Give me liberty or give me death!" in a speech at the Virginia Convention, Richmond, on March 23, 1775. The quote comes from his speech on May 30, 1775.

4. Abolitionists and African American rights advocates Frederick Douglass (ca. 1818–1895), Gerrit Smith (1797–1874), William Lloyd Garrison (1805–1879), Lucretia Mott (1793–1880), Wendell Phillips (1811–1884), and Sojourner Truth (1797–1893).

5. For a general discussion of Abolition, see James Brewer Stewart, *Holy Warriors: The Abolitionists and American Slavery* (New York: Hill and Wang, 1976); and Benjamin Quarles, *Black Abolitionists* (New York: Oxford University Press, 1969).

6. Henry Clay (1777–1852) was a senator and representative from Kentucky. He became known as the Great Compromiser for his ability to find compromise between the North and the South on the issue of slavery, especially in 1820 and 1850.

7. Daniel Webster (1782–1852) was a politician who was elected to the U.S. House and Senate from New Hampshire and Massachusetts.

8. Charles Sumner (1811–1874) was a senator from Massachusetts who was a vocal antislavery advocate and a leader of the Radical Republicans during the Civil War and Reconstruction. Fortune gave a strong address on the memory of Charles Sumner, in which he also promoted the need for the creation of a civil rights organization. See *Hartford Telegram*, January 11, 1884; and *New York Globe*, January 19, 1884. For more on Sumner, see chapter 6, note 5.

9. Preston Brooks (1819–1857) was a congressman from South Carolina who famously attacked Charles Sumner on the floor of the Senate in 1856. See Manisha Sinha, "The Caning of Charles Sumner: Slavery, Race, and Ideology in the Age of the Civil War," *Journal of the Early Republic* 23 (2003): 233–62.

10. John Brown (1800–1859) was a radical abolitionist who led twenty-one followers in an attack on the federal arsenal in Harper's Ferry, Virginia, on October 16, 1859 with the intention of liberating and arming slaves. Fortune wrote a poem about Brown while visiting Kansas and published it in the *Age* in 1907. See "With John Brown in Kansas," *New York Age*, September 19, 1907. For more on John Brown, see chapter 6, note 6.

11. Stephen A. Douglas (1813–1861) of Illinois defeated Abraham Lincoln in the 1858 Illinois Senate race but lost to Lincoln in the presidential election of 1860 as one of the Democratic nominees. Douglas served as representative from Illinois from 1843 to 1847 and as senator from 1847 to 1861. In relation to slavery Douglas promoted the popular sovereignty doctrine and became famous for proposing the Kansas Nebraska Act in 1854. For more on Douglas, see Robert W. Johannsen, *Stephen A. Douglas* (New York: Oxford University Press, 1973).

12. For the text of the debates, see Robert W. Johannsen, ed., *The Lincoln-Douglas Debates of 1858* (New York: Oxford University Press, 1965). For discussion of the debates in the context of the period, see James M. McPherson, *Battle Cry of Freedom: The Civil War Era* (New York: Oxford University Press, 1988), 181–88.

13. Benjamin F. Butler (1818–1893) was a Massachusetts politician who was a member of the House of Representatives and later governor of the state. During the Civil War, his administration occupied Union-controlled New Orleans.

14. Joint Select Committee to Inquire into the Condition of Affairs in the Late Insurrectionary, *Report of the Joint Select Committee to Inquire into the Condition of Affairs in the Late Insurrectionary States: Made to the Two Houses of Congress February 19, 1872*, vol. 13 (Washington, D.C.: U.S. Government, 1872). It should be noted that Fortune's father, Emanuel Fortune Sr., gave testimony for the inquiry. See also Trelease, *White Terror*.

15. On October 16, 1883, the Supreme Court ruled the Civil Rights Act of 1875 unconstitutional. Although the Act had not been fully enforced, it had protected all Americans, regardless of race, in their access to public accommodations and facilities such as restaurants, theaters, trains, and other public transportation, and protected the right to serve on juries. See *Civil Rights Cases*, 109 U.S. 3 (1883).

16. George T. Downing (1819–1903) was an African American abolitionist and entre-

preneur. Downing became a supporter of the Democratic Party after the Reconstruction.

17. Frederick Douglass, "Southern Barbarism," in *Life and Writings of Frederick Douglass*, ed. Philip S. Foner (5 vols.; New York: International Publishers, 1950), IV, 430–42.

18. Prominent African American Republicans, Frederick Douglass (1818–1895), John R. Lynch (1847–1939), Blanche K. Bruce (1841–1898), John Mercer Langston (1829–1897).

19. Matthew 25:23.

8

The Kind of Education the Afro-American Most Needs

In his article "The Kind of Education the Afro-American Most Needs," published in Hampton Institute's *Southern Workman*, Fortune emphasizes the importance of industrial education. This idea was promoted by schools such as Hampton and Booker T. Washington's Tuskegee Institute and by Fortune himself in his 1884 *Black and White*. As in his argument laid out in *Black and White,* Fortune does not undervalue the necessity of higher education but rather calls for both to be employed for the betterment of the race.

The Kind of Education the Afro-American Most Needs —*Southern Workman* 27, no. 1 (1898): 4–6

The question of popular education has received more general attention from the states and from individuals and from philanthropic organizations North and South, East and West, during the past thirty years than any other question of vital moment.[1] Interest in other questions of national concern has occupied the public attention for a brief period, and has then subsided, from one cause and from another, having been either rejected as dangerous to the general welfare or accepted by enactment into law; but there has been no subsidence of interest anywhere in the subject of education, in all of its multiform phases, from the kindergarten to the university, from the munificence of the state to the munificence of the individual. The conviction that the perpetuation of the republic depends upon the intelligence of its citizenship has been, and is, the mainspring of this interest, of this movement for the general diffusion among the masses of the people of the principles of a liberal education. The impulse is and has been national in character and scope. It has grown with the national growth, and had reached such proportions and strength as to serve as an object lesson, to admire and to imitate, to all the nations of the earth. Indeed, the educational system of the United States has become its chief glory and defense.

In how far the abolition of slavery, thirty-two years ago, and the incorporation into the national life of 4,500,000 people, who had served an apprenticeship of 245 years in slavery, and who were destitute, as far as it was possible to make an estimate, of all the requirements of successful citizenship, served to arouse the people of the country to the imminent and menacing danger of an illiterate electorate, and to stimulate them to do all in their power to educate it, cannot be easily estimated; but that it operated powerfully with gratifying results is admitted by all candid persons conversant with the facts. It is true that the public and private interest which aroused the North especially, to the importance of lifting into the glorious sunlight of knowledge the great mass of Afro-Americans who had so long stumbled and fallen and groveled in the darkness of ignorance and superstition and immorality, with which the institution of slavery was compelled to hedge itself about in order to insure existence, has no parallel in the history of mankind. We seek in vain for philanthropy so instant and generous and continuous, and for missionary spirit so noble and capable and self-sacrificing, as that which answered the Macedonian cry that came out of the log cabins of the South,

> When the war drum throbbed no longer, and
>   the battle flags were furled,
> In the parliament of man, the federation of the
>   world.[2]

And what a Herculean task was theirs! The New England men and women who went into the waste places of the South, following closely upon the heels of the warlike host that stacked their arms at Appomattox Court House, formed an army as heroic as ever went forth under the standard of the cross to "redeem the human mind from error."[3] No wealth could have purchased the service and the sacrifice they undertook for God and humanity, and no memorial of affection or granite shaft can ever adequately commemorate their works. There are some services and sacrifices which it is impossible to reward. These evangels went into a hostile country, armed with Puritan faith and New England culture, and by singleness of purpose and gentleness of character disarmed the intense prejudice of the whites and won the respect and confidence of the suspicious blacks, who had been educated in the hard school of slavery to distrust all Greeks, even those bearing gifts. And who shall blame them, seeing that they had been robbed of liberty and labor and virtue, and all other things that men most prize by these same Greeks! But in the progress of time all this was changed, and prejudice and suspicion were transformed into respect and confidence.

What have been the results? After thirty years of effort there are 25,615 Afro-American teachers in the schools of the South, where there was hardly one when the work began; some 4,000 men have been prepared, in part or in whole, for the work of the Christian ministry, and a complete revolution has been effected in the mental and moral character of Afro-American preachers, a service which no one can estimate who is not intimately informed of the tremendous influence which these preachers exercise everywhere over the masses of their race; the professions of law and medicine have been so far supplied that one or more representatives are to be found in every large community of the South, as well as in the North and West, graduates for the most part of the schools of the South; and all over the South I have found men engaged in trade occupations whose intellects and characters were shaped for the battle of life by the New England pioneers who took up the work where their soldier brothers laid it down at the close of the war. But the influence of these teachers upon the character, the home life, of the thousands who are neither teaching, preaching, nor engaged in professional or commercial pursuits, but are devoted to the making of domestic comfort and happiness for their husbands and children, in properly training the future citizens of the republic, was one of the most necessary and far reaching that was exercised, and the one which today holds out the promise for the best result in the years to come.

All of this work was foundation work—cultivating the intellect and shaping the character of a race, making it fit for the glorious privileges and the exacting responsibilities of citizenship. It is not necessary to enlarge upon the thoroughness with which the work was done. Every Afro-American home and school-house and church in the South bears testimony to it, and will continue to do so for years to come. It was the sort of education that was most needed at the time and under the conditions that prevailed, and which will not prevail again. Most of it was what is called higher education, in which the cultivation of the mind and the shaping character were the leading features. The absence of these in all directions was a sufficient warrant for the methods of education that were adopted and pursued. It was not necessary to educate men in the skilled trades or in the science of agriculture, and the like, because they had had no other sort of education in the long school of experience, from 1620 to 1865—from the auction block at Jamestown to the school-house in every district. The avidity with which the children of the old slaves devoured the contents of Webster's blue-back speller and McGuffey's series of readers astonished their friends and confounded their enemies, and has continued to do so to the present time, albeit new books and new methods have replaced the old ones.

But we have come upon a new phase of Afro-American development, which necessarily calls for a different sort of education to properly meet its requirements. We do not need any fewer graduates from the schools of higher learning, because teachers and preachers and professional men are still needed, to fill new places or to take the places of those who fall by the wayside; but we need to educate men and women more and more in the purely bread-winning occupations. The very existence of the schools of higher learning and the crowded nature of their capacity is the strongest argument that can be urged for more training of the hand and less training of the head of the great mass of students, a majority of whom are unfitted for mental pursuits and ultimately fail in them as successful bread-winners. It is a truthful but a startling fact that the skilled trades which were controlled at the close of the war and for some twenty years after, for the most part, by Afro-American mechanics, in all the Southern States, have passed into other hands. Instead of following the trades of their fathers the sons have gone into the ministry, into pedagogy, into the professions, and the like. This was all right, as long as there was a demand in such occupations, but it is not all right now when those occupations have become so overcrowded that employment in them is most difficult to obtain. In the city of Atlanta, where I write this, I know of half a dozen college graduates who want to teach in the city schools but can find no opening. It is even so in other cities and in other employments requiring the higher educational test. We have got to differentiate the mass seeking education, the same as we differentiate factory hands into classes or groups, according to their aptitudes. The idea, which has prevailed since the war, that any sort of black boy is fit to receive a college education, is the antithesis of that other idea, which found acceptance just after the war that no sort of black boy was fit to receive a college education. Both ideas were based in error, and both have worked incalculable injury. Out of this confusion has grown the common saying among us: "What is the use of giving a ten dollar education to a five cent boy?"

In the *New England Magazine* for October, 1897, Dr. A. D. Mayo,[4] who has spent the best years of his life in educational work in the Southern States, puts the idea I wish to convey, as follows:

Of course a great need of the Southern Negro youth is a training in the new industrial education. I say "the new industrial education." For, after a very practical and effective style, the colored citizen of the United States has already graduated with respectable standing from a course of two hundred and fifty years in the university of the old-time type of manual labor. The South of today is what we see it, largely because the colored men and women, at least during the past two hundred and fifty years, have not been lazy "cumberers of the ground," but the grand army of labor that has wrestled with nature and led these sixteen states "out of the woods" thus far on the high road to prosperity.

But the new industrial education places the emphasis on the last word: education. It teaches that all effective work done by the hand is first done by the soul. It is the man that works the hand, not the hand that works the man. No ordinary system of labor, however plodding, faithful, and persistent, can develop the resources of the least American State, unless it is organized and directed by intelligence, character, and trained executive ability.

This view of the matter is bound to draw unto itself thousands who are now wedded to the theory of higher education, and it will do so because it has its basis in common sense and in necessity. We need captains in the skilled trades in all the states of the South, men trained in technical knowledge to direct and control the vast army of workers who have never seen the inside of a school-house. This need is made all the more apparent by the almost total disappearance of the old apprenticeship system, so that now it is no longer possible for a boy to learn his father's trade in the old way, largely because of the rules enforced by trades union organizations and the revolution wrought in most trades by inventions of one sort and another. We no longer make shoes and harness or build houses and bridges, and the like, as our fathers did. Invention has revolutionized it all, and he who would master any branch of it must take a regular scientific course in it. It is impossible for the old-time farmer to compete with a new one who has been grounded in the science of agriculture.

That education is best for a man, always, which stimulates most of his peculiar genius, and enables him to become the most useful citizen in the occupation he selects. A thorough acquaintance with the conditions which now rule in the Southern States, where a majority of Afro-Americans reside, convinces me that what the masses most need at this stage of their development is skilled captains of industry. We have been making teachers and preachers and professional men for three decades, and most of them are engaged in the work that was waiting for them when the war closed, but a close observer sees plainly that they are in danger of starvation unless more attention shall be given to the industrial and commercial sides of life, unless these graduates of the higher schools of learning—who are largely in the nature of social parasites, producing nothing but consuming everything—have a commercial and industrial element to feed upon. This may be a blunt way of putting it, but it is none the less true. We need educated farmers, mechanics, and tradesmen in the South today more then we need the graduates of higher schools of learning, because we have done little else than manufacture the latter since the war; and what to do with the higher learning after they have got it is fast becoming a burning question.

The growth and popularity of such industrial schools as Hampton and Tuskegee, and the interest everywhere being manifested in industrial training by the young men and women of the race, together with the interest manifested in this phase of education by individual philanthropists, and by trustees of the Peabody, Slater, Hand, and other Funds, are most encouraging signs of the times. But the most encouraging sign of all is that parents are arousing themselves to the importance of giving their children practical education, and that so many young men and women are making heroic sacrifices on their own account to secure such an education as will best fit them for the battle of life. Events have signally justified the wisdom and prophetic foresight of General Armstrong,[5] the first article of whose creed was that education of the head and education of the hand are equally necessary and should go together; and I believe that most of the schools maintained for the so-called higher education of Afro-American youth will be forced ultimately to recognize the force of this view of the subject and act upon it.

Notes

1. For a summary of the discussion, see James D. Anderson, *The Education of Blacks in the South, 1860–1935* (Chapel Hill: University of North Carolina Press, 1988); Louis R. Harlan, *Separate and Unequal: Public School Campaigns and Racism in the Southern Seaboard States, 1901–1915* (New York: Atheneum, 1969); and Herbert G. Gutman, "Schools for Freedom: The Post Emancipation Origins of Afro-American Education," in *Power and Culture: Essays on the American Working Class*, ed. Ira Berlin, 260–97 (New York: Pantheon Books, 1987).

2. Alfred, Lord Tennyson (1809–1892), *Locksley Hall*.

3. Henry Wadsworth Longfellow (1807–1822), *The Arsenal at Springfield*.

4. Amory Dwight Mayo (1823–1907) was a clergyman and educator who became

prominently involved in southern education after the Civil War. Fortune is quoting his "Colored Youth of the South, How Shall They Be Educated?" *New England Magazine* 23 (October 1897): 213–25.

5. Samuel C. Armstrong (1839–1893) was an educator who founded Hampton Institute in Hampton, Virginia, in 1868. For more on Armstrong, see Anderson, *The Education of Blacks in the South, 1860–1935*.

9

The Negro's Place in American Life at the Present Day

In his essay "The Negro's Place in American Life at the Present Day," written for the Booker T. Washington–edited *The Negro Problem*, Fortune summarizes the situation in which the African American community finds themselves, discussing the loss of rights, disfranchisement, and industrial slavery. In this essay, however, despite Fortune's usual themes of race unity, race pride, and agitation for political and civil rights, the editor's message is essentially one of gradualism, not the immediate demand of rights of his earlier years and his later *Negro World* editorials. In the end, Fortune optimistically looks at the future, arguing that being "mindful, therefore, of the Negro's two hundred and forty-five years of slave education and unrequited toil, and of his thirty years of partial freedom and less than partial opportunity, who shall say that his place in American life at the present day is not all that should be reasonably expected of him." In essence, he is trying to win the respect of the white audience in this essay. Fortune explains how far the race has come and recognizes that there is still some work to do, but at the same time he makes the point that such a condition does not justify abandonment of the principles of the Constitution by white America.

The Negro's Place in American Life at the Present Day —*The Negro Problem,* **ed. Booker T. Washington, 211–34 (New York, 1903)**

There can be no healthy growth in the life of a race or a nation without a self-reliant spirit animating the whole body; if it amounts to optimism, devoid of egotism and vanity, so much the better. This spirit necessarily carries with it intense pride of race, or of nation, as the case may be, and ramifies the whole mass, inspiring and shaping its thought and effort, however humble or exalted these may be,—as it takes "all sorts and conditions of men"[1] to make up a social order, instinct with the ambition and the activity which work for "high thinking and right living,"[2] of which modern evolution in all directions is the most powerful illustration in history. If pride of ancestry can, happily, be added to pride of race and nation, and these are re-enforced by self-reliance, courage and correct moral living, the possible success of such people may be accepted, without equivocation, as a foregone conclusion. I have found all of these requirements so finely blended in the life and character of no people as that of the Japanese, who are just now emerging from "the double night of ages"[3] into the vivifying sunlight of modern progress.

What is the Negro's place in American life at the present day?

The answer depends entirely upon the point of view. Unfortunately for the Afro-American people, they have no pride of ancestry; in the main, few of them can trace their parentage back four generations; and the "daughter of an hundred earls"[4] of whom there are probably many, is unconscious of her descent, and would profit nothing by it if this were not true. The blood of all the ethnic types that go to make up American citizenship flows in the veins of the Afro-American people, so that of the ten million of them in this country, accounted for by the Federal census, not more than four million are of pure negroid descent, while some four million of them, not accounted for by the Federal census, have escaped into the ranks of the white race, and are re-enforced very largely by such escapements every year. The vitiation of blood has operated irresistibly to weaken that pride of ancestry, which is the foundation-stone of pride of race; so that the Afro-American people have been held together rather by the segregation decreed by law and public opinion than by ties of consanguinity since their manumission and enfranchisement. It is not because they are poor and ignorant and oppressed, as a mass, that there is no such sympathy of thought and unity of effort among them as among Irishmen and Jews the world over, but because the vitiation of blood, beyond the honorable restrictions of law, has destroyed, in large measure, that pride of ancestry upon which pride of race must be builded. In no other logical way can we account for the failure of the Afro-American people to stand together, as other oppressed races do, and have done, for the righting of wrongs against them authorized by the laws of the several states, if not by the Federal Constitution, and sanctioned or tolerated by public opinion. In nothing has this radical defect been more noticeable since the War of the Rebellion than in the uniform failure of the people to sustain such civic organizations as exist and have existed, to test in the courts of law and in the forum of public opinion the validity of organic laws of States intended to deprive them of the civil and political rights guaranteed to them by the Federal Constitution. The two such organizations of this character which have appealed to them are the National Afro-American League, organized in Chicago, in 1890, and the National Afro-American Council, organized in Rochester, New York, out of the League, in 1898.[5] The latter organization still exists, the strongest of its kind, but it has never commanded the sympathy and support of the masses of the people, nor is there, or has there been, substantial agreement and concert of effort among the thoughtful men of the race along these lines. They have been restrained by selfish, personal and petty motives, while the constitutional rights which vitalize their citizenship have been "denied or abridged"[6] by legislation of certain of the States and by public opinion, even as Nero fiddled while Rome burned. If they had been actuated by a strong pride of ancestry and of race, if they had felt that injury to one was injury to all, if they had hung together instead of hanging separately, their place in the civil and political life of the Republic to-day would not be that, largely, of pariahs, with none so poor as to do them honor, but that of equality of right under the law enjoyed by all other alien ethnic forces in our citizenship. They who will not help themselves are usually not helped by others. They who make a loud noise and courageously contend for what is theirs, usually enjoy the respect and confidence of their fellows and get, in the end, what belongs to them, or a reasonable modification of it.

As a consequence of inability to unite in thought and effort for the conservation of their civil and political rights, the Afro-American Negroes and colored people have lost, by fundamental enactments of the old slave-holding States, all of the civil and political rights guaranteed them by the Federal Constitution, in the full enjoyment of which they were from the adoption of the War Amendments up to 1876–7, when they were sacrificed by their Republican allies of the North and West, in the alienation of their State governments, in order to save the Presidency to Mr. Rutherford B. Hayes of Ohio.[7] Their reverses in this matter in the old slave-holding States, coupled with a vast mass of class legislation, modelled on the slave code, have affected the Afro-American people in their civil and political rights in all of the States of the Republic, especially as far as public opinion is concerned. This was inevitable, and follows in every instance in history where a race element of the citizenship is set aside by law or public opinion as separate and distinct from its fellows, with a fixed status or caste.

It will take the Afro-American people fully a century to recover what they lost of civil and political equality under the law in the Southern States, as a result of the reactionary and bloody movement begun in the Reconstruction period by the Southern whites, and culminating in 1877,—the excesses of the Reconstruction governments, about which so much is said to the discredit of the Negro, being chargeable to the weakness and corruption of Northern carpet-baggers, who were the master and responsible spirits of the time and the situation, rather than to the weakness, the ignorance and venality of their Negro dupes, who, very naturally, followed where they led, as any other grateful people would have done. For, were not these same Northern carpet-baggers the direct representatives of the Government and the Army which crushed the slave power and broke the shackles of the slave? Even so. The Northern carpet-baggers planned and got the plunder, and have it; the Negro got the credit and the odium, and have them yet. It often happens that way in history, that the innocent dupes are made to suffer for the misdeeds and crimes of the guilty.[8]

The recovery of civil and political rights under the Constitution, as "denied or abridged" by the constitutions of the States, more especially those of the old slave holding ones, will be a slow and tedious process, and will come to the individual rather than to the race, as the reward of character and thrift; because, for reasons already stated, it will hardly be possible in the future, as it has not been in the past, to unify the mass of the Afro-American people, in thought and conduct, for a proper contention in the courts and at the ballot-box and in the education of public opinion, to accomplish this purpose. Perhaps there is no other instance in history where everything depended so largely upon the individual, and so little upon the mass of his race, for that development in the religious and civic virtues which makes more surely for an honorable status in any citizenship than constitutions or legislative enactments built upon them.

But even from this point of view, I am disposed to believe that the Negro's civil and political rights are more firmly fixed in law and public opinion than was true at the close of the Reconstruction period, when everything relating to him was unsettled and confused, based in legislative guarantees, subject to approval or disapproval of the dominant public opinion of the several States, and that he will gradually work out his own salvation under the Constitution,—such as Charles Sumner,[9] Thaddeus Stevens,[10] Benjamin F. Butler,[11] Frederick Douglass,[12] and their co-workers, hoped and labored that he might enjoy. He has lost nothing under the fundamental law; such of these restrictions, as apply to him by the law of certain of the States, necessarily apply to white men in like circumstances of ignorance and poverty, and can be overcome, in time, by assiduous courtship of the schoolmaster and the bank cashier. The extent to which the individual members of the race are overcoming the restrictions made a bar to their enjoyment of civil and political rights under the Constitution is gratifying to those who wish the race well and who look beyond the present into the future: while it is disturbing the dreams of those who spend most of their time and thought in abortive efforts to "keep the 'nigger' in his place"—as if any man or race could have a place in the world's thought and effort which he did not make for himself! In our grand Republic, at least, it has been so often demonstrated as to become proverbial, that the door of opportunity shall be closed to no man, and that he shall be allowed to have that place in our national life which he makes for himself. So it is with the Negro now, as an individual. Will it be so with him in the future as a race? To answer that we shall first have to determine that he has a race.

However he may be lacking in pride of ancestry and race, no one can accuse the Negro of lack of pride of Nation and State, and even of county. Indeed, his pride in the Republic and his devotion to it are among the most pathetic phases of his pathetic history, from Jamestown, in 1620, to San Juan Hill, in 1898. He has given everything to the Republic,—his labor and blood and prayers. What has the Republic given him, but blows and rebuffs and criminal ingratitude! And he stands now, ready and eager, to give the Republic all that he has. What does the Republic stand ready and eager to give him? Let the answer come out of the mouth of the future.

It is a fair conclusion that the Negro has a firmer and more assured civil and political status in American life to-day than at the close of the Reconstruction period, paradoxical as this may appear to many, despite the adverse legislation of the old slave-holding States, and the tolerant favor shown such legislation by the Federal Supreme Court, in such opinions as it has delivered, from time to time, upon the subject, since the adoption of the War amendments to the Federal Constitution. Technically, the Negro stands upon equality with all other citizens under this large body of special and class legislation; but, as a matter of fact, it is so framed that the greatest inequality prevails, and was intended to prevail, in the administration of it by the several States chiefly concerned. As long as such legislation by the States specifies, on the face of it, that it shall operate upon all citizens equally, however unequally and unjustly the legislation may be interpreted and administered by the local courts, the Federal Supreme Court has held, time and again, that no hardship was worked, and, if so, that the aggrieved had his recourse in appeal to the higher courts of the State of which he is a citizen,—a recourse at this time precisely like that of carrying coal to New Castle.

Under the circumstances, there is no alternative for the Negro citizen but to work out his salvation under the Constitution, as other citizens have done and are doing. It will be a long and tedious process before the equitable adjustment has been attained, but that does not much matter, as full and fair enjoyment of civil and political rights requires much time and patience and hard labor in any given situation, where two races come together in the same governmental environment; such as is the case of the Negro in America, the Irishman in Ireland, and the Jew everywhere in Europe. It is just as well, perhaps, that the Negro will have to work out his salvation under the Constitution as an individual rather than as a race, as the Jew has done it in Great Britain and as the Irishman will have to do it under the same Empire, as it is and has been the tendency of our law and precedent to subordinate race elements and to exalt the individual citizens as indivisible "parts of one stupendous whole."[13] When this has been accomplished by the law in the case of the Negro, as in the case of other alien ethnic elements of the citizenship, it will be more gradually, but assuredly, accomplished by society at large, the indestructible foundation of which was laid by the reckless and brutal prostitution of black women by white men in the days of slavery, from which a vast army of mulattoes were produced, who have been and are, gradually, by honorable marriage among themselves, changing the alleged "race characteristics and tendencies" of the Negro people. A race element, it is safe and fair to conclude, incapable, like that of the North American Indian, of such a process of elimination and assimilation, will always be a thorn in the flesh of the Republic, in which there is, admittedly, no place for the integrality and growth of a distinct race type. The Afro-American people, for reasons that I have stated, are even now very far from being such a distinct race type, and without further admixture of white and black blood, will continue to be less so to the end of the chapter. It seems to me that this view of the matter has not received the consideration that it deserves at the hands of those who set themselves up as past grand masters in the business of "solving the race problem," and in accurately defining "The Negro's Place in American Life at the Present Day." The negroid type and the Afro-American type are two very distinct types, and the sociologist who confounds them, as is very generally done, is bound to confuse his subject and his audience.

It is a debatable question as to whether the Negro's present industrial position is better or worse than it was, say, at the close of the Reconstruction period. As a mass, I am inclined to the opinion that it is worse, as the laws of the States where he is congregated most numerously are so framed as to favor the employer in every instance, and he does not scruple to get all out of the industrial slave that he can; which is, in the main, vastly more than the slave master got, as the latter was at the expense of housing, feeding, clothing and providing medical service for his chattel, while the former is relieved of this expense and trouble. Prof. W. E. B. DuBois,[14] of Atlanta University, who has made a critical study of the rural Negro of the Southern States, sums up the industrial phase of the matter in the following ("The Souls of Black Folk," pp. 39–40):

"For this much all men know: Despite compromise, war and struggle, the Negro is not free. In the backwoods of the Gulf States, for miles and miles, he may not leave the plantation of his birth; in well-nigh the whole rural South the black farmers are peons, bound by law and custom to an economic slavery, from which the only escape is death or the penitentiary. In the most cultured sections and cities of the South the Negroes are a segregated servile caste, with restricted rights and privileges. Before the courts, both in law and custom, they stand on a different and peculiar basis. Taxation without representation is the rule of their political life. And the result of all this is, and in nature must have been, lawlessness and crime."

It is a dark and gloomy picture, the substitution of industrial for chattel slavery, with none of the legal and selfish restraints upon the employer which surrounded and actuated the master. And this is true of the entire mass of the Afro-American laborers of the Southern States. Out of the mass have arisen a large number of individuals who own and till their own lands. This element is very largely recruited every year, and to this source must we look for the gradual undermining of the industrial slavery of the mass of the people. Here, too, we have a long and tedious process of evolution, but it is nothing new in the history of races circumstanced as the Afro-American people are. That the Negro is destined, however, to be the landlord and master agriculturist of the Southern States is a probability sustained by all the facts in the situation; not the least of which being the tendency of the poor white class and small farmers to abandon agri-cultural pursuits for those of the factory and the mine, from which the Negro laborer is excluded, partially in the mine and wholly in the factory. The development of mine and factory industries in the Southern States in the past two decades has been one of the most remarkable in industrial history.

In the skilled trades, at the close of the War of the Rebellion, most of the work was done by Negroes educated as artisans in the hard school of slavery, but there has been a steady decline in the number of such laborers, not because of lack of skill, but because trade unionism has gradually taken possession of such employments in the South, and will not allow the Negro to work alongside of the white man. And this is the rule of the trade unions in all parts of the country. It is to be hoped that there may be a gradual broadening of the views of white laborers in this vital matter and a change of attitude by the trade unions that they dominate. Can we reasonably expect this? As matters now stand, it is the individual Negro artisan, often a master contractor, who can work at his trade and give employment to his fellows. Fortunately, there are a great many of these in all parts of the Southern States, and their number is increasing every year, as the result of the rapid growth and high favor of industrial schools, where the trades are taught. A very great deal should be expected from this source, as a Negro contractor stands very nearly on as good footing as a white one in the bidding, when he has established a reputation for reliability. The facts obtained in every Southern city bear out this view of the matter. The individual black man has a fighting chance for success in the skilled trades; and, as he succeeds, will draw the skilled mass after him. The proper solution of the skilled labor problem is strictly within the power of the individual Negro. I believe that he is solving it, and that he will ultimately solve it.

It is, however, in the marvelous building up of a legal, comfortable and happy home life, where none whatever existed at the close of the War of the Rebellion; in the no less stupendous development of church life, with large and puissant organizations that command the respect and admiration of mankind, and owning splendid church property valued at millions of dollars; in the quenchless thirst of the mass of the people for useful knowledge, displayed at the close of the War of the Rebellion, and abating nothing of its intense keenness since, with the remarkable reduction in the illiteracy of the mass of the people, as is eloquently disclosed by the census reports—it is in these results that no cause for complaint or discouragement can be found. The whole race here stands on improved ground over that it occupied at the close of the War of the Rebellion; albeit, even here, the individual has outstripped the mass of the race, as it was but natural that he should and always will. But, while this is true and gratifying to all those that hope the Afro-American people well, it is also true, and equally gratifying that, as far as the mass is concerned, the home life, the church and the school house have come into the life of the people, in some sort, everywhere, giving the whole race a character and a standing in the estimation of mankind which it did not have at the close of the war, and presaging, logically, unless all signs fail, a development along high and honorable lines in the future; the results from which, I predict, at the end of the ensuing half century, builded upon the foundation already laid, being such as to confound the prophets of evil, who never cease to doubt and shake their heads, asking: "Can any good thing come out of Nazareth?"[15] We have the answer already in the social and home life of the people, which is so vast an improvement over the conditions and the heritage of slavery as to stagger the understanding of those who are informed on the subject, or will take the trouble to inform themselves.

If we have much loose moral living, it is not sanctioned by the mass, wedlock being the rule, and not the exception; if we have a vast volume of illiteracy, we have reduced it by forty per cent. since the war, and the school houses are all full of children eager to learn, and the schools of higher and industrial training cannot accommodate all those who knock at their doors for admission; if we have more than our share of criminality, we have also churches in every hamlet and city, to which a vast majority of the people belong, and which are insistently pointing "the way, the light and the truth"[16] to higher and nobler living.

Mindful, therefore, of the Negro's two hundred and forty-five years of slave education and unrequited toil, and of his thirty years of partial freedom and less than partial opportunity, who shall say that his place in American life at the present day is not all that should be reasonably expected of him, that it is not creditable to him, and that it is not a sufficient augury for better and nobler and higher thinking, striving and building in the future? Social growth is the slowest of all growth. If there be signs of growth, then, there is reasonable hope for a healthy maturity. There are plenty of such signs, and he who runs may read them, if he will.

Notes

1. From the Book of Common Prayer: "O God, the Creator and Preserver of all mankind, we humbly beseech thee for all sorts and conditions of men."

2. Pilgrim, "The Valley of the Quest," in *Theosophical Siftings*, vol. 2 (London: Theosophical Publishing Society, 1889–90).

3. George Gordon, Lord Byron (1788–1824), *Childe Harold's Pilgrimage*.

4. Alfred, Lord Tennyson (1809–1892), *Lady Clara Vere de Vere*.

5. For information on the activities of these organizations and Fortune's relation to them, see Emma Lou Thornbrough, *T. Thomas Fortune: Militant Journalist* (Chicago: University of Chicago Press, 1972); and Shawn Leigh Alexander, "'We Know Our Rights

and Have the Courage to Defend Them': Agitation in the Age of Accommodation, 1883–1909" (Ph.D. diss., University of Massachusetts–Amherst, 2004).

6. U.S. Constitution. Fortune is referencing the 14th Amendment of the U.S. Constitution.

7. Rutherford B. Hayes (1822–1893) served as U.S. president from 1877 to 1881. The certification of his election was preceded by the Compromise of 1877, which led to the withdrawal of federal troops from the occupied southern states, Florida, Louisiana, and South Carolina.

8. For more on the situation African Americans were facing, see Thornbrough, *T. Thomas Fortune*; Alexander, "We Know Our Rights"; August Meier, *Negro Thought in America, 1880–1915: Racial Ideologies in the Age of Booker T. Washington* (Ann Arbor: University of Michigan Press, 1963); Robert L. Factor, *The Black Response to America: Men, Ideals, and Organization, from Frederick Douglass to the NAACP* (Reading, Mass.: Addison-Wesley, 1970); Leon F. Litwack, *Trouble in Mind: Black Southerners in the Age of Jim Crow* (New York: Alfred A. Knopf, 1998); C. Vann Woodward, *The Strange Career of Jim Crow* (New York: Oxford University Press, 1966); Edward L. Ayers, *The Promise of the New South: Life after Reconstruction* (New York: Oxford University Press, 1992); and Michael Perman, *Struggle for Mastery: Disfranchisement in the South, 1888–1908* (Chapel Hill: University of North Carolina Press, 2001).

9. Charles Sumner (1811–1874) was a senator from Massachusetts who was a vocal antislavery advocate and a leader of the Radical Republicans during the Civil War and Reconstruction. Fortune gave a strong address in memory of Charles Sumner, in which he promoted the need for the creation of a civil rights organization. See *Hartford Telegram*, January 11, 1884; and *New York Globe*, January 19, 1884. For more on Sumner, see chapter 6, note 5.

10. Thaddeus Stevens (1792–1868) was a Republican member of the U.S. House of Representatives from Pennsylvania and a prominent member of the Radical Republicans during Reconstruction.

11. Benjamin F. Butler (1818–1893) was a Massachusetts politician who was a member of the House of Representatives and later governor of the state. During the Civil War his administration occupied Union-controlled New Orleans.

12. Frederick Douglass (ca. 1818–1895) was an escaped slave who became a prominent abolitionist, editor, and author. Douglass rose to become the most influential African American of the nineteenth century. For more on Douglass, see Benjamin Quarles, *Frederick Douglass* (New York: Atheneum, 1974); David W. Blight, *Frederick Douglass' Civil War: Keeping Faith in Jubilee* (Baton Rouge: Louisiana State University Press, 1989); and Waldo E. Martin, *The Mind of Frederick Douglass* (Chapel Hill: University of North Carolina Press, 1984). Fortune wrote a moving article on Douglass after his passing; see T. Thomas Fortune, "Mr. Douglass' Peculiar Greatness," *AME Church Review* 12 (1895): 108–13. He also delivered a poem honoring Douglass at the Douglass monument dedication ceremony in Rochester, New York, on September 14, 1898. A portion of this poem is published as the introduction to part 2 of this volume, "Civil Rights and Race Leadership." For the entire poem, see John W. Thompson, *An Authentic History of the Douglass*

Monument: Biographical Facts and Incidents in the Life of Frederick Douglass (Rochester, N.Y.: Rochester Herald Press, 1903).

13. Alexander Pope (1688–1744), *An Essay on Man*.

14. W.E.B. Du Bois (1868–1963) was a civil rights activist, educator, sociologist, and historian. For more on Du Bois during this period, see August Meier, *Negro Thought in America*; Elliott Rudwick, *W.E.B. Du Bois: Propagandist of the Negro Protest* (New York: Atheneum, 1978); and David Levering Lewis, *W.E.B. Du Bois: Biography of a Race, 1868–1919* (New York: Henry Holt and Company, 1993). Fortune is quoting from Du Bois' *The Souls of Black Folk*.

15. John 1:46.

16. John 14:6: "I am the way, the truth, and the life." Fortune uses "light" in place of "life."

10

The Voteless Citizen

In the following essay Fortune discusses the consequences of the disfranchisement of the African American population and calls upon the community to fight for their right to vote and for all their rights "securely anchored in the Constitution." According to the editor, the community needed to stop looking outside for assistance: "His reliance must mainly be upon himself." To add substance to his argument, in the second section of the essay Fortune dissects the 1879 *North American Review* symposium "Ought the Negro to Be Disfranchised? Ought He to Have Been Enfranchised?"

The Voteless Citizen — *Voice of the Negro* 1, no. 9 (1904): 397–402

I. It has been seldom in the history of mankind that the verdict of a nation, deliberately arrived at, after a long and illuminating discussion of all of the phases of it, has been reversed by the deliberate act of the same people. Upon this fact of history we have the axiom that revolutions seldom go backward. The emancipation of the African slaves by the United States was not a spontaneous act; it was the logical outcome of quite a century of agitation of the question by all shades of thought of the whole people, by far some of the ablest men of the south being in favor of it up to the time when the politicians, aided by the invention of the cotton gin, made an issue of it to further the political prestige of their section of the country, if not their own. It was but natural that Thomas Jefferson should be opposed to the institution of slavery, although he was a slave-holder, as he imbibed his democracy from the high priests of the French Revolution, as also did Thomas Paine, the basic principle of whose philosophy was the equality of all men under the law; and these two men, with Alexander Hamilton, the master mind of the whole American movement for a federal union based upon the consent of the governed, had more to do with shaping the Declaration of Independence and the Constitution as it has come down to us, than any other of the great men of the period. But that the influence of Thomas Jefferson was second only to that of Alexander Hamilton in the whole movement may easily be accepted as a fact of our history.

If Hamilton, Jefferson and Paine could have had their way about it, African slavery would have disappeared from the states of the federal union when the organic law was finished by the Philadelphia convention and the United States assumed their place in the commonwealth of nations. That their wishes in this matter were not deferred to, along with those of other men as able and broad-minded, has cost the republic more in vital energy, in money values and in the sacrifice of life than all the other questions passed upon finally in the perfected Constitution.

The emancipation of the slaves was a deliberate act of the American people, a culmination of the consideration of the subject in all its phases from the foundation of the republic, in the progress of which the good relations of the states in the federal union were often in peril of disruption. This is especially true of the period beginning with the Compromise era from 1835 to 1856, when the supreme court, through Chief Justice Roger B. Taney,[1] defined the attitude of the government towards the slave question in such wise as to remove it from the domain of sophomoric discussion and legislative prestidigitation, giving it a fixed place in the federal system which could only be changed or revoked by the sovereign people in an amendment of the organic law. The attitude of the court, that "it is held to be good law and precedent that a black man had no rights that a white man is bound to respect," not only sobered by shocked the American people, although any other conclusion at the time would have convulsed them. The friends of freedom were astounded and nonplussed while the slave power was jubilant. These latter were rudely awakened from their revelry, however, by John Brown's raid on Harper's Ferry in 1859. It came their turn to be astounded and nonplussed; they were more than this; they were demoralized. John Brown's raid was the answer which the people of the north and west gave to the people of the south, who had laid down the slave-law through Chief Justice Taney, although the people of the north and the west are not as yet tired of disavowing that old Ossowatomie spoke for them.[2] That Chief Justice Taney's opinion and John Brown's raid demoralized the slave south and precipitated the war of the rebellion and thus hastened the emancipation of the slaves is but to reason from cause to effect.

When the Thirteenth Amendment, abolishing slavery, was adopted, it followed as a natural and logical sequence that the Fourteenth and Fifteenth amendments should also be adopted, because it is inconceivable that so large a body of citizens should be left without protection of the ballot; and this view of the matter was emphasized by the high-handed acts of the state governments growing out of the policy of President Andrew Johnson, in which the southern white men showed that they were determined to reenslave the Negroes, and from which grew the reconstruction policy as an inevitable result of the tyrannical course. As they had forced the war of rebellion and thus made the abolition of slavery possible, so, by their conduct, with the connivance of President Johnson, they made the reconstruction policy possible. The phases of the matter; this point of view, has been stated with brilliant effect by Hon. Carl Schurz,[3] in *McClure's Magazine*, for January last.

"The government of the union was in duty and honor bound," Mr. Schurz says, "to maintain the emancipation of the slaves and to introduce free labor. The solution of such a problem would have been extremely difficult under any circumstances. It was in this case especially complicated by the partial failure of the Freedmen's Bureau, and still more by the decided encouragement given to the reactionary tendency prevailing among the southern whites, by the attitude of President Johnson, which permitted the southern whites to expect that they would soon have the power to reestablish something similar to slave labor."

Having abolished slavery by the Thirteenth amendment and enfranchised the freedman by the Fourteenth and Fifteenth Amendments, the revolution begun by Benjamin Lundy[4] in 1815, at St. Clairsville, Va., when he established the "Union Humane Society," was consummated, and the equality of all citizens under the Federal Constitution became a fixed fact in the law and equity of the United States, where it will remain forever, however much states acting in their several capacities and within the limitation prescribed by the Federal Constitution, may qualify it by one make-shift and another. And this aspect of the matter should seal up the mouths of those who insist that the adoption of the Fourteenth amendment was a mistake, because, first, the adoption of it was necessary to make effective the Thirteenth Amendment; second, and if it had not been adopted when it was, it never would have been adopted, and third, having once been adopted and become a part of the organic law, it never will be repealed.

II. But, in dealing with the Negro question, the white men of the southern states have never exercised that saneness and magnanimity for which in other matters of vital moment they have become noted. An evil genius has always seemed to have dictated their policy and shaped their conduct.

Disaster after disaster had not taught them the soberness of wisdom and generous humanity, so that we have come to expect an exhibition of these no more than we expect figs of thistles. The opinions expressed in *The North American*, for March, 1879, in a symposium on the subject: "Ought the Negro to be Disfranchised? Ought he to have been Enfranchised?" bars out this view.

The Hon. James G. Blaine[5] opened the discussion in a clean-cut statement of the case. On the first proposition he stated his conclusion as follows:

"And these amendments can not be annulled until two-thirds of the senate and two-thirds of the house of representatives of the United States shall propose and a majority of the legislatures or conventions of twenty-nine states shall, by affirmative vote, approve the amendment. In other words, the Negro can not be disfranchised so long as one vote more than one-third in the United States senate, or the one vote more than one-third in the house of representatives shall be recorded against it, and if these securities and safeguards should give way, then the disfranchisement could not be effected so long as a majority in one branch in the legislatures of only ten states should refuse to assent to it and refuse to assent to a convention to which it might be referred. No human right on this continent is more completely guaranteed than the right against disfranchisement on account of race, color or previous condition of servitude, as embodied in the Fifteenth Amendment to the Constitution of the United States."

On the second proposition he stated his conclusion as follows:

"For myself, I answer the second question in the affirmative with as little hesitation as I answered the first in the negative. And if the question were again submitted to the judgment of congress I would vote for suffrage in the light of experience with more confidence than I voted for it in the light of experiment.

"The one sure mode to remand the states that rebelled against the Union to their autonomy was to give suffrage to the Negro; and that autonomy will be complete, absolute, and unquestioned whenever the rights that are guaranteed by the constitution of the republic shall be enjoyed in every state as the administration of justice was assured magna charta—promptly and without delay; freely and without sale; completely and without denial."

While the other republican contributor to the symposium, Hon. James A. Garfield,[6] agrees substantially with Mr. Blaine's views, Mr. Wendell Phillips[7] powerfully arraigned the government and the Republican party for treachery and cowardice in dealing with the suffrage and other rights of the Afro-American people. The Democratic contributors were Hon. L. C. Q. Lamar, of Mississippi;[8] Governor Wade Hampton, of South Carolina;[9] Alexander H. Stephens, of Georgia;[10] Thomas A. Hendricks, of Indiana,[11] and Montgomery Blair, of Maryland.[12] Mr. Lamar,[13] says:

"He (Mr. Blaine) lays down with force and clearness his propositions: 1. That the disfranchisement of the Negro is a political impossibility under any circumstances short of revolution. 2. The ballot in the hands of the Negro, however its exercise may have been embarrassed and diminished by what he considers, erroneously, a general southern policy, has been to that race a means of defense and an element of progress. I agree to both propositions. In all my experience of southern opinion I know of no southern man of influence or consideration who believes that the disfranchisement of the Negro on account of race, color or previous condition of servitude is a political possibility."

All of the other representative democrats a party to the discussion, substantially agree with the opinions of Mr. Lamar, as here quoted, with the exception of Montgomery Blair, who, strangely enough, was a member of President Lincoln's cabinet and was present when he read the Emancipation Proclamation to it. At that time, in 1879, none of these men believed that the Negro would or should be disfranchised. That was the general attitude, not only of southern mind, but of the national democratic mind. After the republicans had sacrificed the southern state governments, in 1876, to save the electoral votes for Rutherford B. Hayes,[14] an Ohio republican marplot of whom we have since had a sickening succession—the country settled down to the belief that the suffrage question in the southern states would gradually adjust itself, as it had done in other states of the union, under abnormal stress, by state regulations bearing alike upon all the citizenship and within the limitations defined by the Federal Constitution. Southern men pleaded that the question be left to them and that they would settle it in fairness at all concerned. It was in the nature of a solemn covenant which the southern whites entered into the people of the republic. In his Boston address, after the delivery of which he went home to die, Henry Woodfen Grady, of Georgia,[15] said:

"Can we solve it (the race problem)? The God who gave it into our hands, He alone can know. But this, the weakest and wisest of us do know, we cannot solve it with less than your tolerant and patient sympathy—with less than the knowledge that the blood that runs in your veins is ours—and that when we have done our best, whether the issue be lost or won, we shall feel your strong arm about us and hear the beating of your approving hearts."

But this persuasive eloquence, like all that he uttered, and like most that the white south has ever uttered on this question, was but the siren's voice. It pleaded for confidence, for time, for freedom from outside intervention, not to keep faith, not to work for the betterment of all and to create a condition in which the scales of justice could be balanced evenly between whites and blacks; but in order that they might forge the conditions encouraged by Andrew Johnson after the war of the rebellion and which the reconstruction policy was inaugurated to wipe out any forever thereafter to make impossible. The good advice to Thomas A. Hendricks, in the symposium to which I have referred, has been ignored, and a persistent effort has been made to destroy the results of war of the rebellion by subtle laws, made organic by snap judgment and in defiance of the explicit guarantees of the Federal Constitution. How complete has been the disfranchisement of the race by the southern states is stated with judicial precision by Mr. Wilford H. Smith,[16] of New York, an Afro-American lawyer of great ability, who has appeared several times before the Federal Supreme Court in cases growing out of the southern disfranchisement laws, as follows: ("The Negro Problem," 83–85.)[17]

"These restrictions fall into three groups. The first comprises a property qualification—the ownership of $300 worth or more of real or personal property (Alabama, Louisiana, Virginia, and South Carolina); the payment of a poll tax (Mississippi, North Carolina, Virginia); an educational qualifications—the ability to read and write (Alabama, Louisiana, North Carolina.) Thus far, those who believe in a restricted suffrage everywhere, could perhaps find no reasonable fault with any one of these qualifications, applied either separately or together. But the Negro has made such progress that these restrictions alone would perhaps not deprive him of effective representation. Hence the second group. This comprises an "understanding" clause—the applicant must be able to "read, or understand when read to him, any clause of the constitution" (Mississippi), or to read and explain, or to understand and explain, when read to him, any section of the constitution (Virginia); an employment qualification—the voter must be regularly employed in some lawful occupation (Alabama); a charter qualification—the voter must be a person of good character who "understands the duties and obligations of citizens under a republican (!) form of government" (Alabama). The qualifications under the first group are left to the discretion and judgment of the registering officer, for in most instances these are all requirements for registration, which must precede voting.

"But the first group, by its own force, and the second group, under imaginable conditions, might exclude not only the Negro vote, but a large part of the white vote. Hence, the third group, which comprises a military service qualification—any man who went to the war willingly or unwillingly, in a good cause or a bad, is entitled to register (Alabama, Virginia); a prescriptive qualification, under which are included all male persons who were entitled to vote on January 1, 1867, at which date the Negro had not yet been given the right to vote; a hereditary qualification (the so-called "grandfather" clause), whereby any son (Virginia), or descendant (Alabama) of a soldier, and (North Carolina) the descendant of any person who had a right to vote on January 1, 1867, inherits that right. If the voter wish to take advantage of these last exceptions to a general rule, he must register within a stated time, whereupon he becomes a member of a privileged class of permanently enrolled voters, not subject to any of the other restrictions."

Since the article by Mr. Smith was written last year, Maryland has been added to the disfranchising and proscribing States. The Federal Congress and Supreme Court have, so far, justified, by toleration or equivocation, the measures adopted by the Southern States to deny or abridge the right to vote on account of race, color or previous condition of servitude, and this condition is likely to continue for an indefinite time; that ultimately the laws of the States will conform to the laws of the United States, which are fundamental and specifically mandatory on the States, is a reasonable conclusion. The general interest and welfare are too directly involved in the issue to admit of a perpetuation of the existing irregularities. While the Fourteenth and Fifteenth Amendments to the Federal Constitution remain a part of the fundamental law of the land, it will be impossible for any State permanently to disfranchise any portion of its citizenship "on account of race, color or previous condition," and such disfranchisement as obtains or may obtain, directly or indirectly, for such cause, must by the nature of it be temporary in duration, subject to the modification or disappearance of the provoking causes, such as too general illiteracy or poverty, or both.

III. While accepting the fact that the Afro-American citizen is disfranchised in all of the Southern States, by fundamental enactment of those States, and that the Federal Congress and Supreme Court have acquiesced in such disfranchisement, for the time being, and while admitting the hardships which are entailed upon the Afro-Americans by such disfranchisement and acquiescence, we have the assurance that the fundamental law of the land remains unchanged, and will remain unchanged, as Mr. Blaine had so forcibly pointed out in the quotation I have made in this article from the *North American Review*. From year to year a larger and larger number will pass into the voting body, by reason of the steady growth in intelligence and possession of property and development of strong self-reliant character, without which intelligence and property are of no value.

We know to our sorrow that a voteless citizen is a pariah, to be victimized by individuals and mobs and by legislators, and that he must put up with injustice which makes the blood boil with indignation. A body of citizens so large as that of the Afro-American people in the Southern States would never with the ballot in their hands be subject to separate car laws, separate school laws, separate penal institution regulations—separate everything that arrogance and insolence, uncurbed by fear of retaliation at the ballot-box, are disposed to heap upon the defenseless. Class legislation and mob law could not flourish in a condition where the victims possessed power to vote out of office those who make and enforce class laws and tolerate the excesses of individuals and mobs. As Hon. James A. Garfield[18] puts it, "the ballot was given to the Negro not so much to enable him to govern others as to prevent others from misgoverning him. Suffrage is the sword and shield of our law, the best armament that liberty offers to the citizen." The truth of this has demonstrated in the past fifteen years, since the utterance was published, during which time the Afro-American citizen has been robbed of his civil and political rights by legislatures, and is now mistreated and wronged and murdered by any white man or collection of white men who for personal or selfish ends have a mind to so do, as a result of that robbery.

Having our rights securely anchored in the Constitution of the United States, I can well close this article with the conclusion of the Hon. Thomas A. Hendricks, a Democrat of the Democrats (*North American Review*, March, 1879),[19] as follows: "I am not able to see why the subject of Negro suffrage should be discussed. It must be known to all that the late amendments will not be, cannot be, repealed. There is but the duty upon all to make the political power now held by the enfranchised race the cause of the least evil, and the greatest possible good to the country. The Negro is now free, and is the equal of the white man in respect to his civil and political rights. He must now make his own contest for position and power. By his own conduct and success he will be judged. It will be unfortunate for him if he shall rely upon political sympathy for position, rather than upon duties well and intelligently discharged. Everywhere the white race should help him, but his reliance must mainly be upon himself."

Yes; "his reliance must mainly be upon himself." How can we most effectually hammer this fact into his head?

Notes

1. Roger B. Taney (1777–1864) was chief justice of the U.S. Supreme Court from 1836 to 1864. He authored the majority decision in *Dred Scott v. Sandford*, 60 U.S. 393 (1856).

2. John Brown (1800–1859) was a radical abolitionist who led twenty-one followers in an attack on the federal arsenal in Harper's Ferry, Virginia, on October 16, 1859, with the intention of liberating and arming slaves. Fortune wrote a poem about Brown while visiting Kansas and published it in the *Age* in 1907, "With John Brown in Kansas," *New York Age*, September 19, 1907. For more on Brown, see chapter 6, note 6.

3. Carl Schurz (1828–1906) was a journalist, author, Union soldier, Republican politician, and editor of the *New York Evening Post*. Fortune is referring to an article by Schurz, "Can the South Solve the Negro Problem," *McClure's Magazine* 22 (January 1904): 259–84.

4. Benjamin Lundy (1789–1839) was a Quaker abolitionist and editor of the abolitionist newspaper *Genius of Universal Emancipation*. For more on Lundy, see chapter 6, note 2.

5. James G. Blaine (1830–1893) was a Republican politician from Maine who ran for president in 1884 and lost to Democrat Grover Cleveland. Fortune is citing Blaine's article, "Ought the Negro to Be Disenfranchised? Ought He to Have Been Enfranchised?" *North American Review* 128 (March 1879): 225–34.

6. James A. Garfield (1831–1881) was a Republican politician who was elected president of the United States in 1881. Garfield was shot in office on September 19, 1881.

7. Wendell Phillips (1811–1884) was a distinguished abolitionist and antislavery orator. Fortune wrote a moving obituary of Phillips. See *New York Globe*, February 9, 1884. For more on Phillips, see chapter 6, note 4.

8. Lucius Quintus Cincinnatus Lamar (1825–1893) was a Mississippi Democratic senator from 1877 to 1885 and justice of the Supreme Court from 1888 to 1893.

9. Wade Hampton (1818–1902) was a Democratic governor of South Carolina from 1876 to 1879 and a senator from 1879 to 1891.

10. Alexander H. Stephens (1812–1883) was a Democratic representative from Georgia who served from 1873 to 1883.

11. Thomas A. Hendricks (1819–1885) was elected the twenty-first vice president of the United States as Grover Cleveland's running mate in 1884.

12. Montgomery Blair (1813–1883) was a Democratic politician and lawyer from Maryland.

13. For Lamar's comments, see L.Q.C. Lamar, "Ought the Negro to Be Disenfranchised? Ought He to Have Been Enfranchised?" *North American Review* 128 (March 1879): 231–40.

14. Rutherford B. Hayes (1822–1893) served as U.S. president from 1877 to 1881. The certification of his election was preceded by the Compromise of 1877, which led to the withdrawal of federal troops from the occupied southern states, Florida, Louisiana, and South Carolina.

15. Henry W. Grady (1850–1889) served as managing editor of the *Atlanta Constitution* in the 1880s and used his position to promote the New South program of northern investment, southern industrial growth, diversified farming, and white supremacy. Grady delivered a speech on December 12, 1889, the "Race Problem in the South." For the full text of the speech, see the *Atlanta Constitution*, December 15, 1889.

16. Wilford H. Smith was a lawyer and civil rights activist. Smith often worked with Booker T. Washington, and among other cases he represented Jackson W. Giles in two suits supported by the Afro-American Council and Booker T. Washington, *Giles v. Harris*, 189 U.S. 475 (1903), and *Giles v. Teasley*, 193 U.S. 146 (1904), challenging the disfranchisement legislation in Alabama.

17. Fortune is citing Wilford H. Smith's article "The Negro and the Law," in *The Negro Problem*, ed. Booker T. Washington, 125–60 (1903; repr., New York: Arno Press, 1969).

18. James A. Garfield, "Ought the Negro to Be Disenfranchised? Ought He to Have Been Enfranchised?" *North American Review* 128 (March 1879): 244–50.

19. Thomas A. Hendricks, "Ought the Negro to Be Disenfranchised? Ought He to Have Been Enfranchised?" *North American Review* 128 (March 1879): 267–70.

PART 2

Civil Rights and Race Leadership

Frederick Douglass

For he was large in stature and in soul and head
True type of New America, whose sons, 'tis said,
The western world shall have as glorious heritage—
That they shall write in history's fadeless, truthful page
Such deeds as ne'er before have wrought for liberty
And all the arts of peace—the strongest of the free!

And every depth he braved, and every height he trod
From earth's alluring shrines to the presence of his God;
And he was cheered by children's confidence and trust,
A tribute never withheld from the true and just;
And woman's sympathy was his, the divine power
That rules the world in calmest and stormiest hour!

To him all weakness and all suffering appealed;
'Gainst none such was his brave heart ever steeled.
And pleading womanhood for honest rights denied
No champion had of sturdier worth to brave wrong's pride—
To claim for her in all the fullest measure true
Of justice God ordained her portion, as her due.

He needs not monument of stone who writes his name
By deeds, in diamond letters, in the Book of Fame—
Who rises from the bosom of the race to be
A champion of the slave, a spokesman of the free—
Who scorns the fetters of a slave's degrading birth
And takes his place among the giants of the earth.

From John W. Thompson, *An Authentic History of the Douglass Monument*, 86–88

11

The Virtue Of Agitation

In his editorial, "The Virtue of Agitation," written in August 1883, Fortune calls upon the race to demonstrate that they are willing to fight for their rights. It is important to note that the editorial was written a few months before the Supreme Court ruled the Civil Rights Act of 1875 unconstitutional and before the riot in Danville, Virginia. These two watershed events signaled the "revolution gone backward" that Fortune discussed after the 1876 election of Rutherford B. Hayes.

The Virtue of Agitation —*New York Globe*, **August 18, 1883**

We believe in dissatisfaction; we believe in the manifold virtues of agitation.[1] Wrongs spring up and gain a solid footing as naturally as the dews of heaven descend upon the grasses of the field. The propensity to tyranize is a predominant element in the human nature; it springs from the all absorbing sentiment of self-interest and self-preservation. It is as strong in the affairs of civilized society as in savage society. The struggle to get on top is instinctive. Around the great prizes in the lottery of life the giants contend with fury and havoc, but the masses of mankind humbly battle for a place to sleep, clothes to cover them and food to sustain them. And this is the most desperate contention. They not only contend one with the other but they often forget their mutual woes and takes arms against the giant vultures which gnaw away their vitals.

Thus the Helots of Sparta strove time and again to liberate themselves from the tyranny of their masters, and the plebeians of Rome contended even unto death against the encroachments of the patrician Shylocks.[2] The grapple of the masses with the few who managed to rise to the infamy of tyrants has always been of the most sanguinary character. While the result has not always appeared to incline to the side of the masses it has, however, really done so. To the clamors of the masses, and ceaseless contention, the British people owe that large measure of freedom they enjoy. Out of the fury, fanaticism and carnage of the French Revolution,[3] the people rose stronger and freer, and when the last remnant of the name of Napoleon sinks into the oblivion out of which the great Bonaparte came, they will be still stronger and freer. And the Russian masses will yet cease to feel the heel that crushes and to hear the voice that blights with its very breath. Ireland will yet stand up free and equal with the other members of the government of which she forms a part. The tendency of the world's history has always been in the direction of larger intelligence and freedom of the masses.

In our own country the conflict of wrong and right has been long and bloody. Around the battle-fields of Bunker's Hill and Yorktown, and Manassas and Appomattox the masses contended and conquered; and so they will always, if they fight on the side of right.

Agitation does not always lead to an appeal to arms. Peace has its triumphs, and often they are more substantial than those that follow the victorious card of Napoleon or Wellington. Our history in this country dates from the moment that restless men among us became restless under oppression and rose against it. From Denmark Vesey[4] to Nat Turner,[5] from the flight of Frederick Douglass[6] and Henry Highland Garnet,[7] from the blood hounds of Maryland to the present time the voice of the race has been heard on the lecture platform and on the field of battle protesting against the injustice heaped upon the race. It has had its effect. Agitation, contentions, ceaseless unrest, constant aspiring—A race so moved must prevail. There is no half-way ground between right and wrong. The one or the other must obtain, and prevail.

Mental inertia is death. Indifferent acquiescence in wrong is death. Tame submission to outrage is death. Agitation, constant protesting, always standing up to be counted, to be heard, or to be knocked down—this spirit breeds respect and dulls the edge of tyranny. We should learn that the aggressive man, the man who is always ready to contend for what is his, is the man who gets what is his.

In politics, in business, in social intercourse we want to show more manhood, a deeper appreciation of the philosophy of life. We must learn to lean upon ourselves; we must learn to plan and execute business enterprises of our own; we must learn to venture our pennies if we would gain dollars. We must wake up. We spend too much time and money in frivolity. Fortunes and reputation are not made in that way.

Notes

1. Fortune often urged his readers to stand up and defend their rights. In December 1883 he wrote an editorial in which he reprinted the 1873 New York statute that outlawed discrimination in public accommodations. He urged: "Colored men of New York, stand your ground on the civil rights business." Further, he exclaimed, "In New York, South Carolina, let colored men assert their rights, and if they have to die in defending them, or bankrupt themselves, better a dead man or a pauper who dared to assert his manhood, than a living slink who prized his miserable life and money above the right to live as a man." See *New York Globe*, December 29, 1883.

2. The usurer in Shakespeare's *The Merchant of Venice*.

3. French Revolution (1789–1799).

4. Denmark Vesey (1767–1822) was a freed African slave who conspired to lead a slave revolt in Charleston, South Carolina, in 1822. For more on Vesey, see chapter 6, note 7.

5. Nat Turner (1800–1831) was an enslaved African who led a slave rebellion in Southampton County, Virginia, in 1831. Fortune published a poem honoring Turner in 1884, "Nat Turner," *AME Church Review* 1 (October 1884): 101, and "Nat Turner," *Globe*, October 18, 1884. For more on Turner, see chapter 6, note 8.

6. Frederick Douglass (ca. 1818–1895) was an escaped slave who became a prominent abolitionist, editor, and author. Douglass rose to become the most influential African American of the nineteenth century. Fortune wrote a moving article on Douglass after his passing; see T. Thomas Fortune, "Mr. Douglass' Peculiar Greatness," *AME Church Review* 12, no. 1 (1895): 108–13. Fortune also delivered a poem honoring Douglass at the Douglass monument dedication ceremony in Rochester, New York, on September 14, 1898. A portion of this poem is published as the introduction to section 4 of this volume. For the entire poem, see John W. Thompson, *An Authentic History of the Douglass Monument: Biographical Facts and Incidents in the Life of Frederick Douglass* (Rochester, N.Y.: Rochester Herald Press, 1903). For more on Douglass, see chapter 9, note 12.

7. Henry Highland Garnet (1815–1882) was an escaped slave who became a powerful abolitionist and orator. In 1843, at the National Negro Convention in Buffalo, New York, Garnet called for armed insurrection to free the slaves. For more information on Garnet, see Earl Ofari, *"Let Your Motto Be Resistance": The Life and Thought of Henry Highland Garnet* (Boston: Beacon Press, 1972); and Sterling Stuckey, *Slave Culture: Nationalist Theory and the Foundations of Black America* (New York: Oxford University Press, 1987).

12

Civil Rights and Social Privileges

"Civil Rights and Social Privileges" is an excellent example of Fortune's strength as an essayist. In this article he urges the community to develop the "dynamitic element" and agitate for their civil rights, which, according to Fortune, "are all such as affect the whole people, and are regulated by them in their collective capacity as a government." He argues that the move of white Americans to conflate civil rights with social privileges should not go unnoticed. He calls on the community to react and demand the rights which are theirs as co-equal citizens of the country. One such person who was attempting to conflate the two was Henry W. Grady, editor of the *Atlanta Constitution;* and he in particular became an object of Fortune's wrath in this essay. In reply to Grady's appeal to the North to leave the race question to the South, Fortune quipped, "Unlike in times past, *we have a voice; and we propose to make that voice heard,* in all future phases of the discussion of the race question."

In the essay Fortune also praises the actions of African resistance to colonial rule and acknowledges that such a fight may come to America, to which the author declares, "Let it come; I do not fear it." Furthermore, the editor acknowledges the necessity of reparations for the crimes committed by whites against blacks.

Civil Rights and Social Privileges —*AME Church Review* 2 (1886): 119–31

If any person should ask me in what essential element Afro-American character was most deficient, I would unhesitatingly respond *the dynamitic element*; that is, the element of character which represents an injury promptly, and in a way most characteristic of the *lex loci*. If I were asked, further, why the Afro-American was so deficient in this element of character, possessed in such large measure by our trans-atlantic kinsmen of the past as well as of the present, I would point him to the history of American slavery for two hundred years prior to 1865; during which time the object of all law, regulation and custom being to reduce the Afro-American character as much as possible to the condition of a pliant tool in the hands of a cruel but expert master. I do not think my interrogator, after perusing that history, would require further explanation for the phenomenal absence of the dynamitic element in our character.

Courage is one of the most striking peculiarities in the character of the savage. His absolute disdain of fear, and his vigilant readiness at all times to expose himself to danger in defense of what he regards as his natural rights, are facts notorious in the history of savage peoples. The persistent courage of the North American Indians has, indeed, decimated them from the countless millions of three centuries ago to a bare handful to-day; but no man can be found who will not applaud that savage bravery,—which recognized in every conflict it waged with the bull-dog tenacity, avarice and cruelty of the usurping and intolerant European a priority of ownership in the soil and usufruct of this grand continent. Had the Indian been less courageous he would have, perhaps, multiplied in numbers, not as a freeman, but as a slave; for it would have been strictly in harmony with the white man's predilection to take advantage of such cowardice to enslave the coward. It is my candid opinion that a dead savage, who dies defending his natural and prescriptive rights, is a far nobler object than the miserable slave who has neither the courage to die nor to live like a man.

There are two elements of Anglo-Saxon character which have enabled that people to dominate wherever they have planted the standard of St. George, *i.e.*, avarice and courage. In the wake of victorious armies the missionary, with his Holy Bible, and the commercial shark, with his rum jug and gewgaws, have trudged; the one to redeem the spiritual man from the sin of death, the other to condemn the physical man to eternal torments of the flesh and the spirit. The commercial instinct of the Anglo-Saxon has blunted his every sense of honesty, fair play and humanity; so that the empire of India, as the expense of rivers of guiltless blood, has been made tributary to his selfish schemes. The presence of the Anglo-Saxon on this continent, while not the primary outgrowth of the selfish commercial spirit, was largely so; the introduction here of African slavery, and in the West Indies as well, was due wholly to this ungodly inspiration. The most striking exhibition we have witnessed of late of this predominant idiosyncrasy, was British interference in the affairs of Egypt; where, to insure British Shylocks[1] in the principal and interest of moneys advanced to a most profligate and besotted government, a defenseless people were put under tribute and mulcted of their scanty earnings. The Soudan country, in no sense justly tributary to the Egyptian government, was also desolated in the selfish and fool-hardy attempt to force blood out of a turnip.

The Anglo-Saxon plants himself behind the sacred cross of Christ to conquer weak and defenseless peoples with, apparently, no other object than the ignoble one of usurping the ancient liberties of such forcibly compelling them to labor for the aggrandizement of alien tyrants.

These usurpers have the impudence to assure such injured people that their enslavement is a far better condition than their savage state; since a slave who dwells in the midst of our so-called Christian civilization, it is assumed, has much more to be grateful for than the free man of the boundless forest and prairies, in his nude, yet happy, condition of savagery. Such thinly spun sophistry as this was incessantly dinned into the ears of the African slaves of our country, prior to the issuance of the Emancipation Proclamation, from a thousand pulpits said to have been sacred to the service of the most High, and by other agencies whose selfish interest were father to the thought they blushed not to proclaim. And, strange as it may appear, there have not been wanting within very recent years multiloquent persons of intelligence and presumptive piety who have not hesitated to herald it as their firm belief that the all-wise and all-just Father had this in view when he permitted our expatriation to this country where our inextricably hybrid Anglo-Saxon population has dominated and fleeced everything from a red Indian and a negro African to a yellow Chinaman.

In whatever quarter of the globe the Anglo-Saxon has secured a controlling influence he has used it to enrich himself at the expense of the subject people. He has at no time been fettered by quibbles of conscience. The natural and prescriptive rights of others have never been regarded as a barrier to the attainment of his selfish purposes. In India, in Australia, in Africa, in North America, in the Islands of the Sea, the object has always been the same, the means identical. Weak and defenseless peoples have been their prey. Indeed, so deep-rooted is their propensity to enrich themselves at the expense of others that, when they could find no victims among alien people, they have not hesitated to fleece and tyrannize over each other. The people who enjoy immunity from the inordinate greed and propensity to tyrannize inborn in the Anglo-Saxon character are only such as are too powerful to be victimized. If you are not of Anglo-Saxon blood, you must become such through the tortuous by-ways of hybridity,—race metamorphosis, amalgamation, or through other ethnological channels for the extinction or absorption of race individuality. You cannot preserve your race individuality and dwell under the same governmental vine and fig tree with the Anglo-Saxon; and that, too, whether he comes to you or you go to him. It would seem to have passed into a proverb that Rome is altogether too small to contain, at the same time, Caesar and Pompey. It is reported of Julius Caesar[2] that, on returning from one of his brutal German campaigns, he remarked, in passing an Alpine village, "I would rather be *first* here than *second* at Rome."[3] The sentiment reveals the true character of the man. His spirit, it would seem, has fallen upon the Britons he so heartily despised.

It is not my purpose, in the limits of this article, to traverse the first settlement of this continent, nor the introduction here of African slavery by the whites of England and various other countries of Europe. Nor is it necessary, so well-known are these important matters of history. From the foundation of our government to 1865, the people of African origin in the United States had no other than a slave status; or, as Chief Justice Taney[4] states it in the opinion of the court (Dred Scott *versus* Sandford, in December, 1856):

"In the opinion of the court, the legislation and histories of the times, and the language used in the Declaration of Independence, show that neither the class of persons who had been imported as slaves, nor their descendants, whether they had become free or not, were then acknowledged as a part of the people, nor intended to be included in the general words used in that venerable instrument."*

Again in further defining the status of Afro-Americans, the court held that:—

"They had for more than a century been regarded as beings of an inferior order, and altogether unfit to associate with the white race, either in social or political relations, and so far inferior that they had no rights which the white man was bound to respect, and that the negro might justly lawfully be reduced to slavery for his benefit."†

This barbarous opinion prevailed up to the termination of the Great Rebellion, and subsequent years, during which the African slave was manumitted in all the territory of the United States, and enfranchised by proclamation and the adoption of the thirteenth, fourteenth and fifteenth amendments by the several States. By the happy provisions of these proclamations and amendments, the Afro-American was lifted from the abject

---
* Howard Reports, page 407.
† Ibid. 407.

condition of absolute and tormenting servitude, with no honorably defined status in the social compact, to a full-fledged citizen, with *co-equal* rights as such before the law and in all the avenues of civil life. The extremely cruel and barbarous laws and precedents upon which Chief Justice Taney was enabled to predicate the opinion of the court in the case of Dred Scott *versus* Sandford, had each and every one been swept away—made utterly null and void and inoperative—by the results of the war, and the incorporation into the fundamental law of the land, by adoption, of the amendments; in so far forth, indeed, that all previous interpretations of the constitution, relating to the rights of citizens of the United States and of the States had become obsolete.

Indeed, the powers of the Federal Government were very greatly and vitally enlarged by the amendments, not only as to their letter, but as to their spirit as well. This, as a matter of course, was to have been anticipated, since the war was fought to decide the right of a State to secede from the Federal compact, because of real or fancied injury, without the consent of all, or a majority of the members of that compact. Yet there are many persons, learned and others, who insist upon construing the Federal constitution from the standpoint of 1856, instead of from the standpoint of 1876 in the matter of the relation which the citizens of States bear to the Federal Government. I may add that the present Supreme Court Bench, with the single exception of Mr. Justice Harlan,[5] favor the Taney construction in this pregnant and vital particular.

Overriding the obvious letter and spirit of the constitutional amendments in the matter of the relations of the citizens of States to the Federal Government, the Supreme Court, in passing upon the Constitutionality of the Kuklux and Civil Rights laws, laid it down that the State was sovereign within its own territory; and that the citizens of States must look to the commonwealth wherein they reside for protection to life, limb and property, and for the conceding and yielding of other matters of civil import—such, for instance, as were defined in the Civil Rights laws and Kuklux law, overruled by the Supreme Court—since, as is maintained, the Federal Government is powerless, under the Constitution, *even as amended*, to interfere in the internal civil and purely municipal affairs of States;—except in cases of appeal, where there was reasonable ground for the assumption that such wronged citizen had no recourse in the courts of the States for injuries sustained; that is to say, the complainant must show that not only was he outraged in his common right by a fellow-citizen, but that by denying him proper redress in law the State became also, in fact, *particeps criminis*. These decisions proceed, it would seem, upon the same theory which obtains in cases of insurrection or rebellion within the jurisdiction of States, that the Federal authority can take no cognizance of or proceed to suppress such insurrection or rebellion until the lawful authority of such State appeals for assistance to the Federal Government, proclaiming thereby its inability longer to enforce law and order, and abdicating, for the time being at least, its functions as a sovereign to the Central or Federal authority.

The very arduous nature of the work before the thoughtful men of the race will be more readily appreciated, apprehended and mastered if we shall study diligently the doctrine of citizenship as laid down by the Supreme Court in the cases here cited. It will appear obvious to the most obtuse that the power of the Federal authority in the jurisdiction of States,—in the matter of proper protection of life and limb and property, and the enforcement of the full measure of such civil rights as inhere in the citizen by reason of his citizenship—is as impotent as a new born infant; and that, further, it would appear, in so far as these matters are concerned, he might just as well not be a citizen of the United States. Perhaps, no other instance is recorded in the annals of mankind where a government was powerful to confer but impotent to enforce the full measure of right and justice which attach to the manumission and enfranchisement of a wrong and defrauded class.

It is very true that the amendments forever inhibiting slavery in the territories of the United States, and conferring upon the manumitted class the power and dignity of citizenship, while emanating *from* the Federal authority, had to be submitted *to*, and ratified *by*, the States severally before receiving the force and effect of fundamental and irrevocable law. While, therefore, apparently, we owe to the Federal Government the boon of manumission and enfranchisement, it is to the States severally, the Federal Executive and Congress concurring, we are indebted; if, indeed, a sense of obligation can obtain in a case where that is returned which could not, in law or equity, justly have been alienated, usurped or withheld in the first instance.

I am among the few who maintain that, since the American people, in their Colonial as well as in their Federal capacity, legalized, or sanctioned, by acquiescence, or statutory enactment, the crime of holding property in man, they are responsible to the African people of this country for the principal and compound interest thereupon of the wages of each such slave, or his descendant, for at least the time covered by the adoption of the Federal Constitution (1787) and the manumission of the slave (1865); and that, until such principal and interest are paid to the last penny the American white man should cease to reproach us because of our poverty, ignorance, or mendacity. What we are the white man made us. He should not disclaim his workmanship. What we may be in the future will be largely the result of our own workmanship; and this we should not forget. Recognizing the vast labor to be performed, bearing in mind the tremendous consequences pendent upon the result of that labor, we should labor, so build, that our children shall have nothing to complain of when they are called upon to take up the work when we lay it down.

It comes with exceeding bad grace for the thief to arraign his hapless victim for being impecunious. And, yet, this is the true history of the dealings of the Anglo-Saxon race with all the people it has subjugated and fleeced. The history of the poor Indian in this country bears a melancholy resemblance to that of our own; especially in the feature of being forcibly robbed of labor, of freedom, and (in the case of the Indian) of priority of ownership of the soil. But the depravity of Anglo-Saxon character in this particular is so deep-seated and ramifying that, perhaps, we should not expect it to regard its disposition to dominate and fleece weaker people as a sin or a crime; perhaps we should not expect a people whose sense of justice and fair dealing is so marvelously blunted to acknowledge their past faults, or to recognize the existence of present ones,—or appeals to their selfish interests; or by arousing that sense of justice which, however obtuse and callous, is still found, in large or small measure, to be existent in all the multitudinous ethnical divisions of the human race.

To successfully cope with the Anglo-Saxon race, requires the possession of equal brain, cunning and courage. He yields nothing from a bare sense of equity. He concedes that you have inherent and common rights, but the concession is forced out of him by four years of the most sanguinary warfare; and, if you would enjoy these common rights which he concedes belong to you, he makes you contend for them one by one at the ballot-box, in the jury panel, on the palace car, on steamboats, at the threshold of hotels, and even at the doorway of the churches which he has created to propagate the doctrine of the "Fatherhood of God, and the brotherhood of man," enunciated in the byways of Palestine by the meek and lowly Nazarene. It requires brains, courage and cunning to cope with the Anglo-Saxon. He yields only to the force of circumstances. "Give him an inch, he'll take an ell." So he will. The disposition to dominate the pilfer "is bone of his bone, and flesh of his flesh."

Until such time as we thoroughly master the underlying actuating motives of Anglo-Saxon character, and turn upon him artillery of the same manufacture and power that he has so long used against us with such deadly effect, he will continue to dominate and fleece us. There can be no evasion of the issue on our part. We must have culture, wealth, courage and cunning, and we must use them as other people have done from the uprising of the Helots of Sparta (464 B.C.) to the tremendous uprising of the giants of intellect in this country, beginning with Benjamin Lundy (in 1815).[6] Whatever be the weapons employed, intelligence and courage are necessary to success. I do not believe in, or advise, violence. The logic of peace should always be thoroughly exhausted before an appeal is made to the barbarous agency of destruction, to enforce respect for those rights which inhere in man and which are guaranteed to him by the system of government of which he is a co-equal member. Our road to success lies (1) through an intelligent apprehension of our common rights, as defined by the Federal Constitution and by the Constitution of the State of which we may be citizens; because, while the Federal Constitution affirms who shall be citizens, and prohibits any discrimination as between citizen and citizen, the State actually defines the measure and quality of such citizenship, and it thereby enabled, through the ignorance or the weakness of particular classes, to make (as is frequently done in the South) discrimination laws which are odious and grievous to be borne; and (2) sufficient courage to maintain the sanctity and inviolability of such defined rights. Things should be called by their proper names, and no fear of offending the sense or lacerating or exasperating the feelings of wrongs-doers should deter us from speaking the truth, defending the right, protesting against outrage.

I admire the Irishman's persistent, courageous struggle for the same measure of right and justice enjoyed by the other constituent members of the British kingdom. In saying this, I do not desire to be construed as endorsing the more violent features which have characterized the struggle of the Irish people for justice. And, yet, truth compels the affirmation that such violence was frequently the logical evolution of the attending circumstances and conditions. There are times when oppressed people have no other medium through which to make their protest heard than that of violence. In such cases the righteous end aimed at must justify the means employed. It is the ceaseless, earnest recognition of the truism that "eternal vigilance is the price of liberty"[7] which I admire in the elements which go to make up Irish character, and which I sincerely regret is not possessed in larger measure by our own people in this country. No man respects a coward; he is despised by even the members of his own household. All history teaches that courage and intelligence are the complement of each other, in the obtaining as in the maintenance of freedom; and this is as true of individuals as of nations or races.

A discussion of the question of civil rights, with special reference to those withheld from us, was provoked by an article on "The Freedom's Case in Equity," by Mr. George W. Cable,[8] of New Orleans, in the January "Century Magazine," and a subsequent article from the pen of the same author appeared in the "Century" for September, under the suggestive caption, "The Silent South." In these two articles Mr. Cable thoroughly and courageously defines and discusses the subject of Civil Rights. The position assumed by Mr. Cable is, *in the present stage of our development*, the correct one; and we may be allowed to express, not surprise, but gratification and pleasure, at having a champion, sprung out of the very bosom of southern society, so thoroughly armed to combat the narrowness, perversity and cruelty of his own race. Surely, Rev. John Jasper[9] is correct, metaphorically if not logically, in his famous declaration that "the sun does move."

One of the most astounding things about the current discussion of the Civil Rights question is, the habitual and malicious disposition of those who would withhold them from us to confound social privileges with civil rights. This is peculiarly true of the position taken by Mr. Henry W. Grady[10] in his "In Plain Black and White" article, in the April "Century."[11] Mr. Grady expends all the wit and ingenuity he had mastered in a long residence in the South, and as editor of a leading but hide-bound Georgia newspaper, to confuse the matter,—for the very obvious purpose of giving a bare semblance of rationality for the absurd prejudices he rushed forward to champion. Every line of his argument bristles with evidence that he was all too conscious of the untenability and utter unrighteousness of the cause he urged. After a careful perusal of his labored arguments, we are more disposed to laugh at the ludicrous straits to which he is reduced than to sympathize with him. The platitudes upon which he would predicate a solution of the question fell still born.

Mr. Grady's arguments would have sounded reasonable, from his point of view, thirty years ago; to-day they sound like the mouthings of an old man in the last stage of his dotage. He contends that the races should be compelled to live as far apart as possible,—as far apart as the North and South poles,—unmindful, apparently, that for centuries the two peoples have sustained toward each other the closest and dearest relations, in all the avenues of life; and that, as a consequence; the entire African race in this country has not only had its blood tainted but *actually corrupted* by unholy contact with his much vaunted "superior race." Let Mr. Grady but adjust his eye-glasses and look about him in the city of Atlanta, and he will discover at a glance that the white people of his State, (one of the meanest in the whole Union), and of the entire nation, have gone too far in polluting the blood of the race to turn back now. What they began at the end of a cat-o-nine tails, to satisfy the most beastly instinct of unrestrained power, we shall continue as a right, which the law and educated public opinion will yet sanction as eminently just and proper.

Again, in concluding his platitudinous array of sophistical logic, Mr. Grady appeals to the North to leave the race question to "*us*" and "*we*" will settle it. So *we* will; but the *we* Mr. Grady had "in his mind's eye" will not be permitted to settle it alone. Not by any means, Mr. Grady. Not only the White *we*, but the Colored *we* as well, will demand a share in that settlement; nor will the settlement be permitted to proceed and to be adjusted on the biased basis laid down by Mr. Grady and his school of false prophets. There is a correct interpretation of this matter which *we* will strenuously insist shall be given. This sober, earnest, emphatic declaration may wound Mr. Grady's preconceived conviction of the "eternal fitness of things," but we mean what we say. Exigencies of the moment may suggest make shifts and compromises, but the ceaseless purpose will be to see that the great principle is not lost sight of, but shall so keep pace with the progress of the adjudication that the final settlement will be in the strictest sense a complete conformity to absolute justice to all the parties concerned.

We protest against the current treatment of this momentous question by which we are completely counted out, or regarded as other than passive or acquiescent factors. Unlike in times past, *we have a voice, and we propose to make that voice heard*, in all future phases of the discussion of this race question. *The race is here; it will stay here*; it is most vitally concerned; and it insists, and will do so more and more, upon its proper share in the settlement of all questions affecting its constitutional and natural rights and its material and other concerns. We insist that, as American citizens, we have coequal right, whether it be social or civil, with all our fellow citizens, and that we shall be permitted to enjoy such in the same manner and to the same extent, as others. The absurdity of the claims set up by those who oppose our enjoyment of what even they concede belongs to us, is most apparent; and it is extremely *bizarre* that they should have studied us and the measure of knowledge we have acquired since the war, to so little purpose as to deem us wholly incapable of apprehending the weak as well as the salient features of such claims. The whites of this country ignore utterly a patent fact, which was most aptly expressed by Mr. J. Stahl Patterson in the following deliverance:

"Even now they are no longer Negroes. One-third has a large infusion of white blood; another third has less, but still some, and of the other third it would be difficult to find an assured specimen of pure African blood."*

This diagnosis being correct, and we are free to accept it, the Anglo-Saxon should understand that the people whom he would defraud, and upon whom he would impose specious and illogical arguments to justify such fraud, have, aside from the quick intelligence derived from their African origin, a very copious admixture of the shrewd cunning of his own blood to hoodwink, in the mixed African population in this country.

We desire it to be distinctly understood that we make no boast of this admixture. We came by it not of our seeking or connivance. It was forced upon us like our slavery; and, mainly because of the manner of coming into possession of it, we regard it as far more of a curse than a blessing. But we have this admixture of blood, and in a far greater measure than is generally accepted. It is useless to attempt to hide it from ourselves, or to permit the dishonest white man, who forced it upon us, to hide it from himself. We will make him reap the whirlwind, since he was so imprudent as to sow to the wind.

The disposition to confound civil rights and social privileges, shown in the published utterances of nearly all our opponents, is to be discredited, especially at this stage of the question; since it is absolutely indispensable, in the statues of any people, to build first the material, then the ornamental feature, because social privileges can only be appreciated by those intellectually and peculiarly circumstanced to take advantage of them. Not only have the whites to learn and to accept as irrevocably binding this obvious truism, but the colored people as well. The man who craves for universal social equality must go to savage tribes to find it. The lines upon which our distorted civilization proceeds do not permit of any Spartan communism. Lycurgus is at a discount. The inductive philosophers, with Bacon at the head, have the ear of our progress; and the Darwinian theory of the survival of the fittest is forced upon the weak by law and custom, and used by the strong and crafty to oppress and rob mankind; as if it were not the first, the underlying, principle of organized society, the social compact, to insure every member of it in absolute security of his life and liberty, and in the unincumbered

---

* Popular Science Monthly, Oct., 1881, p. 789. [Fortune is referring to J. Stahl Patterson, "Increase and Movement of the Colored Population, Part 1 & 2," *Popular Science Monthly* 19 (October 1881): 665–75; and 784–90. Ed.]

pursuit of such labor as will yield him the necessary subsistence to make these objects a blessing instead of a curse. Link the theory of Darwin[12] and that of Malthus[13]—who maintained, in substance, that procreation is a crime, since the pressure of population lessened, instead of augmenting, subsistence—and you have the very worst phases of barbarism accepted and incorporated into our civilization by the sophisms of the schoolmen and doctrinaires. It is true that the Malthusian theory has been discredited by advanced thinkers; still, when we remember that all law and usage favor the Darwinian theory, it is readily to be seen that Malthus is correct, as far as he goes. The two theories are, naturally, the complements of each other. The condition which makes either theory plausible has its basis in the very foundation of our civilization.

The selfish and malicious attempt to confound social privileges and civil rights will not succeed. The thing is altogether too transparent; the inutility of it too obvious. To say that I shall enjoy *full* civil rights, and that I shall not enjoy *any* social privilege is one of those contradictions against which logic has been specially reduced to a science, and which we are more amused than surprised to see advanced by men who pretend to stand at the top of the ladder of everything. Yet, so we find it.

The matter of civil rights and social privileges may be reduced to a very simple proposition: Civil rights comprise all public benefits sought to be obtained by or insured to individuals by the organization of mankind into government for mutual protection and advantage; and in which no member possesses a legal prerogative to enjoy any larger share of such public benefits, or to enjoy any peculiar benefits not common to each and all of his fellow-citizens. This is, or should be, the primal object of all organized government; and, in so far as it fails to compass this object, it fails in the essential element of its creation. These are defined and secured to the citizen by constitutional and statutory enactment. They are primarily and essentially matters which society regulates through laws enacted by its legally constituted tribunals; for law, according to Sir William Blackstone,[14] "in its most general and comprehensive sense signifies a rule of action."* Again; "law is properly defined to be a rule of civil conduct, prescribed by the supreme power in a State, commanding what is right and prohibiting what is wrong."†

This definition of law being accepted, it will be seen that it would be directly in contravention of equity to prescribe one rule of conduct for me and

---

* Sharswood's Blackstone, p. 38. [Fortune is referring to his volume of William Blackstone's *Commentaries on the Laws of England Four Books* (London: Sherwood, Jones, 1823). Ed.]
† Ibid., p. 44

another for my neighbor; that is to say, my neighbor shall enjoy a certain public benefit, but I shall not. In our government the theory is that no man shall have advantage before the law to the detriment of his neighbor. The theory and the practice are often sorely out of joint with each other. This appears painfully true when a black citizen and a white citizen disagree and appeal to the judiciary to decide as between them; and especially is this true in the South. In the North and West matters are on a much more satisfactory basis.

If we may accept as correct the definition as laid down, that civil rights are all such as come within the purview of government, or the expressed will of the aggregate membership of the social or civil compact, by direct or indirect vote, we shall have little or no difficulty in arriving at what are social rights, or, more properly, social privileges. Civil Rights,—all such rights as are, in their nature, essential to the happiness and convenience of the whole people and to preserve the unity and impartiality of the laws,—are not to be denied to one individual, or to a class, without jeopardizing the rights of all the people, since infraction of a common rule by one person, or class leads to contempt of the rule. Denial of civil rights to one is a menace to the rights of all. Barring the free passage-way to the ballot box of one individual or class, is a common injury; invidious discrimination in the accommodation and convenience of travel; in places licensed for public amusement and comfort; the enforcement of separate schools, to the maintenance of which the supreme law and the theory of government presumed that one citizen contributes as much as another; the enactment of miscegenation laws, when the marriage institution is universally recognized as a civil contract, except in Catholic governments, wholly within the purview and supervision of the law, and which operates upon all classes alike,—such purely civil rights every man, by reason of his citizenship in these benefits, public in their nature, and operating directly upon the constitution of society, is a flagrant miscarriage of justice, a perversion of the rights of citizenship, and a direct blow at the personal liberty of the citizen.

I do not candidly believe that white men themselves are convinced that one tithe of the nonsense they put forth on this question imposes upon the intelligence and humanity of the world. Having the constitutional disposition to deny rights they know to be common in their nature and scope, they do not hesitate to impose them upon the vanity of the narrow-minded of their own class, and upon the ignorance and helplessness of the colored people. Upon this same theory the English nation has for centuries dominated and robbed the Irish people, and forced from the abject victims, who compose their Indian dependencies, forty per centum of their hard earnings, by the imposition of outrageous taxation upon everything,—from the water they drink to the miserable black bread they eat. After this high-handed usurpation and robbery, the English people have the supreme impudence to prate of the inestimable advantage such people derive from contact with superior civilization!

When we observe the precipitation with which European nations are making haste to assert and have recognized claims to African territory, it is difficult to suppress a sigh at the prospect of the millions of treasure and streams of blood which will be sacrificed in some future epoch by the outraged people of that continent in wringing from the grasp of the white man their usurped domain and liberties. The conflict will come. We have already had a foretaste of it in Dahomey, Zuzuland and Soudan. Let it come; I do not fear it. I feel that the future will develop an African Empire as potential in every sense as that carved out of the disintegrated elements of the Germanic States by the wisdom and nerve of Bismarck; and the time will come when the European who now braves and bullies the savages of the Dark Continent will cringe and fawn to a mighty people, mobilized into a coherent and aggressive government.

The white races have braved and bullied the darker hued children of Adam from time immemorial; so long, indeed, that they have persuaded themselves that God colored them white for the express purpose of dominating the rest of mankind. This self-sufficiency and cruelty have paved with human sacrifices the pathway of progress, from the earliest dawn of recorded history to the present time. But we have reason to believe that a new page in history has been turned, and that the crouching animal so long hunted and outraged will turn in the years now upon us and fight it out on the line of brawn, intellect and shrewdness. Africa is the last, the only great continent which has not been permeated with the vitality, the genius, the culture and the enterprise of high Christian government; and when her turn at domination shall come, as come it must, may she not soar to greater heights of power, wealth and humanity than that of any other power which has preceded her in the "paths of glory?"

One thing is assured: We are citizens of the United States, and of the States in which we reside, and by virtue of this we are copartners in all the benefits of government. Even so narrow-minded a logician as Mr. Grady will be compelled to acknowledge this much. The question raised then, is not upon our right to a co-equal enjoyment of such benefits as attach to citizenship, but upon such privileges as our opponents are pleased to denominate social rights,—rights which inhere in the man, not in the government—and as many of these common rights, of a civil nature, as they can, by any species of sophistical legerdemain, muster under the banner of social privileges. That is to say, in one breath they make haste to admit that we are, by reason of our citizenship, entitled to *full* civil rights, but in the next arrogate the prerogative of transposing as many of these civil rights as they see fit to deny to the column of social privilege. Was syllogism ever before drawn upon to do service in a more transparently selfish purpose? Was sophistry ever before perverted in a more outrageously flagrant sense? It takes a white man to so attenuate argument, to so pilfer from one side of the scales in the interest of the other. With him the stereotyped formula is, "heads I win; tails you lose." Colored men are expected, even exhorted, to swallow this nauseous admixture of nonsense without so much as a grimace! The thing is supremely ridiculous, absurd, presumptuous. It presupposes a state of mental aberration or idiocy on our part which may have once obtained, but which has long since given place to something higher, nobler, grander, more comprehensive and assertive, to which Mr. Grady's journalistic intuition will readily furnish "a local habitation and a name."

I think I have very clearly indicated what are civil rights, and what are social privileges. To summarize the argument; Civil rights are all such as affect the whole people, and are regulated by them in their collective capacity as a government. Social privileges, on the contrary, are regulated wholly by individual tastes and inclinations, and are in no sense subject to the cognizance or supervision of government. Every citizen has a co-equal right in all benefits of government; but every citizen has not on this account, a legal right to demand or expect the concession of any social privilege. The one he can force by legal process; the other he must win by conduct, position, superior abilities, affluence. The possession of these in large measure will bring all the social privilege worth the having. That we possess them in such small measure and in such isolated instances, is to be attributed the present unsatisfactory social status of the race.

Notes

1. The usurer in Shakespeare's *The Merchant of Venice*.
2. Gaius Julius Caesar (102?-44 B.C.) was a Roman military and political leader who ruled Rome from 49 to 44 B.C.
3. Common quote by Caesar. Fortune may be quoting Plutarch, either in *Roman Lives* or *The Fall of the Roman Republic*.

4. Roger B. Taney (1777–1864) was chief justice of the U.S. Supreme Court from 1836 to 1864. He authored the majority decision in *Dred Scott v. Sandford*, 60 U.S. 393 (1856).

5. John Marshall Harlan (1833–1911) was a Supreme Court justice from 1877 to 1911. He was known as the "great dissenter" during his tenure, in part because of his positions on civil rights. For more on Harlan, see Tinsley E. Yarbrough, *Judicial Enigma: The First Justice Harlan* (New York: Oxford University Press, 1995). Fortune praised Harlan's dissent from the majority ruling in the *Civil Rights Cases*. See *New York Globe*, November 24, 1883.

6. Benjamin Lundy (1789–1839) was a Quaker abolitionist and editor of the abolitionist newspaper *Genius of Universal Emancipation*. For more on Lundy, see chapter 6, note 2.

7. Wendell Phillips (1811–1884) was a distinguished abolitionist and antislavery orator. Fortune wrote a moving obituary of Phillips. See *New York Globe*, February 9, 1884. Fortune is citing his speech before the Massachusetts Anti-Slavery Society in 1852. For more on Phillips, see chapter 6, note 4.

8. George Washington Cable (1844–1925) was a novelist, essayist, and reformer. See George W. Cable, "The Freedman's Case in Equity," *Century* 29 (1885): 409–18, and "The Silent South," *Century* 30 (1885): 674–92. Both essays were republished in George W. Cable, *The Negro Question: A Selection of Writings on Civil Rights in the South*, ed. Arlin Turner (New York: W. W. Norton, 1958). Fortune republished portions of "The Freedman's Case in Equity" and praised the piece in an editorial in the same issue of the *Freeman*. See *New York Freeman*, January 17, 1885. Cable's article and Henry W. Grady's response continued to be discussed throughout much of the year. See, for example, *New York Freeman*, January 31, March 28, April 11, April 18, June 6, September 19, and November 28, 1885.

9. John Jasper (1812–1901) was an African American Baptist minister who formed the Sixth Mount Zion Baptist Church in Richmond, Virginia, in 1867 and became nationally famous after delivering his "Sun Do Move" sermon in 1878.

10. Henry W. Grady (1850–1889) served as managing editor of the *Atlanta Constitution* in the 1880s and used his position to promote the New South program of northern investment, southern industrial growth, diversified farming, and white supremacy. Grady was one of Fortune's constant targets. See, for example, *New York Age*, November 30, December 21 and 28, 1899.

11. Henry W. Grady, "In Plain Black and White," *Century* 29 (1885): 909–18.

12. Charles Darwin (1809–1882) was an English naturalist who gained fame with his work on the origin of species and natural selection.

13. Thomas R. Malthus (1766–1834) was an English demographer and political economist whose work on population growth influenced many, including Charles Darwin.

14. William Blackstone (1723–1780) was an English jurist and educator who wrote the monumental four-volume *Commentaries on the Laws of England* (1765–1769).

13

Afro-American League Convention Speech

The following is the address Fortune gave before the inaugural convention of the Afro-American League in Chicago on January 25, 1890. The league was the nation's first national civil rights organization and a group whose creation Fortune had called for since 1884. In the speech he outlines the organization and its agenda. In many ways this organization and the program that Fortune is outlining would be echoed in the formation of other organizations in the years to follow, including the Afro-American Council, the Constitution League, the Committee of Twelve, the Niagara Movement and the National Association for the Advancement of Colored People.

Afro-American League Convention Speech —*New York Age,* **January 25, 1890**

Ladies and Gentlemen of the Afro-American Leagues[1]—We are met here to-day, representatives of 8,000,000 freemen, who know our rights and have the courage to defend them. We are met here to-day to emphasize the fact that the past condition of dependence and helplessness upon men who have used us for selfish and unholy purposes, who have murdered and robbed and outraged us, must be reversed.

It is meet and proper that we have met for such high purpose upon the free soil of Illinois. It was here that Elijah Lovejoy,[2] the first martyr of freedom's sacred cause, died that we might be free. It was here that Abraham Lincoln[3] lived, and in this soil he sleeps, having died "that the Nation shall under God, have a new birth of freedom, and that the government of the people, by the people and for the people shall not perish from earth."[4] It was here that John Alexander Logan,[5] like Saul of Tarsus, was convicted of his error in persecuting the people of the Lord, and buckled on his sword and went forth to lead the volunteer hosts in freedom's fight, pausing not until struck down at his post of duty by the angel of death; he, too, sleeps in the imperial soil "where law and order reign," "where government is supreme." And we do not forget the living sons of this soil who fought in freedom's ranks when we mention here the names of Gen. Walter Q. Gresham,[6] or Private Fifer,[7] the Chief Executive of this Commonwealth, and of his generous opponent, Gen. John M. Palmer.[8]

Upon such historic ground, surrounded by the spirits of such famous dead, and cheered by the presence of such living friends of the black soldiers who followed where they led—

> Into the jaws of death,
> Into the mouth of hell—[9]

borne down in the wild charges, baptized with fire and shot and shell, contending like heroes from freedom's priceless smile, shall we not take fresh courage? Shall we not bravely buckle on the armor and march with unhesitating step, with unfaltering hearts to the convention before us for absolute justice under the constitution? By the name of Elijah Lovejoy, embalmed in song and story; by the name of Abraham Lincoln, which shall illustrate and illuminate the pages of history brightest in the annals of our glory; by the names of the black heroes who died at Battery Wagner, Fort Pillow and the awful crater at Petersburg—by the names of those honored dead I conjure the spirit of universal emancipation to be with us here, and to enthuse us with the devotion to high principle which Wm. Lloyd Garrison[10] emphasized when he exclaimed, "I am in earnest; I will not equivocate, I will not retreat a single inch—and I will be heard."

Fellow-members of the League, I congratulate you upon your presence here. I congratulate you upon the high resolve, the manly inspiration, which impelled you to this spot. I congratulate you that have aroused from the lethargy of the past, and that you now stand face to face, brave men and true, with the awful fact that "who would be free themselves must strike the blow."[11] I congratulate you that you now recognize the fact that a great work remains for you to do, and that you are determined, with the countenance of Jehovah, to do it. And, finally, I congratulate myself that I have been chosen as the humble spokesman to voice at this time and in this manner the high resolves which move you as one man to perfect an organization which shall secure to ourselves and to our children the blessings of citizenship so generally denied us.

The spirit of agitation which has brought us together here comprehends in its vast sweep the entire range of human history. The world has been rocked in the cradle of agitation from Moses to Gladstone. The normal condition of mankind is one of perpetual change, unrest and aspiration—a contention of the virtues against the vices of mankind. The great moving and compelling influence in the history of the world is agitation, and the greatest of agitators was He, the despised Nazarene, whose doctrines have revolutionized the thought of the ages.

The progress of mankind has been greatest in eras of most unrest and innovation. Iconoclasm has always been the watchword of progress.

It was an idle dream of the poet that time would ever come in the history of the race

When the war drum beats no longer,
  When the battle flag is furled,
In the parliament of nations,
  The federations of the world.[12]

Equally fatuous was Longfellow's lament that

Were half the power that fills the world with
  terror,
Were half the wealth bestowed on camps and courts
Given to redeem the human mind from error,
There were no need of arsenals and forts.[13]

Apathy leads to stagnation. The arsenal, the fort, the warrior are as necessary as the school, the church, the newspapers and the public forum of debate. It is a narrow and perverted philosophy which condemns as a nuisance agitators. It is this sort of people who consider nothing to be sacred which stands in the pathway of the progress of the world. Like John crying in the wilderness, they are the forerunners of change in rooted abuses which revolutionize society.

Demosthenes, thundering against the designs of Philip of Macedon upon the liberties of Greece; Cicero, holding up to scorn and ridicule the schemes of Cataline against the freedom of Rome; Oliver Cromwell,[14] baring his sturdy breast to the arrows of royalty and nobility to preserve to Englishmen the rights contained in Magna Charta; Patrick Henry,[15] fulminating against the arrogant and insolent encroachments of Great Britain upon the rights of the American colonies; Nat Turner,[16] rising from the dust of slavery and defying the slave oligarchy of Virginia, and John Brown,[17] resisting the power of the United States in a heroic effort to break the chains of the bondsman—these are some of the agitators who have voiced the discontent of their times at the peril of life and limb and property. Who shall cast the stone of reproach at these children of the race? Who shall say they were not heroes born to live forever in the annals of song and story?

Revolutions are of many sorts. They are either silent and unobservable, noiseless as the movement of the earth on its axis, or loud and destructive, shaking the earth from centre to circumference, making huge gaps in the map of earth, changing the face of empires, subverting dynasties and breaking fetters asunder or reviewing them anew.

Jesus Christ may be regarded as the chief spirit of agitation and innovation. He himself declared, "I come not to bring peace, but a sword."[18]

St. Paul, standing upon Mars Hill, read the death sentence of Grecian and Roman mythology in the simple sentence, "Whom ye ignorantly worship Him I declare unto you."[19]

A portion of mankind remains always conservative, while the other portion is moved by the spirit of radicalism; and no man can predict where the conflict may lead when once the old idea and the new one conflict, and must needs appeal to the logic of revolution to arbitrate between them. Few Romes are large enough to hold a Caesar and a Brutus. The old idea and the new idea, the spirit of freedom and the spirit of tyranny and oppression cannot live together without friction. The agitator must never be in advance of his times. The people must be prepared to receive the message that he brings. The harvest must be ripe for the sickle when the reaper enters the field.

As it was in ancient Greece and Rome, so it is in modern Europe and America. The just cause does not always prevail. The John Browns and Nat Turners do not always find the people ready to receive the tidings of great joy they bring them.

Martin Luther,[20] opposing the vice and corruption and superstition of the religion of his times, putting in motion influences which aroused all Christendom, needed only to have failed in his self-imposed reformation to have died by the tortures of the thumb-screw and the rack of the Inquisition.

Nothing succeeds like success, nothing is more severely condemned than failure.

Napoleon Bonaparte,[21] at the head of a million soldiers, firmly seated upon the throne of the Bourbons of France, is courted and flattered and feared by the whole of Europe. Whipped at Waterloo, his vast armies scattered and demoralized, exiled to a rock in the Atlantic Ocean, chained as Prometheus, all pronounce him a Corsican adventurer, a base upstart, a human monster.

It does not pay to fail.

Napoleon Bonaparte was the avenging Nemesis of the mediaeval conditions of government and society. He heralded the reaction against abuses in civil and ecclesiastical administration which had been the slowly developed fungi of centuries. It is always the most drastic medicine that kills the deep-seated disease—or the patient. We yet live in the swim of that tremendous revolution. To it we may trace the dominating impulses that lead to the independence of the United States, the independence of Hayti and San Domingo, the independence of the South American Republics, the abolition of slavery in the British West Indies, the liberation of the Russian serfs, the abolition of slavery in this country, the recent manumission of Brazilian slaves, and that agitation for larger individual freedom, battling against the incubus of conservatism,—whether in the garb of tyranny in the state, oppressions of the nobility, superstitious and unjust assumptions of priestly inquisitors, as in Europe, or of arrogant and insolent intolerance, as in the United States.

Agitations are inevitable. They are as necessary to social organism as blood is to animal organism. Revolutions follow as a matter of course. Each link in the long chain of human progress is indelibly marked as the result of revolution. The thunder storm clarifies the atmosphere and infuses into the veins of all animal life new vigor and new hope. Revolutions clarify the social and civil atmosphere. They sober the nation; they sharpen the wits of the people; they mark rights and privileges which have been the bone of contention all the more precious, because of the severe labor which consecrated them anew to ourselves and to our posterity. The benefits that come to us as the rewards of our genius, untiring industry, and frugality are more highly and justly prized than benefits that come to us by indirection and without our seeking. The spendthrifts of our society are those who reap where others have sown, who spend what others have toiled to amass.

The aspirations of the human soul, like the climbing vine, are forever in the line of greater freedom, fuller knowledge, ampler possessions. These aspirations find always opposing aspirations. It is true of nations seeking after greater reforms. To accomplish these agitations is necessary.

The imperial eagle, the emblem of our National prowess and unconquerable aspiration, builds his nest in the loftiest peaks of the highest mountains. He knows his supreme power and he exercises it. His eaglets, when they burst from the chrysalis which had nurtured their infancy, gaze first into the face of the lordly sun. The first law of the eagle's nature is aggressiveness. Resistance remains the most pronounced characteristic of his existence.

Wherein does the eagle differ from the strong nations of the world?

The revolutionary intuitions of mankind are fundamental and sleepless. It is because of this fact that agitators like the Roman Gracchi, the German Luther, the British Cromwell, the American John Brown and William Lloyd Garrison, for examples, cut such a considerable figure in the history of every nation and every epoch. It is the discontent, the restlessness, the sleepless aspiration of humanity, voiced by some braver, some more far-seeing member of society, some man ready to be a martyr to his faith or wear the crown of victory, which keep the world in a ferment of excitation and expectancy, and which force the adoption of those reforms which keep society from retrograding to the conditions of savage life, from which it has slowly and painfully moved forward. There can be no middle ground in social life. There must be positive advancement or positive decline.

Social growth is the slowest of all growths.

Fellow-members of the League, it is matter of history that the abolition of slavery was the fruit of the fiercest and most protracted agitation in the history of social reforms. Begun practically in 1816 by Benjamin Lundy,[22] having been the chief bone of contention at the very birth of the republic, the agitation for the emancipation of the slave did not cease until Abraham Lincoln issued the Emancipation Proclamation in 1863. When emancipation was an established fact, when the slave had been made a freeman and the freeman had been made a citizen, the Nation reached the conclusion that its duty was fully discharged. A reaction set in after the second election of Gen. Grant[23] to the presidency in 1872, and terminated after the election of Mr. Hayes[24] in 1876, when the Afro-American citizen was turned over to the tender mercies of his late masters—deserted by the Nation, deserted by the party he had served in peace and in war, left poor and defenseless to fight a foe who had baffled the entire Nation throughout four years of bloody and destructive war.

Patient as a slave, heroic as a soldier, faithful to every trust as a citizen, and faithful above all to the country his valor aided to consecrate anew to the great destiny treason had attempted to destroy, and to the great party God had used to consummate His gracious purposes, even when that party had deserted him, had offered him as a sacrifice upon the altar of expediency and selfish advantage, the Afro-American in every situation has proved himself true to the duty imposed upon him—true to his country, true to his friends, rising always and at all times to the sublime principles which are at the bed-rock of the Federal union. In sunshine and in storm, in the prosperity of peace, and in the convulsion and devastation of war, he has shown that he is a man and a brother.

His sublime faith in the Government, his implicit obedience to the law, his undeviating devotion to the party which led him as Moses led the children of Israel out of the house of bondage—all this, the noblest conduct of which men are capable, has been used against him as a crime instead of a virtue, as a badge of servility rather than as an ensign of the greatest nobility, hitching upon him the sobriquets of cowardice and ignorance. Is it cowardice in a society governed by law to wait upon the eternal justice of the law to vindicate its outraged majesty? In the Afro-American it has been so charged. Is it a crime, a badge of ignorance, to be loyal to friends and consistent in hatred of tireless foes? In the Afro-American it has been so charged.

Ladies and gentlemen, we have been robbed of the honest wages of our toil; we have been robbed of the substance of our citizenship by murder and intimidation; we have been outraged by enemies and deserted by friends; and because in a society governed by law, we have been true to the law, true to treacherous friends, and as true in distrust of our enemies, it has been charged upon us that we are not made of the stern stuff which makes the Anglo-Saxon race the most consummate masters of hypocrisy, of roguery, of insolence, of arrogance, and of cowardice, in the history of races.

Was ever a race more unjustly maligned then ours? Was ever a race more shamelessly robbed than ours? Was ever a race used to advance the political and pecuniary fortunes of others as ours? Was ever a race so patient, so law abiding, so uncomplaining as ours?

Ladies and gentlemen, it is time to call a halt. It is time to begin to fight fire with fire. It is time to stand shoulder to shoulder as men. It is time to rebuke the treachery of friends in the only way that treachery should be rebuked. It is time to face the enemy and fight him inch for every right he denies us.

We have been patient so long that many believe that we are incapable of resenting insult, outrage and wrong; we have so long accepted uncomplaining all that injustice and cowardice and insolence heaped upon us, that many imagine that we are compelled to submit and have not the manhood necessary to resent such conduct. When matters assume this complexion, when oppressors presume too far upon the forbearance and the helplessness of the oppressed, the condition of the people affected is critical indeed. Such is our condition today. Because it is true; because we feel that something must be done to change the condition; because we are tired of being kicked and cuffed by individuals, made the scapegoats of the law, used by one party as an issue and by another as a stepping stone to place and power, and elbowed at pleasure by insolent corporations and their minions, corporations which derive their valuable franchises in part by consent of these very people they insult and outrage—it is because of the existence of these things that we are assembled here to-day—determined to perfect an organization whose one mission shall be to labor by every reasonable and legal means to right the wrongs complained of, until not one right justly ours under the Constitution is denied us.

Ladies and gentlemen, I stand here to-day and assert in all soberness that we shall no longer accept in silence a condition which degrades our manhood and makes a mockery of our citizenship. I believe I voice the sentiments of each member of the League here assembled when I assert that from now and hence we shall labor as one man, inspired with one holy purpose, to wage relentless opposition to all men who would degrade our manhood and who would defraud us of the benefits of citizenship, guaranteed alike to all born upon this soil or naturalized by the Constitution which has been cemented and made indestructible by our blood in every war, foreign or domestic, waged by this grand Republic. And it is our proud boast that never in the history of this government has an Afro-American raised the hand of treason against the star spangled banner. Loyal in every condition to the flag of the Union—as slave, as contraband of war, as soldier and as citizen—we feel that we have a right to demand of the government we have served so faithfully the measure of protection guaranteed to us and freely granted to the vilest traitor or who followed Robert E. Lee.[25] There are Afro-American veterans in every State in the Union, of whom it may be said:

> If you asked from whence they came,
>   Our answer it shall be,
> They came from Appomattox
>   And its famous apple tree.

In the name of these veterans, who like their white comrades went back to their homes after the toils of war and mingled in the pursuits of peace, aiding by their industry to pay the enormous debt contracted to vindicate the right of every man born on this soil to be free indeed—in the name of these veterans who wore the blue, we appeal here to-day to the loyal people of the Nation, to frown upon the manifold wrongs practiced upon us, and to give their sympathy and their support to the movement we have met to inaugurate to combat these wrongs. It is reproach to this Nation that one man entitled to the protection of the laws should be outraged in his person or in his property, and be unable to get redress. It is a shame and disgrace to the entire people that the arm of the government, which is long enough to reach the naturalized Irishman in British dungeons, to ward off the conscriptions of the German government when it would lay unholy hands upon a naturalized German—I say it is a shame and a disgrace that the government has the power to protect the humblest of its citizens in foreign lands and has not the power to protect its citizens at home—if we have a black face. Venerable prelates of the church have been insulted and outraged by corporations; refined and delicate women have been submitted to the grossest indignity on the public highway; men and women are lynched and flogged every day; and a million voters are practically disfranchised, have no representation in Federal or State legislature; and we are told by the supreme court of the land that the government which made the citizen and conferred co-equal rights upon him has no power to protect him in the vital matters here recited. If this be true, if it be true that the power which can create has no power to protect the creature, then it is high time that it secure to itself the necessary power. We appeal to the Nation, which fears a righteous God and loves justice, to judge if our contention here is unreasonable, and we here demand of the party now in power, which has promised so much and which enjoyed our best confidence and our support in the past, that it make good the promises made, that it pay us for our confidence and support in the past, or abide the consequences. We are weary of the empty promises of politicians and the platitudes of national conventions, and we demand a fulfillment of the stipulations in the bond as a condition of our further confidence and support. We do not mince our words here. For the constitutional opponents of our rights we have no faith, no confidence, and no support, and of professed friends we here demand that they perform their part of the contract, which alone can justify the sacrifices we have been called upon to make. If it cannot do this, then it has ceased to be the party of Lincoln, of Sumner,[26] of Wilson, and of Logan, and deserves to die, and will die, that another party may rise to finish the uncompleted work, even as the Whig party died that the Republican party might triumph in the Nation.

I am no hero worshipper. Parties are not things sacred to me. They are brought into existence by men to serve certain ends. They are the creatures and not the creators of men. When they have fulfilled the objects for which they were created or when they prove false to the great purpose for their creation, what further use are they? None certainly to us if they do not give us in return for our support the measure of justice and consideration in party management and benefits commensurate with the service we render. I do not speak here as a partisan; I speak as an Afro-American, first, last, and all the time, ready to stab to death any party which robs me of my confidence and vote and straightway asks me "what are we going to do about it?" I have served the Republican party, the Prohibition party, and the Democratic party, and I speak with the wisdom of experience when I declare that none of them cares a fig for the Afro-American further than it can use him. In seeking to rebuke false friends we often make false alliances. If we shall serve the party and the men, as Afro-Americans, who serve us best, in the present posture of our citizenship, we shall follow the dictates of the highest wisdom and the most approved philosophy. It will be sound policy on the part of the Leagues here assembled to leave the local Leagues free to pursue such political course in its immediate community as the best interests of the race will seem to dictate. In National affairs it does not seem wise to me for the League to commit itself officially to any party. Let parties commit themselves to the best interest of Afro-American citizens, and it will then be time enough for us to commit ourselves to them. We have served parties long enough without benefit to the race. It is now time for parties to serve us some, if they desire our support.

I am now and I have always been a race man and not a party man. Let this League be a race league. To make it anything else is to sow the seed of discord, disunion, and disaster at the very beginning of our important work. We stand for the race, and not for this party or that party, and we should know a friend from a foe when we see him.

And now, ladies and gentlemen, it is time that I confine myself to the special matters which have moved us to congregate in this proud city of the West.

There come periods in the history of every people when the necessity of their affairs makes it imperative that they take such steps as will show to the world that they are worthy to be free, and therefore entitled to the sympathy of all mankind and to the co-operation of all lovers of justice and fair play. To do this they must unequivocally show that while they may solicit the sympathy and co-operation of mankind, they have the intelligence and courage to know what are their rights and manfully to contend for them, even though that sympathy and co-operation be ungenerously denied them.

I am in no sense unmindful of the vastness of the undertaking; but this instead of being a drawback, is rather an incentive to prosecute the matter with more earnestness and persistence.

I now give in consecutive order the reasons; which in my opinion justify the organization of the National Afro-American League, to wit:

1. The almost universal suppression of our ballot in the South, and consequent "taxation without representation," since in the cities, counties and States where we have undisputed preponderating majorities of the voting population we have, in the main, no representation, and therefore no voice in the making and enforcing the laws under which we live.

2. The universal and lamentable reign of lynch and mob law, of which we are made the victims, especially in the South, all the more aggravating because all the machinery of the law making and enforcing power is in the hands of those who resort to such outrageous, heinous and murderous violations of the law.

3. The unequal distribution of school funds, collected from all taxpayers alike, and to the equal and undivided benefits of which all are alike entitled.

4. The odious and demoralizing penitentiary system of the South, with its chain gangs, convict leases and indiscriminate mixing of males and females.

5. The almost universal tyranny of common carrier corporations in the South—railroad, steamboat and other—in which the common rights of men and women are outraged and denied by the minions of these corporations, acting under implicit orders in most cases, as well as by common passengers, who take the matter in their own hands as often as they please, and are in no instances pursued and punished by the lawful authorities.

6. The discrimination practiced by those who conduct places of public accommodation, and are granted a license for this purpose, such as keepers of inns, hotels and conductors of theatres and kindred places of amusement, where one man's money, all things being equal, should usually be as good as another's.

7. The serious question of wages, caused in the main by the vicious industrial system in the South, by the general contempt employers feel for employees, and by the overcrowded nature of the labor market.

These matters reach down into the very life of our people; they are fundamentally the things which in all times have moved men to associate themselves together in civil society for mutual benefit and protection, to restrain the rapacious and unscrupulous and to protect the weak, the timid and the virtuous; and whenever and wherever a condition of affairs obtains when these principles are disregarded and outraged, it becomes the imperative duty of the aggrieved to take such steps for their correction as the condition of affairs seems to warrant.

I know, ladies and gentlemen of the league, that those who are looking to do this organization, loyal people in every section of the country for some sensible action which shall assist in solving the great problems which confront us, as well as the croaking, skeptical few, who do not expect that we shall be able to advance or to accomplish anything which shall survive the hour of our adjournment, have their eyes upon us. I have confidence in the great race of which I am proud to be a member. I have confidence in its wisdom and its patriotism, and its self-sacrifice for the common good. I have faith in the God who rules in the affairs of men, and who will not leave us alone to our own devices if we shall make an honest effort to assist ourselves. Thus fortified in my faith, what have I to propose as remedies for some if not all of the evils against which we have to contend? It shall not be said that I have called you here to a barren feast; it shall not be said by friend or foe that I am an impracticable visionary, a man chasing shadows—a man who denounces the fearful structure in which we abide and would tear it down without offering at least a substitute to replace it.

I have pondered long and seriously on the evils which beset us, and I have sought, as light was given me, for an antidote to them if such there be. I lay them before you, and you are here to adopt or reject them. I propose, then,

(1) The adoption by this league of an Afro-American Bank, with central offices in some one of the great commercial centers of the republic and branches all over the country. We need to concentrate our earnings, and a bank is the proper place to concentrate them. And I shall submit a bank scheme which I have devised in the hope to meet the requirements of the situation.

I propose (2) the establishment of a bureau of emigration. We need to scatter ourselves more generally throughout the republic.

I propose (3) the establishment of a committee on legislation. We need to have a sharp eye upon the measures annually proposed in the Federal and State legislatures affecting us and our interests, and there are laws everywhere in the republic the repeal of which must engage our best thought and effort.

I purpose (4) the establishment of a bureau of technical industrial education. We need trained artisans, educated farmers and laborers more than we need educated lawyers, doctors, and loafers on the street corners. The learned professions are over-crowded. There is not near so much room at the top as there was in the days of Daniel Webster.

And I propose (5) lastly the establishment of a bureau of co-operative industry. We need to buy the necessaries of life cheaper than we can command them in many States. We need to stimulate the business instinct, the commercial predisposition of the race. We not only want a market for the products of our industry, but we want and must have a fair, and a living return for them.

To my mind the solution of the problems which make this league a necessity is to be found in the five propositions here stated. Their successful execution will require the very highest order of executive ability and the collection and disbursement of a vast sum of money. Have we brains and the necessary capital to put these vast enterprises into successful motion? I think we have. There are 8,000,000 of us in this country. Some of us are rich and some of us are poor. Some of us are wise and some are foolish. Let us all—the rich and the poor, the wise and the foolish—resolve to unite and pull together, and the results will speak for themselves. Let us destroy the dead weight of poverty and ignorance which pulls us down and smothers us with the charity, the pity, and the contempt of mankind, and all other things will be added unto us.

I think this League should have its stronghold in the Southern States. It is in those States that the grievances we complain of have most glaring and oppressive existence; it is in those States that the bulk of our people reside. The League in the North and West will serve to create public opinion in those sections and to coerce politicians into taking a broader view of our grievances and to compel them to pay more respect to our representations and requests than they have ever done before. This will follow fast upon organization and capable management; because we have learned by experience that intelligent sympathy can only be created by intelligent agitation, and that the respect of politicians can only be secured by compulsion, such alone as thorough organization can bring to bear. In the North and West we are not restrained in the free exercise of the ballot, but aside from this what benefit accrues to us? Elections come and pass, parties are successful or defeated, but the influence of the race remains simply worthless, the victor and the vanquished alike treating us with indifference or contempt after the election. Every year the indifference and contempt are shown in more pronounced and different ways. It is only by proper organization and discipline that anything to our advantage can be accomplished. In the South like results will follow, save in larger measure, and perhaps at greater cost to individual members of the League, since free speech and action are things which must be fought for there. It cannot be denied that in the South free speech and free action are not tolerated. The white men of that section, in defiance of all constitution and law, have taken affairs into their own hands, and crush out, or attempt to do it, all opinions not in accord with theirs. And this is not only true in matters of a political nature, but of an economical nature.

It is stated by those who ought to know that the colored laboring masses of the South are fast falling into a condition not unlike in its terrible features the chattel slavery abolished by constitutional enactment.

We have it in the newspapers and we have it from the lips of our own men fresh from all sections of the South that the condition of the Afro-American laborers of their section is simply atrocious and appalling, that the employers of such labor, backed up by ample legislation are by all the machinery of the law, and tyrannical in the conduct of their affairs, in so far that colored laborers have no "appeal from Caesar drunk to Caesar sober."

The people suffer in silence. This should not be. They should have voice. The grievances they are forced to suffer should be known of all the world and they must be. An organization national in its ramifications, such as we propose, would be such a voice, so loud that it would compel men to hear it; for if it were silenced in the South, it would be all the louder in the North and the West.

Whenever colored men talk of forming anything in which they are to be the prime movers and their grievances are to be the subjects to be agitated, a vast array of men, mostly politicians, and newspaper editors, more or less partisan, and therefore interested in keeping colored voters in a helpless state as far as dis-organization and absence of responsible leadership can effect this, cry aloud that "colored men should be the last persons to draw the color line." So they should be; so they have been; and they would never have drawn any such line, or proposed that any such line be drawn, if white men had not first drawn it, and continue to draw it now in religion, in politics, in educational matters, in all moral movements, like that of temperance for instance. We have not drawn the color line. The A. M. E. Church, did its founders establish it because they did not care to worship with the co-religionists? Not a bit of it. They established that magnificent religious organization as a rebuke and a protest against the peanut gallery accommodations offered by white Christians, so-called, to colored Christians. The same spirit actuated the founders of the Zion A. M. E. Church and the Colored M. E. Church.

It was not the colored Christians, but the white Christians, who, to their eternal shame and damnation, drew the color line, and continue to draw it, even unto this hour. Turn to the Masonic, the Odd Fellows and the Knights of Pythias orders—did colored men draw the line in these? Did they set up colored lodges all over the country because they did not wish to fraternize with the white Orders? The answer can be inferred when it is stated that white Masons, white Odd Fellows and white Knights of Pythias even at this hour refuse to fraternize with or recognize the legality or regularity of the orders their actions caused Afro-Americans to establish. Do Afro-Americans desire separate Grand Lodges in the Temperance Order? Did they ask for such? No! But the British and American Good Templars have re-united, and the only condition on which the American order would consent the re-union was that the British order would acknowledge that its action of thirteen years ago in seceding from the order on the color question was not odious and unsound in principle.

Ladies and gentlemen, let us stand up like men in our own organizations where color will not be a brand of odium. The eternal compromises of our manhood and self-respect, true of the past, must cease. Right is right, and we should at no time, or under any circumstances compromise upon anything but absolute right. If the white man cannot rescue our drunkards and evangelize our sinners except by insulting us, let him keep away from us. His contamination under such conditions does us more harm than good. It is not we who have drawn the color line. That is pure nonsense.

Take our public schools—take the schools and colleges throughout the land; who draw the color line in these? Is there an Afro-American school of any sort in the South where a white applicant would be refused admission on account of his color? Not one! Is there a white school in the South where a colored applicant would not be refused admission on account of his color? Not one! The thing is plain. The white man draws the color line in everything he has anything to do with. He is saturated with the black mud of prejudice and intolerance.

Leadership must have a following, otherwise it will run to seed and wither up, be of no benefit to the race or to the persons possessing the superior capacity. An army without a general is a mob, at the mercy of any disciplined force that is hurled against it; and a disorganized, leaderless race is nothing more than a helpless, restless mob.

All those men who have profited by our disorganization and fattened on our labor by class and corporate legislation, will oppose this Afro-American League movement. In the intensity of their opposition they may resort to the coward argument of violence; but are we to remain forever inactive, the victims of extortion and duplicity on this account? No, sir. We propose to accomplish our purposes by the peaceful methods of agitation, through the ballot and the courts, but if others use the weapons of violence to combat our peaceful arguments, it is not for us to run away from violence. A man's a man, and what is worth having is worth fighting for. It is proudly claimed that "the blood of the martyrs is the seed of the Church."[27] Certainly the blood of anti-slavery champions was the seed of Garrison's doctrine of "the genius of universal emancipation." Certainly the blood of Irish Patriots has been the seed of Irish persistence and success; certainly the blood of Negro patriots was the seed of the independence of Hayti and San Domingo; and in the great revolution of our own country the cornerstones of American freedom were cemented with the blood of black patriots who were not afraid to die; and the refrain which celebrates the heroism and martyrdom of the first men who died that the American colonies might be free will reverberate down the ages.

> Long as in freedom's cause the wise contend
> Dear to your country shall your fame extend;
> While to the world the lettered stone shall tell
> Where Caldwell, Attucks, Grey and Maverick fell[28]

Attucks,[29] the black patriot—he was no coward! Toussaint L'Ouverture[30] —he was no coward! Nat Turner—he was no coward! And the two hundred thousand black soldiers of the last war—they were no cowards! If we have work to do, let us do it. And if there come violence, let those who oppose our just cause "throw the first stone." We have wealth, we have intelligence, we have courage; and we have a great work to do. We should therefore take hold of it like men, not counting our time and means and lives of any consequence further than they contribute to the grand purposes which call us to the work.

And now, ladies and gentlemen, in concluding the pleasant task set before me here by your kindness, I would reduce the whole matter, so far as this league is concerned to the following proposition: A large portion of our fellow citizens have determined that the material, civil and political rights conferred upon Afro-Americans by the 13th, 14th, and 15th amendments to the Federal Constitution shall not be enjoyed by the beneficiaries of them. To all practical intents and purposes these rights have been denied and are withheld, and especially so in the Southern States. That the majority shall not rule; that the laborer shall be robbed of his wages without redress at law; that the citizen shall enjoy no common and civil rights a brute would not scorn; that the principle of taxation and representation are inseparably correlated is without force in fact, as regards Afro-Americans—here is the work before us.

As the agitation which culminated in the abolition of African slavery in this country covered a period of fifty years, so may we expect that before the rights conferred upon us by the war amendments are fully conceded, a full century will have passed away. We have undertaken no child's play. We have undertaken a serious work which will tax and exhaust the best intelligence and energy of the race for the next century.

Are we equal to the task imposed upon us?

If we are true to ourselves, if we are true to our posterity, if we are true to our country, which has never been true to us, if we are true to the sublime truths of Christianity, we shall succeed—we cannot fail.

We shall fight under the banner of truth. We shall fight under the banner of justice. We shall fight under the banner of the Federal Constitution. And we shall fight under the banner of honest manhood. Planting ourselves firmly upon these truths, immutable and as fixed in the frame-work of social and political progress as the stars in the heavens, we shall eventually fight down opposition, drive caste intolerance to the wall, crush out mob and lynch law, throttle individual insolence and arrogance, vindicate the right of our women to the decent respect of lawless rowdies, and achieve at last the victory which crowns the labors of the patient, resourceful, and the uncompromising warrior.

And may the God of Nations bestow upon us and our labors His approving smile and lead us out of the house of bondage into the freedom of absolute justice under the Constitution.

Notes

1. For more on the Afro-American League, see Emma Lou Thornbrough, *T. Thomas Fortune: Militant Journalist* (Chicago: University of Chicago Press, 1972); Robert L. Factor, *The Black Response to America: Men, Ideals, and Organization, from Frederick Douglass to the NAACP* (Reading, Mass.: Addison-Wesley, 1970); and Shawn Leigh Alexander, "'We Know Our Rights and Have the Courage to Defend Them': Agitation in the Age of Accommodation, 1883–1909" (Ph.D. diss., University of Massachusetts–Amherst, 2004).

2. Elijah Parish Lovejoy (1802–1837) was an abolitionist and journalist who was murdered for his antislavery position in Alton, Illinois, on November 7, 1837. For more on Lovejoy, see Paul Simon, *Freedom's Champion—Elijah Lovejoy* (Carbondale: Southern Illinois Press, 1994).

3. Abraham Lincoln (1809–1865) was the sixteenth president of the United States. He oversaw the Union during the American Civil War and signed the Emancipation Proclamation in 1863.

4. Abraham Lincoln, *Gettysburg Address*, November 19, 1863.

5. John A. Logan (1826–1886) was a major general in the Union army. He ran as James G. Blaine's vice presidential nominee in 1884.

6. Walter Q. Gresham (1832–1895) was a politician, judge, and Union soldier from Indiana.

7. "Private" Joseph W. Fifer (1840–1938) was a Union soldier and served as Illinois governor from 1889 to 1893.

8. John M. Palmer (1817–1900) was a Union army general and Illinois governor from 1869 to 1873.

9. Alfred, Lord Tennyson (1809–1892), *The Charge of the Light Brigade*.

10. William Lloyd Garrison (1805–1879) was an abolitionist, editor of the *Liberator*, and founding member of the American Anti-Slavery Society in 1833. The quote is from his first issue of the *Liberator*, January 1, 1831. For more on Garrison, see chapter 6, note 3.

11. George Gordon, Lord Byron (1788–1824), *Childe Harold's Pilgrimage*.

12. Alfred, Lord Tennyson (1809–1892), *Locksley Hall*.

13. Henry Wadsworth Longfellow (1807–1882), *The Arsenal at Springfield*.

14. Oliver Cromwell (1599–1658) was an English military leader and politician and English head of state from 1653 to 1658.

15. Patrick Henry (1736–1799) was the colonial orator and statesman who declared "Give me liberty or give me death!" in a speech at the Virginia Convention, Richmond, on March 23, 1775.

16. Nat Turner (1800–1831) was an enslaved African who led a slave rebellion in Southampton County, Virginia, in 1831. Fortune published a poem honoring Turner in 1884, "Nat Turner," *AME Church Review* 1 (October 1884): 101, and "Nat Turner," *Globe*, October 18, 1884. For more on Turner, see chapter 6, note 8.

17. John Brown (1800–1859) was a radical abolitionist who led twenty-one followers in an attack on the federal arsenal in Harper's Ferry, Virginia, on October 16, 1859, with the intention of liberating and arming slaves. Fortune wrote a poem about Brown while visiting Kansas and published it in the *Age* in 1907, "With John Brown in Kansas," *New York Age*, September 19, 1907. For more on Brown, see chapter 6, note 6.

18. Matthew 10:34; Alfred, Lord Tennyson (1809–1892), *Queen Mary*.

19. Acts 17:23.

20. Martin Luther (1483–1546) was a leader of a religious revolt in the sixteenth century.

21. Napoleon Bonaparte (1769–1821) was a French military leader and later emperor of France, 1799–1804.

22. Benjamin Lundy (1789–1839) was a Quaker abolitionist and editor of the abolitionist newspaper *Genius of Universal Emancipation*. For more on Lundy, see chapter 6, note 2.

23. Ulysses S. Grant (1822–1885) was a Union army general and eighteenth president of the United States.

24. Rutherford B. Hayes (1822–1893) served as U.S. president from 1877 to 1881. The certification of his election was preceded by the Compromise of 1877, which led to the withdrawal of federal troops from the occupied southern states, Florida, Louisiana, and South Carolina.

25. Robert E. Lee (1807–1870) was a Confederate general during the Civil War.

26. Charles Sumner (1811–1874) was a senator from Massachusetts who was a vocal antislavery advocate and a leader of the Radical Republicans during the Civil War and Reconstruction. Fortune gave a strong address in memory of Charles Sumner, in which he also promoted the need for the creation of a civil rights organization. See *Hartford Telegram*, January 11, 1884; and *New York Globe*, January 19, 1884. For more on Sumner, see chapter 6, note 5.

27. Quintus Septimius Florens Tertullianus (Tertullian) (ca. 155–230) was a third-century author and church leader. The quote comes from *Apologeticum*.

28. The above words appear on a stone placed above the location where the first martyrs of the Boston Massacre (March 5, 1770) were buried.

29. Crispus Attucks (ca. 1723–1770) was an African American killed at the Boston Massacre. For more information on Attucks and the black community during the revolutionary era, see Benjamin Quarles, *The Negro in the American Revolution* (Chapel Hill: University of North Carolina Press, 1996); James Oliver Horton and Lois E. Horton, *In Hope of Liberty: Culture, Community, and Protest among Northern Free Blacks, 1700–1860* (New York: Oxford University Press, 1997); and Gary B. Nash, *The Forgotten Fifth: African Americans in the Age of Revolution* (Cambridge, Mass.: Harvard University Press, 2006).

30. Toussaint L'Ouverture (1743–1803) was a leader of the Haitian revolution. For more on L'Ouverture and the Haitian revolution, see chapter 6, note 26.

14

Are We Brave Men or Cowards?

Written for the short-lived *Monthly Review*, edited by Charles Alexander, this essay is Fortune's strong condemnation of the race for failing to support the Afro-American League in particular and, more generally, to organize for their "civil, political, or commercial welfare." He calls on the race to stop looking for the assistance and guidance of whites and to organize from within. Moreover, he calls on the race to set aside their egos and create an organization of both leaders and followers for the betterment of the community. He believes that organization is possible, but he wonders if the leadership and the masses are up for the challenge.

Are We Brave Men or Cowards? —*Monthly Review* 1, no. 6 (1894): 178–81

It is the very general disposition of mankind to regard with a degree of suspicion or contempt men or races who wait for others to do for them what they can and ought to do for themselves. It is a remarkable fact that in the United States and in the British West Indies the African has been more largely the recipient of the benevolence of other races than as the architect of his own fortunes. Especially is this true in the matter of human freedom, except in the island of Hayti; the boon of freedom has come to him as the result of the agitation and labors of others rather than his own. It cannot be for lack of courage, for in comparatively recent times the African in Africa has demonstrated a courage of warfare which has commanded the respect and admiration of universal mankind. But it remains a fact that West Indian emancipation and American emancipation and Brazilian emancipation have come through the agitations and efforts directed largely without instead of within the forces of the African masses.[1]

In the United States, it is true, there are instances where the slave made a valiant and commendatory effort to throw off the yoke which doomed him to a life of servile and unrequited toil. But the great anti slavery conflict which resulted in his emancipation was, in the main, the inception and the development of Anglo-American rather than Afro-American genius and persistence.

In the accomplishment of the magnificent result, it is true, we took an honorable, and in the final analysis, a decisive part in peace and in war; but the forces were directed and controlled by others than ourselves. Since the war we have looked to treacherous parties to enforce for us Constitutional guarantees of citizenship and manhood rights, without comporting ourselves with the necessary wisdom and foresight to insure the cession of what we clamored for. As a consequence, with a population which entitles us to forty-four representatives in the National Congress, we have but one, and in State and Municipal Governments we have representations which may be regarded as a parody upon what we are entitled to and what any other race would insist upon having. In matters of education we have relied almost entirely upon the philanthropy of others to supply the sinews of war, which has brought out a Christian expression of unselfishness which must remain the admiration of all times. Our most commendable effort had been displayed in religious activity, which has resulted in more than three millions of church membership, with thousands of church edifices, and not one banker, or merchant, or manufacturer of the first magnitude in all the Republic.

The weakness of the race had been shown to a distressing extent in the inability of the race to organize in any way for its civil, political or commercial welfare. This inability, coupled with the vast amount of charity, of which we have been the recipients, has had the natural effect of producing in the minds of our fellow-citizens the belief that we are what Goldsmith aptly described as "children of a larger growth,"[2] hence to be regarded as children are regarded, as "wards of the nation," as objects of charity, as footballs of politicians, as victims of lust and the playthings of depraved individuals who have no respect for law and order and no regard for human life. This condition had produced the following results: (1) We are disfranchised in every Southern State and exercise, consequently, little influence in States where we are not disfranchised. (2) Mob and lynch law prevails to such an extent that a black-man is murdered every day in the year without any process of law, and the country at large regards the extraordinary phenomenon as a matter of course. (3) Although our taxes go into the common fund, we are, in most cases, forced to attend separate and inferior schools with terms less by far than those our white fellow-citizens enjoy. (4) In most of the Southern States we are compelled to ride in separate cars, which have become infamous as "Jim Crow cars," because they are inferior beyond the power of expression, and filthy and indecent to the lowest degree. (5) In all of the Southern States there are separate marriage laws, which place a premium upon the dishonorable relations of the sexes and fill the country with a race of children without respectable parentage, leading necessarily to a loose system of morality, which vitiates the whole system. (6) The penal system of every Southern State is a blot upon the honor of the Republic, and is a fruitful schoolhouse of immorality and crime, and leads to the imposition of long terms of imprisonment for trivial offences, for the purpose of supplying cheap contractors. It is a notorious fact that in the convict camps of the South there is no proper separation of the sexes, and it has been shown by more than one investigation that the white guards of these camps have assisted in degrading the females placed in their charge.

It would be useless to include in these major designations the vast number of minor ways by which the whites have succeeded in degrading black-free-men to a condition in comparison of which the condition of black slaves was a happy one. I am sure that this statement is not an exaggerated one; I am sure from observation of my own and from a close study of the conditions covering a period of a quarter of a century. The entire legal machinery of the Southern States has been twisted by white men who control it to degrade black-men and women under the forms of law. The press and the pulpit are in league in this matter, so that condonation and extenuation of barbarous and criminal practices have become so common that it is no longer possible to get the truth out of the mouths of either of these prime factors in the moulding of public opinion; and the press and the pulpit of the north are almost as bad as those of the south in suppressing the truth or apologizing for the condition upon which the truth abides. Indeed, we may reasonably conclude that a conspiracy had been entered into on the part of those who mould public opinion to ignore the extraordinary condition of affairs which has been built upon the tradition of slavery. The protest of one woman in Great Britain did more in ninety days to arouse the press and pulpit of the United States than the protests of one million agencies here during the past twenty years.[3] Why? Because the nation's honor and credit abroad have been damaged.

The great need of the times is well directed agitation which will vex the soul of the nation until it shall be aroused to a sense of its duty. Who is to provoke this agitation? There are no white William Lloyd Garrisons[4] and Horace Greeleys[5] in journalism, or Wendell Phillips[6] and Anna Dickinsons[7] upon the lecture platform, or Thaddeus Stevens[8] and Charles Sumners[9] in legislative halls to do it. The white men of the north have buried the bloody shirt, have forgotten the crime of rebellion, and in the pursuit of commercial and political gain have allowed Henry W. Grady[10] to declare in Fanueil Hall that the whites of the south would rule the south, and brook no outside interference, even as they allowed Bob Toombs[11] to call the roll of his slaves at the foot of Bunker Hill monument. Under the circumstances, it is useless for us to look to white men to fight for black man's rights. If we don't do it ourselves it will not be done. How shall we do it? We can only do it through the medium of organization, the approved method of reaching the consciences of men. Can we have such organization? I once believed we could, and undertook, through the Afro-American League, to supply it. The venture was not an absolute failure, but it never accomplished anything of what its promoters intended that it should accomplish. Why? Because the men who had aforetime been regarded as the leaders of the race refused to give it their countenance and support. Why? The answer is short and pointed, and it is nothing of honor or of glory to their reputations. While the masses cried for justice, they looked on in amusement, even as Nero fiddled while Rome burned, and the masses seeing the indifference of the leaders, and having no one to guide them in the matter, were distrustful, and gave nothing of support calculated to make the movement a success. But all this was four years ago. We have learned much and we have suffered much during that time. The steel has entered deep into our souls. Are we ready to do what we refused to do four years ago? We shall see. An effort will be made to get an authoritative expression of the masses in this matter. A League, national in character, with a hundred thousand members who would support it loyally, could in time bring about the correction of every wrong, of every injustice, of every outrage perpetrated upon the race. But to do this we must have men good to lead, and men good to follow, all of whom will back up their protestations with money necessary to keep the legal machinery of the nation hot, working in our behalf. The opportunity is ours. Will we improve it?

Notes

1. Mary Church Terrell (1863–1954) wrote a strong critique of Fortune's essay, claiming that the editor had gone too far in his characterization of the race. See Mary Church Terrell, "Re: Are We Brave Men or Cowards," *Woman's Era* 2 (1895): 3–4.

2. Oliver Goldsmith (1728–1774); although Fortune is attributing the line to Goldsmith, it is also often linked to John Dryden (1631–1700), *All for Love*.

3. Fortune is referring to Ida B. Wells-Barnett (1862–1931) and her 1893 and 1894 trips to England, where she spoke about the horrors of lynching. For more on Wells-Barnett, see Ida B. Wells-Barnett, *Crusade for Justice: The Autobiography of Ida B. Wells*, ed. Alfreda M. Duster (Chicago: University of Chicago Press, 1970); Wells-Barnett, *Southern Horrors and Other Writings: The Anti-Lynching Campaign of Ida B. Wells, 1892–1900*, ed. Jacqueline Jones Royster (Boston: Bedford Books, 1996); Linda O. McMurry, *To Keep the Waters Troubled: The Life of Ida B. Wells* (New York: Oxford University Press, 1998); and Patricia A. Schechter, *Ida B. Wells-Barnett and American Reform, 1880–1930* (Chapel Hill: University of North Carolina Press, 2001).

4. William Lloyd Garrison (1805–1879) was an abolitionist, editor of the *Liberator*, and founding member of the American Anti-Slavery Society in 1833.

5. Horace Greeley (1811–1872) was founder and editor of the *New York Tribune*.

6. Wendell Phillips (1811–1884) was an abolitionist who associated with William Lloyd Garrison.

7. Anna Dickinson (1842–1932) was an abolitionist who became the first woman to speak before Congress in 1864.

8. Thaddeus Stevens (1792–1868) was a representative from Pennsylvania who was a vocal antislavery advocate and leader of the Radical Republicans during the Civil War and Reconstruction.

9. Charles Sumner (1811–1874) was a senator from Massachusetts who was a vocal antislavery advocate and a leader of the Radical Republicans during the Civil War and Reconstruction. Fortune gave a strong address in memory of Charles Sumner, in which he also promoted the need for the creation of a civil rights organization. See *Hartford Telegram*, January 11, 1884; and *New York Globe*, January 19, 1884. For more on Sumner, see chapter 6, note 5.

10. Henry W. Grady (1850–1889) served as managing editor of the *Atlanta Constitution* in the 1880s and used his position to promote the New South program of northern investment, southern industrial growth, diversified farming, and white supremacy. Grady was one of Fortune's constant targets. See, for example, *New York Age*, November 30, December 21 and 28, 1899.

11. Robert A. Toombs (1810–1885) was a Georgia politician who became a leading secessionist in the U.S. Senate on the eve of the Civil War and was the major architect of Georgia's redemptive constitution in 1877. For more on Robert Toombs, see Ulrich B. Phillips, *Life of Robert Toombs* (New York: Macmillan Company, 1913); and William Y. Thompson, *Robert Toombs of Georgia* (Baton Rouge: Louisiana State University Press, 1966).

15

Mob Law in the South

In the summer of 1897, Fortune wrote "Mob Law in the South" for the *Independent*, appealing to the nation for assistance in ending the brutal acts of lynching. He extols the actions of Ida B. Wells-Barnett and her internationalization of the issue—an act he supported early on as he and the Afro-American League held meetings to raise money for her travels. Fortune also employed Wells-Barnett when she fled the South after the 1893 lynching of her friends and the firestorm that her editorials started. In the end, Fortune, like Wells-Barnett, placed the blame for the continued lynchings squarely on the apathy and silence of the nation.

Mob Law in the South —*Independent,* **July 15, 1897**

When Miss Ida B. Wells[1] went to England, a few winters ago, she horrified the British public by a plain, straightforward story of the prevalence of mob law in the United States, and especially in the Southern States. She had herself been a victim of the mob spirit. Her newspaper property at Memphis Tenn., which it had taken her years of hard labor and self-denial to build up, was destroyed in an hour, and she was warned to remain away from Memphis or take the consequences. Why? Because she had the courage to denounce, in her newspaper, the lynching of three of her acquaintances, reputable young men, one of them a letter mail carrier, who were lodged in jail at Memphis for defending their grocery store from the assaults of what they believed to be white ruffians, instigated by a rival white concern, but who turned out to be special constables, deputed to arrest the three young men on a trumped-up charge, and for the special purpose of breaking up their business.

The recital of this simple story, and of hundred of others like it, by Miss Wells, so excited the public mind of Great Britain that public meetings were held all over England and Scotland, which eventuated in the organization of an Anti-Lynching Society, in which such men were interested as the Duke of Argyle, Henry Labouchére, Justin McCarthy, the Rev. Charles F. Aked, Earl Russell, of the *Chronicle*, and many others. The interest manifested by the British people in agitation was felt in this country; but instead of arousing a responsive sympathy and cooperation on the part of press and people here, it aroused, with reasonable exceptions, a spirit of bitter resentment that the people of Great Britain should interest themselves in our domestic affairs, as if the interests of humanity can be circumscribed by race or nationality.[2]

The public opinion and the newspapers of the Southern States were particularly outspoken and malignant against Miss Wells and the people of Great Britain. The chivalry of Memphis, which had not scrupled to hound a weak woman out of their community, and to destroy her property, because she had fearlessly denounced wrong and outrage, and because God had endowed her with "a skin not colored as their own," pursued her beyond the ocean. The British newspaper offices were flooded with Southern newspaper articles intended not to disprove the story that Miss Wells told, but to prove that she was a moral leper and unworthy of credence. In this infamous business of seeking to deny the truth and to blast the woman's character who told it, the Memphis *Daily Commercial* was easily foremost.[3] The vulgarity and mendaciousness of its utterances upon the subject were such as should not enter any Christian home; but as they were intended to justify the bloody work of the mob and to vindicate Southern honor, whatever that may now mean in the South, and as the woman assailed was of the black and not of the white race, the publications were considered to be in good taste by the people of Memphis, for whom it spoke. As an evidence of the esteem and affection in which it is held its editor was elected to Congress at the November election by the people of Memphis. When shall we have an end of mob law, if the vile champions of it are selected by their fellow citizens to represent them in the highest legislative body of the Republic?

The agitation started in Great Britain three years ago, and which gave promise of effecting some permanent good, has, to all intents and purposes, subsided. The reception which the American people gave the agitation dampened the enthusiasm of the British people, and very naturally. It is in the first place our business, as Christian individuals and as a Christian nation, to see to it that all our people enjoy the protection of the laws, as guaranteed by the Federal Constitution and made obligatory upon the several States by that fundamental charter of our republican form of government. It is for us to see to it that no one of the many races that make up our population is made the object of systematic persecution and spoliation of life and property, as the Jews are in Russia and the Armenians are in Turkey and the Cubans are by the Spaniards in Cuba; and when we fail to do it the rest of the world has a justifiable right to cry aloud and spare not, even as we have done and are doing against Russia and Turkey and Spain. As no man can live to himself alone, so can no nation. "One touch of nature makes the whole world kin,"[4] and the telegraph wire and the printing-press register the heart-throbs of universal mankind every second in a minute and every minute in an hour and every hour in a day. "Am I my brother's keeper?"[5] can be asked now, as when asked by Cain when the world was young, only to shirk responsibility for wrong-doing of one sort or another.

We have been robbing and murdering the Indians and the Africans from the foundation of the Government, doing it as individuals and as a nation; and we are still doing it. The Southern States at least, by failing to punish the miscreants, think it consistent and proper to shoot an Afro-American, without as well as with provocation. Judge Albion W. Tourgée,[6] and other friends of justice and humanity, have utterly failed to touch the national conscience, so that by their silent acquiescence the whole people become a party to the slaughter of Afro-Americans, for one cause or another, from the day that Robert E. Lee[7] surrendered his sword to Ulysses S. Grant[8] to the present day. We cannot shirk the responsibility nor the exceeding odium of our silent toleration of "every day's report of wrong and outrage," which had gone up from the South for thirty years. We may plead as Cain pleaded, but the blood of our brother will remain upon our hands.

From 1865 to 1876, Afro-Americans were slaughtered in all the Southern States by the organized bands of murderers, styling themselves the Ku-Klux Klan, Knights of the White Camellia, and the like, for political reasons ostensibly; and there are men in the Federal Senate and House of Representatives to-day, honored by their fellow members and looked upon and trusted by the nation, who have led those bands on their missions of murder and incendiarism, and who, in any normal condition of society, would have been hanged dead by the neck ten or twenty years ago, "Righteousness exalteth a nation, but sin is a reproach to any people."[9] The crimes of the Ku-Klux Conspiracy have been preserved to posterity in thirteen bulky volumes of "Congressional Reports,"[10] and when the historian of the future reaches that epoch of our national chronicles, he will shudder at the black depravity of it.

Under the specious plea of Home Rule the Ku-Klux mob carried death, destruction and terror everywhere. Like the Spaniards in Cuba to-day, they spared neither male nor female, old nor young; all alike were butchered, all alike despoiled. The absolute destruction of the Afro-American's right of the elective franchise, which had been conferred upon him by the whole American people, who was the object of the conspiracy. The nation put the seal of its approval upon the object achieved in so cowardly and bloody a manner, in 1876, when it withdrew the Federal troops from the South and recognized the legality of the usurped governments of South Carolina, Florida and Louisiana.

When all the State governments of the South had been violently wrestled from the control of the enfranchised Afro-Americans and the Northern allies, the "Carpetbaggers"; when the white men of the South had recovered control of all the machinery of municipal, county and State government, the general belief was that mob law would cease and that the Afro-American, despoiled of political rights and power, would be allowed to live in peace under his vine and fig-tree. But the belief was not realized. The mob spirit was not chased out. The average number of Afro-American men, women, and children lynched in the Southern States in the past twenty years, from 1876, is one hundred; two thousand people murdered in two decades by the inhabitants of Christian States of a Christian nation. Hundreds have been murdered of whose taking off no record was made in the public press, while thousands have been starved and tortured to death in the stockades and the chain-gangs of the penal system, Siberian in its rigors and fatality. Thus to the slaughter of the mob is added judicial murder. How great this latter is can be ascertained by reading the report of the commission appointed to investigate the convict lease system of Georgia, recently submitted.

The Northern newspapers do not keep track of the doings of the mob in the Southern States. They sometimes make brief mention of them. They only give extensive space to them when some unusually atrocious act is perpetrated, like the burning and flaying of a man at Paris, Tex.,[11] three years ago, or the storming of the jail and the lynching of eleven Italians four years ago at New Orleans,[12] or the lynching of two men at Columbus, Ga.,[13] last summer, and the like; but those who spend much time in the Southern States, as I do, know that the newspapers make report nearly every day of some execution by the bloody mob. But a few weeks ago the whole population of Mayfield, Ky.,[14] was under arms to repel a threatened uprising of Afro-Americans, who had been infuriated by the lynching of one of their number for an alleged crime, and for the malicious shooting of several others as an outgrowth of the same affair, charged with no crime whatever.

The charge that these lynchings, which increase instead of decrease from month to month, are provoked by the perpetration of criminal assault, will not bear the test of analysis. A man was lynched in Florida, a little while ago, because he was suspected of burning a house; and not long since a preacher was taken from his pulpit, in the same State and lynched for no assignable reason whatever. A black man will be lynched in the Southern States whenever a few white men decide that they want some excitement out of the ordinary. The black man charged with any sort of crime or who has incurred the enmity of some white man, is hit upon as the victim.

Only two Governors of Southern States have set their faces resolutely against that law; they are Governor T. O'Ferrall, of Virginia,[15] and Governor William Y. Atkinson, of Georgia.[16] These men have rendered splendid service to the South by the resolute opposition to the mob spirit. Their example is worth a ton of percept. South Carolina has an Anti-Lynching law, and Governor John Gary Evans[17] is trying to enforce its provisions.

The mob spirit grows upon what it feeds. It is rapidly demoralizing Southern society; it long ago demoralized and discouraged the Afro-American portion of it, who feel that they are deserted by the nation and by the State and especially by the State which makes haste to mass armed troops at any given point to protect the white mob from the threatened vengeance of black men goaded to desperation.

Is there no appeal to Caesar drunk to Caesar sober? Is it as true to-day as it was in 1856, as proclaimed by Chief-Justice Roger B. Taney,[18] that "the black man has no rights that a man is bound to respect"?

Notes

1. Ida B. Wells-Barnett (1862–1931) was a journalist and civil rights activist who was best known for her antilynching activism. For more on Wells-Barnett, see chapter 14, note 3.

2. Wells-Barnett went to England in 1893 and 1894 to lecture on the horrors of lynching. See Linda O. McMurry, *To Keep the Waters Troubled: The Life of Ida B. Wells* (New York: Oxford University Press, 1998); and Patricia A. Schecter, *Ida B. Wells-Barnett and American Reform, 1880–1930* (Chapel Hill: University of North Carolina Press, 2001).

3. Fortune is referring to the letter written by newspaper editor John Jacks, president of the Missouri Press Association, in which he defended the white South and maligned black women for their immorality. See McMurry, *To Keep the Waters Troubled*; Schecter, *Ida B. Wells and American Reform*; and Beverly Guy-Sheftall, *Daughters of Sorrow: Attitudes toward Black Women, 1880–1920* (Brooklyn, N.Y.: Carlson, 1990). These attacks led to the unification of the women's clubs and the creation of the National Association of Colored Women (NACW). See McMurry, *To Keep the Waters Troubled*; Schecter, *Ida*

B. Wells and American Reform; Guy-Sheftall, *Daughters of Sorrow*; and Paula Giddings, *When and Where I Enter: The Impact of Black Women on Race and Sex in America* (New York: Bantam Books, 1985).

4. William Shakespeare (1564–1616), *Troilus and Cressida*.

5. Genesis 4:9.

6. Albion W. Tourgée (1838–1905) was an abolitionist, lawyer, author, and civil rights activist who later represented Homer Plessy in the landmark *Plessy v. Ferguson* case in 1896. Tourgée published *A Fool's Errand, by One of the Fools* (New York: Fords, Howard, & Hulbert, 1879) and its addendum *The Invisible Empire* (New York: Fords, Howard, & Hulbert, 1880). Tourgée had often spoken out against lynching, and in 1894 he and African American supporters secured the passage of an antilynching bill in Ohio. Much of Tourgée's civil rights work during this period was done with his organization, the National Citizens Rights Association, formed in 1892 with goals similar to Fortune's Afro-American League. See Otto H. Olsen, *Carpetbagger's Crusade: The Life of Albion Winegar Tourgée* (Baltimore: Johns Hopkins Press, 1965); and Mark Elliott, *Color-Blind Justice: Albion Tourgée and the Quest for Racial Equality from the Civil War to Plessy v. Ferguson* (New York: Oxford University Press, 2006).

7. Robert E. Lee (1807–1870) was a Confederate general during the Civil War.

8. Ulysses S. Grant (1822–1885) was a Union army general and eighteenth president of the United States.

9. Proverbs 14:34.

10. Joint Select Committee to Inquire into the Condition of Affairs in the Late Insurrectionary, *Report of the Joint Select Committee to Inquire into the Condition of Affairs in the Late Insurrectionary States: Made to the Two Houses of Congress February 19, 1872*, vol. 13 (Washington, D.C.: U.S. Government, 1872). It should be noted that Fortune's father, Emanuel Fortune Sr., gave testimony for the inquiry. See also Allen W. Trelease, *White Terror*.

11. Henry Smith was lynched on February 1, 1893, in Paris, Texas. The *New York Sun*, a paper Fortune was working for at the time, published a description and reaction to the brutal killing. *New York Sun*, February 2, 1893.

12. Eleven Italians acquitted of a "mafiosi"-type killing were lynched in the city on March 13, 1891. See *New Orleans Picayune,* March 14, 15, 16, 1891.

13. Jesse Slayton and Will Miles were lynched by a mob in Columbus in Muscogee County, Georgia, on June 1, 1896. They were accused of rape. See Brundage, *Lynching in the New South: Georgia and Virginia, 1880–1930* (Urbana: University of Illinois Press, 1993).

14. James Stone and George Finley were lynched in Mayfield, Kentucky, on December 21 and 22, 1896, respectively. See George C. Wright, *Racial Violence in Kentucky, 1865–1940: Lynchings, Mob Rule, and "Legal Lynchings"* (Baton Rouge: Louisiana State University Press, 1990).

15. Charles T. O'Ferrall (1840–1905) was governor of Virginia from 1894 to 1898. For information on O'Ferrall's position on lynching, see Brundage, *Lynching in the New South*.

16. William Yates Atkinson (1854–1899) was governor of Georgia from 1894 to 1898. For information on Atkinson's position on lynching, see Brundage, *Lynching in the New South*.

17. John Gary Evans (1863–1942) was governor of South Carolina from 1894 to 1897. Although South Carolina had recently passed antilynching legislation, the legislation did not end the brutal crime as quickly as Fortune may have expected. The incidents of lynchings in South Carolina steadily increased throughout the final decade of the nineteenth and into the first decade of the twentieth centuries. See George B. Tindall, *South Carolina Negroes, 1877–1900* (Baton Rouge: Louisiana State University Press, 1952); and Terence Finnegan, "Lynching and Political Power in Mississippi and South Carolina," in *Under Sentence of Death: Essays on Lynching in the South*, ed. W. Fitzhugh Brundage (Chapel Hill: University of North Carolina Press, 1997), 189–218.

18. Roger B. Taney (1777–1864) was chief justice of the U.S. Supreme Court from 1836 to 1864. He authored the majority decision in *Dred Scott v. Sandford*, 60 U.S. 393 (1856). Fortune is citing the decision.

16

Immorality of Southern Suffrage Legislation

In the following piece, written for the *Independent*, Fortune outlines the argument against the southern states' disfranchisement legislation. Beginning in 1890 with Mississippi, the southern governments began rewriting their constitutions and effectively disfranchising their African American population. In 1898, the same year Fortune is writing this essay, the Supreme Court upheld Mississippi's suffrage amendment in *Williams v. Mississippi*, and Louisiana passed its own franchise legislation, instituting what became known as the "grandfather clause."

Immorality of Southern Suffrage Legislation —*Independent*, **December 1, 1898**

In view of the proposition to rob the negroes of North Carolina of the right of suffrage it is well to recall the last constitutional robbery, that of Louisiana.[1]

If it had been the purpose of the controlling influences of the Constitutional Convention of Louisiana to devise a fundamental suffrage law which should be just and fair to all of the heterogeneous elements of the citizenship of the State the task would have been a comparatively easy one. Friendly advice and counsel were showered upon the convention by men of both races eminent in the thought and effort of Southern life. To have followed the straight and narrow path it was not at all necessary to give ear to the advice and counsel of men of the North and West—men who are habitually but erroneously regarded as being antagonistic to the best interests of the Southern people. In an open letter addressed to the convention, February 19th, 1898, Mr. Booker T. Washington[2] of Alabama, the most noted, popular and conservative Afro-American in the country, said among other things:

"The negro does not object to an educational or property test, but let the law be so clear that no one clothed with State authority will be tempted to perjure and degrade himself by putting one interpretation upon it for the white man and another for the black man. Study the history of the South and you will find that where there has been the most dishonesty in the matter of voting there you will find to-day the lowest moral condition of both races. First, there was the temptation to act wrongly with the negro's ballot, with the carrying of concealed weapons, with the murder of a negro, and then with the murder of a white man, and then with lynching. I entreat you not to pass such a law as will prove an eternal millstone about the necks of your children.

"No man can have respect for government and officers of the law when he knows deep down in his heart that the exercise of the franchise is tainted with fraud. . . .

"I beg you, further, that in the degree that you close the ballot box against the ignorant you open the school house."

Dr. J. L. M. Curry[3] is a Southern man. He was a member of the Confederate Congress. President Cleveland made him Minister to Spain. No man in the country has done more to advance the cause of education in the Southern States than he, and to-day he is the faithful and trusted representative of the trustees of the Peabody and Slater funds. Dr. Curry addressed the Constitutional Convention at New Orleans with special reference to proposed suffrage legislation. Among other things he said:

"The negroes, unlike alien immigrants, are here not of their own choosing, and their civil and political equality is the outcome of our subjugation. Neither their presence nor their civil equality is likely to be changed in our day. The negroes will remain a constituent portion of Southern population and citizenship. What are to be our relations to them? Are they to be lifted up or left in the conditions of discontent, ignorance, poverty, semi-barbarism? Shall one race have every encouragement and opportunity for development for the highest civilization and the other be handicapped and environed with insurmountable obstacles to progress? Are friction, strife, hatred less likely with the negro under stereotyped conditions of inferiority than by the recognition and stimulation of whatever capacities for progress he may possess? Shall we learn nothing from history? Do Ireland and Poland furnish us no lessons? . . .

"Attach, if you please, the restraining qualification upon suffrage; make it a boon, a reward for intelligence and industry; affix to it any conditions you please which the public weal may demand, but do not make it impossible to attain to the privilege. That would be dishonest, and neither communities nor men can afford to be dishonest."[4]

Mr Washington's letter was more generally quoted and commented upon and approved by the responsible press of the country, North and South, than any similar expression from an Afro-American.[5] The New Orleans *Times-Democrat*, the leading newspaper of the State, adopted the view of the matter as presented by him, and urged the convention to do so. But the convention had not got itself together for the purpose of dealing honestly and fairly by all the elements of the citizenship. The only excuse for its existence was the undisguised purpose of devising a way to disfranchise as many black voters as possible and as few white ones as possible. That was its avowed object. Its members did not hesitate to avow it from the housetops, and, when the time came, to give their avowal the force and effect of fundamental law. The immorality of it did not worry them, nor the demoralizing influence it would inevitably have upon the whole people of the State. Despite prayers and protests the convention adopted a suffrage law, the gist of which is as follows:

Section 3 provides for an educational qualification.

Section 4 provides that "if he be not able to read and write, as provided by section 3, then he shall be entitled to register and vote if he shall, at the time he offers to register, be the *bona fide* owner of property assessed to him at a valuation of not less than $300 on the assessment roll of the current year in which he offer to register, or on the roll of the preceding year if the roll of the current year shall then have been completed and filed, and on which, if such property be personal only, all taxes due shall have been paid. The applicant for registration under this section shall make oath before the registration officer or his deputy that he is a citizen of the United States and of this State, over the age of 21 years; that he possessed the qualifications prescribed in section 1 of this article, and that he is the owner of property assessed in this State to him at the valuation of not less than $300; and if such property be personal only, that all taxes due thereon have been paid."

"Section 5. No male person who was on January 1, 1867, or at any date prior thereto, entitled to vote under the Constitution or statutes of any State of the United States wherein he then resided, and no son or grandson of any such person not less than 21 years of age at the date of the adoption of this Constitution, and no person of foreign birth who shall have been naturalized prior to the first day of January, 1898, shall be denied the right to register and vote in this State by reason of his failure to possess the educational or property qualification prescribed by this Constitution; provided, he shall have resided in this State for five years next preceding the date at which he shall apply for registration, and shall have registered in accordance with the terms of this article prior to September 1, 1898; and no person shall be entitled to register under this section after said date."

It is hardly conceivable that a convention of intelligent men of any American commonwealth would devise and adopt any legislation so obviously immoral and demoralizing as this suffrage law. Both of the Senators in Congress for Louisiana give it as their opinion that section 5 was unconstitutional, and would be so construed by the Federal Supreme Court, while the New Orleans *Times-Democrat* denounced the enactment as a whole as the work of political demagogs and tricksters.[6]

Section 5 is supposed to conflict with the provisions of section 1 of article 14 and of section 1 of article 15 of the Federal Constitution, the latter section reading as follows:

"The right of citizens of the United States to vote shall not be denied or abridged by the United States or by any State on account of race, color or previous condition of servitude."

This amendment was not adopted until March 30, 1868. The Thirteenth Amendment, abolishing slavery, was adopted December 18, 1865. While giving suffrage to white men, and to their sons and grandsons who were entitled to vote prior to January 1, 1867, and to all foreigners naturalized prior to January 1, 1898, section 5 of the Louisiana suffrage law disfranchises all Afro-Americans who were enfranchised by the Fifteenth Amendment, adopted March 20, 1868. It does this not only as to the letter of the law but as to the spirit of it, as expressed by those who adopted it, and which is a part of the discussion of the convention and which must influence the Federal Supreme Court in passing the validity of it.

Mississippi, South Carolina[7] and Louisiana have now adopted constitutions whose suffrage clauses were avowedly designed and intended to, and which do, disfranchise the bulk of their Afro-American citizenship, which in each of these three States is numerically greater than their Anglo-American citizenship. The suffrage clauses of the Constitutions of Mississippi and South Carolina are just as immoral and demoralizing as that of Louisiana.[8]

It is worthy of note and an element of positive discouragement that the Federal Supreme Court, in the case of Williams against the State of Mississippi,[9] has affirmed the constitutionality of the suffrage clauses of the new Constitution of Mississippi, and with expressions of antagonism to the Afro-American citizen as extreme and repugnant as those of Chief Justice Roger B. Taney,[10] delivered in 1856, in the famous case of Dred Scott against

Sanford, when it was affirmed that when the Constitution was adopted negroes were regarded as an inferior race who had "no rights that a white man was bound to respect." The decision was rendered by Mr. Justice McKenna,[11] who was promoted to the bench from the office of Attorney-General by President McKinley.[12]

As far as the Federal Supreme Court is concerned we have not advanced one inch from this dictum since it was delivered forty-two years ago, as every piece of supplementary legislation based upon the war amendments—which necessarily revolutionized all law and precedent based upon the civil and political rights of citizens of the United States—passed by the Congress has been declared null and void by the Federal Supreme Court.

The immorality of such suffrage legislation as has been adopted by Mississippi, South Carolina and Louisiana is apparent upon its face, while Congress had thus far neglected to reduce the representation of such States, as provided in section 2 of article 14.[13] We are undoubtedly drifting into a condition of affairs in this matter which will inevitably provoke serious trouble. It is not possible to rob the black man of his rights without robbing the white man, and North Carolina and South Carolina are just now proving that fact.

Notes

1. It is important to note that while Fortune is writing this article the newly formed Afro-American Council, whose executive committee he directs, is beginning to formulate a challenge to the Louisiana suffrage legislation. During its existence the Council also challenged the suffrage amendments of Alabama and Virginia. See Shawn Leigh Alexander, "The Afro-American Council and Its Challenge of Louisiana's Grandfather Clause," in *Radicalism in the South since Reconstruction*, ed. Chris Green, Rachel Rubin, and James Smethurst, 13–38 (New York: Palgrave, 2006); and Alexander, "'We Know Our Rights and Have the Courage to Defend Them': Agitation in the Age of Accommodation, 1883–1909" (Ph.D. diss., University of Massachusetts–Amherst, 2004). North Carolina would ultimately disfranchise its African American population in 1900 by amendment. Louisiana disfranchised its African American population in 1898 by a constitutional convention. The process Louisiana used became known as the "grandfather clause," which exempted from the literacy and property tests those entitled to the vote as of January 1, 1867. See Michael Perman, *Struggle for Mastery: Disfranchisement in the South, 1888–1908* (Chapel Hill: University of North Carolina Press, 2001); August Meier, *Negro Thought in America, 1880–1915: Racial Ideologies in the Age of Booker T. Washington* (Ann Arbor: University of Michigan Press, 1963); and C. Vann Woodward, *Origins of the New South, 1877–1913* (Baton Rouge: Louisiana State University Press, 1951).

2. Booker T. Washington (1856–1915) was the founder and head of Tuskegee Institute (1881) and founder of the National Negro Business League (1900). Washington was

propelled to the position of *the* African American leader by both whites and blacks after his 1895 Atlanta Exposition address, where he seemingly accepted segregation. For the full text of the letter, see Booker T. Washington, "An Open Letter to the Louisiana Constitutional Convention," in *The Booker T. Washington Papers*, ed. Louis R. Harlan and Raymond Smock (Urbana: University of Illinois Press, 1975), 4:381–84. For more on Washington, see Louis R. Harlan, *Booker T. Washington: The Making of a Black Leader, 1856–1901* (New York: Oxford University Press, 1972); Harlan, *Booker T. Washington: The Wizard of Tuskegee, 1901–1915* (New York: Oxford University Press, 1983); and Meier, *Negro Thought in America*.

3. Jabez Lamar Monroe Curry (1825–1903) was a colonel in the Confederate army during the Civil War, Alabama representative to the Confederate Congress, Alabama state representative (1847, 1853–57), U.S. representative (1857–61), and minister to Spain, 1885–88. Following the Civil War he became a supporter of education for both races, and after 1890 Curry also served as agent of the John F. Slater Fund for African American education.

4. *Official Journal of the Proceedings of the Constitutional Convention of the State of Louisiana, Held in New Orleans, Tuesday, February 8, 1898* (New Orleans: J. J. Hearsey, 1898).

5. See *New Orleans Times-Democrat*, February 21, 1898; *New Orleans Picayune*, February 21, 1898; *Springfield Republican*, February 22, 1898; *Boston Globe*, February 21, 1898; *Atlanta Constitution*, February 26, 1898; *Chicago Tribune*, February 21, 1898; *New York Times*, February 21, 1898; and *Washington Post*, February 21, 1898.

6. *Washington Post*, May 13, 1901.

7. Mississippi passed its disfranchisement legislation in 1890, using a combination of literacy, property requirements, and an understanding clause. South Carolina passed disfranchisement legislation in 1895, following Mississippi's plan. See Perman, *Struggle for Mastery*; Woodward, *Origins of the New South*; and George B. Tindall, *South Carolina Negroes, 1877–1900* (Baton Rouge: Louisiana State University Press, 1952).

8. For a discussion of their immorality and unconstitutionality, see John L. Love, *The Disfranchisement of the Negro* (Washington, D.C.: American Negro Academy, 1899); and John Hope, *Negro Suffrage in the States Whose Constitutions Have Not Been Specifically Revised* (Washington, D.C.: American Negro Academy, 1905).

9. *Williams v. Mississippi*, 170 U.S. 213 (1898).

10. Roger B. Taney (1777–1864) was chief justice of the U.S. Supreme Court from 1836 to 1864. He authored the majority decision in *Dred Scott v. Sandford*, 60 U.S. 393 (1856).

11. Joseph McKenna (1843–1926) was a California representative from 1885 to 1892, U.S. attorney general from 1897 to 1898, and justice of the Supreme Court from 1898 to 1925.

12. William McKinley (1843–1901) was a Republican politician and twenty-fifth president of the United States, 1897–1901.

13. Fortune would later argue against Congress reducing representation, believing that the tactic would backfire. The issue was hotly contested during the 1904 election and became a splintering issue in the Afro-American Council. See Alexander, "We Know Our Rights."

17

False Theory of Education Cause of Race Demoralization

In this July 1904 essay, Fortune calls attention to the fact that there are educated men who "have been saturated with the notion that their paramount mission in life is to lift up the race." This, according to Fortune, has created a race of leaders rather than a group of faithful followers "to execute the wise policies of capable men." In the end, Fortune concludes that this sort of education has paralyzed "the thought and action of the race."

False Theory of Education Cause of Race Demoralization —*Colored American Magazine* 7, no. 7 (1904): 473–78

The writer was present at the commencement exercises, at Hampton Institute, a few years ago, when a theory of education, which has been persistently inculcated in all the academic and collegiate schools founded and maintained for the education of Afro-American youth, since the War of Rebellion, was emphasized in a painful manner, as far as the writer was concerned.[1] I do not wish to have it understood that this theory of education was or is knowingly inculcated in our schools; it appears to be a matter of unconscious inculcation, hammered into the students from start to finish of the prescribed course of study by the words of professors and outside speakers in addressing the student body, so that ultimately the students come to regard it as a fixed principle of the school course and of their life-work. Much of the misdirected effort of the graduates of Afro-American schools, in the past quarter of a century, is traceable, in some sort, to this theory of education; which I may define as educating the student away from the principle that his first object in life should be the building up of his individual character and material well-being, substituting instead the necessity of devoting all of his time and talents to the building up of the character and material well-being of his race, as the first rule of action.

The incident, at Hampton Institute, to which I wish to direct attention, as being the false theory of education which has caused so much of misdirected effort, was illustrated in the addresses of the two principal graduates of the class; one being an Afro-American and other an Onandago Indian, whose reservation home was near Syracuse, New York.

The Negro was the first speaker. There was nothing in his looks or speech to differentiate him from the average academic graduates. He was short of stature, fat, and his face was indicative of abounding good nature. Genius did not flash from his eyes nor resound in his periods as he held the auditory spellbound. His address was pitched in a high-key of devotion to and sacrifice for others, although the speaker did not appear capable of doing more than the ordinary work that falls to an educated man, with an appetite for good eating and plenty of it and a disposition to take life easy, looking at the humorous rather than the serious side of life's struggle. When he reached the peroration of his essay, the student struck the theatrical attitude usual in oratorical heroics, and exclaimed, in substance:

"I shall go out from these sacred walls with one great idea uppermost in my mind; I shall go back and mingle with my people and devote my life to lifting them up. I shall seek to give to them of the knowledge with I have gathered here, for the first rule of every educated man's conduct should to do what he can to lift up his people."

That is the substance of what he said on that subject, although the same thought ran all through his essay. I was impressed, but sadly. The fact is, the young man had had no money when he reached Hampton Institute four years prior to his graduation; he had been assisted all through his school course by Northern philanthropy and work given him by the school, the clothes in which he graduated had been given to him, and the car-fare in his pocket necessary to enable him to reach his home and the field of his proposed Atlasan labors had been sent to him by relatives as poor as he. I have never heard of the student since, and I dare say he is still tugging away at building up his own character and fortunes; for, unless a man first lift himself up, how can he lift up others? Of course, the well informed reader will point to Booker T. Washington as a shining example of this sort of education, for he did not have a shirt to his back when he reached Hampton Institute, and there are others; but there are exceptions to every rule, and the fact that the theory of education which produced him, and a few others of lesser conspicuity, is the proper sort is refuted by the fact that it has produced so few of his kind and so many who have been and are staggering through life, laboring earnestly, perhaps, but as poor and inconsequental as when they left their alma maters, with little more influence on the general mass of the people than if they had not graduated from any school of learning. Their efforts had been misdirected. They had striven to lift up others before lifting up themselves, and so remained on a dead level of effort and achievement.

In his recent address to the students of Tuskegee Institute, Bishop Galloway, of Mississippi,[2] eloquently inculcated the theory that the students had a special mission, that the eyes of the world were upon them, and that they should do what they could to lift up their race. The good bishop meant well, for his heart beats in the right place. The students he exhorted have no special mission, but simply the mission of the average American citizen who has enjoyed the advantages of a liberal education; and eyes of the world are not upon them, and will not be, until they do something which will attract general attention, whether in their town, or county, or state, or in the nation. The eyes of the world do not rest upon the obscure, but upon those who, by achievement in the development of their individual fortunes, are in position to help others, and this can not be done by wasting a life of effort striving to lift up a whole race and neglecting first to lift up the individual self.

The next speaker at the Hampton Institute commencement was an Onandago Indian. He looked just like all other Indians I had seen; and most Indians look alike to me. His essay was pitched on similar lines to those of the first speaker, and his peroration was the same. He was going right back to the Onandago Reservation and devote his life to lifting up his people. Now, this Indian's car-fare from Syracuse to Hampton Institute had been paid by the Federal Government, which has always been more generous to the Red Indian than the Black African, his tuition, food, and clothing had been paid for by the Government, and the ticket on which he traveled back to his home in Western New York will have been paid for by the Government when he turned his face towards it. How could a man, even a proud Indian, so circumstanced and hedged about, get it into his head, except by a false theory of education, that he could lift up his race, or anybody else, before he had first lifted up himself? He started out in life with his head twisted by a false idea which would hamper all of his efforts and, more than likely, frustrate them one by one, until he should round out the number of his days, a soured old man because he had made a failure of his life in all that he had prized most in the basic philosophy of his education.

It is worthy of note that the Negro and Indian are the only race elements of the American citizenship who are taught that their chief mission in life is to lift up their race. Other elements of the citizenship are taught from the nursery to the graduating hour at school that the chief end of effort is to develop the individual to the utmost, and that in so far as this is done will he and society at large be benefited; that by lifting up himself he will be able to lift up others, as the units make the whole and not the whole the units; as the individuals make the aggregate citizenship, and not the aggregate citizenship the individuals; as the success of the race or the nation depends not upon the untied effort of all, as such, but upon the efforts of the several individuals constituting the race or nation, as such, proceeding invariably upon individual and not national or race initiative.

It may reasonably be argued that this view of the matter is the sublimation of selfishness. Granted. The progress of mankind is based in selfish and not magnanimous effort, the individual units working out the evolutionary processes independently of each other and often unconsciously, the sum total of their efforts making for general progress, prosperity and happiness without their conscious connivance. Looked at as a whole, the sum total appears to be the result of conscious design and effort, and is placed to the credit of the whole race or nation, whether for good or evil; but, as a matter of fact, the result is due to individual initiative and selfishness, with no conscious thought of benefiting the race or nation, as the case may be.

That the Indian and the Afro-American have been the victims of this false theory of education, which is not hitched upon any other element of the American citizenship, is due wholly to the fact that education had been designed, directed and paid for, for the most part, by good people, worthy of praise, who regard the Indian and the Afro-American people as peculiar people, not like other people, who require peculiar standards of education, as they are to occupy a peculiar place in the life of the American citizenship. When the products of this theory of education come into close contact with the every-day exactions of society they find that they are not prepared for them, there being nothing peculiar about them, a uniformity of requirement prevailing from bootblacking to book-keeping, and the book-keeping to the administrative positions dominating in the social and civil order. The origin of this theory is essentially religious. The good people who have been at the bottom of the educational initiative and support of the Afro-American and Indian, and who have been intensely religious in their own convictions, and have made the missionary aim in thought and effort the corner stone of their system of education ethics, in which, preparation for the life that is, and living and sacrificing for others was regarded as of more moment and nobility than living and sacrificing for self. In all of the institutions maintained for the education of Afro-American youth the atmosphere of religious sanctity even now is as intense as in the Puritan days of New England, when all men and women were weighted down with the burden of the hereafter and dread of what it held in store for them, so that the present was so full of terrors as to rob if of all pleasures of the most innocent character. The theory of education, therefore, that obtains and has obtained, not only makes sacrifice for others and lifting up of others the rules of living, but by the nature of it, has fostered and encouraged a subsidiary rule, that of hypocrisy, a large element of which will be found to demoralize the conduct of a larger percentage of the educated among the Afro-American people, because all men are not religious to the extent of willingness to make it the ruling passion of life, and when they have it forced upon them, and they are unable to escape from it, they become insincere, hypocritical in thought and ultimately in conduct.

In 1874, the writer left the grounds of Howard University, preferring to room and board on the outside rather than submit to the religious tyranny practiced upon resident students. Besides the two religious services in the chapel each day, each meal service, with Bible reading and a "grace" as long and often longer than the average prayer; and there were some five different religious societies maintained among the students, suggested by the college authorities, with which all students were expected to affiliate, and were affected in their class standing if they did not do it. I contended then that I did not matriculate at the college for the purpose of learning how to die, but how to live, and that the requirements of the religious observances took up so much time as to leave little for the prescribed course of studies, while the religious atmosphere was so intense as to make worldly matters seem inconsequential, inducing a mental depression which amounted to habitual sadness, if lived in long enough. I preferred not to live in it, and I have not regretted that I did so. I know a score of men who were students with me at the time conformed strictly to the rule; they were looked upon as hypocrites then and they have lived the lives of hypocrites since, occupying a dead level of achievement in the vain-glorious struggle to lift up the race. If they had had a proper sort of education in manliness and self-respect and self-interest; they would have made strong and useful men; as it has turned out, many of them are less than leeches, always ready with a scheme to benefit the race, and a willingness to accept the money from some one else necessary to make the scheme a success, with no honest intention of applying the funds for the purpose which they were solicited and given. And before I went to Howard University, and was attending the Stanton Institute, at Jacksonville, Florida, a northern man who had done much for the school offered me a scholarship at Atlanta University if I would promise to become a preacher or teacher when my education was completed. I refused the offer and would do so again under similar conditions, because I know that there are no elements of a preacher or teacher in my make-up. Some of the young men who did accept the bounty and conditions of this good man have been acting the part of hypocrites ever since, and some of them are as rank failures in everything they have attempted to do as would be easy to find.

And we have preachers and school teachers by the thousand all over this country who have no fitness for the work in which they are engaged, and have measurably failed in it, but who, having accepted an education with the understanding, expressed or implied, that they would preach or teach, have stuck to their work and justified their conscience, if not the expectations of those who paid for their education. These people would have made splendid success, unburdened by the obligation to build up their race, if they had been left free to follow the bent of their own genius.

And there is a broader aspect of the evil. A system of education cannot turn out a succession of graduates for a quarter of a century, each one inflated with the notion that he is the chosen instrument for the uplifting of his race, a leader of men manufactured out and out by a process of education, who, in the world of action, needs only to blow one blast upon his bugle horn to have his thousand liege followers rise up, as did Rhoderick Dhu's[3] men, apparently out of the ground, without creating a cult, so to speak. We have it in evidence everywhere as a protuberant, truculent and obnoxious assumption of leadership of all sorts of conditions of men, in all sorts of situations, graduates of schools of all sorts, some of which have not drilled the graduates in a moderate mastery of the mother tongue and in the ethics of domination, some of whom are not even prepared to be good followers under wise guidance. It was Napoleon Bonaparte, I believe, who declared that a man who did not know how to obey is not fit to command. It is a fair conclusion that this is the condition of the Afro-American people to-day. Its educated men have been saturated with the notion that their paramount mission in life is to lift up the race, and they go about that mission as persons having authority. The young graduate just out of school has the affliction in as aggravated and provoking form as the old one, who has struggled through years of discouragement to live up to his education, covered all over with the scars of defeat, with nothing but the ruling passion that he is an authorized "lifter" left as his stock in trade. And these people have scattered the heresy broadcast through the ranks of the ignorant mass, so that it is difficult not to find an Afro-American without a mission to lift up his race, to be a leader of thought and effort, and not a faithful follower to execute the wise policies of capable men, the latter being given little opportunity to make themselves felt and heard.

The extent to which the demoralization of this false theory of education has gone can easily be estimated by any one who will attend any sort of gathering of Afro-Americans where the work in hand requires deliberation and action, and, therefore, a semblance of organization. Every man in the gathering imagines that he should be made chairman, and is indisposed to vote for anyone as long as he thinks he has a chance of succeeding, and then he will probably throw his influence to the least competent man in the gathering in order to get even with the modest man who is probably the only man fit to be selected. And the defeated men always feel that they have been defrauded of their dues and stand ready at the first opportunity to obstruct the orderly transaction of business or to break up the assemblage. This is not only true of small gatherings without consequence, but of great national assemblages as well. Church conferences and great quadrennial conferences are marred by the same display of bumptious ambition to dominate without brains or character, or substantial reputation in achievement, to warrant it. And when an organization is finally perfected everybody has an idea and insists upon having an hour or more in which to talk about it, and when ruled or voted out of order will create an uproar which the police may have to quell with a display of clubs and pistols.[4]

Where every educated man feels that he is authorized to lift the race up, because he is educated that way, and the mass of the people have become inoculated with the same deadly disease, we have a condition in which every man feels that he is as good and knows as much as his neighbor, and refuses to follow if not allowed to lead. Demoralization, therefore, paralyzes the thought and action of the race. That is the situation to-day.[5]

How are we to get back to first principles? How are we to educate the youth of the race so as to get the best results, not in the lifting up of the race, but in the lifting up of the individual? How are we to spread broadcast the fact that ability, character and experience are working capital which youth and ignorance do not posess and cannot resist without being dashed to pieces? How are we to get rooted in our education the fact that while "all men are created equal, and endowed by their creator with certain unalienable rights," this equality disappears absolutely in the progress from childhood to manhood, when most are fitted to follow and precious few are fitted to lead?

With the race full of educated men, there are yet few to follow most men striving to pull down everybody, in the hope to reap some selfish advantage in the confusion; so that the enemies of the race have it at a fearful disadvantage and are wreaking havoc with its character, and with its civil and political and manhood rights. The individual must lift up himself before he can lift up the race.

Notes

1. For a summary of education in the post–Civil War South, see James D. Anderson, *The Education of Blacks in the South, 1860–1935* (Chapel Hill: University of North Carolina Press, 1988); Louis R. Harlan, *Separate and Unequal: Public School Campaigns and Racism in the Southern Seaboard States, 1901–1915* (New York: Atheneum, 1969); and Herbert G. Gutman, "Schools for Freedom: The Post Emancipation Origins of Afro-American Education," in *Power and Culture: Essays on the American Working Class*, ed. Ira Berlin (New York: Pantheon Books, 1987), 260–97.

2. Charles B. Galloway (1849–1909) was a bishop of the Methodist Episcopal Church, South.

3. Rhoderick Dhu was a Scottish Highlands rebel chief of Clan Alpine and sworn enemy of King James V. Rhoderick Dhu was memorialized in Sir Walter Scott's poem *The Lady of the Lake*.

4. Here Fortune is referring to the Boston Riot, which occurred when Booker T. Washington spoke before a National Negro Business League meeting at the AME Zion Church in Boston, Massachusetts. At the meeting, William Monroe Trotter and his associates tried to get Washington to answer questions regarding his stated policy on race relations. For more on the riot, see Elliott M. Rudwick, "Race Leadership Struggle: Background of the Boston Riot of 1903," *Journal of Negro Education* 31 (1962): 16–24; Rudwick, *W.E.B. Du Bois: Propagandist of the Negro Protest* (New York: Atheneum, 1978); August Meier, *Negro Thought in America, 1880–1915: Racial Ideologies in the Age of Booker T. Washington* (Ann Arbor: University of Michigan Press, 1963); Louis R. Harlan, *Booker T. Washington: The Making of a Black Leader, 1856–1901* (New York: Oxford University Press, 1972); Stephen R. Fox, *The Guardian of Boston: William Monroe Trotter* (New York: Atheneum, 1970); David Levering Lewis, *W.E.B. Du Bois: Biography of a Race, 1868–1919* (New York: Henry Holt, 1993); and Shawn Leigh Alexander, "'We Know Our Rights and Have the Courage to Defend Them': Agitation in the Age of Accommodation, 1883–1909" (Ph.D. diss., University of Massachusetts–Amherst, 2004).

5. It is important to note that this piece was written shortly after Fortune resigned from the Afro-American Council, where he had noted similar frustrations with the leaders of the race. See chapter 20. Fortune also argued along similar lines in his *Age* column, "Fortune's Weekly Talks," in 1890. He stated, "The colored people of this country have never had a great popular leader, in the sense that we speak of Parnell or Gladstone . . . a leader whom the people trusted and should sustain as loyally in the day of defeat as in

the day of victory." "Why is this so," the editor asked, "I think it is due to the fact that we are a race of leaders! Every man regards himself as a natural captain, and therefore scorns to be led or advised." "If he can't lead and advise a host," Fortune explained, "he will lead and advise himself." *New York Age*, October 29, 1887. See also *New York Age*, November 19, 1887.

18

Failure of the Afro-American People to Organize

In this 1906 editorial, Fortune reflects on the attempts of the race to organize civil rights organizations. He examines his own efforts to create the Afro-American League and the efforts of those individuals who had tried to sustain the Afro-American Council and the Niagara Movement. Although he acknowledges the importance of their efforts, he concludes that the masses have taken no interest in sustaining the organization and therefore the groups are failures. They need to get the masses aroused, he argues, and stop being windjamming organizations.

Failure of the Afro-American People to Organize —*New York Age*, October 11, 1906

The meeting of the National Afro-American Council,[1] in New York, the current week, brings very sad reflections to the mind of the writer of this article, who has given sixteen years of his life and his means to the effort to organize the Afro-American people for their own protection in "all lawful ways, especially in the courts and in the manufacture of healthy public opinion," and who is compelled to admit, while an annual meeting of the Council is in session, that, for all practical purposes, the effort had been a failure.[2] The time and the money, and above all the enthusiasm, in the work have gone for naught, measured by the standard of results, and results are the only things that count in the estimation of mankind in any given effort for good or for evil. We speak but the sad and solemn truth when we declare that while the National Afro-American Council exists, and will continue to exist, it has no organization in the literal sense, it has not the people behind it, because the people do not appreciate the need of organization. A hundred devoted men and women of the highest character and culture, the self-appointed representatives and spokesmen of ten millions of people, who have stood by the League and the Council for sixteen years, through good and evil report, deserve all of the good things that can be said of them. They deserve well of the race and of the American people; but they are and have been and will be a standing reproach to and an attestation of the backwardness of the Afro-American people, who have persistently refused to second their efforts by moral or financial support, standing indifferently by while their dearest rights under State and Federal Constitutions have been denied or abridged, without any disposition to organize or to contribute even pennies to protect and defend themselves. God helps those who help themselves, and He leaves it to the devil to help the others.

The National Afro-American League was organized in Chicago, January 15, 1890.[3] The convention was one of the largest and most representative Afro-American gatherings in the history of the country. There were brave men and beautiful women in the convention, devotedly loyal and self-sacrificing people who felt the urgent need of effective organization to "protect the best interests of the race by all lawful means and by the creation of healthy public opinion." They were ready to spend and be spent in the work of the League, and they went away from the great city of Chicago bent upon doing what they could to make the League a success. But from the very first they found that the great mass of the Afro-American people did not care for organization and did not respond to their appeals to organize. The writer went up and down the country at his own expense, preaching the gospel of organization. The people came out in large numbers to hear him, and applauded him to the echo, but they contributed practically nothing to the support of the work, often leaving him to pay the traveling expenses, and no organization followed his appeals for organization.

When the work of the League, at Chicago, was made public, George William Curtis,[4] in a strong and exhaustive article in *Harper's Weekly*, declared that if the people would stand behind the League, if they would give it loyal support, it would accomplish a great work for the people, but that if they should not sustain it, if they should allow it to fail, it would prove to be the greatest calamity that they will have sustained since the days of slavery. The prophecy of the great orator and journalist had been literally verified.

When, after three years, the League had become a cipher, because the mass of the people would not sustain it, another effort was made to create a new life and interest in the work of organization, and a League meeting was held in the beautiful city of Rochester.[5] It was not numerously attended, but there were plenty of good men and women there, and they changed the name and gave us a new constitution based upon the fundamental principles of the League. But the masses have taken no more active interest in the organization and maintenance of the Council than they did in that of the League. The same hundred that laid the basis of organization at Chicago have stuck to the work, with the exception of a baker's dozen, who went off by themselves because they were not allowed to boss the work when a majority had pronounced against them, and would do it again under like circumstances. But this is of small moment. The distressing thing is that the masses have not seen the wisdom of organization, and have failed to support the League or the Council, and have given no more hearty response to the efforts of the Niagara Movement people,[6] whose membership, like that of the Council, is made up of about one hundred and fifty intellectual people, loyally devoted to the best interests of the people, but whom the people will in no wise sustain by moral or financial support. The intellectual Afro-American had done what he could to create and sustain the League and Council and the Niagara Movement, but the mass of the people have done nothing to create or to sustain either. This is the bald, sad truth. And it is the keynote of the whole failure of the race to save even a remnant of its civil and political rights in the Southern States, and it is having its civil and political rights in the Northern and Western States encroached upon every hour. "Eternal vigilance is the price of liberty."[7] The people who will not organize and put themselves under the wisest and best of their leaders and contribute of their means to protect what all men regard as the dearest things under government and in the social order, cannot expect other people to look after their interests or to care a rap about them as men and as citizens. That is what has happened to the Afro-American people in the past sixteen years, and they have themselves and not their foes to blame for it. It is a shame and disgrace that it is so; but it is so, and the mass of the race and not the intellectual part of it is responsible for it. A stream can rise no higher than its source, and a handful of intellectual and devoted people cannot drag an inert, indifferent and stupid mass against its will to its proper place in the civil, political and economic life of the Republic. It must do that of its own free will and effort.

The writer honors the brave men and women who have for sixteen years kept alive the spirit of organization, and he deems it an honor to have been able to labor, to spend and to be spent, with them; but he feels that much that has been done has been wasted upon the mass of the Afro-American people, who have not responded to their enthusiasm and devotion and sacrifice; and while he feels the imperative necessity of keeping alive organization, if for no other purpose than that of protest, he is sure that we shall continue to lose out in all directions unless the mass can be aroused to its duty, as the intelligent men and women of the race have seen and done for sixteen years. If this mass cannot be aroused, if it continues to be indifferent to its best interests, if it shall continue to expect others to do for it what it can and should do for itself, then, though the present be dark and unforbidding, the future will be intolerable to the thoughtful men and women of the race. We have talked enough. Let us act, or stop talking.

Notes

1. When this piece was written, the Afro-American Council was holding its sixth annual convention in New York and the Niagara Movement had already held its second annual convention in Harper's Ferry, West Virginia, in August. For information on the activities of these organizations and Fortune's relation to them, see Emma Lou Thornbrough, *T. Thomas Fortune: Militant Journalist* (Chicago: University of Chicago Press, 1972); and Shawn Leigh Alexander, "'We Know Our Rights and Have the Courage to Defend Them'" (Ph.D. diss., University of Massachusetts–Amherst, 2004).

2. Fortune had published an earlier editorial entitled "Let Us Organize Our Strength," calling on the race to put its strength behind the Afro-American Council. See *New York Age*, July 12, 1906.

3. See Fortune's address at the convention, chapter 13. See also Thornbrough, *T. Thomas Fortune*; and Alexander, "We Know Our Rights."

4. George William Curtis (1824–1892) was an essayist and journalist who wrote for a number of publications, including *Harper's Weekly*. *Harper's* was an early supporter of the league idea. Fortune is actually discussing an article that Curtis wrote on the league idea in 1887, not 1890. See *Harper's Weekly*, June 25, 1887; and *New York Freeman*, October 8, 1887.

5. The meeting was held in Rochester to coincide with the dedication of the new Frederick Douglass statue. It was held on September 15, 1898. See Alexander, "We Know Our Rights"; and John W. Thompson, *An Authentic History of the Douglass Monument: Biographical Facts and Incidents in the Life of Frederick Douglass* (Rochester, N.Y.: Rochester Herald Press, 1903).

6. The Niagara Movement was formed in 1905. The group was an outgrowth of the council and developed because of a rift between some members over their perception that Booker T. Washington was controlling and holding back the council. See Alexander, "We Know Our Rights"; and Elliott Rudwick, *W.E.B. Du Bois: Propagandist of the Negro Protest* (New York: Atheneum, 1978).

7. Wendell Phillips (1811–1884) was a distinguished abolitionist and antislavery orator. Fortune wrote a moving obituary of Phillips. See *New York Globe*, February 9, 1884. The quote comes from a speech in Boston, Massachusetts, January 28, 1852. For more on Phillips, see chapter 6, note 4.

19

The Breath of Agitation Is Life

In this 1914 article for the *AME Church Review,* Fortune reflects on the work of race organizations and the value of agitation. He believes that the "breath of agitation is life" and that it should be advocated, but at the same time he believes that those who are not directly involved in agitation should not be criticized. In this he believes that the work of Booker T. Washington and the National Negro Business League are important and should not be dismissed. The most important issue to Fortune is "race unity."

The Breath of Agitation Is Life —*AME Church Review* 31, no. 1 (1914): 5–10

The social organism is so constituted that perpetual and uninterrupted agitation of all of its coordinates makes for life of the whole, while stagnation makes for death. So true is this principle that it permeates and dominates spiritual and material force, so that evolution in every direction is worked out by revolution. The human body is the most perfect organism in existence. All of the members of it work in harmony, when they do, to supply the money necessary to buy the food that makes the blood that fills the heart, "out of the fullness of which the tongue speaks." The moment the members of the body get tired of making the money to renew the blood, the substance of which makes fresh for the body, and the spirit of which makes life for the soul, stagnation sets in and, if not counteracted promptly, produces death of the whole organism, the whole body.

The individual is the unit of the Nation. If the individual is unjust, unfaithful, untrue to himself he will be false to his neighbor; if there be more individuals of a race, of a nation, false to themselves than there are who are true, neighbor will obviously be arrayed against neighbor so that endless strife will ensue, until the issues are determined by a measurement of arms, as in the case of the long and fierce agitation against human slavery in this country, in which the master class were whipped to their knees, but whose short-sighted sons have continued the war against the freeman and citizen, which now confronts the Afro-American people and the Nation, and who are sure to be worsted in the conclusion, as their fathers were in the beginning of the reactionary warfare, begun after the civil war, to make a race of civil slaves to take the place of the race of chattel slaves destroyed forever by the Thirteenth Amendment.

It is an easier task to kidnap savages in their own country and enslave them in a foreign land than it is to enslave free men in their own land and to deprive them of their constitutional rights of manhood and citizenship. The effort to do it, which the sons of the slave fathers began in 1867, and have since labored at with the determination of demons, may take a longer time to settle than it took to settle the question of chattel slavery, but as that was settled right, so will the question of full and equal rights of manhood and citizenship be settled right. "The fight for justice once begun bequeathed is from sire to son."

I believe in the ultimate triumph of the Afro-American people, because I believe in myself, who never undertook anything with the intention of failing in the accomplishment of it, and who never failed in anything I undertook to accomplish. Why? Because I never undertook to do the impossible, and was satisfied when I had accomplished that which was possible. Many people do not appear to be able to know when they have completed their work, or the particular phase of it assigned to them. I am not one of them. I began active work as an agitator, as a journalist, in 1879, and ceased from my work as an agitator in 1907, and resigned from all of the organizations to which I belonged, except as chairman of the Executive Committee of the National Negro Business League[1] and of the Committee of Twelve,[2] because I had finished my work as an agitator, my phase of work of an agitator, and because I had a nervous breakdown, from the efforts of which I am still not free. But I have not ceased to be a journalist, and do not expect to cease to be one; an annalist, a recorder, a thinker, sobered by experience and matured by adversity.

Men have changes of life, the same as women; sometimes late and sometimes early in their existence. When the change comes they either answer. "Here am I," and give up, or challenge the right to be called and fight for the personal, inherent right to continue to live and enjoy the benefits of the experience gained in the first life. It is the same way with races and nations as with individuals. My change came when I was 50 years of age, and was completed when I am 57.[3] A man learns many things in such a struggle not written outside of the Holy Bible. So does a race; so does a nation. The Afro-American citizen is 50 years old. He is having a change of life, but few of them know it or believe it. There is the misfortune. The Nation is having a change of life, but its wise men do not know it; they certainly do not act as if they knew it. There is a danger.

The editor of *The Review* requested me to write an article on my "journalistic career," or the "rise and fall of race organizations," or "the present opportunities of the Afro-American press." In meeting my obligations to writing about either one of the subjects, because of my personal relations to them, and my indisposition to criticise those who have succeeded to the work, he wrote the following paragraph:

"I cannot share your view, wherein you seem to think that your work has been wasted upon an unappreciative generation. Indeed, your conspicuous service is not only known, but cherished, by many thousands whom you do not know, and will never know. Such work as you have done in behalf of the civic, social and intellectual progress of our people cannot be measured by monetary value nor honors bestowed. It may be with you, as with many other builders of humanity, you may have to be dead a long time before the appreciative people hand garlands of flowers on your monument."

Now, then, having ceased to be an agitator, in the old sense, as from 1879 to 1907, what then? I am sure that, as the title to this article indicates, the breadth of agitation is life, and that with equal certainly the breadth of stagnation is death. What is true in this respect of the individual and race is true of the Nation. We might have slavery now if Benjamin Lundy[4] and William Lloyd Garrison[5] had not thundered through the press into the ears of the Nation defiance of slavery, while Phillips[6] and Sumner[7] did the same from the rostrum and Lovejoy[8] and Brown[9] from the grave of martyrdom. But those agitators, who never built a church, schoolhouse or factory, but deliberately went about tearing down those builded with the blood of the black slaves, that others and better ones might be builded with the money and enthusiasm of free men, counted their lives as nothing in the balance against slavery, but gave freely of them that the slaves might have life more abundantly. It has been the supreme virtue of agitators in all ages that they have not feared danger, but courted it, in the effort to right what they considered race or national wrongs. And those men, from Jesus and John Brown, have builded more wisely and permanently for the best welfare of mankind than all of the mammon-builders and teachers of material wealth-getting and keeping, from the money changers in the Temple of David to the unscrupulous gamblers in the Stock Exchanges of Christendom.

There would have been no Republican Party but for the agitation of Lundy, Garrison, Phillips, Sumner, Lovejoy and John Brown, and the valiant hosts that stood with and sustained them; and yet those men were regarded by the leaders of the Republican Party as a lot of crazy fanatics, unbalanced; but when the party denied the principles for which those men lived and died, and went a consorting and hungering after the money to be got out of special privileges and grants to crafty and grafty partisans, it died the death, with only four small States, out of forty-eight, faithful to it unto death. The agitators sow the good seed and the crafty and grafty (what Lord Macauley[10] called "the trimmers") too often come in at the psychological moment and gather the fruit and decry and malign the sowers. The wise agitator, reformer if you will, does not mind that; he knows that after the crafty and grafty have been gorged they will fall by the wayside, as they did in the balloting of greed in 1912. It has always been so with those who have worshiped the golden calf, or who have killed the goose, the principle of co-equality of right, that lays the golden egg.

I was much hurt in feelings two years ago to read an address of Prof. H. T. Kealing,[11] extolling the virtues of the National Negro Business League, the organization of which I suggested to Dr. Washington,[12] in which he said that he had ceased to follow up the meetings of the National Afro-American Council, because he could not see that it had accomplished any good. I was equally surprised to read in The New York News of April 2, 1914, a generous and fair estimate of Bishop Alexander Walters,[13] whom I greatly admire and honor, by Mr. Ralph W. Tyler,[14] the present Organizer of the National Negro Business League, the following impudent statement.

"I ran into the Bishop for the first time up at Detroit at what was possibly the last meeting of any consequence of the late lamented Afro-American Council. At that time the Bishop was at the head of the organization which promised so much and which achieved so little commensurate with the noise it made."

What are the facts? At that very meeting I was instrumental, with the active support of the late Judge D. Augustus Straker,[15] Hon. J. C. Napier[16] and a few others, in throttling the efforts of emissaries of the Association for the Advancement of Colored People to force an indorsement of the proposition to petition Congress to reduce Southern representation because of the disfranchisement of Afro-American citizens by the white Democratic of the Southern States. Great pressure was brought to get the indorsement.[17] After I had defeated it in the Executive Committee, Mr. A. B. Humphrey[18] insisted upon forcing it in open convention, and I whipped it there. I consider that one of the most substantial victories won by the council, because it led to the death of the measure in Congress, Dr. Washington, who had been convinced by me that my view was the correct one, having induced President Roosevelt to tell Congressman Crumpacker and other determined members that he would veto the measure if it was enacted into law. My position was very simple: If we should consent to the proposition to reduce Southern representation it would be no advantage to the disfranchised, but would give congressional sanction to the principle of disfranchisement which other States of the Union, along with the Southern States, would make haste to accept in the desire to get rid of the Afro-American voters. The act of Congress would have worked disfranchisement, at the option of the States, and without appeal by the disfranchised.

If Mr. Tyler was stupid enough not to have recognized the work in this matter alone done by the Detroit meeting of the Council, is it surprising that he should be stupid enough now to be unable to see any good thing it did during its active existence, and to be able to hear through years only the "noise" it made? Certainly not. There are plenty of people just as stupid as Mr. Tyler, and some of them think they are great leaders of great things who are only little leaders of little things, of which they are the littlest. The historian of the race fifty years hence will not be so stupid in estimating the important work of agitation which the National Afro-American League accomplished from its organization, in Chicago, January 15, 1890, to its lingering death as a Council under Bishop Walters, as a Democratic submergence, a few years ago. It died simply because the people did not support it in its youth and strength or its weakness and old age. The Niagara Movement died from the same disease.

It takes a great deal of money to support such an organization, and the people refused to join the local organizations or to pay the assessments, small as they were, to sustain the work. I spent all I made and could persuade friends to give the work, only to see the public interest in it diminish from year to year. But the meetings were great and helpful occasions, when great orations were delivered and ringing addresses to the country were given out, and when the great newspapers of the country gave the proceedings columns upon columns of news and editorial space. There was no compromise with the enemies of the race in what was spoken from platform or drafted in resolutions. There were brave men behind the brave declaration of principles and denunciations of wrongs. The meetings at Chicago, Indianapolis, St. Paul, Rochester, Washington, Philadelphia and Louisville, as well as the one at Detroit, were great gatherings, which kept the race and its wrongs at the hands of the Nation before the people, and served the purpose of its creation, which was to stimulate the thought of the race as to what was the best thing to be done to "keep alive the jewel of freedom."

The period of agitation, from 1890 to 1900, was succeeded by a period of acceptance of the situation for the most part, as it had been crystallized by unjust Southern laws on the race line and public opinion, and the inauguration of the money, property and other material-getting movement, of which Dr. Booker T. Washington became the head, and which I have always supported loyally, but without undervaluing the work of agitation which went before and prepared the way for the business movement. Money and money-getters are always timid and cowardly, where their money is at stake. We all know that. But there was urgent need that we have a period of money-getting, of business building. I was sure when we had got our footing in these that we should again take up the agitation for the civil and political rights denied us. That will be done, perhaps twenty-five years hence, when the people have wealth, as the Jews have it, and a position to draw wealth to them, and with more success than when they were poor in this world's goods, but rich in culture and the courage not afraid of bullets in contention for Justice.

Indeed, Dr. W. E. Burghardt Du Bois[19] has done a great and good work, as have Mr. William Monroe Trotter[20] and his school of Protestants, in keeping alive the breadth of agitation for those precious things in American citizenship about which Dr. Washington and his Business League people do not concern themselves, because, for the time being, they are after making dollars and not after "keeping alive the jewel of freedom." I respect the work being done by Dr. Du Bois and Dr. Washington, and am glad I have been in a position to assist both of them with the work they are doing. None of us should forget that the breath of agitation is life, while the breath of stagnation is death—in the individual, in the race, in the Nation. There is plenty of work before us of all sorts, and we need all the forces now engaged in doing it. What we most need, however, is race unity in the work, each to his task, and a recognition by all of the good each is doing, without harsh and unwarranted criticism of any from envious motives and a desire to gain selfish advantage. Front the common enemy; those of the house should work together, each in his place, as men and brethren.

Notes

1. In 1900 Booker T. Washington formed the National Negro Business League, to promote "commercial, agricultural, educational, and industrial advancement . . . and the commercial and financial development of the Negro." W.E.B. Du Bois first proposed the organization in 1899 in his report to the Afro-American Council as the director of the Council's Business Bureau. For more information, see August Meier, *Negro Thought in America, 1880–1915: Racial Ideologies in the Age of Booker T. Washington* (Ann Arbor: University of Michigan Press, 1963); Louis R. Harlan, *Booker T. Washington: The Making of a Black Leader, 1856–1901* (New York: Oxford University Press, 1972); and Harlan, *Booker T. Washington: The Wizard of Tuskegee, 1901–1915* (New York: Oxford University Press, 1983).

2. The Committee of Twelve was a civil rights organization that formed out of the Carnegie Conference of 1904. For more information, see Harlan, *Wizard of Tuskegee*; and Shawn Leigh Alexander, "'We Know Our Rights and Have the Courage to Defend Them': Agitation in the Age of Accommodation, 1883–1909" (Ph.D. diss., University of Massachusetts–Amherst, 2004).

3. For a summary of Fortune's life, see Emma Lou Thornbrough, *T. Thomas Fortune: Militant Journalist* (Chicago: University of Chicago Press, 1972).

4. Benjamin Lundy (1789–1839) was a Quaker abolitionist and editor of the abolitionist newspaper *Genius of Universal Emancipation*. For more on Lundy, see chapter 6, note 2.

5. William Lloyd Garrison (1805–1879) was an abolitionist, editor of the *Liberator*, and founding member of the American Anti-Slavery Society in 1833. For more on Garrison, see chapter 6, note 3.

6. Wendell Phillips (1811–1884) was a distinguished abolitionist and antislavery orator. Fortune wrote a moving obituary of Phillips. See *New York Globe*, February 9, 1884. For more on Phillips, see chapter 6, note 4.

7. Charles Sumner (1811–1874) was a senator from Massachusetts who was a vocal antislavery advocate and a leader of the Radical Republicans during the Civil War and Reconstruction. Fortune gave a strong address in memory of Charles Sumner, in which he also promoted the need for the creation of a civil rights organization. See *Hartford Telegram*, January 11, 1884; and *New York Globe*, January 19, 1884. For more on Sumner, see chapter 6, note 5.

8. Elijah Parish Lovejoy (1802–1837) was an abolitionist and journalist who was murdered for his antislavery position, in Alton, Illinois, on November 7, 1837. For more on Lovejoy, see chapter 13, note 2.

9. John Brown (1800–1859) was a radical abolitionist who led twenty-one followers in an attack on the federal arsenal in Harper's Ferry, Virginia, on October 16, 1859, with

the intention of liberating and arming slaves. Fortune wrote a poem about Brown while visiting Kansas and published it in the *Age* in 1907, "With John Brown in Kansas," *New York Age*, September 19, 1907. For more on Brown, see chapter 6, note 6.

10. Lord Thomas Babington Macaulay (1800–1859) was an English Whig lawyer, politician, essayist, poet, and popular historian. Macaulay was active in the Anti-Slavery and Parliamentary Reform movements.

11. Hightower Theodore Kealing (1860–1918) was an educator and journalist who was the editor of the *AME Church Review* from 1896 to 1912.

12. Booker T. Washington (1856–1915) was an educator, political leader, and author who founded Tuskegee Institute in 1881 and became the most influential African American leader of the later-nineteenth and early-twentieth centuries. For more on Washington, see chapter 16, note 2.

13. Alexander Walters (1858–1917) was a bishop in the African Methodist Episcopal Zion church and civil rights activist who was president of the Afro-American Council off and on throughout its existence, 1898–1909. For more on Walters, see Alexander Walters, *My Life and Work* (New York: Fleming H. Revell, 1917); and George Mason Miller, "'A This Worldly Mission': The Life and Career of Alexander Walters (1858–1917)" (Ph.D. diss., State University of New York at Stony Brook, 1984).

14. Ralph Waldo Tyler (1859–1921) was a journalist and businessman from Columbus, Ohio.

15. David Augustus Straker (1842–1908) was a lawyer, politician, civil rights activist, and writer. For more on Straker, see Dorothy Drinkard Hawkshawe, "David Augustus Straker, Black Lawyer and Reconstruction Politician, 1842–1908" (Ph.D. diss., Catholic University of America, 1974).

16. James Carroll Napier (1845–1940) was an entrepreneur and civil rights advocate. For more on Napier, see Herbert L. Clark, "James Carroll Napier: National Negro Leader," *Tennessee Historical Quarterly* 49 (1990): 243–52.

17. When Fortune mentions the Association for the Advancement of Colored People, he is not talking about the NAACP; he is discussing the Afro-American Council. It may be a bit of a Freudian slip on the part of Fortune as the NAACP's principles are similar to the Council's and his Afro-American League, and he may be trying to drive that point home. For more information on the council and the meeting in Detroit, in particular the issue of supporting legislation to reduce the franchise in accordance with the Fourteenth Amendment, see Alexander, "We Know Our Rights."

18. Andrew B. Humphrey was secretary of the Constitution League, a civil rights organization founded in 1904 and led by John Milholland.

19. W.E.B. Du Bois (1868–1963) was a civil rights activist, educator, sociologist, and historian. For more on Du Bois in this period, see chapter 9, note 14.

20. William Monroe Trotter (1872–1934) was a journalist and civil rights activist who, through the editorial page of his newspaper, the *Boston Guardian* (1901), became a leading critic of Booker T. Washington. For more on Trotter, see Stephen R. Fox, *The Guardian of Boston: William Monroe Trotter* (New York: Atheneum, 1970).

20

The Quick and the Dead

Written in 1916, "The Quick and the Dead" is an interesting piece in which Fortune tries to cement his place in African American history. Written in response to George Forbes' article and the *Review*'s own editorial on the passing of Booker T. Washington, Fortune asserts that he and not Washington is the successor of Frederick Douglass in the realm of race leadership. He separates the history of race leadership into three parts: 1841–1884, led by Douglass, 1884–1904, led by himself, and 1904–1915, led by Washington. In this piece Fortune also tries to separate himself from Washington's lack—at least in public—of political agitation. Fortune acknowledges his support for Washington and his policies, but he states that he was never hindered in what he sought to pursue.

The Quick and the Dead —*AME Church Review* 32, no. 4 (April 1916): 247–50

In the A. M. E. Church Review for January, 1916, I find two references to the death, the life and the influence of Dr. Booker T. Washington[1] that demand correction of the historical record. As I am personally concerned that the historical record should be made up and kept correctly, I thank you for the opportunity to correct it. Speaking of the death of Mr. Frederick Douglass, in 1895, Mr. George W. Forbes[2] says ("The Passing of Booker T. Washington," pp. 190–2):

> Odysseus had passed over the Acheron and none was left to bend the bow of Ulysses. But a new order of things, with a new leader, was already on the horizon. Even if Price[3] had lived it is doubtful if he should have held the leadership. He would have at least been but a feeble echo of Douglass, and Douglass was in the end but a linger-

ing voice of the anti-slavery agitation which had led up to and been thrashed out in the results of the Civil War. The coming of Booker T. Washington, therefore, with the Atlanta speech in this very same year of Douglass' death, was due more to the changed order of things than to the chance of the speech.

In your editorial, "The Prophet of a New Age" (p. 208) you say:

> "Doctor Washington was called forth at a pivotal hour. The Garrisons and Sumners and Douglasses, with all that noble band of philanthropists and humanitarians, had had their hour. Booker T. Washington caught the spirit and vision of the new age. Questions of Liberty, Justice and Equality, and freedom of opportunity must now retire from the center of the stage. All black Americans must henceforth seek to be useful in practical service to their white neighbors."

You and Mr. Forbes both leave a historical blank of twenty-four years, from 1880–1904, in the leadership of the race, which marks the turning point of the race from slave conditions to those of freedom and opportunity, to be filled in. The idolatry of Doctor Washington has gone to such absurd extremes as to murder all men of the race who divide his labors and influence from those of Mr. Douglass.[4] I knew them both. They each had feet of clay, and were also intensely human, sensitive to the last degree as to their own position and equally intolerant and scornful of the others.

The leadership of the race should be divided into three parts, as follows: From 1841, when Mr. Douglass made his first address, to 1884, when he married Miss Helen Pitts,[5] and lost what influence he had with the race on that account; the astounding position being very generally by the race, as well as by white people, that Mr. Douglass had no more right to marry a white women than Doctor Washington had a long time after to dine with a white president at the White House. It was a period of the Colored American, which Mr. Douglass had been the spokesman for and never the leader of from 1841. In fact, Mr. Douglass confined his activities after the war to losing all the money he had saved in the effort to establish the New National Era at Washington, and in trying to make some more for his old age on the lecture platform and holding federal positions. It is good that he was wise enough to do so; otherwise he would have died as the fool dieth, a pauper. All the time of his residence in Washington Mr. Douglass' leadership was contested by Mr. John Mercer Langston,[6] Professor Richard Theodore Greener[7] and others, who thought that they were bigger men than Mr. Douglass.

The Afro-American period of leadership began in 1880, when, at the age of 24 years, I became an editor in New York.[8] I had for advisors in the work from the start Mr. Douglass, Mr. Langston, Professor Greener, and others. The twenty years, from 1880 to 1900, were devoted entirely to the work of agitation for independence in politics, especially in the northern and western States, for civil rights in public places of amusement and accommodation, and for the abolition of separate schools for the races. Every one of these objects was accomplished, and we have the fruits of them now. In the contention for independence in politics[9] I had the assistance of able men, such as James Monroe Trotter and William H. Dupre, of Boston; George T. Downing, of Rhode Island; Peter H. Clark, of Ohio; J. Milton Turner, of Missouri; William Still and Robert Purvis, of Pennsylvania,[10] and others; none of which claimed that he led me, and that I did not lead them, as the newspaper files of the time will show; the platform being the address I delivered at the National Afro-American Press Association meeting in the Fifteenth Street Presbyterian Church, at Washington, in 1884.

These objects having been attained, a foundation having been laid, which endures until this day, another phase of the work, the organized phase, was attempted by me when the National Afro-American League was organized at Chicago, January 15, 1890.[11] It was one of the largest meetings ever held upon this continent by men of the race. The address I delivered as temporary chairman, and the constitution adopted, incorporated the idea of independence in politics, equality of rights of all matters, civil and political, and the encouragement of industrial and academic education and business development. Mr. George William Curtis,[12] editor of Harper's Weekly, and one of the ablest and most public-spirited men of his time, in an editorial page broadside declared that the league met all of the requirements of the Afro-American people, and that if they failed to sustain it and make it a power for good the progress and development of the race would be retarded for half a century.

The race did not support the Afro-American League. It was a drain on my limited financial resources from the start to finish, and left me impoverished when I relinquished the work of it, as the following letter will show:[13]

    Maple Hall,
    Red Bank, N. J., March 28, 1904

To Mr. William H. Steward,
    First Vice-President,
    National Afro-American League, Louisville Ky.

My dear Sir: I herewith tender my resignation as president of the National Afro-American Council. I am gratified in doing so to know that the high office would fall into no worthier hands than your own.

Through my efforts, assisted by devoted men and women, the Council was organized at Chicago January 15, 1890, and was reorganized at Rochester, N. Y., in 1898; but from the beginning the organization has been kept in existence, and its devoted officers have done what they could, with small response from the masses of the race, to stem the fearful tide of civil and political and material degradation of the race to a condition of pariahs in the citizenship of the Republic. I have grown old and impoverished in the long struggle, and I must now take heed of my age and precarious health to devote my time and energies to repairing my personal fortunes in the interest of my immediate family.

I have an abiding faith that right and justice will prevail in the end, and, if I had the health and the money and the youth to continue the struggle—with the deadly apathy of the mass of the race and the malignant antagonism and vituperation of many thoughtful men of the race—to combat, I should continue to fight on to the end; but I have neither the health, money nor youth at my disposal, and I relinquish the herculean labor to others, who may easily prove more devoted and successful in the work than I have been.

To the loyal men and women who have labored with me in the work of the organization, those who are dead and those who are living, my heart will always cling with deep affection. None braver or more self-sacrificing ever labored for the welfare of the race that did not respond to their courage and sacrifice.

In my own way I shall continue to labor as in the past, for the highest aspirations of the race, for nobler manhood and for perfect equality of citizenship of all men.

Upon the same day I resigned from the position of chairman of the executive committee of the National Afro-American Press Association, but retained the positions of chairman of the executive committed of the committee of twelve[14] and the National Negro Business League,[15] resigning from the latter at the Baltimore meeting in 1909, I think. It was some satisfaction to me that the meetings of the league kept the press of the country busy discussing the rights and wrongs of the Afro-American people, the meetings of the annual conventions at Washington, Indianapolis, Philadelphia, St.

Paul, Louisville and Detroit being largely attended and effective nationally in arousing discussion, which is the primary purpose of any agitation.

Doctor Washington[16] did not assume active leadership until 1904, when I got out of the way, and then he became the leader of the Negro race and not the Afro-American people, as Mr. Douglass had been the leader of the Colored Americans, who have neither race nor people, being ethical nondescripts, derelicts of the indistinguishable mixed multitude no man can number. Doctor Washington and I became acquainted some time in 1893, and thereafter were the closest of friends and co-workers, down to the meeting of the Business League, in 1907, at Topeka, and he had my advice and criticism of every article and speech and book that he wrote. We had a working understanding that I should pursue the radical course I had always pursued and that he would pursue the course of diplomacy he had mapped out for himself, but he would not write or speak any sentiment I disapproved as injurious to him or the race. He undertook the organization of the Business League upon my advice, as Mr. J. H. Lewis, of Boston, had suggested it to me, and I left that I had more organization work already on my hands than I could manage. He attended the St. Paul and Louisville meetings of the Afro-American League upon my invitation, but he never advised me as to any policy that I should pursue or the character of any address I should make.

The first misunderstanding between Doctor Washington and me came when he got into politics as the adviser extraordinary of President Roosevelt and began the suggestion of southern white men as officeholders in the south with the purpose of displacing all Afro-Americans in the south and giving a few of them high positions in the north.[17] He protested against my unsparing condemnation of President Roosevelt for discharging the battalion of the twenty-fifth infantry by the Brownsville order, for which President Roosevelt took the sole responsibility in a letter to Doctor Washington, which has never been published, which I read and advised that he publish, because it was not marked "private," and the circumstances of the situation warranted and demanded the publication of it.[18]

I had not recovered from the climatic effects of the trip to the Philippine Islands, 1901–2, when my health began to fail in 1904.[19] It failed utterly in 1907, and after the Topeka meeting of the Business League I was compelled to dispose of the New York Age and began the long struggle to recover my nervous control, which is now, ten years after, quite complete. After the loss of the Age and health, Doctor Washington did not have any further use for me, and we only met some five times after that, the last at the marriage of his youngest son, in Washington, last winter. We did not fall out and quarrel; we were on speaking terms to the last, but he had no further use for me in his business, because I had lost my health and newspaper, and because with my assistance he had been able to reach to the point of leadership where he did not want friends to advise him, but persons to do what he wanted done. He was the leader of the Negro people from 1904 to 1915, but without their selection or election, and because white men labeled him leader after the Atlanta address in 1895, and gave him plenty of money to carry out the purposes of his leadership. I helped to make him leader, having finished the work I had to do in two sections of ten years each, and if I had to go over it all again I would do for him just what I did do, because I thought then, and think now, that we needed to build up the educational and business interests of the race, so that it might have some intelligence and money to back up its much-talked about justice and equality in the citizenship of the nation. An ignorant and pauper race cannot ever command its own self-respect or that of the rest of mankind. Doctor Washington was a very great man. He did a very great work; but it was not such work as Mr. Douglass did from 1841 to 1880; nor such work I did from 1880 to 1904. I had everything in common with Mr. Douglass and his methods and nothing in common with the policies of Doctor Washington, especially his personal and political ones. His work was necessary to be done, and I helped rather than hindered him in the doing of it.

Notes

1. Booker T. Washington (1856–1915) was the founder and head of Tuskegee Institute (1881) and founder of the National Negro Business League (1900). Washington was propelled to the position of *the* African American leader by both whites and blacks after his 1895 Atlanta Exposition address, where he seemingly accepted segregation. For more on Washington, see chapter 16, note 2.

2. George W. Forbes (1864–1927) was a journalist and civil rights activist who with William Monroe Trotter formed the *Boston Guardian* in 1901.

3. Joseph Charles Price (1854–1893) was an educator and civil rights activist who was elected the first president of the Afro-American League in January 1890. Price was the president of Livingston College in North Carolina. In many ways he was viewed as the individual who bridged both schools of racial thought at the time, both "radical and conservative." At the 1903 conference of the Afro-American Council, it was a picture of Price placed on the stage opposite Booker T. Washington's that silenced William Ferris

and William Monroe Trotter. See William J. Walls, *Joseph Charles Price* (Boston: Christopher Publishing, 1953); August Meier, "Negro Racial Thought in the Age of Booker T. Washington, circa 1880-1915" (Ph.D. diss., Columbia University, 1957), 234-41; and Shawn Leigh Alexander, "'We Know Our Rights and Have the Courage to Defend Them'" (Ph.D. diss., University of Massachusetts-Amherst 2004).

4. Frederick Douglass (ca. 1818-1895) was an escaped slave who became a prominent abolitionist, editor, and author. Douglass rose to become the most influential African American of the nineteenth century. Fortune wrote a moving article on Douglass after his passing; see T. Thomas Fortune, "Mr. Douglass' Peculiar Greatness," *AME Church Review* 12 (1895): 108-13. He also delivered a poem honoring Douglass at the Douglass monument dedication ceremony in Rochester, New York, on September 14, 1898. A portion of this poem is published as the introduction to part 2 of this volume, "Civil Rights and Race Leadership." For the entire poem, see John W. Thompson, *An Authentic History of the Douglass Monument: Biographical Facts and Incidents in the Life of Frederick Douglass* (Rochester, N.Y.: Rochester Herald Press, 1903). For more on Douglass, see chapter 9, note 12.

5. In 1884 Frederick Douglass married Helen Pitts, a white woman. Many in the community criticized Douglass, but Fortune defended his right to marry anyone he wished. See *New York Globe*, February 3, March 15 and 23, 1884. For more on the subject, see Benjamin Quarles, *Frederick Douglass* (New York: Atheneum, 1974); David W. Blight, *Frederick Douglass' Civil War: Keeping Faith in Jubilee* (Baton Rouge: Louisiana State University Press, 1989); and Waldo E. Martin, *The Mind of Frederick Douglass* (Chapel Hill: University of North Carolina Press, 1984).

6. John Mercer Langston (1829-1897) was an educator, politician, and civil rights activist. In 1864 Langston was elected president of the National Equal Rights League, which campaigned for black suffrage. He later served as the dean of Howard University's law department and was appointed U.S. minister to Haiti in 1877. In 1888 he ran for Congress in Virginia and won his seat after a year-and-a-half battle, serving for only six months. For more information on Langston, see chapter 6, note 37.

7. Richard T. Greener (1844-1922) was the first African American to graduate from Harvard University (1870). Greener later taught at the University of South Carolina and Howard University before becoming U.S. consul and diplomat to India and Russia. For more on Greener, see chapter 4, note 2.

8. For information on this period of African American social and political thought, see August Meier, *Negro Thought in America, 1880-1915: Racial Ideologies in the Age of Booker T. Washington* (Ann Arbor: University of Michigan Press, 1963); and Robert L. Factor, *The Black Response to America: Men, Ideals, and Organization, from Frederick Douglass to the NAACP* (Reading, Mass.: Addison-Wesley, 1970). See also Emma Lou Thornbrough, *T. Thomas Fortune: Militant Journalist* (Chicago: University of Chicago Press, 1972).

9. For discussion of Fortune's independence in politics, see Thornbrough, *T. Thomas Fortune*; and William Seraile, "The Political View of Timothy Thomas Fortune: Father

of Black Political Independence," *Afro-Americans in New York Life and History* 2 (1978): 15-28. See also chapters 6 and 7 in this volume.

10. James Monroe Trotter (1842-1892) was a Union army officer, political activist, and politician; William H. Dupre (1839-1871) was an abolitionist and government worker; George Thomas Downing (1819-1903) was an abolitionist, civil rights activist, and businessman; Peter Humphries Clark (1829-1925) was an abolitionist, civil rights activist, and educator; James Milton Turner (1839-1915) was a civil rights activist, politician, and educator; William Still (1821-1902) was an abolitionist, civil rights activist, entrepreneur, and writer; Robert Purvis (1810-1898) was an abolitionist.

11. For the text of the speech, see chapter 13.

12. George William Curtis (1824-1892) was an essayist and journalist who wrote for a number of publications, including *Harper's Weekly*. *Harper's* was an early supporter of the league idea. Fortune is actually discussing an article that Curtis wrote on the league idea in 1887, not 1890. See *Harper's Weekly*, June 25, 1887; and *New York Freeman*, October 8, 1887.

13. For more on Fortune's departure from the Afro-American Council, see Thornbrough, *T. Thomas Fortune*; Alexander, "We Know Our Rights"; Factor, *Black Response to America*; and Louis R. Harlan, *Booker T. Washington: The Wizard of Tuskegee, 1901-1915* (New York: Oxford University Press, 1983). See also T. Thomas Fortune to Emmett Scott, March 28, 1904, *Booker T. Washington Papers*.

14. The Committee of Twelve was a civil rights organization that formed out of the Carnegie Conference of 1904. For more information, see Harlan, *Wizard of Tuskegee*; and Alexander, "We Know Our Rights."

15. In 1900 Booker T. Washington formed the National Negro Business League, to promote "commercial, agricultural, educational, and industrial advancement... and the commercial and financial development of the Negro." W.E.B. Du Bois first proposed the organization in 1899 in his report to the Afro-American Council as the director of the Council's Business Bureau. For more information, see Meier, *Negro Thought in America*; Louis R. Harlan, *Booker T. Washington: The Making of a Black Leader, 1856-1901* (New York: Oxford University Press, 1972); and Harlan, *Wizard of Tuskegee*.

16. For more on Booker T. Washington and race leadership during this period, see Louis R. Harlan, *Making of a Black Leader*; Harlan, *Wizard of Tuskegee*; Meier, *Negro Thought in America*; and Factor, *Black Response to America*.

17. See Thornbrough, *T. Thomas Fortune*; and Harlan, *Wizard of Tuskegee*.

18. In the summer of 1906, the U.S. Army placed three companies of the Twenty-fifth Infantry, one African American, at Fort Brown in Brownsville, Texas. Racial tensions rose, and on August 13 there was a shooting in the town. Black soldiers from the Twenty-fifth Infantry were blamed. After an investigation, despite protest from many within the African American community, the government dismissed the soldiers. For more information on the Brownsville Affair, see John D. Weaver, *The Brownsville Raid* (New York: W. W. Norton, 1970); Ann J. Lane, *The Brownsville Affair: National Crisis and Black Reaction* (Port Washington, N.Y.: Kennikat Press, 1971); Emma Lou Thornbrough, "The

Brownsville Episode and the Negro Vote," *Mississippi Valley Historical Review* 44 (1957): 469–93; Thornbrough, *T. Thomas Fortune*; Meier, *Negro Thought in America*; and Harlan, *Wizard of Tuskegee*.

19. For information on Fortune's trip to the Philippine Islands, see Thornbrough, *T. Thomas Fortune*. See also Fortune's own writings on the trip: T. Thomas Fortune, "The Filipino [Part I]," *Voice of the Negro* 1 (1904): 93–99; "The Filipino [Part II]," *Voice of the Negro* 1 (1904): 199–203; and "The Filipino—across Luzon [Part III]," *Voice of the Negro* 1 (1904): 240–46.

21

A Man without a Country

In this 1926 editorial, Fortune makes it clear that while the goal of the Universal Negro Improvement Association (UNIA) and Marcus Garvey may be the redemption of Africa, the race throughout the diaspora must fight for the social, civil, and economic rights wherever they are located.

A Man without a Country —*Negro World,* **July 3, 1926**

In all of the world there is no more miserable person than one who can be said to be a man without a country. Edward Everett Hale[1] has pictured for us the character of such a man, his sense of isolation, of despair, and we cannot but sympathize with such a man and rejoice when we are not as he. But, perhaps, there are more Negroes and Jews in the world who feel that they are persons without a country than any other race groups, as they find themselves scattered in the vine and leaf of every nation's life. It has been the despair and horror of such persons, who felt or were made to feel that they were persons without a country and were oppressed and persecuted in the countries where they were born. Millions of British Negro subjects feel that way, not only in the West Indies, but in Africa itself, and many Negro citizens of that United States as well. Whatever their status may be they still feel that they are residing in a far country, and among strangers, and long for a country of their own, peopled and governed by and for them. It is a natural feeling.

In the last issue of The Negro World, in the editorial leader, entitled, "Redeeming Africa," we were made to say that "We have often said," instead of "We have often heard of it said that the Negro is a man without a country, and has no standing as a citizen or subject in the countries where he resides." What "we have often said" and what "we have often heard it said" do not convey the same thought by any means. In the body of the article the misstatement in the opening sentence is made very apparent, must leave some confusion in the mind of the reader.

In his front page article in the last issue of The Negro World, President-General Marcus Garvey[2] succinctly explained and enlarged upon this question of a man without a country.[3] He said:

> But to fight for African redemption does not mean that we must give up our domestic fights for political justice and industrial rights. It does not mean that we must become disloyal to any government or to any country wherein we were born. Each and every race outside of its domestic national loyalty has a loyalty to itself; therefore, it is foolish for the Negro to talk about not being interested in his own racial, political, social and industrial destiny. We can be as loyal American citizens or British subjects as the Irishman or the Jew, and yet fight for the redemption of Africa, a complete emancipation of the race.

This statement by the President General covers the ground entirely and leaves no room for confusion. And it is important that there should be no confusion on this vital matter. Nationalization in Africa is the main objective, but in reaching it we cannot sacrifice our social, civil and economic values in the countries where we have been scattered as British subjects, French subjects, and the like, and as citizens of the United States, with out privileges and immunities specifically guaranteed by the Federal Constitution, and which no State may "deny or abridge." And the more we value our opportunities, the more we save and have, the better able will we be to assist the Universal Negro Improvement Association in its program of race upbuilding and national rehabilitation.

Notes

1. Edward Everett Hale (1822–1909) was an author, reformer, and Unitarian clergyman. In 1863 he published his short story, "A Man Without A Country," in *Atlantic Monthly* 12 (December 1863): 665–79.

2. Marcus Garvey (1887–1940) was a journalist, entrepreneur, and leader of the Universal Negro Improvement Association (UNIA), a black political and economic nationalist organization founded in Jamaica in 1914. In 1917 Garvey moved the headquarters of the UNIA to Harlem.

3. Marcus Garvey, "The Negro's Place in World Reorganization," *Negro World*, March 24, 1923. Republished as "Emancipation of the Race," *Negro World*, June 26, 1926.

22

Segregation and Neighborhood Agreements

In this editorial, Fortune acknowledges that the Supreme Court's decision in *Corrigan v. Buckley*, in which the Court upheld the practice of restrictive covenants, and the recent race riots and denial of African Americans' rights in Arkansas and Michigan are signs that African American social and political rights have not improved. He argues, in fact, that the nation has not grown since the Taney Court and its Dred Scott ruling. The community, according to Fortune, may have no recourse but to resort to the "primitive law of self-defense." Such a condition should not "prevail in any civilized country," he argues, but getting "mobcrats to understand they will be met with violence in the same way and as often as they resort to it" may again be the only option for the African American citizen.

Segregation and Neighborhood Agreements —*Negro World*, June 5, 1926

The Federal Supreme Court has . . . just ruled that neighborhood agreements among white citizens not to sell real estate to Negroes violates no constitutional guarantee, but is justified on the ground that owners of property are free to make such agreements in order to protect their interests.[1] What a number of citizens may combine to do, the court holds, in the matter of disposal of their property, is a personal right which does not involve any constitutional principle. If the discrimination were made by a State, instead of a lot of neighbors, we are led to infer, the case would be different, as the constitution covers the acts of States between themselves. It is a very fine distinction, and such as the Supreme Court has always been able to advance where the rights of Negroes and white citizens conflict. Then the rule established by the Supreme Court in the case of Dred Scott vs. Sanford, in 1856, still holds, that "it is held to be good law and opinion that the black man had no rights that a white man is bound to respect." The court has not got far from this Taney opinion, although the Civil War destroyed slavery and enfranchised the Negro, giving him the like standing in the constitution as that enjoyed by white citizens.

If a dozen or more white citizens should agree that the Negro citizens of their community should not be allowed to vote, and should prevent them from doing so, and the State should not interfere, with or without the existence of a State law, it would be on a par with neighborhood agreements that Negroes should not be allowed to buy real property in the community, and should prevent them from doing so, and the Supreme Court would hold, in the absence of a State law justifying such agreements or failure to prosecute such offenders, that no constitutional right of the aggrieved had been violated. That was the construction of the law in the Philips county, Arkansas,[2] mob murders, and in the Sweet cases at Detroit, Mich.,[3] the Negroes being shot to death for protesting in a lawful meeting against the extortion of planters in the Arkansas cases, when a hundred were prosecuted and imprisoned as to certain of their members, while even were prosecuted in the Michigan cases for defending themselves and their property from mob violence. That is to say, the white persons who provoked the mob violence in both cases were allowed to go scott free, without arrest or prosecution, while the Negroes were arrested and prosecuted unto death.

According to the Supreme Court ruling, the Negro citizen has no appeal or redress. If he does not defend himself and property he can be murdered and despoiled, and if he does defend himself and property he is arrested and placed in jeopardy of his life and property. We get this construction of the matter by the facts in the Arkansas and Michigan cases, and it throws the Negro back on the primitive law of self-defense, and it looks as if he will get no redress unless he appeals to it. The individual will suffer but the race will benefit, by getting mobocrats to understand they will be met with violence in the same way and as often as they resort to it. No such condition should prevail in any civilized country, and except where the Negro is the victim, it does not prevail.

Notes

1. *Corrigan v. Buckley*, 271 U.S. 323 (1926). Private racial restrictive housing covenants in Washington, D.C., were upheld. The case was dismissed for lack of substantial federal question under the Due Process (Fourth Amendment) and Equal Protection (Fourteenth Amendment) clauses. For more on the fight against restricted covenants and the

NAACP's participation in the struggle, see Mark R. Schneider, *"We Return Fighting": The Civil Rights Movement in the Jazz Age* (Boston: Northeastern University Press, 2002).

2. For more information on the race riot in Helena, Arkansas, see Schneider, *"We Return Fighting"*; and "The Real Cause of Two Race Riots," *Crisis* 19 (December 1919): 56.

3. In 1925, Detroit physician Ossian Sweet moved his family into a white neighborhood. When a mob approached his home, he and his family defended themselves and in the process shot a white man. It became a celebrated case for the NAACP as they defended Sweet. For more information, see Kevin Boyle, *Arc of Justice: A Saga of Race, Civil Rights, and Murder in the Jazz Age* (New York: Henry Holt, 2004); and Schneider, *"We Return Fighting."*

PART 3

Race and the Color Line

We Bear the Cross

We bear the cross, endure the pain,
And rise from hopeless hope again,
Though hopeless still;
For death alone can crush the soul,
Which hopes at last to reach the goal
   By force of will.
What though the storms of life assail,
And sinking souls around us wail
   Disconsolate!
If there be one with constant heart,
To help us bear our little part,
   We smile at fate.
Then bear awhile the ills that come;
Bid truant thought no more to roam;
   But cheered by love,
Sustained by hope, the way pursue,—
Unto ourselves, others true,
Our love to prove.

New York Freeman, June 12, 1886

23

John Brown and Nat. Turner

The following two editorials are Fortune's side of a debate with Frederick Douglass Jr. over the need for African Americans to erect a monument in honor of John Brown. While Fortune sees the necessity of honoring Brown, he does not see the need of the African American community to give their pennies to perpetuate the memory of the Sage of Osawatomie. Instead, evoking a sense of race pride, Fortune calls on the community to honor Nat Turner, a forerunner of Brown and "a black hero." Fortune questions why every time the community "move[s] that somebody's memory be perpetuated, that somebody's memory is always a white man's." It is such demonstrations of "the absence of race pride and race unity," argues Fortune, "which makes the white man despise black men all the world over."

John Brown and Nat. Turner —*New York Age,* **January 12, 1889**

The *Washington National Leader*, of which Mr. Frederick Douglass, Jr.,[1] is associate editor, recently wanted to know if it was not almost time that the colored people were doing something to perpetuate the memory of John Brown.[2]

We think not. We think John Brown's memory is strong enough to perpetuate itself even if all the Negroes in the universe were suddenly to become extinct. His memory is a part of the history of the government. It is embalmed in a thousand songs and stories. Your own father, Mr. Douglass, has written a lecture on the life of John Brown, which will help along the perpetuation of that great good man. A German scholar has just given a brochure to the world, which competent critics declare the most judicial and thorough study of the character of John Brown ever produced.

No; John Brown's memory stands no immediate prospect of vanishing into oblivion.

But there is another, a fore-runner of John Brown, if you please, who stands in more need of our copper pennies to be melted down into a monument to perpetuate his memory than John Brown. We refer of course to Nat Turner,[3] who was executed at Jerusalem, Northampton County, Virginia, for inciting and leading his fellow slaves to insurrection long before John Brown invaded Kansas and planned an unfortunate raid on Harper's Ferry.

Nat. Turner was a black hero. He preferred death to slavery. He ought to have a monument. White men care nothing for his memory. We should cherish it.

It is quite remarkable that whenever colored men move that somebody's memory be perpetuated, that somebody's memory is always a white man's.

Young Mr. Douglass should mend his ways in this matter. His great father will some day have a monument which he will have eminently deserved, and it will have been built by the pennies of colored people. White people build monuments to white people.

Nat. Turner —*New York Age,* January 29, 1889

Fred Douglass, Jr., in the *National Leader,* exhibits too much temper in replying to our editorial suggesting a monument to Nat. Turner instead of one to John Brown. It indicates that we touched the Achillean weak spot in his armor.

"That Nat. Turner has been dead many years" is almost equally true of John Brown. John Brown lost his life in urging and leading an insurrection of slaves. Nat. Turner at an earlier date did the same. The conduct of the one was no more heroic than that of the other. The whites have embalmed the memory of John Brown in marble and vellum, and Fred Douglass, Jr., now wants the colored people to embalm it in brass; while the memory of the black hero is preserved neither in marble, vellum nor brass.

What we protest against is Negro worship of white men and the memory of white men, to the utter exclusion of colored men equally patriotic and self-sacrificing. It is the absence of race pride and race unity which makes the white man despise black men all the world over.

We do not draw the color line. Fred Douglass, Jr., knows that his insinuation in this regard is a baseless invention. We simply insist that in theory "do unto others as you would have them do unto you" is splendid, but that in practice the philosophy of conduct is "do unto others as they do unto you," the sooner to make them understand that a dagger of the right sort has two edges, the one as sharp of blade as the other.

We yield to none in admiration of the character and sacrifices of John Brown. The character and sacrifices of Nat. Turner are dearer to us because he was of us and exhibited in the most abject condition the heroism and race devotion which have illustrated in all times the sort of men who are worthy to be free.

Notes

1. Frederick Douglass Jr. (1842–1892) was a journalist and son of Frederick Douglass.

2. John Brown (1800–1859) was a radical abolitionist who led twenty-one followers in an attack on the federal arsenal in Harper's Ferry, Virginia, on October 16, 1859, with the intention of liberating and arming slaves. Fortune wrote a poem about Brown while visiting Kansas, "With John Brown in Kansas," *New York Age,* September 19, 1907. Also, despite his disagreement with Frederick Douglass, Jr., Fortune did like John Brown and his legacy. He evokes his memory in a number of instances, many of which are included in the volume, and in May 1900 when the Afro-American Council was celebrating Brown's centennial Fortune gave a rousing speech in New York City. See *New York Times,* June 4, 1900. For more on Brown, see chapter 6, note 6.

3. Nat Turner (1800–1831) was an enslaved African who led a slave rebellion in Southampton County, Virginia, in 1831. Fortune published a poem honoring Turner in 1884, "Nat Turner," *AME Church Review* 1 (October 1884): 101, and "Nat Turner," *Globe* October 18, 1884. For more on Turner, see chapter 6, note 8.

24

The Color Line

In this early editorial, the young Fortune responds forcefully to the *New York Sun*'s critical comments about the way in which the African American community separate themselves from the white community or draw the color line. In his response, Fortune demonstrates his call for racial unity and race consciousness. He calls on the community to continue to draw the line and be proud of their black skin. They are acting out of their own interest, he explains, similar to the Irish and German immigrants. Moreover, he argues, the color line in the South and increasingly in the North is drawn by the white community, not the black.

The Color Line —*New York Globe*, **June 2, 1883**

In your issue of the 22nd inst you grow serious in an editorial headed the "Color Line." You have noted from time to time, with fidelity and apparent solicitude, the growing tendency among colored people to seek association among themselves socially, religiously, and politically. It appears to me that the *Sun* puts too much stress upon this tendency.

The tendency among us is neither unique nor ominous. It has been illustrated in the history of every tribe and nation of which history has taken cognizance. Where two or more races are brought together on the same soil and are subject to the same governmental authority, amalgamation and assimilation have been the slow growth of time. It is almost needless to point to the peculiar idiosyncrasies of the Alexandrian Jews, who for centuries maintained their racial and social integration in the midst of an alien and hostile people. The heterogeneity of the Roman population, and the acrimonious conflicts arising therefrom, are as marked in the history of that great people as the gradual absorption which at length welded them into an empire, which only yielded to the unprecedented floods of barbarians which ultimately worked the downfall of the Roman Government. The Russian Jew is to-day more persecuted, despised, and isolated than the African is in the United States, while the German Jew is not wholly free from the malice, hate and persecution of his Teutonic fellow citizens.[1] The persecution and ostracism which have followed the Anglo-Celts of Ireland, and the distinctive raciality and social and political integration of that people, dwelling in the midst and ruled by Anglo-Saxon government for centuries, is among the most striking illustrations history furnishes of what the mongrel American type of man would call the "drawing of racial lines."[2]

Even in our land, where everybody is supposed to be a part of one harmonious whole, an Irishman remains an Irishman, brings with him his Catholic religion, prefers his own race above all others, and, even when casting a ballot of an American freeman, he is resolving in his active mind ways and means by which to liberate his unhappy country from the thraldom of British oppression. The German American sticks to his beer, his German frau, and his Lutheran Church, and, after a century of American citizenship, sings with gusto and fond recollections the glories of his fatherland.

The race tendency is true of all the diverse peoples associated under our Government as one people, and the attempt of newspapers and individuals to mark out a "special" tendency for the African is dictated sometimes by malice and oftener by profound ignorance of the history and peculiar idiosyncrasies of races. A man always feels safer and more at ease in his own home than in the home of his best friend; and the disposition of a race to perpetuate itself by marriage and social affiliation is one of the most natural as well as one of the most thoroughly understood of ethnological phenomena.

Among the Africans in the United States, and especially in the South, to which the *Sun* turns its editorial telescope, the tendency among us to isolation in church and social and political sentiment is accelerated by many causes, among them miscegenation laws, political tyranny and intolerance, and the anti-Christian spirit which obtains in white churches. The white pseudo professors of religion in that section are peculiarly diabolical toward colored Christians who attend their churches. They have seats set apart for colored Christians in the extreme rear of the church, or far out of sight in the gallery. "Alas! for the rarity of Christian charity;"[3] these prospective white angels want nothing whatever to do with prospective black angels. Before I would sacrifice my sense of manhood by accepting such special treatment in the North or South, I would live and die outside of the communion of the Church of Christ. It is for these reasons that colored men establish and maintain separate religious denominations, in which they can serve God without at the same time reflecting upon the narrow Christian interpretation of white men. There is a great deal of religion in this country which serves the devil, and every time a black man goes into a white church or convocation it shows itself.

As far as political unity of action is concerned, the colored man will preserve his clannishness until all parties teach him that they neither desire to use him as a tool nor to degrade him as a man. The common instinct of man and brute is to concentration when danger is apprehended. The colored people are resolving themselves out of the habits of slavery into the habits of free men as fast as it is possible for them to do so, and the time is at hand when the colored man will be proud of the black skin which is the index of his African extraction, and the honorable political, social and religious status which he will have made in this country under disadvantages which the white man is absolutely incapable of appreciating.[4]

Notes

1. John Higham, *Strangers in the Land: Patterns of American Nativism, 1860–1925* (New York: Atheneum, 1963); Matthew Frye Jacobson, *Whiteness of a Different Color: European Immigrants and the Alchemy of Race* (Cambridge, Mass.: Harvard University Press, 1998); Jacobson, *Barbarian Virtues: The United States Encounters Foreign Peoples at Home and Abroad, 1876–1917* (New York: Hill and Wang, 2000); Jacobson, *Special Sorrows: The Diasporic Imagination of Irish, Polish, and Jewish Immigrants in the United States* (Berkeley: University of California Press, 2002).

2. Kerby A. Miller, *Emigrants and Exiles: Ireland and the Irish Exodus to North America* (New York: Oxford University Press, 1985).

3. Thomas Hood (1799–1845), *The Bridge of Sighs*.

4. Fortune was still arguing along similar lines in the final years of his life. In a 1927 editorial for his *Norfolk Journal and Guide* column, "The Way of the World," Fortune argued that the color line was being drawn tightly throughout the United States and Europeanized sections of Africa and that the "races discriminated against, whether African or Asiatic origin, are being aroused as never before to the necessity of getting together and fighting for a square deal." *Norfolk Journal and Guide*, July 9, 1927.

25

The Afro-American

In his 1890 article "The Afro-American," Fortune explains his use of the term "Afro-American," which, he explains, includes anyone of African origin who is "not ashamed of his race," over "Negro" or "colored" as a designation for the race. The purpose of writing the article was to respond to a piece written by Senator John T. Morgan of Alabama in which he referred to the term "Afro-American" as a reference exclusively used for mulattoes. Fortune took the opportunity to correct the senator and also to address fully the issue of the mixing of the races, a problem that, Fortune explains, is on the hands of the southern white man. Fortune also addresses the issue of social privileges and civil rights, a topic discussed in greater detail at other times, including in his 1885 article "Civil Rights and Social Privileges" (chap. 12).

The Afro-American —*Arena* 3, no. 13 (1890): 115–18

As I am, in some sense, responsible for the term "Afro-American,"[1] in the general application of it to the Afro-American League, organized January 15, 1890, at Chicago, I wish to correct an error into which Senator John T. Morgan[2] allowed himself to lapse in discussing "The Race Problem in the United States," in the September number of THE ARENA. Senator Morgan:

"The Afro-Americans, as the mulattoes describe themselves, believe that the precedent has been set, by their foremost man, which they can follow, with the aid of the politicians, that will secure their incorporation, by marriage, into the white families of the country. These vain expectations will be followed with the chagrin of utter disappointment, and will increase their discontent."

Senator Morgan displays the same amount of recklessness in the general discussion of the "Race Problem" that he exhibits in specifically defining the term "Afro-American." He is so saturated with prejudice and hatred of race that the violence of his argument of fact is worth as much as, and no more than, his argument of fiction, figments of his brain.

As a matter of fact, the term "Afro-American" was first employed by advanced thinkers and writers of papers devoted to the interests of Africans in the United States, as the most comprehensive and dignified term in sight to cover all the shades of color produced by the anxiety of the white men of the South to "secure their incorporation," without "marriage, into the 'black' families of the country." If the Morgans of the South had been as virtuous, as earnest to preserve the purity of Anglo-Saxon blood before, and even since, the war, as the Senator from Alabama now insists, there would be no mulattoes in the Republic to give them "a Roland for an Oliver."

But the term "Afro-American" was never intended to apply in the circumscribed sense implied by Senator Morgan. It was intended to include all the people in the Republic, of African origin. It does include them. It has been adopted, and is used, almost generally, by the leading newspapers. The term "negro" signifies black. Not three-eighths of the people of African parentage in the United States are black. If they were, there is no negro race. "Colored" may mean anything or nothing, from extreme white to extreme green; and, in any event, as applied to a race, is a misnomer from every point of view, without force or dignity. Both terms are used by writers everywhere as common nouns and in a contemptuous sense, just as Senator Morgan uses them. African is a proper name; it has a race behind it; and no writer will venture to treat it as a common noun. The same is true of the term "Afro-American," which includes every man, woman, and child in the country who is not ashamed of his race, and who insists that he shall be honorably designated as other races are.

When the Hon. Frederick Douglass[3] exercised his undoubted right of choice to select a second wife, and took a white lady of splendid social position and acknowledged literary attainments, nearly every one of the one hundred and seventy-five Afro-American newspapers condemned him for it. The paper I edited at the time was one of the few that maintained that Mr. Douglass did perfectly right in exercising his personal preference in selecting his wife. I know that the masses of the people were in sympathy with the indignant protests hurled at Mr. Douglass. The scaffolding under the "precedent" upon which Senator Morgan rears such an imposing edifice thus falls to the ground, upon its ambitious architect, and the "Afro-American," mulatto, and others, standing on the outside of the wreck, can afford to laugh him to scorn.

It is not true, as Senator Morgan insists, that Afro-Americans desire to "secure their incorporation, by marriage, into the white families of the country." I maintain that the facts are all against Senator Morgan. The extensive hybridization of the race, all too true, in the country, is due to white men, not to black men, who exercised, when they had it in their power to do so, their brutal authority, and who now exercise their influence of wealth and of social position to corrupt the women of the race, who everywhere are regarded as the weaker vessels. White men have not shown the same manly honor and Christian self-denial in this respect that Afro-American men have done, nor do they now. Any one familiar with the facts as Senator Morgan is, knows this to be true and deplores it. The best white blood of the South has for two hundred years gone into the black race; and if it now and in the future returns to plague those who sowed to the wind, is it not highly puerile for these men now to whine like babies over their supposed misfortune, and appeal to the rest of mankind for sympathy, where they deserve but contempt?

It is impossible for two races to live as close together as the Anglo-Saxons and the Afro-Americans do in the South without the actual fact of miscegenation asserting itself. Laws prohibiting legal unions but aggravate the matter. They may circumscribe, they cannot stamp out the existence of the fact, I will not say the evil. It is true in the South, in the British and Spanish West Indies, in Brazil, in Africa itself, where whites and blacks are brought into contact. If any explanation were needed, it is furnished in the famous couplet of William Cowper:

"Fleecy locks and black complexion
   Cannot forfeit Nature's claim;
Skins may differ, but affection
   Dwells in white and black the same."[4]

I never saw, and Senator Morgan never saw, an Afro-American who desired social equality with any Anglo-Saxon who did not want it with him. Afro-Americans do not seek it; they do not desire it, except when it comes, as it must ever come, by reason of the mutual likes and dislikes of all the parties concerned. Most southern white men confound civil rights with social privileges. Even so good a lawyer as Senator Morgan does this. What, then, is to be expected of the baser sort? If one of these men pays for a section in a sleeping car, or a seat in an ordinary coach, the moment a black or yellow face appears upon the scene, he imagines he owns the entire car, and proceeds to assert his preposterous claim in the most savage and brutal manner. The same is true in an eating house. When Afro-Americans protest against this monstrous confounding of things, Senator Morgan, and those who share his views, cry aloud, on the floor of the Congress, and in the pages of THE ARENA and other literary agents, "The niggers want social equality!" "We must protect our women!" and the like. Astounding is it that a whole nation of sixty million people can and do listen with patience to this sort of hypocrisy and humbug!

The Afro-American of to-day is a new creature. Senator Morgan knows very little about him. He lives apart from him. He has no social and little business association with him. He sees him as he goes to and fro in the town he visits once a year at his home, and in Washington, where he resides the greater part of the year, but he has small contact with him. The eminent men of the race, residing in Washington, for instance,—such as Frederick Douglass, Minister Resident and Consul General to Hayti; Ex-Minister John M. Langston, John R. Lynch, Fourth Auditor of the Treasury; Ex-Senator B. K. Bruce, Ex-Register of the Treasury, Recorder of Deeds of the District; Dr. James M. Townsend, Recorder of the General Land Office; Mr. John F. T. Cook, Superintendent of the "colored" schools of the district; Bishop John M. Brown, and a hundred others at the Capital I could mention, men in whose homes are to be found as much culture, refinement, and evidences of wealth as can be found in the homes of the best Anglo-Saxons in the South,—what does Senator Morgan know about these men, who reflect in their successes the possibilities of the race?

The men who have in the past talked most about the "Race Problem," have distorted the facts to fit their bed of Procrusters' prejudice, and misrepresented the real condition, the real sentiments, the real aspirations, of the people they arraign before the bar of public opinion and condemn unheard as aliens, as an incumbrance upon the face of the earth, and consign with the stroke of the pen to Africa, to the West Indies, to anywhere,—except to the South, where they are, where they belong, and where they are going to abide, in sunshine and in shadow, until the great Republic shall go the way of Babylon, of Greece, and of Rome, "the Niobe of nations."[5]

There are two sides to every question. The Afro-American,—who is not all black nor all yellow, but a good deal of both complexions,—understands his side of it.

Notes

1. The debate over the name which the community would use had become more heated in the late-nineteenth and early-twentieth centuries. Fortune promoted the term "Afro-American," as demonstrated in this essay. He was backed by individuals such as Bishop Alexander Walters, who stated that they should be defined by a term "which defines the country, the race to which they belong, and not by the color which distinguishes them from the rest of mankind. We are Afro-American," Walters argued, "not colored Americans or Negro Americans." Others, such as Alexander Crummell, John Edward Bruce, Booker T. Washington, and W.E.B. Du Bois preferred the term "Negro." Crummell considered the term Afro-American "a bastard, milk and water term," and John E. Bruce thought that "Afro-American" and "colored" were used by those who were "neither fish, nor fowl, nor good red herring" and any other term than Negro was an effort by "hybrids" to distinguish themselves from others within the race. As the twentieth century progressed, most used the term Negro as long as it was capitalized, "a proper noun" and not a "common noun," as Fortune would argue. Both Du Bois and Washington subscribed to this logic. For a discussion of the debate over the use of the terms, see, among others, Robert Terrell to John E. Bruce, September 29, 1896, and Alexander Crummell to John E. Bruce, March 22, 1898, *John E. Bruce Papers*, Schomburg Center for Research in Black Culture of the New York Public Library; Booker T. Washington to Hamilton Holt, May 31, 1907, *Booker T. Washington Papers*, Schomburg Center for Research in Black Culture of the New York Public Library; Alexander Walters, *My Life and Work* (New York: Fleming H. Revell, 1917), 200–201; "Afro-American," *St. Paul Appeal*, May 16, 1891; "A Minuscule," *AME Church Review* 21 (1904): 126–40; "Shall Negro Begin with a Capital 'N'?" *AME Church Review* 21 (1904): 192–94; "By What Name Shall We Be Called," *Southwestern Christian Advocate*, April 13, 1905; John E. Bruce, "'Negro,' 'Colored,' or 'Afro-American,'" and "Who Are We," in *The Selected Writings of John Edward Bruce: Militant Black Journalist*, ed. Peter Gilbert, (New York: Arno Press, 1971), 50–52, 106–8; Willard B. Gatewood Jr., *Aristocrats of Color: The Black Elite, 1880–1920* (Bloomington: Indiana University Press, 1990); Glenda Elizabeth Gilmore, *Gender and Jim Crow: Women and the Politics of White Supremacy in North Carolina, 1896–1920* (Chapel Hill: University of North Carolina Press, 1996), 15; Leon F. Litwack, *Trouble in Mind: Black Southerners in the Age of Jim Crow* (New York: Alfred A. Knopf, 1998), 458–63.

2. John Tyler Morgan (1824–1907) was a Democratic senator from Alabama who served from 1877 to 1907. Morgan, "The Race Question in the United States," *Arena* 10 (September 1890): 385–98. For more on Morgan, see Joseph A. Fry, *John Tyler Morgan and the Search for Southern Autonomy* (Knoxville: University of Tennessee Press, 1992).

3. Frederick Douglass (1818–1895) was an escaped slave who became a prominent abolitionist, editor, and author. Douglass rose to become the most influential African American of the nineteenth century. Douglass married Helen Pitts in 1884. Fortune published an editorial on the subject on February 2, 1884, in the *New York Globe*. For more on Douglass' second marriage, see Benjamin Quarles, *Frederick Douglass* (New York:

Atheneum, 1974); Waldo E. Martin, *The Mind of Frederick Douglass* (Baton Rouge: Louisiana State University Press, 1984); and David W. Blight, *Frederick Douglass' Civil War: Keeping Faith in Jubilee* (Baton Rouge: Louisiana State University Press, 1989).

4. William Cowper (1731–1800), *The Negro's Complaint.*

5. George Gordon, Lord Byron (1788–1824), *Childe Harold's Pilgrimage.*

26

Whose Problem Is This?

In this 1894 essay for the *AME Church Review,* Fortune outlines the racial situation of the day. He does not see the problem as being substantially different from those that faced the country before the Civil War. These issues, argues Fortune, are "as much a menace to national liberty and the preservation of the union of the states as was the problem of slavery." He discusses five problems—disfranchisement, mob and lynch law, miscegenation laws, separate coach legislation, and the convict lease program. These issues, according to Fortune, are affecting the "honor and credit" of the nation, and the country should address them. In the end, however, although Fortune sees the problem as an issue the government and the country as a whole need to address, he also deems it necessary for the race to organize and support its organizations that are employed in the act of educating the nation. Such a comment is a reference to Fortune's Afro-American League, which had collapsed the previous year on the national level.

Whose Problem Is This? —*AME Church Review* 11, no. 2 (1894): 253–61

Revolutions, like time, it has been said, never go backwards. However, this may be, if the revolution begun by Benjamin Lundy[1] and William Lloyd Garrison,[2] and culminating at Appomattox Court House, has not gone backward since 1876, in all respects, it is undeniable that it has done so as to some of its phases. There is nothing truer than that in all those matters affecting the life, liberty and citizen rights of Afro-Americans with which they were clothed by the three war amendments to the Federal Constitution, we have steadily lost ground in the past two decades in the Southern States where the large mass of the race reside, and must continue to reside for a number of years to come, and perhaps for all time. If we shall continue to lose ground in those States during the next two decades as we have done in the past two, in the vital matters of civil and political rights, our condition will be more hopeless and desperate than it was in 1856, when Chief Justice Taney[3] declared "that it has been held to be good law and precedent that a black man has no rights which a white man is bound to respect." It is not necessary to be an alarmist, to take refuge in an ultra-pessimism, to reach such a conclusion, because all existing facts, based upon existing conditions, plainly and logically point to such an unforbidding ultimation.

Regarded from this point of view, it is vital to the discussion to ascertain whose problem is this, ours or the Nation's, as upon the answer depends the solution of the issues involved for or against us. Mr. Frederick Douglass[4] remarked some time ago that there is no "Negro problem" but that the problem to which he is related is the Nation's problem. Technically, this definition is sound, although at the time it was enunciated I did not so regard it. True it is that all of our effort since the war, has been based upon the presumption that there is a "Negro problem" and that such relation as the Nation at large bore to it, was incidental rather than fundamental; and, contending upon this line, we have encountered defeat and mortification at every step of the way. The Nation has not heeded when we protested, when we cried out against injustice and outrage, because, taking our cue from the enemy, we have labored with all our resources to convince the Nation at large that its interest in the matter was purely sentimental. We are a busy people; and we seldom trouble ourselves about the misfortunes of others. We become interested only, and often reluctantly, when it is clearly demonstrated that the misfortunes of others affect us in some way. It was because of this that Mr. James G. Blaine[5] anathematized the suffrage villainies of the Southern States, because those suffrage villainies had led to his defeat for the Presidency in 1884. He did not open his mouth upon those suffrage villainies until they had been successfully employed (as they had been employed in other days against Henry Clay,[6] Daniel Webster[7] and Stephen A. Douglas[8]) to destroy forever the most cherished political dream of his life. It was a selfish lamentation, but selfishness, in the main, is the mainspring of human aspiration and conduct among all peoples, as the history of mankind conclusively proves.

As long as the abolition of slavery rested upon the sentiment that slavery was wrong, that it was repugnant to the genius of republican institutions, that it made brutes of master and slave, the conscience of the nation could not be reached and its voice was as silent as the sleepers in the catacombs of old Egypt. Lundy was imprisoned in Baltimore; Garrison was stoned and rotten-egged in Boston; Lovejoy[9] was murdered at Alton and John Brown[10] at Harper's Ferry—each one looked upon as a crazy John crying in the wilderness, as a noxious weed shaken by the wind; and under the monstrous provisions of the Fugitive slave law, men were chased all over the Continent and bound and gagged and remanded to a condition infernal from every point of view; but the Nation tolerated all this, and more, feeling that it had only a sentimental interest in the matter. When the liberty of white men began to be invaded, when the right of petition and freedom of speech were assailed in the Congress and the champions of these struck down in their seats, when a determined effort was made to steal the political representation of Kansas and Nebraska to the end that the slave power might control the legislation of the Republic, and when it was conclusively shown that slave labor degraded and depreciated white labor, all which came out in joint debates between Abraham Lincoln and Stephen A. Douglas—when it was made clear that the abolition of slavery was not a matter of abstract sentiment, but that it was a national question, affecting the political liberties and the bread and butter of all the people, then the institution of slavery was doomed, and not until then.[11] The issues of the conflict were decided in favor of the largest lump of Selfishness.

Now, does the contention upon which we are engaged to-day differ in any essential point from the contention against slavery and the aggressions of the slave power? I do not think that it does. The elements of injustice and wrong, political and industrial, which culminated in the war of the Rebellion and the suppression of the slave power, are present in every aspect of the problem that confronts the nation to-day, and is as much a menace to national liberty and the preservation of the union of the states as was the problem of slavery, intrenched as it was behind John C. Calhoun's[12] States' Rights theories and Bob Toombs'[13] insolence and swagger. The tail of the serpent has been crushed, but its head has not even been bruised. The right of every man in the Republic to be free has been fought out and won; the right of every freeman to enjoy all the manhood and constitutional rights of citizenship is still as unsettled as when Robert E. Lee[14] surrendered his sword to Ulysses S. Grant;[15] and in this statement of the case abides the fight in which we are now engaged, and have been since the first Ku-Klux rode on his midnight ride of murder and incendiarism. Do the issues involved constitute an Afro-American problem or a National problem? Do they affect us alone or all the people of the Nation? Let us see.

(1.) The entire race in the Southern States is disenfranchised. A voteless citizen in a Republic is an unprotected citizen, and denial to him of his suffrage rights affects the suffrage rights of every other citizen. Upon this point Mr. Blaine said in 1884: "There cannot be political inequality among the citizens of a free Republic; there cannot be a minority of white men in the South ruling a majority of white men in the North." But they do it, and have done it for twenty years. Mr. Lincoln declared: "This nation cannot endure half slave and half free."[16] In a recent speech in the Federal Senate, Senator William E. Chandler[17] showed that Afro-American voters were entitled to 44 representatives in the Congress, and have really only one, although there are seven Republican Representatives from the South. Using these 44 votes in Congress and the electoral colleges, the South dictates the Democratic nominees for the Presidency and elects them and then controls the majority power in the Congress, to the damage and demoralization of Northern and Western financial and industrial interest, as has been shown by the terrible sea of despair the Republic has passed through since March 4, 1892. These 44 votes are controlled as absolutely against the interest of the North and West as was the slave vote conceded to the South under the first article of the Federal Constitution. This fact alone makes the problem to-day a National one.

(2.) Mob and lynch law[18] has established itself upon the rule of Ku-Kluxism, through the terrorizations of which the suffrage rights of Afro-Americans were destroyed. An effort is being made to show that the Southern States are not dominated by mob law and that lynchings occur in the main because of criminal assaults upon white women; but the effort will prove of no avail, because the accessible facts are all against the assumption, no more than 25 per cent of lynchings being chargeable to this alleged offense, showing that the mob spirit is due to other causes than the one alleged. No one familiar with the facts will claim that Afro-Americans have the same consideration in Southern courts of law that Anglo-Americans have, or that they are not subject to mob outrages upon the slightest provocation. The whites have control of all the machinery of the law, and yet have fostered mob law to such an extent that the lives of white men are becoming almost as cheap as the lives of black men have long been held. This condition of affairs affects the credit and the honor of the whole nation, at home and abroad, foreign periodicals having advised people not to go into such communities to live, or to invest their money in such because of the disrepute into which law and lawful authority have been allowed to lapse. When matters reach this stage the whole nation becomes affected in its good name and credit and can no longer remain silent without becoming a party to the mob law system.

(3.) The miscegenation laws[19] of the Southern States affect the morality of all the people of the Republic, and are at the very bottom of most of the rape charges and lynchings for criminal assault which occur in the Southern States. The natural affections of men and women are cut off from the sanction of the law, and all the evils resulting from such a condition naturally follow.

The miscegenation laws should be repealed, and the marriage and divorce laws of the country should be made by the Federal Congress, having uniform operation in all the states. It is an outrage upon American citizenship that a marriage contract made in New York should be invalidated if the parties enter upon Virginia or other southern territory. As I have said, these miscegenation laws corrupt the morality of the entire people, besides entailing infinite hardship upon innocent and often defenseless people.

I do not wish here to deny that there are cases of rape in the South; nor do I wish to be understood as assailing the virtue of Southern white women; but that all the criminal assaults are committed by black men is presumption which the facts disprove; and that all white women in the South are better than the white woman in the North and West could only be advanced by a race of libertines who reduced the raping of black women to a science and pursued it from the introduction to the abolition of slavery. But we shall have nothing but crimination and recrimination along this line of argument. The main point is that criminal assault is a capital offence in all the Southern States and that the law should be allowed to take its proper course, whether the criminal be black or white, in cases of rape as well as in cases of chicken stealing, and that there never is any justification of mob and lynch law, as a transient expedient or an established institution. The whole nation has been scandalized at home and abroad, and damaged in its good name and credit, by the lawless record of the Southern States, beginning with Ku-Kluxism in 1868 and terminating in the lynch law system, which is now the burning issue in America and Europe. The cry of "Rape" is a pretext, a falsehood on its face, just as was the cry of "Down with the Carpet-bagger and Negro Domination," from 1868 to 1876. The main object has been, since the close of the war to the present, to destroy the political rights of Afro-Americans, to degrade them in their manhood, and to appropriate their labor now as it was appropriated in the days of slavery. Any excuse that will justify these crimes, which affect the people of all the country, is hit upon and employed with a genius and persistency never before equaled in a warfare so infamous. The cry of rape is one of these blasting excuses.

(4.) Separate schools[20] are an injustice which affects all the people, and violates one of the first principles of republican government. Taxation is levied and collected in common, and there can be no equal distribution of the common fund, except by an equal participation in its benefits. The inequality in the distribution of the Southern school funds is opposed to the genius of our institutions and an injustice to all taxpayers, who are made to support two school systems when one would be sufficient. Separate car laws are like unto separate school laws, only that they are in direct conflict with laws of contract, and impose hardships upon railroad and steamboat carriers as well as upon their patrons which give them common ground of complaint and protest. The object of the law is to degrade our manhood by defrauding us of our legal, common and manhood rights. That the Nation has permitted the condition of affairs to become hitched upon the Republic as firmly as was the institution of slavery is a National disgrace.

(5.) Under the operations of the convict lease system[21] of the South labor is systematically degraded and crime encouraged. Honest wage earners are forced into competition with labor the wages of which cannot be dignified by the term wages without a frightful stretch of the imagination, and by the operations of which the wage earners of the entire country are damaged and degraded. And the laws in the South, defining and regulating the relations of employers and employees are as binding and exacting and degrading as the laws that governed the relations of master and slave. As the latter were regarded as a degradation of the free labor of the North so will the former come to be regarded in the progress of the existing contention.

Lynch law is but a manifestation of the distemper; by simply removing that we shall not destroy but cauterize the disease; but it is interesting to note that an anti-lynching and anti-caste society has been established in Great Britain, as the result of the splendid efforts of Miss Ida B. Wells,[22] and that similar societies are being organized in this country. But until the nation realizes that the condition of affairs in the Southern States is a menace to national honor and credit we shall clamor for justice in vain. All honor to Georgia for passing an anti-lynching law, and to the good people of Louisiana, who are striving to have one passed; and all honor to Congressman Henry W. Blair[23] for introducing a measure in the House of Representatives calling for an investigation of the entire subject of lynching. It is the Nation's problem; let the Nation know the facts in the way made and provided by our Constitution for ascertaining them.

But because it is the Nation's problem we are in no sense absolved from supporting such agencies as are being employed to educate the Nation to a sense of its duty and obligation.

Notes

1. Benjamin Lundy (1789–1839) was a Quaker abolitionist and editor of the abolitionist newspaper *Genius of Universal Emancipation*. For more on Lundy, see chapter 6, note 2.

2. William Lloyd Garrison (1805–1879) was an abolitionist, editor of the *Liberator*, and founding member of the American Anti-Slavery Society in 1833. For more on Garrison, see chapter 6, note 3.

3. Roger B. Taney (1777–1864) was chief justice of the U.S. Supreme Court from 1836 to 1864. He authored the majority decision in *Dred Scott v. Sandford*, 60 U.S. 393 (1856). For more information on the *Dred Scott* decision, see Paul Finkelman, ed., *Dred Scott v. Sandford: A Brief History with Documents* (Boston: Bedford Books, 1997).

4. Frederick Douglass (ca. 1818–1895) was an escaped slave who became a prominent abolitionist, editor, and author. Douglass rose to become the most influential African American of the nineteenth century. Fortune is referring to Douglass' comments on the negro problem that were repeated in various locations. See for example, Frederick Douglass, "The Negro Problem," n.d. *Frederick Douglass Papers*, Library of Congress; and Douglass, "The Nation's Problem," 16 April 1899, in Howard Brotz, ed. *African-American Social & Political Thought 1850–1920* (New Brunswick: Transaction Publishers, 1992), 311–328. Fortune wrote a moving article on Douglass after his passing; see T. Thomas Fortune, "Mr. Douglass' Peculiar Greatness," *AME Church Review* 12 (1895): 108–13. For more on Douglass, see chapter 9, note 12.

5. James G. Blaine (1830–1893) was a Republican politician from Maine who ran for president in 1884 and lost to Democrat Grover Cleveland. For his views on suffrage rights, see Michael Perman, *Struggle for Mastery: Disfranchisement in the South, 1888–1908* (Chapel Hill: University of North Carolina Press, 2001).

6. Henry Clay (1777–1852) was a senator and representative from Kentucky. He became known as the Great Compromiser for his ability to find compromise between the North and the South on the issue of slavery, especially in 1820 and 1850.

7. Daniel Webster (1782–1852) was a politician who was elected to the U.S. House of Representatives and the Senate from New Hampshire and Massachusetts.

8. Stephen A. Douglas (1813–1861) was a politician from Illinois who defeated Abraham Lincoln in the 1858 Illinois Senate race but lost to Lincoln in the presidential election of 1860 as one of the Democratic nominees. Douglas served as Illinois representative from 1843 to 1847 and as a senator from 1847 to 1861. In relation to slavery Douglas promoted the popular sovereignty doctrine and became famous for proposing the Kansas

Nebraska Act in 1854. For more on Douglas, see Robert W. Johannsen, *Stephen A. Douglas* (New York: Oxford University Press, 1973).

9. Elijah Parish Lovejoy (1802–1837) was an abolitionist and journalist who was murdered for his antislavery position, in Alton, Illinois, on November 7, 1837. For more on Lovejoy, see chapter 13, note 2.

10. John Brown (1800–1859) was a radical abolitionist who led twenty-one followers in an attack on the federal arsenal in Harper's Ferry, Virginia, on October 16, 1859, with the intention of liberating and arming slaves. Fortune wrote a poem about Brown while visiting Kansas and published it in the *Age* in 1907, "With John Brown in Kansas," *New York Age*, September 19, 1907. For more on Brown, see chapter 6, note 6.

11. For the text of the Abraham Lincoln–Stephen Douglas debates, see Robert W. Johannsen, ed., *The Lincoln-Douglas Debates of 1858* (New York: Oxford University Press, 1965). For discussion of the debates in the context of the period, see James M. McPherson, *Battle Cry of Freedom: The Civil War Era* (New York: Oxford University Press, 1988), 181–88.

12. John Caldwell Calhoun (1782–1850) was a South Carolina politician, representative, senator, and vice president who promoted states' rights on the issue of slavery. For more on Calhoun, see John Niven, *John C. Calhoun and the Price of Union: A Biography* (Baton Rouge: Louisiana State University, 1988). For more on Calhoun and states' rights, see Manisha Sinha, *The Counterrevolution of Slavery: Politics and Ideology in Antebellum South Carolina* (Chapel Hill: University of North Carolina Press, 2000).

13. Robert A. Toombs (1810–1885) was a Georgia politician who became a leading secessionist in the U.S. Senate on the eve of the Civil War and was the major architect of Georgia's redemptive constitution in 1877. For information on Toombs and Calhoun, see Sinha, *The Counterrevolution of Slavery*. For more on Toombs, see chapter 14, note 11.

14. Robert E. Lee (1807–1870) was a leading Confederate general during the Civil War.

15. Ulysses S. Grant (1822–1885) was a leading Union general during the Civil War and was elected the eighteenth president of the United States (1869–1877).

16. Abraham Lincoln, "House Divided" speech, Springfield, Illinois, June 16, 1858.

17. William Eaton Chandler (1835–1917) was a New Hampshire Republican senator who served from 1887 to 1901. See Perman, *Struggle for Mastery*.

18. Joint Select Committee to Inquire into the Condition of Affairs in the Late Insurrectionary, *Report of the Joint Select Committee to Inquire into the Condition of Affairs in the Late Insurrectionary States: Made to the Two Houses of Congress February 19, 1872*, vol. 13 (Washington, D.C.: U.S. Government, 1872). See also Ida B. Wells-Barnett, "Lynch Law in America," *Arena* 23 (1900): 15–24; Wells-Barnett, *Southern Horrors and Other Writings: The Anti-Lynching Campaign of Ida B. Wells, 1892–1900*, ed. Jacqueline Jones Royster (Boston: Bedford Books, 1997); John E. Bruce, *The Blood Red Record* (Albany: Argus Company, 1900); W. Fitzhugh Brundage, "Mob Violence: North and South, 1865–1940," *Georgia Historical Quarterly* 75 (Fall 1991): 748–70; Brundage, *Lynching in the New South: Georgia and Virginia, 1880–1930* (Urbana: University of Illinois Press, 1993); and Allen W. Trelease, *White Terror: The Ku Klux Klan Conspiracy and Southern Reconstruction* (Baton Rouge: Louisiana State University Press, 1995).

19. Joel Williamson, *New People: Miscegenation and Mulattoes in the United States* (New York: Free Press, 1980).

20. For a summary of the discussion, see Louis R. Harlan, *Separate and Unequal: Public School Campaigns and Racism in the Southern Seaboard States, 1901–1915* (New York: Atheneum, 1969); and James D. Anderson, *The Education of Blacks in the South, 1860–1935* (Chapel Hill: University of North Carolina Press, 1988).

21. Pete Daniel, *The Shadow of Slavery: Peonage in the South, 1901–1969* (Urbana: University of Illinois Press, 1972); David M. Oshinsky, *Worse than Slavery: Parchman Farm and the Ordeal of Jim Crow Justice* (New York: Free Press, 1996); and Matthew J. Mancini, *One Dies, Get Another: Convict Leasing in the American South* (Columbia: University of South Carolina Press, 1996).

22. Ida B. Wells-Barnett (1862–1931) was a journalist and civil rights activist who was best known for her antilynching activism. For more on Wells-Barnett, see chapter 14, note 3.

23. Henry William Blair (1834–1920) was a representative and senator from New Hampshire from 1879 to 1891.

27

The Latest Color Line

In this essay, published both in the *New York Sun* and the *Liberia Bulletin,* Fortune takes issue with those who seem, according to him, to be attempting to create a color caste system in the United States. Fortune begins his critique with an attack on Edward Blyden, who claimed that the race problem in America was caused by conflict between mulattoes and whites, not blacks and whites. Fortune proceeds to take issue with the American Negro Academy, an organization he feels will cause a "separation of the black and mulattoes," particularly through its preference for the term "Negro" over "Afro-American." The editor warns that drawing another color line in American society will hurt the race as a whole. "No friend of the Afro-American race can fail to forget," he said, "that the black and yellow people of the United States will have their problem of manhood further complicated by a color line. They have enough trouble as matters stand without borrowing more."

The Latest Color Line —*New York Sun,* May 16, 1897, and *Liberia Bulletin* no. 11 (November 1897): 60–65

When Dr. Edward W. Blyden,[1] of West Africa, was in the United States a few years ago he made a lecture trip through the Southern States, and wherever he spoke he managed to give great offense to the mixed members of his audience by the extreme position he took on the relations of the races at the South. The matter culminated at Charleston, where Dr. Blyden is accused of having said that the pure blacks and the whites got along very well together, and that all the trouble between the races was caused by the mulattoes. This statement of the learned African brought down upon his head an avalanche of disclaimer on the one hand and of anathema on the other. At that time the question of black and yellow people had not been raised in such a way as to provoke discussion of any sort; but the question existed just the same, and flourished nowhere more pronouncedly than at Charleston. As I have seen no disclaimer from Dr. Blyden, I have accepted the statement as having been made by him. Charleston was a bad place to make it, and he was made to feel that fact in short order. He has not been at Charleston since, and it is not likely that he will again go there for a long time to come. If he does, people on the spot have told me he will have a warm reception.

For a number of years there has been very little said in the public prints on the subject of the feeling between the blacks and mulattoes of the country. On the surface the family has been an entirely harmonious and happy one as far as its internal affairs are concerned; but appearances are often deceptive. In this case they were decidedly so. The feeling between the pure blacks and all the shades up to that of the white—and there are a lot of white Afro-Americans in this country—has existed all the time, even in the days of slavery, and the feeling has attained more intensity since the close of the war and by the changed conditions which were brought about by the results of the war. Thoughtful men of the Afro-American race have watched this manifestation with more or less apprehension as being the most dangerous element that could possibly be injected into the already complex problem, and have done what they could to restrain it within bounds, but their labors have been barren of good results. They have had their labor for their pains.

The social conditions in the United States have had more to do with shaping the matter than any other influence. Unfortunately for all concerned, black is not a popular color in the United States when used by nature in the skin of a child of Adam. This was true before the war and it is as true today, perhaps in larger measure, because it is believed that the pure blacks and the whites of the country are further apart now in all the relations of life than they were in the days of slavery, although even then the Afro-American people of mixed blood were almost universally preferred for the lighter work of the house and the like by Southern planters and merchants and professional men and statesmen, while the pure blacks were generally condemned to the rougher work of the field and the like. This fact alone helped to make a breach between the pure blacks and their mixed brethren, which often led to dramatic situation of the most thrilling character. It also served another purpose, which is not generally considered in estimating the relative position of the blacks and the mulattoes since the war—it gave the mulattoes the advantage of contact with the best and strongest influences in Southern life, with its wealth and culture and refinement. They were, therefore, in position to improve themselves, and they did, as has been amply demonstrated in the usually prominent part they have taken in all departments of activity since there, in state and in church. The extent to which they have been concerned has been and is noticeable. The advantages they enjoyed before the war are not to be underrated in this result, although they may not be entirely responsible for it. At any rate, this conspicuousness of the Afro-American colored people in all relations of the national life is at the root of the argument for cleavage between them and the blacks which is just now gaining sufficient lung power to make itself heard and ridiculous. Strangely enough, it is the blacks who are doing the most talking and protesting and fulminating with verbose resolutions defining their position and organizing societies to preserve the purity of their blood and see to it that the blacks get their share of the good things going and coming which fall to the Afro-American "on account of race, color, and previous conditions of servitude."[2]

Washington is just now the storm center. The District of Columbia contains an Afro-American population of 80,000, one-half of whom are of mixed blood, some of them so white as to be clean out of the black family by all the rules of ethnological classification; but they cling to the race, with all the disadvantage that it naturally entails, disadvantages that no one can properly estimate who has not labored under them. Indeed, the fidelity of this class of the Afro-American population to their race has been and is one of the most beautiful things in our national life. All the more pity is it, therefore, that there should be any disturbing influence at work to mar it, not only from the race point of view, but also because the mixed-blooded people have always stood between the prejudice of the whites and the blacks, softening the prejudice, and acting a sort of connecting link, however the blacks may regard the matter from the contrary point; and these mixed-blooded people everywhere in the United States have always looked with the greatest abhorrence upon race prejudice, as such, and hoped that it would gradually disappear as a disturbing factor in the development of the race on the continent. It is not to be denied that of late years there has been less mixing in all ways than formerly between the black and colored people in all the large centers of population, and that especially is this true in the social relations, the marriage and giving in marriage of the people. This social segregation, as I have observed it in the large cities of the country for many years, has constantly grown more pronounced and observable, owing, in large part, to the causes already stated and the further cause that, being better prepared by the education received in the school of slavery to meet the conditions of freedom, the mixed-blooded people have profited materially from the special advantages they have enjoyed. The nature of their employment has been lighter and, in the main, more profitable. Still, the general disfavor that falls upon the pure black, because he is black, has much to do with it. In Washington race prejudice is almost as general as it is in Richmond or Atlanta or New Orleans, and the man with a black face finds himself at war with organized society in all the relations of life, being debarred from privileges of all sorts without which life is almost made a perpetual burden, instead of pleasure. This prejudice falls upon the black man in Washington and everywhere else more pronouncedly than upon his brother of mixed blood. It should not be so, but it is so. He notices it, of course, and resents it, as he has a right to do and as he should do, because prejudice of race is unnatural and un-American and should be frowned upon and discouraged by all who hope well for the future of all the children of the Republic, from whatever root of the main trunk they may have sprung in the differentiation of the races. But we do not make facts; they are evolutions of conditions which we do not control. We have to deal with them as we find them.

A newspaper synopsis of the situation in Washington sufficiently explains it to be reproduced here. It is as follows:

"Negroes in the District of Columbia have themselves drawn the color line, the cleavage being between the pronounced blacks and mulattoes. The blacks are the aggressors. Their grievance is that all the places of emolument in the District, notably in the management of the colored schools, are monopolized by the mulattoes, although the latter are a small minority of the colored population. It is asserted that nearly all the teachers in the Negro schools are of a light shade of color, in the proportion of seven to one, it is claimed, and the blacks desire this proportion reversed. The agitation has directed attention to the antagonism between the branches of the Negro race, which has existed since the days of emancipation and appears to be on the increase. In addition to monopolizing official places, the mulattoes have the more desirable positions in private employ. Two, three, four, or more members of a mulatto family will be frequently found drawing Government pay, while others will be receiving compensation in private employ which the blacks have never been able to attain. This class of the colored people has a society of its own. In several sections of the city whole blocks are given up to their occupancy, their homes are well furnished and appointed, and their incomes are sufficiently large to enable them to indulge not only in comforts, but luxuries. It is alleged by the blacks that the lighter-hued Negroes look down upon them. This is acknowledged to be measurably true, and has much to do with the jealousy and bitterness of feeling displayed. The trouble was brought to the attention of President Cleveland by a committee of the blacks, just before he went out of office, and it is now alleged that his refusal to reappoint Commissioner Ross grew out of the Commissioner's favoritism to the mulattoes. Following up this claimed victory, a committee has been appointed to wait upon President McKinley."

This is a very fair estimate of the situation, as far as it relates to the capital of the nation, and a very ugly and disagreeable picture it is. It forebodes no good to the Afro-American citizen. It presages a condition of affairs such as obtains in most of the West Indian islands, where the lines are drawn between the blacks and mulattoes as strongly as they are drawn between the blacks and whites of our Southern States. These lines have, in the History of Hayti and San Domingo at least, led to the bloodiest results and even to revolutions in the State. Indeed, those who know declare that the greatest drawback to the progress of the independent West Indian islands is the existence of this perpetual row between the blacks and the mulattoes, who spend so much time watching and fighting each other that they have no time left to develop the resources of their country and insure a stable government, without which progress in any State is impossible.

A society has been organized in Washington called "The American Negro Academy,"[3] which, while it has not for its object a separation of the blacks and the mulattoes, will ultimately work out that result. The officers of the academy are the Rev. Alexander Crummell,[4] D. D., president; J. W. Cromwell,[5] secretary. The objects are: (1) The promotion of literature, science, and art; (2) the culture of a form of intellectual taste; (3) the fostering of higher education; (4) the publication of scholarly works; (5) the defense of the Negro against vicious assaults. The academy is pledged to opposition to the term Afro-American and insists upon the integrality and perpetuity of the black race as such. In the second paper published by the academy W. E. Burghardt Du Bois,[6] a professor in the University of Pennsylvania and the author of a scholarly work published under the auspices of Harvard University, of which he is an alumnus, discusses "The Suppression of the African Slave Trade."[7] In defining the objects of the academy, and discarding the term of Afro-American, he says: "The term 'Negro' is, perhaps, the most indefinite of all, combining the mulattoes and zamboes of America and the Egyptians, Bantus, and Bushmen of Africa." Again: "The Negroes, the blacks;" and, further: "For the development of Negro genius, of Negro literature and art, of Negro spirit, only Negroes bound and welded together, Negroes inspired by one vast ideal, can work out in its fullness the great message we have for humanity." All of which sounds well enough, but is absolutely unattainable in a country where Anglo-Saxon ideals of literature and art and everything else predominate and will to the end of the chapter, absorbing to themselves all that makes for national beauty and strength; and an amusing phase of the matter is that Mr. Du Bois is not black at all, but brown, and did not take a black woman to wife. Dr. Crummell and Mr. Cromwell are both unmixed in blood, but both of them married mulatto women; and it is very generally the case that those black men who clamor most loudly and persistently for the purity of the Negro blood have taken to themselves mulatto wives. This is also the case with Dr. D. W. Culp, of Jacksonville, Fla., who makes a strong plea for the perpetuation of the Negro race type in the United States in the April number of the *Arena* magazine;[8] he married a woman so white that no one would suspect that she was an Afro-American, although he is one of the purest types of the Negro to be found, ranking in this respect with Dr. Crummell and Mr. Cromwell. Black men who want to preserve the Negro type should not marry mulatto women; but, while they preach purity of race very generally, and are very sensitive on the question of color, they marry most often in a way to destroy the logic of their preaching.

No friend of the Afro-American race can fail to forget that the black and yellow people of the United States will have their problem of manhood and citizenship further complicated by a color line in a color line. They have enough trouble as matters now stand without borrowing more.[9]

Notes

1. Edward Wilmot Blyden (1832–1912) was born in St. Thomas. He moved to Liberia and became an educator and statesman who promoted the ideas of African nationalism, Pan-Africanism, and African American emigration to Africa. See Edward Wilmot Blyden, *Christianity, Islam and the Negro Race* (London: W. B. Whittingham, 1887); Blyden, *Black Spokesman: Selected Published Writings of Edward Wilmot Blyden*, ed. Hollis Ralph Lynch (London: Cass, 1971); and Ralph Hollis Lynch, *Edward Wilmot Blyden: Pan-Negro Patriot 1832–1912* (New York: Oxford University Press, 1967).

2. Fifteenth Amendment to the U.S. Constitution.

3. The American Negro Academy was an educational society, formed in 1897, that sought to promote science, art, literature, and higher education, publish scholarly works, and defend the black population from vicious attacks. For information on the American Negro Academy, see Alfred A. Moss, *The American Negro Academy: Voice of the Talented Tenth* (Baton Rouge: Louisiana State University Press, 1981).

4. Alexander Crummell (1819–1898) was an African American Episcopalian priest, missionary, scholar, and educator. Crummell spent twenty years in Liberia as a mis-

sionary and educator and promoted the Christianization and civilization of Africa. In 1873, Crummell returned to the United States and founded and served as pastor of St. Luke's Episcopalian Church in Washington, D.C. He later taught at Howard University (1895–1897) and founded the American Negro Academy in 1897. For more information on Crummell, see chapter 2, note 1.

5. John Wesley Cromwell (1846–1927) was a journalist, lawyer, educator, author, and civil rights activist who founded the newspaper the *People's Advocate* in 1876 and among other things was a prominent member of the Bethel Literary and Historical Association in Washington, D.C.

6. W.E.B. Du Bois (1868–1963) was a civil rights activist, educator, sociologist, and historian. Fortune is referring to Du Bois' essay, "Conservation of the Races." See W.E.B. Du Bois, *The Conservation of Races,* American Negro Academy Occasional Papers, no. 2, 1897. For information on this essay and Du Bois' relationship to the American Negro Academy, see David Levering Lewis, *W.E.B. Du Bois: Biography of a Race, 1868–1919* (New York: Henry Holt and Company, 1993), 168–74.

7. W.E.B. Du Bois, *The Suppression of the African Slave-Trade to the United States of America, 1638–1870* (1898; repr., New York: Russell and Russell, 1965).

8. D. W. Culp, "The Past and the Future of the American Negro," *Arena* 57, no. 89 (1897): 786–99.

9. John E. Bruce responded to Fortune's article, see *Star of Zion*, December 2, 1897. See also Alexander Crummell to John E. Bruce, December 9 and 15, 1897, *John E. Bruce Papers*, Schomburg Center for Research in Black Culture of the New York Public Library. For a discussion of the response of Crummell and Bruce to Fortune's charge, see Ralph L. Crowder, *John Edward Bruce: Politician, Journalist, and Self-Trained Historian of the African Diaspora* (New York: New York University Press, 2004), 39–40.

28

Race Absorption

In his 1901 essay "Race Absorption," Fortune puts forth his belief that the race problem will ultimately be solved by the absorption of the black population into the "American race." According to Fortune this process has already begun. There is no longer a Negroid population; there is only an Afro-American population, he argues.

Race Absorption —*AME Church Review* 18, no. 1 (1901): 54–66

A race problem is an unfortunate and dangerous thing for any nation to have. The Irish people have frittered away their best intellect and energy and weakened and harassed the British Empire for years as a distinctive race problem. The Jewish problem is a source of menace and weakness to Germany and Russia. We have expended untold treasure and life in exterminating the Indian races of the American Continent. For more than a century we have been harassed and perplexed by the Afro-American problem, and every effort we have made to settle it upon the philosophy of injustice and selfishness has been frustrated, sometimes by fire and sword.[1]

What will be the Afro-American's future? Will the Republic absorb him, or will he preserve his race integrality?[2] It must either absorb him, or eject him. The opponents of the theory of absorption are as numerous as leaves in Vallombrosa; while those who favor the theory of ejectment are among the first to recognize the impossibility of the undertaking. The expatriation of eight millions of people after quite two centuries of residence, would be an achievement miraculous from every point of view. The presumption that the Afro-American will remain here, a homogeneous and disturbing element, to the end of the chapter, is one that the most ultra opponent of the theory of absorption would reject.

There is abundant evidence on every hand that the Republic is absorbing the Afro-American, and that he will contribute in no small degree, as Victor Hugo prophesied, to the formation of the future race type of the United

States, about which speculation will yet busy itself. It could not logically be otherwise. We might just as reasonably ignore the influence being exercised in the same direction by other alien races of the population.

The Honorable Charles A. Dana,[3] after a hasty tour through some of the Southern States, gave it as his opinion that the Afro-American is growing darker instead of lighter in complexion; and Mr. James Bryce,[4] Member of Parliament for Aberdeen, has stated it to be his belief that the social relations of whites and blacks in the Southern States are growing less intimate and general every year.

These opinions, even if true in every respect, are no argument against the theory of ultimate absorption. The first step towards an honorable social status is the development of a virtuous manhood. This can never be accomplished by the promiscuous intercourse of races brutalized by miscegenation laws. If the Afro-American is growing darker in complexion, it is good evidence that the license practiced under the slave code is spending its power for evil and that the men and women of both races are becoming more amenable to the higher conception of the marital relation and the parental obligation.

The influence of climate upon physical development, and of culture upon cranial and facial refinement, have been sufficiently demonstrated. The transformation wrought by these influences has been shown to be marvelous. They have had a large influence upon the Afro-American during the past century or more, and they will continue to exercise it, absorbing agents constantly at work, until the Afro-American will bear small resemblance to his African cogener as the latter now bears to his European brother. Other influences, of course, than climate and culture, will contribute to the ultimate absorption of the Afro-American into the warp and woof of American life.

If the accident of color had been eliminated from the problem when the African in the United States was emancipated,—as the badges of servility and servitude hitched upon the Angles by the Norman conquerors were laid aside as fast as they absorbed the invaders into their national life, a half century would have sufficed to place the Afro-American upon civil and industrial equality in our population alongside all other elements. Prejudice against the Afro-American is more the result of previous servitude and present conditions than inherent race antipathy. Gentlemen who believe in the fundamental isolation of the Hamitic race will reject this position; but the facts, which are not governed by race prejudice, sustain it.

The universally accepted dogma of the unity of the human family has nowhere had stronger confirmation than in the ready amalgamation of dissimilar race types in the United States. The African has not been exempt from the absorbing processes. He is not exempt now. He will be far less so in future years, because of improvement in his intellectual and material condition. A social organism capable of receiving and digesting an Indian or Chinaman has not, in times past, shown any incapacity to receive an African and gradually bleach him out.

If the Aborigines of the American Continent had possessed the elements of civilization, if they had been a less belligerent race, instead of having been annihilated by European contact and encroachment, they would have been, very largely, absorbed into the life of the Republic. But the Indian is a child of the forest, not of the boulevard; a child of impulse, not of reflection; a child of leisure, not of toil. The felled forests and the exterminated buffalo drive him into "the Happy Hunting Grounds" of his hopes. That the absorption of the Indian was possible and probable, we have only to recall the case of Rolfe and Pocahontas.[5] But the Indian would not tolerate it. Being a savage in all his fiber, he preferred annihilation to absorption, not through any process of ratiocination, but instinctively.

The Afro-American is different in all his nature from the Indian. His mental aptitudes are similar to those of the white race. He is eloquent, musical, poetic, and philosophical. Like the white races, he will toil when necessity compels him and rest from labor when he can afford to do it. He is accused of being an imitative race; but what race in history has withstood the destructive tendencies of civilization that did not possess in a high degree facility of imitativeness,—adaptivity to environment and receptivity of its influences of whatever sort? Because the Afro-American is imitative, because he absorbs to himself the influences dominant in his surroundings, is one of the strongest arguments that can be advanced in support of the theory that the Republic will eventually absorb and assimilate him, along with the other race forces of the population. Why should we accept this theory in the case of the Celt and the Teuton and reject it in the case of the African? Because, forsooth, the latter has a black and the former has a white skin? Then, what becomes of the accepted dogma of the unity of the human family? No; rather because the Afro-American had been a slave race, and because he is now, in large measure, an ignorant and impecunious race, with a prescribed social status: disbarments which time and opportunity will effectually remove, as they are now doing. They do it in the case of other races. Has experience shown, in this country, that they will not do it in the case of the African?

Slavery taught no more impressive and significant lesson than that, if nature has set up barriers between the black and white races, they are by no means impassable ones, and are contingent, entirely, upon the absolute isolation of the races. Human nature is the same the world over. Like forces gravitate towards each other and are absorbed and resolved by the contact. It is a natural law. As a result, the Afro-American is already a mixed race; otherwise he would not be an Afro-American, but an African. Two hundred and eighty years of isolation from the parent stock, with a century of absolute cessation of reinforcement from the fatherland, and with instant contact with a masterful class whose passions were not restrained by either statute or moral law, could not have resulted otherwise than in corruption of blood. Theory must here give way to demonstrated facts, however, disagreeable. The extent to which this vitiation has obtained, while underrated by superficial theorizers, is not easily ascertainable. Mr. Robert P. Porter, the Superintendent of the eleventh census,[6] is reported to have declared it as his belief, in accounting for the apparent decrease of the Afro-American population as compared with the tenth census,—that quite half a million mixed-blooded Afro-Americans had been counted as white because the census enumerators could not determine that they were black! Professor W. S. Scarborough,[7] an accomplished Afro-American scholar, estimates that twenty per cent of the Afro-American population is of mixed blood. I think this estimate entirely too small. Thirty per cent. would be nearer the truth.

Many gentlemen, who are determined to solve the race problem in accordance with their preconceptions, prejudices and what not, stop a few days in the black belts of Alabama and South Carolina and the Yazoo belts of the Mississippi, and, because they see two millions of Afro-Americans, from the olive to the coal black shade, straightway lose sight of the other six or seven millions scattered all over the Republic, a majority of them residing in urban centers, where the denseness of population works irresistibly for race contact and consequent absorption.

If it be accepted that no more than thirty per cent. of the Afro-American population is of mixed blood, is it not logically deducible that, without further adulteration, the processes of absorption have already gone so far that nothing short of wholesale deportation can avert the ultimate extinction of the African as an integral type in the United States? This may be delayed, but not prevented. If the Afro-American population were reinforced every year by accessions from Africa, such as we have from Italy or Germany, or other European States, the situation would be further complicated; but there is no such reinforcement. Few emigrate, and fewer immigrate.

The trilogy that makes most for absorption of a minority race in contact with a majority race is formed by the following elements: Habitat, language and religion. In a learned article, published not long since, upon the important subject of European immigration. Professor Alessandro Oldrini (of the Geographical Society of Italy and of the Ethnographical Society of France) said: "The man is the son of the land where he is born, above all. Then of his father and mother." If therefore, "the man is the son of the land where he is born:" if he speaks the common language and conforms to the common religion, then, the Afro-American is already a fixed fact in the national life, and must, with the disappearance of the adventitious conditions of ignorance and poverty, which prescribe the industrial and social status, come within the operations of the assimilating agencies constantly at work evolving the national race type. Indeed, as I have already shown, he has been subjected to these agencies, and sensibly and visibly affected by them. The African here is an American by birth, education and religious belief. He takes only an American's interest in Africa and what goes on there. He has no disposition to go to Africa, because he knows nothing of the country, aside from book information. He dreads the climate. He speaks none of the many languages of the country. He is a Chrisitian, not a Mohammedan or heathen.

Professor Oldrini asserts, further, that "It does not take more than a generation to transform an Italian into an American citizen." But the Afro-American has been here not one, but ten, generations. If that has not sufficed to make an Americo-African of him, then, habitat, language and religion avail nothing, and a man is not "the son of the land where he is born, above all."

If the foregoing aspect of the subject had been weighed properly a writer in a recent magazine article would have saved himself the trouble of complaining that Afro-Americans take no interest in Africa and the regeneration of its people. They take as much interest in the subject as other Americans,—the interest that the descendents of an Amsterdam burgher in the tenth generation take in the affairs and the people of Holland. Upon the same theory Bishop Henry M. Turner,[8] of the African Methodist Episcopal Church, is mistaken, when he makes such declarations as the following: "The only remedy is for the self-respecting, self-reliant Negro, conscious of his own worth, to return to the land of his fathers, taking his civilization and Christianity with him, to establish colonies and build up civilized nations in Africa."

Bishop Turner imagines that he is talking about a Negro population, when as a matter of fact, there is no such population in the United States, the absorbing process having evolved an Afro-American population, of which the good Bishop is a distinguished ornament. In Africa, where the Bishop has been in the interest of his church, he was probably regarded as a white man by the natives, or, at least, not as a Negro. The Bishop's dream will hardly materialize. The futile attempts of the American Colonization Society[9] to populate Liberia, on the West Coast of Africa, demonstrates the soundness of the proposition that "the man is the son of the land where he is born."

Another element of absorption has not been sufficiently considered by those who give attention to the solution of the race problem. The bulk of the Afro-American population is concentrated in the Southern States. The whites have always regarded their presence as a source of industrial strength and of social and political weakness; hence they have combined against the Afro-American in all matters of a social and political nature. This had, and is having, its logical effects. Every year the most restless and aspiring of the population of both races are leaving the rural districts and concentrating in the larger cities and towns or removing to the Northern and Westable. The steady depopulation of Memphis, Tenn. of its Afro-American population, beginning with the cowardly lynching of three men a few years ago, is a striking and pointed example.[10] This tendency not only makes for race absorption, because of reasons stated, but it creates a scarcity in the agricultural labor supply, which must be made good for some source. Recourse is had, of course, to the foreign labor supply, a redundancy of which flows into our Atlantic seaboard cities every year,—fifteen millions being Europe's contribution to our labor force from 1820 to 1890. Very few of these fifteen millions have gone to the Southern States. They have taken Horace Greeley's[11] advice and gone West and helped to verify the prophesy of Bishop Berkeley.[12] But there has come a new turn of affairs. The available lands of the great West have been, for the most part, pre-empted. Opportunities in that section are no longer as tempting as in past years. The large cities of the Atlantic seaboard are actually congested with this labor supply. At this juncture the farmers, manufacturers and mine owners of the Southern States are clamoring for laborers. The Italian, it has been found, is more adapted to the farm work of the South than any other European to take the places of the Afro-Americans. In the phosphate and pumice mines of South Carolina and upon the sugar plantations of Louisiana this Italian labor supply has been extensively drawn upon. In a few years other European races will enter the

Southern field and adapt themselves to the requirements of its industrialism.

The introduction of foreign elements into the race and industrial problems of the South will work a three-fold result. (1.) It will break up the conservative aristocracy developed by the slave system, and consequently, democratize the sentiment of the master class and eventually destroy caste rule close of the War of the Rebellion, and are still working, with the old order fighting desperately against the resistless iconoclasm of the new forces. The influx of foreigners will revolutionize the social, political and industrial conditions, and produce an American civilization such as has of late years begun to appear in New England and which is as the breath of life to the great West and Northwest. The competition of foreign labor will compel the Afro-American to scatter himself into other States of the Republic. He has already begun to learn that his lot is made easier where he is found in fewest numbers, and hardest where he is congregated most numerously. In proportion as he isolates himself will the process of absorption be aided and hastened.

As governments are undermined by parasites working at the base, rather than the apex, of the structures, so, also, are races corrupted as to their blood by the contact of their proletarian rather than by their patrician elements. From extensive observations, in all sections of the country, I have reached the (2.) It will force the Afro-American into other occupations than those he has been held to and has monopolized for a long time. (3.) It will hasten the absorption of the Afro-American into the bone and sinew of the Republic.

The slave system, like all variations of the Feudal system, develops an aristocracy, creates large landed estates, and concentrates wealth and power. The Anglo-Saxon population of the Southern States has always been the most undemocratic element in the Republic. The slave system produced caste and class rule; and the consequent degradation of labor not only repelled foreign and New England immigration, but preserved in a remarkable degree the British characteristics and tendencies of the people. Such corruption of blood as obtained was the result of intercourse of the Anglo-Saxon male master and the African slave female. The abolition of slavery was a signal for the democratization of the social and political conditions of the Southern States and for the sub-division of the large landed estates. These forces began to work immediately upon the conclusion that the average European emigrant entertains no prejudice against color. Europeans sometimes acquire it, but always in a qualified degree, and marriages are frequently contracted between them and Afro-Americans, especially in the large cities where they frequently occupy the same tenement houses.

When we consider the relative smallness of the Afro-American population to the whole population; the vitiation of blood that has already taken place; the scattering of the race throughout the States of the Republic, which will become far more general in the future than it has been in the past; and the tendency of races of like social status brought into close contact to contract legal or sentimental relations, the theory of ultimate absorption, and consequent extinction of the African as a race force in the United States will appear to be founded upon reasonable presumptions. The miscegenation laws that disgrace the statute books of most of the Southern States and that place a premium upon libertinism will gradually disappear as the forces I have indicated become more firmly rooted in the social and industrial conditions of those States. The time factor is all-important. Natural forces are never precipitous. They are neither accelerated nor retarded by the exigencies of States or of races.

While all the evidence is corroborative of the theory I have advanced, as far as the Afro-American is concerned, all the other distinct race elements of our citizenship have to confront the same destiny. They are doomed to extinction as race forces and to absorption into the body of the American people. Next to the love of country, the love of race is the strongest element in human nature. The idea of absorption, of extinction as a race, is repulsive. When this is done by a stronger race the repulsion is intensified. But, in a Republic such as ours, there is no other destiny possible to races than absorption. If there is a race element in the population incapable of being absorbed, that element has no place whatever in American life, and will always be regarded as a national menace. We may desire race homogeneity as a matter of sentiment or pride of race as in the case of the Hebrew; a minority race in instant contact with a majority race will be either absorbed or exterminated. Absorption has proceeded so far in this country that the Negroid type has been very nearly destroyed. The cranium, the physiognomy, the physiqiue and the mentality of the race have undergone a more than partial metamorphosis. We have a new type in the Afro-American race. It will not revert to the Negroid type, because it has no chance to do so, while the forces of absorption are in operation in every corner of the Republic, whether we like it or not.

The immorality of the Afro-American people is a theme with which wiseacres on the race question never tire of busying themselves. They never stop to consider that despite miscegenation laws, and despite the fact that the whole race came out of slavery without homes and taught to regard with contempt and aversion the marital relation from a legal point of view, millions of homes have been built up on legal marriage relations since 1865, and are now the pride and the hope of the Afro-American race. It is just to say in this presence and at this time that nothing conduces more to encourage such immorality as the race is guilty of than the miscegenation laws which burden the statute books of all of the States of the South.

The home is the foundation of the State. This is recognized in all civilized lands. It is a scandal of the largest magnitude that every State in this Republic has marriage and divorce laws of its own when the whole matter should be controlled by a Federal marriage and divorce law which should be uniform throughout the States of the Republic. Reform in this respect would do more to improve the morality of the nation than any other reform that occurs to me, and I believe the time is not remote when the people who create public opinion will force this issue to its only logical conclusion. I make reference here to this important matter because the Afro-American people suffer more in their morals and in the rights that inhere in the child from its parent by the existence of miscegenation laws and the diverse marriage and divorce laws of the several states than in any other elements of our citizenship. In the development of the future American type of manhood and citizenship by the irresistible elements of absorption at work constantly and everywhere there should be no barriers in the law which operate disastrously upon the morality of the community or the rights of the child.

Notes

1. Fortune published this article in longer form in 1893 in both the *Los Angeles Times* and the *New York Herald*; see *Los Angeles Times*, July 16, 1893, and *New York Herald*, July 9, 1893.

2. A number of Fortune's contemporaries also believed that the race would one day merge into "the American race." For example, see Frederick Douglass, "The Future of the Colored Race," *North American Review* 141 (May 1886): 437–40; Charles W. Chesnutt, "The Future American," *Boston Transcript*, August 18; August 25; and September 1, 1900. See also Joel Williamson, *New People: Miscegenation and Mulattoes in the United States* (New York: Free Press, 1980).

3. Charles A. Dana (1819–1897) was an American journalist who became nationally recognized as the editor and part owner of the *New York Sun*, a position he assumed in 1868. For more on Dana, see Janet E. Steele, *Sun Shines for All: Journalism and Ideology in the Life of Charles A. Dana* (Syracuse, N.Y.: Syracuse University Press, 1993). For his relationship with Fortune, see Emma Lou Thornbrough, *T. Thomas Fortune: Militant Journalist* (Chicago: University of Chicago Press, 1972).

4. James V. Bryce (1838–1922) was a British jurist, historian, and politician. For more on Bryce, see Edmond S. Ions, *James Bryce and American Democracy, 1870–1922* (London: MacMillan, 1968). For Fortune on Bryce's views, see T. Thomas Fortune, "Prof. James Bryce's Prejudice against African and Polynesian Races," *AME Church Review* 15 (1898): 503–12.

5. John Rolf (1585–1622), an early colonist in North America, is known for marrying Pocahontas (ca. 1595–1617), daughter of the chief of the Powhatan Confederacy, in 1614.

6. Robert P. Porter was the superintendent of the 1890 census. He resigned in 1893.

7. William Sanders Scarborough (1852–1926) was an educator and civil rights activist who served as president of Wilberforce University from 1908 to 1920. For more on Scarborough, see W. S. Scarborough, *The Autobiography of William Sanders Scarborough: An American Journey from Slavery to Scholarship*, ed. Michele Valerie Ronnick (Detroit: Wayne State University Press, 2005); William Sanders Scarborough, *The Works of William Sanders Scarborough: Black Classicist and Race Leader*, edited by Michele Valerie Ronnick (New York: Oxford University Press, 2006); Francis P. Weisenburger, "William Sanders Scarborough: Early Life and Years at Wilberforce," *Ohio History* 71 (1962): 203–26, 87–89; and Weisenburger, "William Sanders Scarborough: Scholarship, the Negro, Religion, and Politics," *Ohio History* 72 (1963): 25–50, 85–88.

8. Henry McNeal Turner (1834–1915) was a bishop in the African Episcopal Church (AME) in Georgia after the Civil War. He was briefly elected to the Georgia legislature during Reconstruction and later advocated African Americans to emigrate to Africa. For more on Turner, see Edwin S. Redkey, *Black Exodus: Black Nationalist and Back-to-Africa Movements, 1890–1910* (New Haven, Conn.: Yale University Press, 1969); and Stephen Ward Angell, *Bishop Henry McNeal Turner and African-American Religion in the South* (Knoxville: University of Tennessee Press, 1992).

9. The American Colonization Society (ACS) was formed in 1817 to send free African Americans to Africa as an alternative to emancipation. In 1822, the society established on the west coast of Africa a colony that in 1847 became the independent nation of Liberia. By 1867, the society had sent more than thirteen thousand emigrants. For more information on the ACS, see Amos J. Beyon, *The American Colonization Society and the Creation of the Liberian State* (Lanham, Md.: University Press of America, 1991); Floyd J. Miller, *The Search for a Black Nationality: Black Emigration and Colonization, 1787–1863* (Urbana: University of Illinois Press, 1975); Edwin S. Redkey, *Black Exodus: Black Nationalist and Back-to-Africa Movements, 1890–1910* (New Haven, Conn.: Yale University Press, 1969); and Claude A. Clegg, *The Price of Liberty: African Americans and the Making of Liberia* (Chapel Hill: University of North Carolina Press, 2004).

10. Fortune is referring to the lynching of Thomas Moss, Calvin McDowell, and Will Stewart, friends of Ida B. Wells who were lynched in March 1893. See Ida B. Wells-Barnett, *Crusade for Justice: The Autobiography of Ida B. Wells*, ed. Alfreda M. Duster (Chicago: University of Chicago Press, 1970), 47–55; Linda O. McMurry, *To Keep the Waters Troubled: The Life of Ida B. Wells* (New York: Oxford University Press, 1998), 130–49.

11. Horace Greeley (1811–1872) was a founder and the editor of the *New York Tribune*. For more on Greeley, see chapter 6, note 17.

12. George Berkeley (1685–1753) was an Anglo-Irish Anglican bishop and philosopher. In his *Verses, on the Prospect of Planting Arts and Learning in America* (1752), Berkeley wrote, "Westward the course of empire takes its way; / The first four acts already past, / A fifth shall close the drama with the day; / Times noblest offspring is the last."

29

Who Are We? Afro-Americans, Colored People or Negroes?

In this article Fortune challenges the notion that African Americans can or should be known as anything other than Afro-American. Written in response to Professor J.W.E. Bowen's assertion that "Negro" is the proper nomenclature for African Americans, Fortune argues that the race are "African in origin and American in birth" and therefore Afro-American. Moreover, he maintains that the word "Negro" is a "common noun" and if used, the race will be the object of "ridicule and contempt." With regard to the term "colored," Fortune dismisses it outright since it is not specific; it can be used to apply to "red, yellow and white people" as well as "black ones." Until "we get this race designation properly fixed in language and literature," Fortune contends, "we shall be kicked and cuffed and sneered at a common noun, sufficiently and contemptuously characterized by the vulgar term Negro."

Who Are We? Afro-Americans, Colored People or Negroes? —
***Voice of the Negro* 3, no. 3 (1906): 194–98**

A Reply to Dr. J.W.E. Bowen[1] in the January *Voice of the Negro*

There would be no confusion about the proper race designation of the people of African origin in the United States if the rule governing in the case of others similarly situated had been applied to them.[2] No such confusion exists in the case of any other of the racial elements that constitute our citizenship. Despite the arbitrary classification of all Europeans as racially homogeneous, there is as much dissimilarity in their race traits and tendencies as there is in the people of Africa, who are divided, for the most part, into tribes instead of nationalities, as in the case of the European peoples. Tribal government is, however, the infant stage of national government. Europeans who have become Americanized are known, and proud to be known, however remote the relation in time, as in origin, British, French, German, and the like. Ask a Continental where he came from and he will answer, unhesitatingly, Europe; ask him further from what country in Europe and he will name the country of his birth. Ask an African newly arrived in the United States where he came from and he will unhesitatingly answer Africa; ask him further what part of Africa and he will name one of its geographical sub-divisions; if you are still unsatisfied and want to know what race he belongs to he will tell you to one of the tribal sub-divisions, as he has and knows no political sub-division—a Vey, a Zulu, a Dahomey race. In short, he will tell you that he is "An African from this or that tribe." It is the same way with the European, the Asiatic and the American as with the African. They all have a geographical and a political relation to the country of their origin, and outside of their country they are referred to by their geographical rather than their political relation. This rule is universally applied to the inhabitants of all of the continents except that of Africa. My contention is that it should also apply to them, when they are racially classified, because there is no reason I have seen advanced why they should not be.

It is by this process of reasoning that I have come to adopt the term Afro-American as the only proper race designation of the people of African origin in the United States. The term has found an abiding place in all of the dictionaries and much of the later literature of the United States. I did not originate the term, if I did force it into popular acceptation. It was first used, as far as I have been able to discover, by Hallam, in speaking of "the Afro-Assyrians." It was first used in this country, I believe, by Mr. E. J. Waring,[3] in a newspaper published by him many years ago at Columbus, Ohio. It is not, therefore, "an hybrid, out of the newspapers gutter." If it is philologically inaccurate, blame Hallam. His shoulders are broad enough—a few feet broader in scholarship and reputation than those of Dr. J. W. E. Bowen, who insists that he is a Negro in a deluge of words most difficult to comprehend, as he has flung them into sentences.

Now, it is one of the isolated instances in the history of mankind that a whole race of people, inhabiting one of the geographical divisions of the earth, have been and are classified as a race, not by their geographical or political division, but by their physical qualities—by color, by hirsute texture and by cranial and facial conformation. The term Negro, adopted from the Latin, has been used, from primitive times, to describe the black people of

Africa as they are or have been; and, so used, it has been treated, and quite properly, as a common noun. It is impossible to get the writers in America, Europe or Asia to treat it as a proper noun. They never will do it, because it is not a term definitive of race affiliates and unities, but of physical peculiarities of race, of which color is the visible and invariable index. No effort of Afro-American publicists will ever be able to convert the term Negro into a proper noun, because, philosophically, it is a common noun. This being the case, and universal interpretation makes it so with the scholars of all lands, how are we to accept it as a race designation, with the dignity which must attach to every race designation? If we should accept it, would not the race always be subjected to the ridicule and contempt of being the only race, dead or alive, which was looked upon and characterized as a common noun? The conclusion is unavoidable, based as it is in the literature of the world for fifteen hundred years.

The term Negro has not even a respectable tribe in Africa to dignify it. The tribe so designated is reputed to be one of the most discredited of all of the African tribes. An American recently returned from Abyssinia told me that if a person should call an Abyssinian a Negro he would fell him in his tracks. He would take it as a term of reproach—as an insult.

As for the term "colored," it may be dismissed from any consideration whatever. It can be applied as appropriately to red, yellow and white people as to black ones. It has neither geographical nor political significance, as applied to a race. It may mean anything and it may mean nothing. As applied to Afro-Americans, it is a cowardly subterfuge—an attempt of the person appropriating it, or to whom it is applied, to convey the impression that he has no race that he cares to acknowledge. I always feel a sort of merciful contempt for the goody-goody Afro-American who insists that he is a "colored person."

There is no reason why the people of African origin in the United States should be termed Negroes or colored people—the one being a misnomer and the other being indefinite, and both being derisive, as the physical characteristics of the people, after two hundred and eighty years of residence in the United States, having undergone a radical change, as to the great mass of them. Outside of the States bordering on the Gulf of Mexico and the Mississippi Valley States, where the bulk of the genuine black people are to be found, it is difficult to come upon a congregation of Afro-Americans in whom the physical qualities ascribed to and defined by the term Negro have not so far been modified or destroyed as to make the application of the term to them not only a misnomer but a rank absurdity. Time, habitat and blood-mixture have produced a new race, approximating much nearer the American than the African type. And, as the years come and go, this will appear even more pronouncedly, as a logical outcome of climate and the blood-mixture forced upon the slave women by the brute lust of the white master, who was the pioneer and most brutal rapist on a gigantic scale on the American Continent, or on any continent, or in any age. We do not need any additional infusion of white blood, although we are getting plenty of it; we need only to intermarry the mixed and pure bloods of the race, as we are doing, ultimately to mix the blood of all the people of African origin on the Continent. To-day we have only Afro-American black and colored people; the time is coming when we shall have only Afro-American colored and white people; and these, ultimately, will disappear into the American people, whose race type is in process of formation; the American type, composed of some of all the tribes and tongues scattered over the earth at the tower of Babel. This is inevitable, as we have no re-enforcement of pure blood from Africa and are ceaselessly mixing blood with all the white races here with whom we live and a part of whom we are.

We are Afro-American black and colored people. I used the term black as synonymous with Negro and the term colored as synonymous with yellow and white, for we have enough Afro-American white people among us to recruit an army with banners. It is not a pleasant thing for a lot of people who get blue in the face whenever they come to contemplate the race question; but they should not blame us, but rather their ancestors, who so industriously planted white seed in black soil. As we sow so shall we reap.

It is the highest importance that we get ourselves straightened out on this question of "Who are We?" We can never give dignity or force to the term Negro, because it is a common noun, defining physical qualities of race; and we can never make it a proper noun in popular usage, because it never can be stretched so as to mean the accepted geographical or political classification of race. In that case, we shall be wise to adhere to first principles and insist that we are African in origin and American in birth; and as habitat, language and religion make for homogeneous citizenship, so the Continent of origin and the Continent of birth must make for classification of race; we are therefore, by the logic of it, Afro-Americans. Until we get this race designation properly fixed in the language and literature of the country we shall be kicked and cuffed and sneered at as a common noun, sufficiently and contemptuously characterized by the vulgar term "Negro."

Notes

1. John Wesley Edward Bowen (1855–1955) was an educator and theologian who taught for a number of years at Gammon Theological Seminary in Atlanta, Georgia.

2. The debate over the name which the community would use had become heated in the late-nineteenth and early-twentieth centuries. Fortune promoted the term "Afro-American," as demonstrated in this essay. He was backed by individuals such as Bishop Alexander Walters, who stated that they should be defined by a term "which defines the country, the race to which they belong, and not by the color which distinguishes them from the rest of mankind. We are Afro-American," Walters argued, "not colored Americans or Negro Americans." Others, such as Alexander Crummell, John Edward Bruce, Booker T. Washington, and W.E.B. Du Bois preferred the term "Negro." Crummell considered the term Afro-American "a bastard, milk and water term," and John E. Bruce thought that Afro-American and colored were used by those who were "neither fish, nor fowl, nor good red herring," and any term other than Negro was an effort by "hybrids" to distinguish themselves from others within the race. As the twentieth century progressed, most used the term Negro as long as it was capitalized, "a proper noun" and not a "common noun," as Fortune would argue. Both Du Bois and Washington subscribed to this logic. For a discussion of the debate over the use of the terms, see chapter 25, note 1.

3. Everett J. Waring (1870–1920) was a journalist and lawyer. While in Columbus, he briefly published a Democratic-leaning paper named the *Afro-American* (dates unknown). He later moved to Baltimore, Maryland, and became a judge and also started the Lexington Savings Bank. For Waring's comments on the term, see *New York Age*, January 2, 1892.

30

We Must Make Literature to Make Public Opinion

In this 1924 editorial Fortune aligns himself with others during the Harlem Renaissance, calling on African Americans "to make our own literature" and to "write the story ourselves."

We Must Make Literature to Make Public Opinion —*Negro World*, **November 22, 1924**

Announcement has been made that young Countee P. Cullen[1] of New York, who is still a student in a New York school, has had accepted and published poems in four of the leading magazines for November. This is a remarkable showing, and would be for a veteran author. The magazines that have accepted his poems for November issues are The American Mercury, which publishes his prize winning poem; Harper's Magazine, The Century and The Bookman.

It will be remembered that young Mr. Cullen had won two prizes in contests for the best poetry of late, and he has now won an entrance into the highest and most exclusive magazines. It is a great gain for him and for the race.

It is good to remember, as Daniel Webster[2] once told a young aspirant for honors at the American bar, that there is always room on the top. And Dr. Washington, who was a philosopher of common sense, once said that if you have something others want they will not be bothered by the color of you but by the price of what you have, and that they would seek you rather than you seek them. It appears to be that way in literature. Young Mr. Cullen has just gone in and offered his poetic wares, and, having been accepted, the best publications of the nation invite him to contribute to their pages, and pay him handsomely for so doing.

As in the case of Roland Hayes,[3] the premier lyric songster of the race, and of Harry Burleigh,[4] the premier composer of the race, Mr. Cullen has not conquered the outworks by sudden onslaught; he has had to plod upwards, as all have to who succeed. The thing is to have the knack of plodding. So many refuse to accept the drudgery of preparing themselves for the work they want to do and are offended when their work is not accepted, with all of its imperfections. The editor is not worried about your race, color or previous condition; what he considers is the work you submit to him for consideration. It has no color. If it is defective in subject and treatment he rejects it. It is your fault and not his.

We must make our own way in literature.[5] If we leave it to others to write about us and what we think and say and do, they will color it from their racial viewpoint, and it will not always flatter us, nor tell the unvarnished truth about us. To get that we must write story ourselves. When I write about white people I always do it from the Negro viewpoint. I can't help it. The white man judges me by his viewpoint and I judge him by mine. I prefer my judgment to his. So would you. If he writes his viewpoint of me and I do not write mine of him, he has the advantage of me in the high court of public opinion, which, in the last analysis, rules the roost.

We are fortunate at this time in having a small group of men and women who are writing from the race viewpoint what the race hopes and aspires to who have the ear of the publishers and of the public, and we owe them much, for they interpret us for those who do not know us and our hopes and aspirations.

Notes

1. Countee P. Cullen (1903–1946) was an African American poet and novelist.

2. Daniel Webster (1782–1852) was a politician who was elected to the House and the Senate from New Hampshire and Massachusetts.

3. Roland Hayes (1887–1976) was an African American concert vocalist.

4. Harry T. Burleigh (1866–1949) was an African American composer and vocalist.

5. Throughout his life Fortune promoted the publication of the race's own literature and history. Fortune actively promoted George Williams' *History of the Negro Race in America, 1619–1880* in the pages of the *Globe* (March 3, 10, 17 and May 12 and 19, 1883), and in his two-part article, "The Negro and His Critics," in the *Age*, June 29 and July 6, 1889, he called upon the race to write their own history and literature. A few months before this piece on Cullen and the promotion of race literature and the arts, Fortune praised Walter White and his *Fire in the Flint* (1924; repr., Athens: University of Georgia Press, 1996), see *Negro World*, October 4, 1924. In 1927 in his *Norfolk Journal and Guide* column, "The Passing Show," Fortune again praised African American writers for writing their own histories, but he called on the race to begin writing on the "period of agitation and organization from 1870 to 1900 . . . the most important period in the history since the Civil War." *Norfolk Journal and Guide*, December 31, 1927.

31

Separate the Douglass and Lincoln Birthdays

Never an avid fan of Abraham Lincoln, in this 1928 editorial Fortune calls on the community to end the practice of celebrating the lives of both Lincoln and Douglass during Negro History Week. "Douglass belongs to us," Fortune proclaims. The race, he argues, should leave Mr. Lincoln to the whites, and "Mr. Douglass should become their priority, an individual praised and honored for all the generations." Fortune's argument is reminiscent of his editorial debate with Frederick Douglass Jr. about John Brown in 1889 and is a good example of Fortune's race pride late in his life (see chap. 23).

Separate the Douglass and Lincoln Birthdays —*Negro World,*
February 25, 1928

The Negro race in the United States has been observing "Negro History Week,"[1] and it is good that it has done so, because we have much history, little of which has been written and most of that has been distorted because those who wrote it were more concerned about concealing the truth than making it plain. And much Negro history, much that is best and most vital, has not been written at all. A race without a written history of its own is much in the position of a dead race, although it may be living. It is that way with the Red Men of the Occident. They have plenty of history, but little of it was transmitted by themselves, and those who have written it have colored it to suit their interests. It is that way with the African races. They had plenty of history, but their records were not written, or were destroyed in some mysterious manner, and most that we have has been scraped together by white people from all sorts of sources and weaved into a story pleasing to white people and seldom satisfactory to black people.

It has become a custom to celebrate jointly the birthdays of Frederick Douglass and Abraham Lincoln as of February 12, with the result that we have been unable to do justice to either of them. The celebrations should be separate. Mr. Douglass belongs to us. He was great enough in all respects for us to make a racial character of him so that he could be held up to our children as a person worthy to be honored and emulated. In order to do this as it should be done, we should celebrate the birthday of Frederick Douglass all by itself, when we could sufficiently render unto him the things that belong to him. The whites will take care of Mr. Lincoln and we can't forget him, and need not, but it is our business to take care of Mr. Frederick Douglass, who lived and labored for us, and died as one of us.

Notes

1. Negro History Week was inaugurated in 1926 by Carter G. Woodson and the Association for the Study of Negro Life and History. For information on the inaugural celebration, see Carter G. Woodson, "Negro History Week," *Journal of Negro History* 11 (April 1926): 238–42. See also Pero Gaglo Dagbovie, *The Early Black History Movement, Carter G. Woodson, and Lorenzo Johnston Greene* (Urbana: University of Illinois Press, 2007).

PART 4

Africa, Emigration, and Colonialism

Then Bartow got a little note,—
    'Twas very queerly signed,—
It simply told him not to vote,
    Or be to death resigned.
Young Bartow thought this little game
    Was very fine and nice
To bring his courage rare to shame
    And knowledge of justice.
"What right have they to think I fear?"
    He to himself did say.
"Dare they presume that I do care
    How loudly they do bray?
"This is my home, and here I die,
    Contending for my right!
Then let them come! My colors fly!
    I'm ready not to fight!

"Bartow Black"—*AME Church Review* 3 (October 1886): 158–59

32

The World in Africa

Fortune often expressed his support for African insurrection. In this 1885 editorial he encourages the El Mahdi forces in their resistance against British occupation. This editorial is not only a strong statement of support for the Sudanese fight for independence; it is also a staunch condemnation of imperialism in general.[1]

The World in Africa —*New York Freeman,* February 14, 1885

It seems that the old saying, "the world is gone after Africa" is just now being literally fulfilled. Nearly every country in the Old World is scrambling for a slice of African soil. "War and rumors of war"[2] on the vast continent of Africa fills columns upon columns of space in the daily newspapers, while magazines and bookmakers are going mad after productions bearing upon Africa and its millions of peoples.

England, as usual is foremost in planting herself in the new El Dorado. She is spending millions of money and carrying fire and sword to thousands of homes to satiate her greed of conquest and of vengeance.

What business has England in the Soudan? What right has she to carry fire and sword and desolation into a country to which she has no more claim than she has upon any one of the sovereignties of South America? As a Christian nation, what right has England in the Soudan with fire and sword and bad whiskey?

England has absolutely no business in the Soudan and she will receive no more than her just deserts[3] if every army she sends there is cut into mince meat by El Madhi.[4]

A corrupt Egyptian government borrowed vast sums of money from capitalists in France and England. The money was squandered in riotous living. When the interest became due the Egyptian government was unable to pay it. Then France and England stepped in to protect their creditor subjects.[5] Heavy taxes were necessarily imposed. This led to complications which made it necessary for England to send an army to coerce the rebellious Egyptians. Having subdued these, dependencies of Egypt rose in insurrection. In attempt to subdue these the English army had penetrated far into Africa and sustained some defeats which have fired the vengeance of the British heart. El Madhi must be subdued and his so-called rebellion terminated, be the cost of blood and treasure what it may.

England may accomplish her purpose. El Madhi may be crushed and the rebellion of which he is the incarnation may be scattered to the four corners of Africa. She has inexhaustible resources of men and money, and can draw upon all appliances of warfare; yet her victory will be a barren one. In the accomplishment of it we trust she will sustain such infinite loss as to deter her somewhat from her commercial mania to impose her tyrannies upon weaker nations than herself.

It is well known that Great Britain is the most relentless of tyrants where she has acquired power. Her commercial interests are paramount. Native governments and refractory peoples are cowed and ruled by the most odious methods. Wherever she predominates, British manufactures, including rum, flourish at the expense of native manhood and independence. Our sympathies are with the Soudanese. They fight for independence of foreign control, for their homes and firesides, and although all odds are against them, we trust they will make it excessively hot for the invaders.

Notes

1. For more of Fortune's support of African resistance over the years, see, for example, *New York Age,* September 12, 1904, June 1 and December 28, 1905, January 31 and September 19, 1907. It is important to note that Fortune spells El-Mahdi, "El-Madhi" in the original text. I have kept his spelling as it appeared in the actual editorial.

2. Matthew 24:6 and Mark 13:7.

3. This is not a typo; Fortune is employing a pun here.

4. The Sudanese had revolted against alien rule since 1881. The first conflict between the Sudanese forces of Muhammad Ahmad El-Mahdi and the corrupt Turco-Egyptian government, backed by Britain, lasted from 1881 until 1885. In 1886, the British invaded the Sudan with an Anglo-British force and were met again by El-Mahdi resistance. See A. Adu Boahen, *Africa under Colonial Domination 1880–1935, General History of Africa,* vol. 7 (Berkeley: University of California Press, 1985). When Muhammad Ahmad El-Mahdi was killed in 1885, Fortune praised his efforts in the pages of the *Age* and described him as the great man who "made it exceedingly warm for the British who desired to gobble up Sudanese territory." *New York Freeman,* July 18, 1885.

5. For a brief description of the events Fortune is describing, see Boahen, *Africa under Colonial Domination.*

33

An African Empire

In this 1887 editorial on European colonization of Africa, Fortune predicts the creation of an "African Empire," an "African Confederation, not unlike that of Germany." He argues that Europeans may have their way on the continent for the time being, but "in the course of time, the people will become educated not only in the grasping and cruel nature of the white man, but in the knowledge of their power, . . ."

An African Empire —*New York Freeman,* **January 15, 1887**

It is written on the wall that there will one day be an African Empire whose extent and power will be inferior to that of no government now denominated as a first-class power. All the indications point to this fact as one of the certainties of the future. Mungo Park,[1] David Livingston,[2] Henry M. Stanley[3] and De Brazza[4] have completely revolutionized accepted opinions of the geography and people of the African Continent, and the indications are abundant that the day is not distant when we shall know as much about that country and people as we know about Russia or Germany. The "Dark Continent" will soon hold within its grasp no secret as to its people, its climate or its varied, exhaustless and priceless resources. In the light of modern explorations and discoveries, the celebrated lines of Bishop Berkeley[5] no longer contain the philosophy of a prophecy, that—

"Westward the course of Empire takes its way;
    The first four acts already past,
A fifth shall close the drama of the day;
    Time's noblest offspring is the last."[6]

    In this Western world empire has already reached out unto the boundless Pacific and unto where the "Oregon hears no sound, save its own dashings;"[7] already the teeming millions upon our continent are crowding upon each other, treading upon each other's heels, and crying aloud that "population is pressing disastrously upon subsistence"—the cry which has for years swelled from the throats of the jostling, starving millions of overpopulated Europe.

Only a few years more and the logic of increasing population and consequent contraction of the volume of the necessaries of life will force upon the governments of the Occident the closing of their Atlantic seaboard against the hungry millions of Europe as they have already been compelled to do on their Pacific seaboard against the countless millions of China and Japan.

The world's area is being constantly contracted by the constant increase of population—not necessarily the area but its capacity to yield the required sustentation made exigent by the increase of mouths to be fed and backs to be clothed. No sooner is a new country discovered,—countries vast in extent of territory like America and Australasia—than they become the objective point of the surplus population of Europe; so that a few years only suffice to fill up the waste places and make further accession of numbers a "grave problem."

Africa is the newest "find." Already the great States of Great Britain and Belgium and Holland have made a lodgment on that continent and begun systematic colonization of their possessions. The grain and gold coast, with Sierra Leone as the centre, is already firmly in the grasp of Great Britain, while the Congo Free State is pushing its way under the patronage of King Leopold[8] of Belgium and the Governorship of Henry M. Stanley. The Transvaal Republic is already firmly rooted by the Dutch Hollanders. Besides, France, Germany and even Italy are seeking territory for purposes of colonization, while the corrupt state of Portugal claims in vain preserves to which it has as just right as any of the other European robbers.

The railroad, the steamboat, the missionary and the rum jug have begun in earnest the conquest of the riches of Africa. The iron heel of the military despot and the oily cunning of the commercial Shylock[9] have already shown the inborn spirit that ever propels them in the bloody wars necessary to break the independence of the people of Dahomey, of the Zululand and Egypt, with its pretended Sudanese possessions; while the tribes of the Congo country have been constantly compelled to choose between abject submission to the invader or complete extermination.

Bloodshed and usurpation, the rum jug and the Bible—these will be the program of the white race in Africa for, perhaps, a hundred years. The whole continent will be put under tribute to European powers, the same as Egypt now is to England and France, and the Shylock will demand at the point of the bayonet the last drop of blood from the prostrate millions. But, in the course of time, the people will become educated not only in the grasping and cruel nature of the white man, but in the knowledge of their power, their priority of ownership in the soil, and in the desperation which tyranny and greed never fail to breed for their own destruction. Out of the convulsions which are sure to come an African Confederation, not unlike that of Germany, will certainly be evolved. It can hardly be prevented, save by Omnipotent interposition. So out of toil and privation and long agony good will eventually come to the swarthy millions of our Fatherland.

Notes

1. Mungo Park (1771–1806) was a Scottish explorer of Africa. Park concentrated much of his exploration in the Niger region.

2. David Livingstone (1813–1873) was a Scottish explorer of Sub-Saharan Africa.

3. Henry M. Stanley (1841–1904) was a British-born American journalist and explorer who was best known for his exploration of the Congo and his search for David Livingston while a reporter for the *New York Herald* (1871). During this third journey (1879–84), he helped to organize the notorious Congo Free State, largely by persuading local chiefs to grant sovereignty over their land to the Belgian king, King Leopold II.

4. Pierre Paul François Camille Savorgnan de Brazza (1852–1905) was a Franco-Italian explorer of the Congo.

5. George Berkeley (1685–1753) was an Anglo-Irish Anglican bishop and philosopher.

6. Berkeley, *Prospect of Planting Arts and Learning in America* (1752).

7. William Cullen Bryant (1794–1878), "Thanatopsis."

8. Leopold II (1835–1909) was king of the Belgians from 1865 to 1909. In the Congo Free State, created in 1885 after the Berlin Conference on Africa (1884–1885), Leopold II brutally ruled and exploited the region. For more on Leopold II, see Adam Hochschild, *King Leopold's Ghost: A Story of Greed, Terror, and Heroism in Colonial Africa* (New York: Houghton Mifflin Company, 1998).

9. The usurer in Shakespeare's *The Merchant of Venice*.

34

Will the Afro-American Return to Africa?

African Americans had at various times debated the idea of emigration outside of the United States, especially in the 1850s and the 1890s. Although Fortune was a supporter of African independence, he did not believe African Americans should return to Africa. When he wrote the following essay for the *AME Church Review* in 1892, the emigrationist ideas of Henry McNeal Turner were gaining some popularity in the African American community. Lynching and mob rule were on the rise, and the nation's federal government continued to do little to prevent the southern states from stripping the black community of social and political rights guaranteed by the Fourteenth and Fifteenth Amendments. Fortune, however, still believed that African Americans should remain in the United States and fight for their civil and political rights.

Will the Afro-American Return to Africa? —*AME Church Review* 8, no. 4 (1892): 387–91

There are some questions absurd to ask and ridiculous to answer; but as most questions propounded are of this kind, sensible men treat them with generous toleration, upon the theory that error cannot long prosper if reason will take the trouble to combat it. People of superficial intelligence would have no occupation if they could not ask questions, which busy and thoughtful people must answer, or witness the triumph of error and humbug and the multitude's worship of them.

Will the Afro-American return to Africa? This question has been asked regularly for more than half a century by people of one sort and another; but, since the war of the rebellion, in the thoughts of some people, especially those engaged in foreign mission work, it has been stereotyped, like the "Jobject!" of Congressman William Steele Holman,[1] for emergent use.

The story is told of three London tailors, who once got off in a corner by themselves and solemnly resolved that they were the people of Great Britain. It was a glorious moment in their lives. That action, silly from every view point, made them famous; and most that we do is an appeal to posterity. Since they lived, resolved and died (even tailors die!), a great many people have laughed at their silliness, but imitated their example.

A handful of people, who imagine that they control the matter entirely, insist that the Afro-American must, will, shall return to Africa. They will not listen to any argument. They will not be moved by any appeal to reason, to facts as stubborn as fate, to barriers as insurmountable as the Alps over which Napoleon climbed into the camp of astonished Austrians. What is the use, these good people contend, of reaching a decision, if you are not going to die by it? Even so must have reasoned the three tailors of Tooley Street. If the Afro-American was not such a stubborn creature, entirely devoted to worship of the flesh-pots of the United States, bent upon questioning the disposition to be made of him by philanthropists and other kindly disposed people, he would act upon the decision that he must go and begin the pilgrimage immediately, regardless of his best interests. The people who insist that we shall go back to Africa are really good people. They mean well, most intermeddlers do, but they are both imprudent and impudent. They have never been to Africa; they do not know anything about the country or its people. They look at the situation from one point of view, and we look at it from another. They will not understand that dreams are dreams, and that facts are facts. They would not be philanthropists if they did. As they spend most of their time thinking for others, often at a comfortable salary, they will not understand why others should bother to think for themselves. And in all sorts of quarters just now, the greatest surprise is manifested because the Afro-American is demonstrating that he has any mind whatever and can use it for thinking purposes. It nearly takes their breath (and occupation, too) away.

Ever since the American Colonization Society[2] was organized, more than a half century ago, for the purpose of accommodating those Afro-Americans who wanted to return to Africa, the question of Afro-American colonization has occupied more or less of the public attention. It was a dream of Henry Clay,[3] who was opposed to slavery, and of Abraham Lincoln,[4] who did not believe that the Afro-American could live here as a freeman, that colonization would solve the problem. Perhaps it would have done so, if the Afro-American, before and since the war, had not set his face against it, as the devil is said to set his against holy water. He would not have it; he will not have it; and all the philanthropists and other good people who want to have it, having decided that he must have it, are simply horrified, cast down, at their wits' end, because of it. They have spent millions of money and years of honest toil, in attempting to put their decision into something they could "point to with pride," and of which they could exultantly exclaim, "I told you so!" but Liberia is all that they have brought forth. I do not wish to be understood as in any way underrating Liberia as a government. There is not enough of it, perhaps. I simply emphasize the fact here, that if the dreams of those who are responsible for its existence had been such as they anticipated and predicted, the country would to-day contain a million or more Afro-Americans, instead of the handful that it does contain. Instead of being an infant in population, it would be a giant. The Afro-American has simply refused to go to Liberia as a race; and when he has gone as an individual, he has, in many instances, returned by the next steamer, as my good friend Bishop Turner[5] is said to have done, although he has been anxious for twenty years for an opportunity to die there.

The Afro-American has reasoned, that if fifteen millions of Europeans have, since 1820, deemed it wise and advantageous to come to the Untied States, it would be wise and advantageous for him to remain here. What was good enough for the oppressed and starving peasants of Europe and the peons of China, was good enough for him, despite the arguments of those who had decided that he must go. This is one view of the matter, and, perhaps, an important one, to a thorough understanding of the colonization failure. Men do not usually run away from opportunities which the rest of mankind are rushing forward to enjoy. The Afro-American is just like other people in this respect. Is he unlike other people in any respect?

Now, what are some of the reasons why Afro-Americans have refused to go to Africa in the past, and have no intention of going in the future? Affecting to believe that there are no reasons against going, the philanthropists and other good people who insist that we must go, will hardly be able to contain themselves when they discover that they have been slumbering in the daylight.

(1) Afro-Americans are not Africans. The slave trade between the United States and Africa ceased in 1808. Since that time a few stragglers have come here, but, in the main, the accessions have been too inconsiderable to enter into calculation at all. In consequence of this, Afro-Americans know, practically, nothing about Africa, and take only a sentimental interest in it and its people. They have forgotten the language of the country and abandoned the religion of its people. They have thrown off all heathenish practices.

(2) Africa is a country without an organized government, an accepted religion, and a uniform language. In a different article from this, I have said that habitat, language and religion prescribe a man's nationality and fix his citizenship.[6] If Africa had a regular government, a great many of us might seek its protection. Civilized men don't abandon organized government for chaos. The population of Africa is supposed to be 100,000,000; the inhabitants speak as many languages as there are tribes. Now, if every one of the 8,000,000 Afro-Americans should go to Africa, would they swallow up the 100,000,000 natives, or would they be swallowed up? Jonah could not swallow the whale, and, therefore, the whale swallowed Jonah.

(3) What assurance have Afro-Americans that they would not starve to death in a country without organized industries, or be slaughtered by hostile natives, or die from the ravages of climatic diseases? Some who have spied out the land relate that each one of these hoodoos has a tooth as sharp as a serpent's, and about as deadly. People go to a new country to better their condition; not to starve or be slaughtered by accommodating natives or an inhospitable climate. Many of these disadvantages will be overcome in time; but they will be overcome by Europeans, with home governments and fabulous wealth behind them. European rule in Africa is no more advantageous then the rule of descendants of Europeans in the United States; and wherever the European goes in Africa, he subjects or exterminates the natives. In the organized European governments in Africa, they are barred out.

(4) Afro-Americans feel that the United States is their country, and that they have as much right to enjoy its advantages as have others of their fellow-citizens. They have labored to build up its grandeur; they have fought and died to defend its honor and to perpetuate its integrity; they own a vast volume of and personal wealth here, which they have acquired by infinite industry and economy; they have a heritage in the government and in the soil, consecrated by the bones of their dead, which have no price and can be purchased with no money; and they find that, in the condition of freedom, their position is growing better and more secure every year, due, mainly, to the development of a more self-reliant and self-supporting manhood and womanhood. While the surplus population of all civilized governments are given a cordial and pressing invitation to come here and enjoy the wealth of our soil and the liberality of our institutions, Afro-Americans cannot understand why they should have a cordial and pressing invitation given to them to betake themselves out of the country. Instead of accepting the invitation as a compliment, they regard it as an insult. If they do not always

proclaim it from the housetops, it is because they consider silence to be the most sarcastic form of contempt. That they should be asked, seriously, to leave a country they had enriched with their toil and defended with their lives, and that grave Senators in the Congress should propose that public money should be placed at their disposal to expedite their self-expatriation, seems to them insult so glaring as to relieve them of the necessity of organized protest. Such baseness carries upon its face a sufficient condemnation and rebuke. It is like asking a coequal heir to abandon his portion of the estate, in order that there may be absolute harmony in the division of the benefaction.

I think these reasons are sufficient to show why Afro-Americans do not, should not, and will not return to Africa.

The sentiment that the Afro-American should return to Africa is by no means general. Far from it. The great mass of our fellow-citizens would oppose any proposition intended to coerce us into leaving the country, if any such was contemplated or proposed. They rightly believe we are old enough to decide the question of residence for ourselves; but a few people, bent upon doing the same thing, can make a great noise. A small spark, dropped in a cow-shed, started a fire that destroyed the greater part of Chicago. And as the three tailors of Tooley Street were convinced that they were the people of England, so a few people in the United States have always presumed to speak for all the people upon questions affecting Afro-Americans. So persistent and ululative have they been that many have accepted the false prophets to be the Simon-pure articles; but the whole race-question in the United States has reached a stage where the Afro-American resents the assumption that he has no tongue, no voice, and no brains in his head. The good people who persist, annually, in getting off in a corner by themselves and resolving for Afro-Americans may delude and impose upon themselves, but the rest of mankind laugh at them.

Over and above the reasons already given to show that Afro-Americans will not return to Africa, as a whole, stands the further reason that it would be a physical impossibility to do anything of the sort. Enough ships could not be put into commission, without demoralizing the commerce of the world, to transport, annually, the natural increase of the Afro-American population. A statistician has been at the pains of demonstrating this fact.

When the question of expatriating Afro-Americans was being discussed in the Congress, a remarkable feature was made prominent. Most of the leading newspapers in the Southern States opposed the proposition and characterized it as being unwise, the consummation of which would disorganize and demoralize the entire industrial system of the South. A great many people, who cannot sleep because of the presence of the Afro-American among them, will not take the trouble to ascertain that the Afro-American is the backbone of the labor force of the South, and that if he should fold his hands and sit down for a week the wheels of Southern industry would cease to turn for that length of time, and that millions of wealth would, in consequence, stand idle throughout the Republic. But what do such people care about facts? Humbug is their stock-in-trade.

Will the Afro-American return to Africa?

He will not.

I will not here enter into a discussion of the missionary question. In the years to come, when we shall not need every decent missionary that we manufacture for home consumption, we will contribute our proper share of noble men and noble women, and of our abundance, to the evangelization of Africa.

Notes

1. William Steele Holman (1822–1897) was an Indiana Democratic representative from 1859 to 1865, 1867 to 1877, and 1881 to 1895.

2. The American Colonization Society (ACS) was formed in 1817 to send free African Americans to Africa as an alternative to emancipation. In 1822, the Society established on the west coast of Africa a colony that in 1847 became the independent nation of Liberia. By 1867, the Society had sent more than thirteen thousand emigrants. For more information on the ACS, see Amos J. Beyon, *The American Colonization Society and the Creation of the Liberian State* (Lanham, Md.: University Press of America, 1991); Floyd J. Miller, *The Search for a Black Nationality: Black Emigration and Colonization, 1787–1863* (Urbana: University of Illinois Press, 1975); Edwin S. Redkey, *Black Exodus: Black Nationalist and Back-to-Africa Movements, 1890–1910* (New Haven, Conn.: Yale University Press, 1969); and Claude A. Clegg, *The Price of Liberty: African Americans and the Making of Liberia* (Chapel Hill: University of North Carolina Press, 2004).

3. Henry Clay (1777–1852) was a senator and representative from Kentucky. He became known as the Great Compromiser for his ability to find compromise between the North and the South on the issue of slavery, especially in 1820 and 1850. Clay was an early supporter of colonization; see Clegg, *Price of Liberty*.

4. For information on Lincoln and colonization, see Abraham Lincoln, "Eulogy on Henry Clay," July 6, 1852; "Speech on the Kansas-Nebraska Act," October 16, 1954; "Speech on the Dred Scott Decision," June 26, 1857; "First Debate with Stephen A. Douglas," August 21, 1858; "First Annual Message to Congress," December 3, 1861; "Message to Congress," April 16, 1862; "Appeal to Border-State Representatives for Compensated Emancipation," July 12, 1862; "Address on Colonization to a Committee of Colored Men," August 14, 1862; "Preliminary Emancipation Proclamation," September 22, 1862; and

"Annual Message to Congress," December 1, 1862. See, Abraham Lincoln, *Speeches and Writings, 1832–1858*, ed. Don E. Fehrenbacher (New York: Library of America, 1989) and Abraham Lincoln, *Speeches and Writings, 1858–1865*, ed. Don E. Fehrenbacher (New York: Library of America, 1989). For more on Lincoln and colonization, see Lerone Bennett, *Forced into Glory: Abraham Lincoln's White Dream* (Chicago: Johnson Publishing Co., 2000).

5. Henry McNeal Turner (1834–1915), a bishop in the African Episcopal Church (AME) in Georgia after the Civil War, was briefly elected to the Georgia legislature during Reconstruction and later advocated that African Americans emigrate to Africa. For more on Turner and his emigrationist ideas, see Redkey, *Black Exodus;* and Stephen A. Angell, *Bishop Henry McNeal Turner and African-American Religion in the South* (Knoxville: University of Tennessee Press, 1992).

6. Fortune wrote on this subject many times. In this volume see "Race Absorption," chapter 28.

35

The Nationalization of Africa

Fortune delivered the following address before the Congress on Africa, held under the auspices of the Stewart Missionary Foundation for Africa of Gammon Theological Seminary, December 13–15, 1895. The general purpose of the conference was to promote interest among African Americans for missionary work in Africa. In his address Fortune expressed greater support for African American missionary work than he had done in his critique of Bishop Turner and his emigrationist plans in 1892 (see chap. 34). At the same time, the editor was critical of economical exploitation of the continent by European powers and warned that something needed to be done to prevent the spread of Europe's control, but Fortune also expressed a belief that colonization would provide some benefits for Africa. Finally, Fortune applied some of his "absorption" philosophy expressed in his 1893 articles in the *Los Angeles Times* and *New York Herald* and later in his "Race Absorption" article (chap. 28) to the continent of Africa. The editor predicted that, although European colonization might have some benefits, ultimately the whites who were colonizing Africa would begin "to be absorbed and assimilated by the vast black majority." This was the destiny of the white minority of Africa, explained Fortune, as was the ultimate assimilation and absorption of blacks by white America. "I know," said Fortune, "that to many this is an abhorrent view of the question, but we are dealing with the philosophy of recorded history and the invariable laws of human conduct and not with the prejudices of men."

The Nationalization of Africa —in *Africa and the American Negro*, ed. J.W.E. Bowen, 199–204 (Atlanta: Gammon Theology Seminary, 1896)

Mr. President, and Ladies and Gentlemen of the Congress:

"The proper study of mankind is man."[1] Man is the simplest and yet the most mysterious mechanism in nature. His physical, mental and spiritual attributes have been the most interesting of his studies in all ages. He has been and he is now, in large part, as much of an enigma to himself as the sphinx, in the sands of old Egypt, reared by black giants of Africa when the world was young, and when color was not the test of manhood or of genius, is now to the students of ethnology and philology. He who contributes in any way to the enlargement of our knowledge of the supreme subject of moment and of interest is a benefactor of his race. That we know as much of the temple in which the Creator has placed the image of himself—grand, mysterious, magnificent—that we know as much of his past history as we do, and of the empires he has reared, and which have long since relapsed into the dust from which they proceeded; that we have been able to follow him from the tower of Babel on the plains of Shinar through the blackness and the mists that envelop human hope and aspiration before we possessed "the letters Cadmus gave,"[2] into the remotest corners of the earth, placing metes and bounds, and to his rise and to his decline and fall, is due as much to the patrons of the arts, the sciences and of letters, as to those who have toiled in the darkness and in the light, weaving the long chain of ratiocination which links the remotest past to the living present, clinching the poet's thought that "All are but parts of one stupendous whole."[3]

As "the heirs of all the ages," as the legatees of the accumulated wealth of sacrifice and of labor which have built up our splendid consensus of knowledge, we stand here to-day with the map of the earth unfolded before us, upon which there are but few black spots into which the explorer has not penetrated and which the philosophical historian has not illuminated as to its people and as to what they have done and have not done. Where our ancestors groped in ignorance and doubt we now walk in the fullness of knowledge and the self-assurance that it gives.

The unity of the human race is no longer a disputed question. That "one-touch of nature makes the whole world kin"[4] is as universally accepted, as the theory that the sun is a stationary orb and that the earth is round. Color of the skin, texture of hair, differences of language and of habitation avail nothing against the demonstration that all mankind proceeded from the same cause and will ultimate in the same effect; that their origin and their destiny are as interlocked and as inseparable as life and death. When so much has been ascertained, when so much has been accepted, when so much shall have become the rule of conduct of individuals and of aggregated societies, of man to man and of government to government, we may rest in the assurance that the dreams of Edward Bellamy, in some remote æon of time, become facts in the intercourse of mankind. The dreams of genius often become realities in "the wreck of matter and the crush of worlds,"[5] in the discoveries of science and of philosophy, in the passing away of old beliefs and of old forms, and in the establishment, as a result of such transformations, of higher ideals of living and of government. All being is but the aspiration of the human soul after perfection. In the savage and in the highest type of civilized man, this philosophy will be found to have been, and to be, exemplified. It has been the touchstone of all the progress which has been made in every department of human effort, from the Chaldean of old, reading the stars, to Benjamin Franklin,[6] harnessing the lightning and Robert Fulton[7] compressing the steam, so that the twain have become the Archimedean lever that unlocks the doors that conceal the treasures of the earth and of the heavens.

The map of Africa is no longer a Chinese puzzle. Its geographical mysteries have been solved. Its mighty lakes and rivers have been traced to their source, and fiction and cupidity have unlocked hordes of treasure by the side of which that of King Solomon's mines was as the vastness of the Atlantic's waste of waters to the smallest stream that, like a silver thread, wanders down the mountain side and sighs itself away into the sands of the desert. Railroads are spanning its immense distances, steamboats are navigating its water-ways, and the electric wire has brought it into talking distance with Europe and America. Its limitless agricultural and mineral resources are being developed for the comfort and the happiness of mankind. Vast States have sprung into being, as if by magic, controlled by European colonists, so that already a South African confederacy has worked its way into the brain of Cecil Rhodes, whose empire is cemented with more human blood and tears than the East Indian empire wrenched into the British Government by the crimes of Lord Clive[8] and Warren Hastings.[9]

Never in the history of mankind has a continent been so rapidly subdued and its waste places made the habitation of civilized governments and its savage inhabitants brought into contact and under the control of civilization. More has been accomplished along these lines in Africa in the past quarter of a century than was accomplished by European colonists in America in the first one hundred and fifty years of their desperate struggles here to subdue the aborigines. Steam and electricity and gunpowder are responsible for this phenomenon. They are conquering forces against which no other forces can prevail. The savage, with his primitive weapons of defense, falls before them as the mists vanish before the all-powerful and all-searching rays of the sun. He must relinquish his sovereignty and his wealth of all sorts when these forces confront him. The heroism of the Ashantee or the Zulu warrior, fighting in defense of his fireside and his country, is wasted when his assagai is opposed to the maxim gun or winchester rifle, or even the old Colt's revolver. We have seen this in the subjugation of the North American Indians, and we are now witnessing it in the case of the Africans.

The extent to which the continent of Africa has been spoliated and delimitated by Europeans is shown in the fact that of 11,360,000 square miles of territory, all of it has been absorbed or is claimed except the 9,700 square miles controlled by Liberia on the west coast. France and Great Britain have already made efforts to absorb this residium, and we have no reason to suppose that when they get ready to absorb it and resolve it into a colony they will not do so. In the philosophy of our civilization might makes right in practice, however much we may disclaim it in theory. In this, as in many other of the Christian virtues, our precept and our example are radically at war.

If the conquest of Africa shall proceed in the next seventy-five years as it has done in the past twenty-five, the whole continent will be as completely under European control, after the lapse of a century, physically and mentally and morally, as it is possible for conquerors to impose their conditions upon the conquered. The vast population of Africa will be brought under Christian influences in new forms of government and habits of thought and of conduct. The whole life of the people will be revolutionized. Ancient beliefs and superstitions and tribal relations and dissimilarity of vernaculars will, in the course of time, be transformed entirely. The demoralizing heterogeneousness which now prevails over the whole continent will give place to a pervading homogeneity in language, in religion, and in government.

WHAT WILL BE THE RESULT IF AFRICANS ARE BROUGHT UNDER CHRISTIAN INFLUENCE?

The physical and mental forces now dissipated in tribal wars, in savage methods of industry, will give place to peaceful administration of government and to concentrated methods of industry. The nationalization of the continent will proceed along these lines as naturally and as surely as did that of Great Britain and Ireland, and as did the Germanic States under the masterful direction of Kaiser William,[10] Prince Bismarck[11] and Count von Moltke.[12] Experience, as the great Virginian proclaimed, is the only light by which we can be guided in a matter so speculative. We can reason only by analogy. Human development proceeds along a straight line.

A common habitation, a common language, a common religion, are the necessary bases of homogeneous citizenship and of autonomous government. They are not possible without these. No government has successfully prevailed without them. It may be that Rome, whose legends overran the world, failed in the end because of the too rapid absorption of alien races possessing dissimilar languages and religions. Absorption was too rapid for proper assimilation, and the mistress of the world perforce died of strangulation. And what a fall was there when "the Niobe of nations,"[13] borne down by the massiveness of its own strength, torn by dissensions from within and surrounded by barbarous hordes from without, her proud eagle, which had circled over the nations of the earth, plucked of his pinions, lay prostrate in the dust, even as Milton's[14] arch fiend which had braved the host of heaven. When so great a giant among the nations of the earth can fall to so low an estate as to furnish the nations of the earth with bootblacks and fruit-venders and organ-grinders, what nation, what people can hope to escape the handwriting on the wall however vaunting their pride, however herculean their strength? Pride goes before a fall, and death lurks in the frame where health is accounted a heritage. "Oh, why should the spirit of mortal be proud!"[15]

The surface of the earth is capable of sustaining so many people. The population of the earth to-day is very little greater than it was a century ago. It will be but a little greater a century hence than it is now. The pressure of population upon subsistence is insistent and relentless. The supreme struggle of mankind is one of life, of subsistence, of preventing death by starvation or exposure. All other objects of life are subordinated to this one. It is the sleepless agent of colonization. It has penetrated the utmost bounds of the globe. It has wrenched from the weak their fertile valleys and luxuriant hillsides; and when they have protested, when they have resisted, it has enslaved them or cut their throats. It has invented all weapons of defense and of offense. It has invented all the machinery to increase the productivity of effort at a minimum cost, of whatever sort.

It was, therefore, but natural that the congested population of Europe should seek an outlet in North and in South America and the islands of the sea and in Asia and in the Australias; and it is but natural that the same congested population, in the desperate pursuit of something to eat and something to wear, should now be seeking an outlet in the virgin continent of Africa, whose vast areas of territory and hordes of population have been the despair of geographers and ethnologists and philologists and antiquarians alike. The book of mystery having been unlocked, mankind has made indecent haste to master its contents. No fear of burning sun and expansive wastes of deserts and savage beasts and black men, the fabled genii of the Arabian Nights' entertainment, has deterred them. They are plunging into the forests and the sandy deserts, braving the deadly miasmas, more fatal than "an army with banners,"[16] fearful that the pearl of great price shall escape them. If we are to give credence to the doleful croakings of many ravens in this country, we should stand in wonderment and awe at the spectacle of caravan after caravan of white men and white women, the flower of Europe's children, winding in a long procession into the black continent, ultimately to impose their civilization upon the continent and to mingle their blood with that of the 300,000,000 children of the sun, the despised black children of the family of races. Their conduct should be inexplicable to these ravens, who insist that black blood and white blood will not mix, although it has so far done so in the West Indies and the United States, that these countries have a yellow streak running through them so thick and so long that only those hopelessly inflicted with blindness fail to see it and to properly account for its existence and to deduce from it the fact that reason, sympathy, affection, and not the color of the skin or texture of the hair, are the tests of the brotherhood, of the unity, of the human race.

"Skins may differ, but affection?
Dwells in black and white the same."[17]

Europe will continue to pour its hungry and ambitious and adventurous children into the continent of Africa in the future as in the past, but there will come a time when self-preservation will dictate a restriction or cessation of the infusion. But even before that time shall have been reached, the white races of Europe who are now subduing savage tribes and laying the foundation of empires upon the ruins of savage villages and imposing their yoke upon the natives, their language and their religions and their forms of governmental administration and their system of commerce and industry—even now the European minority in Africa are beginning to be absorbed and assimilated by the vast black majority. This is inevitable. A minority race in contact with a majority race is doomed to absorption and assimilation. It is the primal element of nationalization. The minority race must exterminate the majority or be exterminated or absorbed by it. This is an iron law. It has been verified in the history of every race and of every nation. It will be verified in the history of Africa. It will be impossible for France to recover Alsace and Lorraine because the population has become Germanized in blood and language and religion. The minority Frank has been absorbed and assimilated by the majority Teuton, even as the invading and conquering Saxon minority was by the conquered Angle majority, and even as the imported and enslaved African black is being absolved by the heterogeneous white races of the United States. The inevitable destiny of the European whites in Africa is absorption and assimilation by the African blacks as surely as the ultimate destiny of the African blacks in the United States is absorption and assimilation by the American whites. I know that to many this is an abhorrent view of the question, but we are dealing with the philosophy of recorded history and the invariable laws of human conduct and not with the prejudices of men. Men are governed by the laws regnant in their environment. They do not make the laws; they cannot control them. If they do not like them, they are free to take themselves into a more congenial atmosphere. If the whites of America did not want to absorb the blacks, they should have left them in Africa; if the European whites do not want to be absorbed and assimilated by the blacks they should remain out of Africa. The matter is a very easy one to decide before the first step is taken; beyond that point it is controlled by "the divinity that shapes our ends, rough hew them as we may."[18] The rigid laws and rules and regulations already adopted by the English, the Germans, the French and the Belgians in Africa to keep the natives in their place will prove as ineffectual to their purpose as such laws and rules and regulations now prove in the United States. The amalgamation of the European in Africa will proceed as surely towards the development of a national type of man as the amalgamation of alien races has proceeded in the United States for two centuries towards the same end. Here we absorb and assimilate the Indian, the European, the Asiatic and the African and grow strong in mental and physical prowess in the process. Indeed, our national strength is to be found in the homogeneity of its heterogeneous race elements, in its common language and in its common religion. The nationalization of Africa will proceed along the same lines as that of the United States is proceeding. What manner of man will be evolved from the process, what sort of national power he will represent, we are already able to judge, inferentially, by the results being worked out in the nationalization of the people of the United States. The intermingling of so many race elements must work for national and spiritual and material strength in Africa as it has done in all the instances with which history has concerned itself.

I believe that the nationalization of Africa will be along English lines, as that of the United States, in its language, from the basic point of view, in its system of government and in its religion. The English language is the strongest of all languages, the most elastic in its structure, the most comprehensive in its use as a vehicle of human thought and expression. The English system of civil government is the best that has been devised, because it allows the greatest possible freedom to the citizen consistent with the safety of the state. The Christian religion is destined to supplant all other religious systems of belief, because it is the best code of moral philosophy ever given to man as an inspiration or as a development, an evolution of the social life of a people.

The English-speaking people are to-day the strongest force in Africa, from the European point of view. They will disappoint the truth of history if they do not ultimately effect a confederation of all the other European forces, including the native forces comprised in each of them. They will be forced into this federation in self-defense, as the American colonists were. History repeats itself. The nationalization of the African confederation which is a foregone conclusion from the facts in the case, will be the first step toward bringing the whole continent under one system of government. Language and religion may not produce a homogeneous people, as stated by the Hon. John H. Smithe[19] yesterday, but habitat, language, and religion will do it in Africa, as they are doing it in the United States.

It is written in the Holy Book that Ethiopia shall stretch forth her hand to God. Is it in the power of men to make of no effect the divine prophecy? Perish the thought. There shall yet be evolved out of the conflicting race elements on the continent of Africa a civilization whose glory and whose splendor and whose strength shall eclipse all others that now are, or that have gone before into the shadows, locked in "the double night of ages,"[20] from which no traveler returns in gladness or in sorrow.

Notes

1. Alexander Pope (1688–1744), *An Essay on Man*.
2. Thomas Bulfinch (1796–1867), "Cadmus—The Myrimidons," in *Bulfinch's Mythology, Age of Fable; or Stories of Gods and Heroes*.
3. Pope, *Essay*.
4. William Shakespeare (1564–1616), *Troilus and Cressida*.
5. Jones Very (1831–80), "Lines on Mount Auburn."
6. Benjamin Franklin (1706–1790) was a scientist, inventor, and diplomat, also one of the Founding Fathers of the United States.

7. Robert Fulton (1765–1815) was an American engineer credited with developing the first steam-powered ship for commercial use.

8. Robert Lord Clive (1725–1774) was a British statesman and military general who established military supremacy of the East India Company in southern India.

9. Warren Hastings (1732–1818) was the first governor general of British India, 1773–1786.

10. William Frederick Louis, William I (1797–1888), ruled Germany from 1861 to 1888 as king of Prussia and German emperor.

11. Otto Eduard Leopold von Bismarck (1815–1898) was a German diplomat and statesman who is credited with unifying Germany.

12. Graf von Moltke (1800–1891) was a German military leader.

13. George Gordon, Lord Byron (1788–1824), "Rome."

14. John Milton (1608–1674) was a British poet, known for his epic poem *Paradise Lost*.

15. William Knox (1789–1825), "Oh, Why Should the Spirit of Mortal Be Proud?"

16. Song of Solomon 6:4 and 6:10.

17. William Cowper (1731–1800), "The Negro's Complaint."

18. William Shakespeare (1564–1616), *Hamlet*.

19. John Henry Smythe (1844–1908) was minister to Liberia, 1878–1881, and editor of the Richmond, Virginia-based *Reformer*. See John H. Smythe, "The African in Africa, and the African in America," in *Africa and the American Negro*, ed. J.W.E. Bowen (Atlanta, Ga.: Gammon Theology Seminary, 1896), 69–84.

20. George Gordon, Lord Byron (1788–1824), "Childe Harold's Pilgrimage."

Postscript

Who refused to hold up his hands? Who refused his wiser youthful leadership? Who withheld the money and bread and clothes due him and his suffering family? We did. Shall we crucify him today for his venality, his weakness, his unbridled passions, his tottering over-aged manhood? No, rather let us bow our heads, for his shame and failure are ours. The lash that goads him, goads us, O Unfortunate!

W.E.B. Du Bois, "The Lash," *Horizon* 1 (May 1907): 5

Selected Bibliography of Fortune's Writings

The following bibliography is a selection of T. Thomas Fortune's writings. Omitted from the list are the numerous editorials he wrote for a number of publications over his forty-seven year career as a journalist and spokesman for the race. These include signed and unsigned editorials in African American publications such as the *New York Globe, New York Freeman, New York Age, Philadelphia Tribune, Colored American Magazine, Amsterdam News, Norfolk Journal and Guide,* and *Negro World* and in white publications such as the *New York Sun* and the *Boston Transcript.* Fortune also sent many signed letters and articles to a number of publications throughout the years, including among others the *Boston Globe, New York Times, New York Herald, Washington Post, Los Angeles Times, Atlanta Constitution, St. Paul Appeal, Wichita Searchlight, Colored American, Cleveland Gazette,* and the *Washington Bee.*

The writings below are listed in alphabetical order. The asterisks preceding the titles indicate those published writings of T. Thomas Fortune that appear in this collection.

Books and Pamphlets

Fortune, Timothy Thomas. 1884. *Black and White; Land, Labor, and Politics in the South.* New York: Arno Press, 1968.

———. *Dreams of Life; Miscellaneous Poems.* 1905. Miami: Mnemosyne, 1969.

*———. *The Negro in Politics: Some Pertinent Reflections on the Past and Present Political Status of the Afro-American, Together with a Cursory Investigation into the Motives Which Actuate Partisan Organizations.* New York: Ogilvie and Rowntree, 1886.

Articles

Fortune, T. Thomas. "Abraham Lincoln." *Colored American Magazine* 4, no. 3 (1902): 253.

———. "The African in Our Politics." *Frank Leslie's Illustrated Newspaper* (1890): 122.

*———. "The Afro-American." *Arena* 3, no. 6 (1890): 115–18.

———. "The Afro-American as He Is." *Open Court* 4, no. 161 (1890): 2535–38.

———. "The Afro-American League." *AME Church Review* 7, no. 1 (1890): 2–6.

———. "Afro-American or Negro?" *Outlook* 62, no. 6 (1899): 359.

———. "The Afro-American Political Giant with the Strength of a Child." *Colored American Magazine* 9, no. 12 (1905): 675–79.

*———. "Are We Brave Men or Cowards?" *Monthly Review* 1, no. 6 (1894): 178–81.

*———. "Civil Rights and Social Privileges." *AME Church Review* 2, no. 3 (1886): 119–31.
———. "The Democratic Return to Power—Its Effect?" *AME Church Review* 1, no. 3 (1885): 219–21.
*———. "False Theory of Education Cause of Race Demoralization." *Colored American Magazine* 7, no. 7 (1904): 473–78.
———. "The Filipino [Part I]." *Voice of the Negro* 1, no. 3 (1904): 93–99.
———. "The Filipino [Part II]." *Voice of the Negro* 1, no. 5 (1904): 199–203.
———. "The Filipino—across Luzon [Part III]." *Voice of the Negro* 1, no. 6 (1904): 240–46.
———. "The Free Coinage of Silver." *AME Church Review* 10, no. 1 (1893): 101–12.
———. "Good Indians and Good Niggers." *Independent* 51 (1899): 1689.
———. "Haytian Revolutions." *Voice of the Negro* 1, no. 4 (1904): 138–42.
———. "How Can the Afro-American Race Help Itself in Constructive Directions?" *Colored American Magazine* 11, no. 6 (1906): 404–5.
*———. "Immorality of Southern Suffrage Legislation." *Independent* 50 (1898): 1576–77.
———. "The Individual as the Unit of Social Power." *AME Zion Quarterly Review* 7, no. 1 (1897): 9–14.
———. "Industrial Education: Will It Solve the Negro Problem?" *Colored American Magazine* 7, no. 1 (1904): 13, 15–17.
———. "Intermarriage and Natural Selection." *Colored American Magazine* 16, no. 6 (1909): 379–81.
———. Introduction to *Black Belt Diamonds: Gems from the Speeches, Addresses, and Talks to Students of Booker T. Washington*. Selected and arranged by Victoria Earle Matthews; Introduction by T. Thomas Fortune. 1898. New York: Negro Universities Press, 1969.
———. "Is the White South Civilized?" *AME Zion Quarterly Review* 1, no. 4 (1891): 283–89.
*———. "The Kind of Education the Afro-American Most Needs." *Southern Workman* 27, no. 1 (1898): 4–6.
———. *The Kind of Education the Afro-American Most Needs*. Tuskegee, Ala.: Tuskegee Institute Print, 1898.
*———. "The Latest Color Line." *Liberia Bulletin*, no. 11 (1897): 60–65.
———. "Mr. Douglass' Peculiar Greatness." *AME Church Review* 12, no. 1 (1895): 108–13.
*———. "Mob Law in the South." *Independent* 49, no. 2537 (1897): 900–901.
———. "Movement of the Afro-American Population from the Southern States." *AME Church Review* 33, no. 3 (1917): 127–30.
*———. "The Nationalization of Africa." In *Africa and the American Negro*, edited by J.W.E. Bowen, 199–204. Atlanta: Gammon Theology Seminary, 1896.
*———. "The Negro's Place in American Life at the Present Day." In *The Negro Problem; a Series of Articles by Representative American Negroes of To-Day*, edited by Booker T. Washington, 213–34. New York: J. Plott, 1903.
———. "New Labor Forces at the South." *Open Court* 5, no. 219 (1891): 1–2.

———. "Old Afro-American and New Negro Journalism." *Favorite Magazine* 9 (1920): 477.

———. "On Syndicating News." *AME Church Review* 8 (1891): 231–42.

———. "Organize! Plan Set Forth by the President and Secretary for Afro-American Council Work." In *Afro-American Council*, edited by Cyrus Field Adams. Cleveland, 1902.

———. "Politics in the Philippine Islands." *Independent* 55 (1903): 2266–68.

———. "Prof. James Bryce's Prejudice against African and Polynesian Races." *AME Church Review* 15, no. 1 (1898): 503–12.

*———. "The Quick and the Dead." *AME Church Review* 32, no. 4 (1916): 247–50.

*———. "Race Absorption." *AME Church Review* 18, no. 1 (1901): 54–66.

———. "The Race Problem: The Negro Will Solve It." *Belford's Magazine* 5 (1890): 489–95.

———. "The Republican Party Platform." *AME Church Review* 9, no. 2 (1892): 126–32.

*———. "The Voteless Citizen." *Voice of the Negro* 1, no. 9 (1904): 397–402.

———. "What Does the White South Expect of the Black South?" *Colored American Magazine* 11, no. 6 (1906): 393–97.

———. "What a Magazine Should Be." *Colored American Magazine* 7, no. 6 (1904): 393–95.

———."What Should Be the Negro's Attitude in Politics?" In *Twentieth Century Negro Literature or a Cyclopedia of Thought on the Vital Topics Relating to the American Negro*, edited by D. W. Culp, 227–31. Atlanta: J. L. Nichols, 1902.

*———. "Who Are We: Afro-Americans, Colored People, or Negroes?" *Voice of the Negro* 3, no. 3 (1906): 194–98.

*———. "Whose Problem Is This?" *AME Church Review* 11, no. 2 (1894): 253–61.

———. "Why We Organized a National Afro-American League." *Afro-American Budget* 1, no. 8 (1890): 231–40.

*———. "Will the Afro-American Return to Africa?" *AME Church Review* 8, no. 4 (1892): 387–91.

Selected Bibliography for Further Reading

Abramowitz, Jack. "Accommodation and Militance in Negro Life, 1876–1916." Ph.D. diss., Columbia University, 1950.

Adeleke, Tunde. *UnAfrican Americans: Nineteenth-Century Black Nationalists and the Civilizing Mission*. Lexington: University Press of Kentucky, 1998.

Alexander, Ann F. *Race Man: The Rise and Fall of the "Fighting Editor," John Mitchell, Jr.* Charlottesville: University of Virginia Press, 2002.

Anderson, James D. *The Education of Blacks in the South, 1860–1935*. Chapel Hill: University of North Carolina Press, 1988.

Angell, Stephen W. *Bishop Henry McNeal Turner and African-American Religion in the South*. Knoxville: University of Tennessee Press, 1992.

Ayers, Edward L. *The Promise of the New South: Life after Reconstruction*. New York: Oxford University Press, 1992.

———. *Vengeance and Justice: Crime and Punishment in the 19th-Century American South*. New York: Oxford University Press, 1984.

Baker, Lee D. *From Savage to Negro: Anthropology and the Construction of Race, 1896–1954*. Berkeley: University of California Press, 1998.

Bauerlein, Mark. *Negrophobia: A Race Riot in Atlanta, 1906*. San Francisco: Encounter Books, 2001.

Bay, Mia. *The White Image in the Black Mind: African-American Ideas about White People, 1830–1925*. New York: Oxford University Press, 2000.

Beatty, Bess. *A Revolution Gone Backward: Black Response to National Politics, 1876–1896*. New York: Greenwood Press, 1987.

Bederman, Gail. *Manliness and Civilization: A Cultural History of Gender and Race in the United States, 1880–1917*. Chicago: University of Chicago Press, 1995.

Blight, David W. *Race and Reunion: The Civil War in American Memory*. Cambridge, Mass.: Harvard University Press, 2001.

Bruce, Dickson D., Jr. *Archibald Grimké: Portrait of a Black Independent*. Baton Rouge: Louisiana State University Press, 1993.

———. *Black American Writing from the Nadir: The Evolution of a Literary Tradition, 1877–1915*. Baton Rouge: Louisiana State University Press, 1989.

Brundage, W. Fitzhugh. *Lynching in the New South: Georgia and Virginia, 1880–1930*. Urbana: University of Illinois Press, 1993.

Cecelski, David S., and Timothy B. Tyson, eds. *Democracy Betrayed: The Wilmington Race Riot of 1898 and Its Legacy*. Chapel Hill: University of North Carolina Press, 1998.

Chase, Hal Scripps. "'Honey for Friends, Stings for Enemies': William Calvin Chase and the Washington Bee, 1882–1921." Ph.D. diss., University of Pennsylvania, 1973.

Cheek, William Francis. "Forgotten Prophet: The Life of John Mercer Langston." Ph.D. diss., University of Virginia, 1961.

Crowder, Ralph L. *John Edward Bruce: Politician, Journalist, and Self-Trained Historian of the African Diaspora.* New York: New York University Press, 2004.

Dailey, Jane. *Before Jim Crow: The Politics of Race in Postemancipation Virginia.* Chapel Hill: University of North Carolina Press, 2000.

———, Glenda Elizabeth Gilmore, and Bryant Simon, eds. *Jumpin' Jim Crow: Southern Politics from Civil War to Civil Rights.* Princeton, N.J.: Princeton University Press, 2000.

Daniel, Pete. *The Shadow of Slavery: Peonage in the South, 1901–1969.* Urbana: University of Illinois Press, 1972.

Dann, Martin E., ed. *The Black Press, 1827–1890: The Quest for National Identity.* New York: Capricorn Books, 1972.

Dittmer, John. *Black Georgia in the Progressive Era, 1900–1920.* Urbana: University of Illinois Press, 1977.

Du Bois, W.E.B. 1903. *The Souls of Black Folk*, eds. David W. Blight and Robert Gooding-Williams. Boston: Bedford Books, 1997.

Factor, Robert L. *The Black Response to America: Men, Ideals, and Organization, from Frederick Douglass to the NAACP.* Reading, Mass.: Addison-Wesley, 1970.

Fishel, Leslie H., Jr. "The North and the Negro, 1865–1900." Ph.D. diss., Harvard University, 1953.

Foner, Eric. *Reconstruction: America's Unfinished Revolution, 1863–1877.* New York: Harper and Row, 1988.

Fox, Stephen R. *The Guardian of Boston: William Monroe Trotter.* New York: Atheneum, 1970.

Franklin, V. P. *Black Self-Determination: A Cultural History of the Faith of the Fathers.* Westport, Conn.: L. Hill, 1984.

Fredrickson, George M. *The Black Image in the White Mind: The Debate on Afro-American Character and Destiny, 1817–1914.* Middletown, Conn.: Wesleyan University Press, 1987.

Fullinwider, S. P. *The Mind and Mood of Black America: 20th Century Thought.* Homewood, Ill.: Dorsey Press, 1969.

Gaines, Kevin K. *Uplifting the Race: Black Leadership, Politics, and Culture in the Twentieth Century.* Chapel Hill: University of North Carolina Press, 1996.

Gaston, Paul M. *The New South Creed: A Study in Southern Mythmaking.* Baton Rouge: Louisiana State University Press, 1970.

Gatewood, Willard B., Jr. *Aristocrats of Color: The Black Elite, 1880–1920.* Bloomington: Indiana University Press, 1990.

———. *Black Americans and the White Man's Burden, 1898–1903.* Urbana: University of Illinois Press, 1975.

Giddings, Paula. *When and Where I Enter: The Impact of Black Women on Race and Sex in America.* New York: Bantam Books, 1985.

Gilmore, Glenda Elizabeth. *Gender and Jim Crow: Women and the Politics of White Su-*

premacy in North Carolina, 1896-1920. Chapel Hill: University of North Carolina Press, 1996.

Godshalk, David Fort. *Veiled Visions: The 1906 Atlanta Race Riot and the Reshaping of American Race Relations*. Chapel Hill: University of North Carolina Press, 2005.

Hahn, Steven. *A Nation under Our Feet: Black Political Struggles in the Rural South, from Slavery to the Great Migration*. Cambridge, Mass.: Belknap Press of Harvard University Press, 2003.

Hair, William Ivy. *Carnival of Fury: Robert Charles and the New Orleans Race Riot of 1900*. Baton Rouge: Louisiana State University Press, 1976.

Hale, Grace Elizabeth. *Making Whiteness: The Culture of Segregation in the South, 1890-1940*. New York: Vintage, 1998.

Harlan, Louis R. *Booker T. Washington: The Making of a Black Leader, 1856-1901*. New York: Oxford University Press, 1972.

———. *Booker T. Washington: The Wizard of Tuskegee, 1901-1915*. New York: Oxford University Press, 1983.

———. *Booker T. Washington in Perspective: Essays of Louis R. Harlan*, ed. Raymond Smock. Jackson: University Press of Mississippi, 1988.

———. *Separate and Unequal: Public School Campaigns and Racism in the Southern Seaboard States, 1901-1915*. New York: Atheneum, 1969.

Higginbotham, Evelyn Brooks. *Righteous Discontent: The Women's Movement in the Black Baptist Church, 1880-1920*. Cambridge, Mass.: Harvard University Press, 1993.

Jacobs, Sylvia M. *The African Nexus: Black American Perspectives on the European Partitioning of Africa, 1880-1920*. Westport, Conn.: Greenwood Press, 1981.

———. "Black American Perspectives on European Imperialism in Africa, 1870-1920." Ph.D. diss., Howard University, 1975.

Justesen, Benjamin R. *George Henry White: An Even Chance in the Race of Life*. Baton Rouge: Louisiana State University Press, 2001.

Kirby, Jack Temple. *Darkness at the Dawning: Race and Reform in the Progressive South*. Philadelphia: Lippincott, 1972.

Lewis, David Levering. *W.E.B. Du Bois: Biography of a Race, 1868-1919*. New York: Henry Holt, 1993.

Litwack, Leon F. *Been in the Storm So Long: The Aftermath of Slavery*. New York: Alfred A. Knopf, 1979.

———. *Trouble in Mind: Black Southerners in the Age of Jim Crow*. New York: Alfred A. Knopf, 1998.

Logan, Rayford Whittingham. *The Betrayal of the Negro: From Rutherford B. Hayes to Woodrow Wilson*. 1965. New York: Da Capo Press, 1997.

McMurry, Linda O. *To Keep the Waters Troubled: The Life of Ida B. Wells*. New York: Oxford University Press, 1998.

McPherson, James M. *The Abolitionist Legacy: From Reconstruction to the NAACP*. Princeton, N.J.: Princeton University Press, 1975.

Meier, August. *Negro Thought in America, 1880-1915: Racial Ideologies in the Age of Booker T. Washington*. Ann Arbor: University of Michigan Press, 1963.

Miller, George Mason. "'A This Worldly Mission': The Life and Career of Alexander Walters (1858–1917)." Ph.D. diss., State University of New York at Stony Brook, 1984.

Mixon, Gregory. *The Atlanta Riot: Race, Class, and Violence in a New South City*. Gainesville: University Press of Florida, 2005.

Moore, Jacqueline M. *Leading the Race: The Transformation of the Black Elite in the Nation's Capital, 1880–1920*. Charlottesville: University Press of Virginia, 1999.

Moses, Wilson J. *Alexander Crummell: A Study of Civilization and Discontent*. New York: Oxford University Press, 1989.

———. *The Golden Age of Black Nationalism, 1850–1925*. Hamden, Conn.: Archon Books, 1978.

Moss, Alfred A. *The American Negro Academy: Voice of the Talented Tenth*. Baton Rouge: Louisiana State University Press, 1981.

Newby, I. A. *Jim Crow's Defense; Anti-Negro Thought in America, 1900–1930*. Baton Rouge: Louisiana State University Press, 1965.

Penn, I. Garland. *The Afro-American Press and Its Editors*. 1891. New York: Arno Press, 1969.

Perman, Michael. *Struggle for Mastery: Disfranchisement in the South, 1888–1908*. Chapel Hill: University of North Carolina Press, 2001.

Rabinowitz, Howard N. *Race Relations in the Urban South, 1865–1890*. Athens: University of Georgia Press, 1978.

Redkey, Edwin S. *Black Exodus: Black Nationalist and Back-to-Africa Movements, 1890–1910*. New Haven, Conn.: Yale University Press, 1969.

Smith, John David, ed. *Anti-Black Thought, 1863–1925*. 11 vols. New York: Garland, 1993.

———. *Black Judas: William Hannibal Thomas and the American Negro*. Athens: University of Georgia Press, 2000.

Swan, Robert J. "Thomas McCants Stewart and the Failure of the Mission of the Talented Tenth in Black America, 1880–1923." Ph.D. diss., New York University, 1990.

Thornbrough, Emma Lou. *T. Thomas Fortune: Militant Journalist*. Chicago: University of Chicago Press, 1972.

Tindall, George B. *South Carolina Negroes, 1877–1900*. Baton Rouge: Louisiana State University Press, 1952.

Toll, William. *The Resurgence of Race: Black Social Theory from Reconstruction to the Pan-African Conferences*. Philadelphia: Temple University Press, 1979.

Washington, Booker T., ed. *The Negro Problem; A Series of Articles by Representative American Negroes of To-Day*. 1903. New York: Arno Press, 1969.

———. *Up from Slavery: An Autobiography*. 1901. Edited with introduction by W. Fitzhugh Brundage. Boston: Bedford Books, 2003.

Williamson, Joel. *The Crucible of Race: Black-White Relations in the American South since Emancipation*. New York: Oxford University Press, 1984.

Wills, David W. "Aspects of Social Thought in the African Methodist Episcopal Church, 1884–1910." Ph.D. diss., Harvard University, 1975.

Woodward, C. Vann. *Origins of the New South, 1877–1913*. Baton Rouge: Louisiana State University Press, 1951.

Index

Africa, xxxi, xxxii, 120, 131, 153, 201–2, 242, 249–50, 259–60, 261–63, 264–69, 271–78. *See also* Liberia; Sudan
Afro-American: as term, xxiv–xxv, xxxviiin50, 215–18, 249–51
Afro-American Council, xxiv, xxvii, xxviii, 94, 134, 169n1, 178n5, 180, 183n1, 187, 195
Afro-American League, xxii, xxiii, xxvii, xxix, xxxii, 94, 134–50, 153–56, 158, 180–83, 188, 194, 196, 215, 221
Alabama, xxix, 108
Alexander, Charles, 153
American Colonization Society, 242, 246n9, 265, 269n1
American Negro Academy, xxvi, 230, 234
Armstrong, Samuel C., 90
Astwood, H.C.C., 64
Atkinson, William Yates, 162
Attucks, Crispus, 149

Berkeley, George, 242, 261
Bismarck, Otto Eduard Leopold von, 275
Blackstone, William, 129
Blaine, James G., 37, 44, 52–61, 63, 66, 76, 77, 106, 107, 109, 222, 224
Blair, Henry W., 6, 226
Blair, Montgomery, 107
Blyden, Edward W., 230–31
Bonaparte, Napoleon, 116, 137, 138, 176, 265
Bowen, J.W.E., xxv, 248–49, 272
Brazza, Pierre Paul François Camille Savorgnan de, 261
Brooks, Preston, 78
Brown, John, xvi, xxv, 28, 45, 70n6, 78, 104, 136, 137, 139, 186, 187, 209–11, 223, 255
Brown, William Wells, 29
Brownsville, Texas, 196
Browne, Hugh M., xviii
Bruce, Blanche K., 56, 64, 81, 218
Bruce, John Edward, xviii, xxiv, xxvi
Bryce, James, 238

Burleigh, Harry, 253
Butler, Benjamin F., 68, 78, 95

Cable, George W., 126
Caesar, Julius, 38, 121, 137
Calhoun, John C. (grandson), 10, 12, 14n3
Calhoun, John C. (South Carolina and U.S. politician), 223, 228n12
Camp, Eugene M., xxi
Chandler, William E., 224
Chase, Salmon, 45
Chase, William Calvin, xviii
Civil rights, 46, 58, 75, 92–100, 115–17, 118–32, 150, 194, 217
Civil Rights Act, 1875, xix, xxxiii, 15–17, 18–23, 44, 52, 65, 79, 115, 122
Civil War, xix, 7, 19, 22, 28, 32, 34, 37, 45, 57, 58, 78, 93, 98, 99, 105, 108, 139, 149, 171, 185, 193, 204, 221, 223, 243, 264
Clark, Peter Humphries, 194
Clay, Henry, 33, 78, 222, 265
Cleveland, Grover, 54, 61–66, 80, 81, 166, 234
Clive, Robert Lord, 273, 279n8
Color line, 147, 148, 210, 212–14, 230–35
Committee of Twelve, 134, 185, 195
Conover, Simon Barclay, 39, 49
Convict Lease, 12–13, 80, 144, 155, 161, 226
Cook, George F. T., 64
Cook, John F., 64
Copiah County, Miss., 63, 66
Corrigan v. Buckley, 203
Cowper, William, 217
Cromwell, John Wesley, xvii, xxxvn14, 234, 235
Cromwell, Oliver, 31, 136, 139
Crum, William D., xviii
Crummell, Alexander, xvii, xxiv, xxvi, 9, 13n1, 234, 235
Cullen, Countee, 253
Culp, D. W., 234

Curry, Jabez Lamar Monroe, 166
Curtis, George William, 181, 183n4, 194

Dana, Charles A., xxi, xxiii, xliv, 238, 245n3
Dancy, John C., xviii
Danville, Va., xxii, 66, 76, 115
Darwin, Charles S., 128, 129
Darwinism, 128, 129
Democratic Party, xxii, 16–17, 19, 20, 24, 32, 33, 46, 54, 57–58, 60, 61–66, 67, 68, 76, 77, 78, 81, 82, 107, 143
Dickinson, Anna, 156
Disfranchisement, xxviii, 59, 61, 103–10, 142, 165–69, 188, 224
Douglas, Stephen, 78, 223
Douglass, Frederick, xvii, xxii, xxiv, xxvi, 27, 29, 42, 43, 56, 62, 64, 66, 74, 77, 78, 79, 81, 95, 113, 116, 192–94, 196–97, 209, 216, 218, 222, 255–56; marriage to Helen Pitts, 193
Douglass Jr., Frederick, xxv, 209–11
Downing, George Thomas, 79, 194
Dred Scott v. Sandford, 16, 17n2, 104, 121, 122, 162, 168–69, 203, 204, 222
Du Bois, W.E.B., xv, xxi, xxiv, xxvi, xxx, 98, 102n14, 189, 234, 235, 281
Dunn, Oscar, 44
Dupre, William H., 194

Education, xvi, xvii, xx, xxii, xxviii, 6–10, 48, 85–90, 92, 154, 171–78, 194, 234
El Mahdi, xxxi, 259–60
Ellenton, S.C., 21, 58
Emancipation Proclamation, 35, 74, 107, 120, 139
Evans, John Gary, 162
Fifer, Joseph W., 135
Fifteenth Amendment, xix, 41, 44, 46, 47, 53, 77, 80, 94, 96, 104–5, 106, 109, 110, 121, 122, 123, 149, 150, 168, 169, 221, 264
Florida, xvi, xviii, 4, 8, 9, 10, 39, 41, 46, 49, 63, 78, 161, 162, 175
Foraker, Joseph B., 59, 65
Forbes, George, 192, 197n2
Fortune, Timothy Thomas, xv–xxxiv; biography, xv–xxxiv; birth, xvi; and Booker T. Washington, xxiii–xxiv, xxviii, xxix–xxx, 192–93, 196–97; education of, xvii–xviii; parents, xvi

Fortune Jr., Emanuel (brother), x, xxiii, xxxi
Fortune Sr., Emanuel (father), xvi, xvii, xxxvn10, 71n19, 83n14, 163n10
Fourteenth Amendment, xix, 41, 44, 46, 47, 53, 77, 94, 96, 104–5, 106, 109, 110, 121, 122, 123, 149, 150, 169, 221, 264
Franklin, Benjamin, 273
Fulton, Robert, 273

Galloway, Charles B., 173
Garfield, James A., 76, 77, 80, 106, 110
Garnet, Henry Highland, 29, 116
Garrison, William Lloyd, 28, 36, 69n3, 77, 135, 139, 149, 156, 186, 187, 193, 221, 223
Garvey, Marcus, xv, xxxi–xxxii, 201, 202, 202n2
George, Henry, xxi, 3, 4
Georgia, 226
Gilliam, E. W., 4, 12
Goldsmith, Oliver, 154
Gracchus, Caius, 45
Gracchus, Tiberius, 45
Grady, Henry W., 107, 118, 126, 127, 131, 132, 156
Grant, Ulysses, 18, 21, 23n4, 35, 42, 46, 59, 76, 78, 139, 160, 223
Greeley, Horace, xvii, xxi, xliv, 35, 71n17, 156, 242
Greene, William Hallett, 63
Greener, Richard T., xvii, 20, 23n2, 56, 193
Gresham, Walter Q., 135

Hale, Edward Everett, 201
Hamburgh, S.C., 21, 58
Hamilton, Alexander, 103, 104
Hampton, Wade, 107
Hampton Institute, 85, 90, 171, 172, 173
Harlan, John Marshall, 122
Hastings, Warren, 273
Hayes, Roland, 253
Hayes, Rutherford B., 18, 21, 41, 42, 46, 76, 77, 79, 80, 94, 107, 115, 139
Helena, Ark., 203–4
Hendricks, Thomas A., 54, 107, 108, 110
Henry, Patrick, 136
Holman, William Steele, 264
Hopkins, Moses A., 61
Howard University, xvii, xxxiii, 50, 175
Hugo, Victor, 237

Ireland, 6, 12, 21, 26, 31, 36, 66, 93, 97, 125, 131, 142, 149, 202, 212, 213, 237
Irish. *See* Ireland
Irish National League, xxxii, 31

Jasper, John, 126
Jefferson, Thomas, 103, 104
Johnson, Andrew, 105, 108

Kealing, Hightower Theodore, 187
King, Samuel George, 68
Ku Klux Klan, xvi, 40, 122, 160, 223–25; Congressional hearings on, xvi, 38, 78, 160

Law, 15, 21, 44, 47, 52, 65, 79
Labor, xx, 3–5, 8, 10–13, 25–26, 28, 67, 98–99, 124, 144, 147, 150, 223, 226, 242–43, 269
Lamar, Lucius Quintus Cincinnatus, 107
Land ownership, xx, 3–5, 8, 9, 98
Langston, John Mercer, 56, 64, 72n37, 81, 193, 194, 218
Lawson, Jesse, xviii
Lee, Fitzhugh, 68
Lee, Robert E. 141, 160, 223
Leopold II (king of Belgium), 262
Liberia, 242, 266, 274
Lincoln, Abraham, xvii, 35–36, 37, 47n2, 78, 107, 134, 135, 139, 142, 223, 224, 255–56, 265
Livingston, David, 261
Logan, John A., 54, 55, 134, 142
Long, Jefferson Franklin, 44
Louis, William Frederick, 275
Louisiana, xxxix, 8, 41, 46, 78, 79, 108, 161, 165, 168, 169, 226, 242
Lovejoy, Elijah, 134, 135, 186, 187, 223
Lundy, Benjamin, 28, 69n2, 105, 125, 139, 186, 187, 221, 223
Luther, Martin, 137
Lynch, John A., 56, 81, 218
Lynching. *See* racial violence

Macaulay, Thomas Babington, 187, 191n10
Magna Charta, 106, 136
Mahone, William, 53, 60, 61, 65
Malthus, Thomas R., 129
Marx, Karl, xxi

Mayo, Amory D., 88
McKenna, Joseph, 169
McKinley, William, 169, 234
Meier, August, xv
Miller, Kelly, xxxiii
Milton, John, 37, 275
Minnesota, xxvii
Mississippi, 78, 165, 168
Mitchell Jr., John, xv–xvi, xxiii
Moltke, Graf von, 275
Morgan, John T., xxiv, 215–17, 219n22
Mott, Lucretia, 77

Napier, James Carroll, 187
National Negro Business League, xxiv, xxv, xxx, 184, 185, 187, 89, 195, 196
Negro Press Association, xxiv, 195
Negrowump, 74–84
Niagara Movement, 134, 180, 182, 188
North Carolina, 165

O'Ferrall, Charles T., 162

Palmer, John M., 135
Park, Mungo, 261
Parker, George W., xviii
Parnell, Charles, xxxii, 31, 70n11, 178n5
Patterson, J. Stahl, 128
Peterson, Jerome B., xxiii
Phelps, James, 13
Phillips, Wendell, 28, 32, 33, 69n4, 77, 106, 156, 182, 186, 187
Pitts, Helen, 193. *See also* Douglass, Frederick
Plessy v. Ferguson, xxviii
Politics, independence in, xix, xx, xxi, xxxii, 27–69, 74–82, 294
Price, Joseph C., xxvii, 192, 197n3
Prohibition Party, 143
Purvis, Charles B., 64
Purvis, Robert, 29, 194

Racial violence, xv, 142, 144, 150, 154, 158–62, 166, 224, 225, 226, 242
Railroad segregation. *See under* segregation
Reconstruction, xvi, xviii, xix, xxxiv, 31, 38, 39, 44, 46, 49, 95, 96, 105, 108
Remond, Charles Lenox, 29
Reparations, xxi, 123

Republican Party, xix–xx, xxi, xxii, xxiii, 15–18, 20–22, 24, 27, 30, 32, 33, 36–39, 41–47, 49–61, 62–68, 74, 76–82, 94, 106–8, 142–43, 159, 187, 224
Revels, Hiram R., 44
Robinson, George Dexter, 68
Rosecrans, W. S., 64

Sampson, Walter J., xviii
Scarbrough, William S., 240, 246n7
School segregation. *See under* segregation
Schurz, Carl, 105
Segregation, 93, 170n2, 197n1, 203–4, 204–5n1, 232–33; railroad, 16, 144, 226; school, 110, 130, 194, 226
Simmons, William, xviii
Slavery, xx, 7, 9, 22, 29, 33, 74, 98, 100, 104, 119, 147, 181, 214, 226, 231, 233, 240
Smith, Gerrit, 36, 77
Smith, John McCune, 29
Smith, Wilford, 108, 109
Smythe, John Henry, 64, 278
Socrates, 45
South Carolina, 10, 12, 19, 20–22, 34, 39, 41, 46, 78, 79, 107, 108, 161, 162, 168, 169, 215, 240, 242
Stanley, Henry M., 261, 262
Stearns, Marcellus Lovejoy, 39, 49
Stephens, Alexander H., 107
Stevens, Thaddeus, 95, 156
Steward, William H., 194–95
Stewart, T. McCants, xxxvin28
Still, William, 194
Straker, David Augustus, 187
Sudan (Soudan), 259–60
Suffrage, xx, xxviii, xxix, 12, 22, 26, 43, 47, 59, 103–11, 165–69, 222, 224
Sumner, Charles, 28, 32, 35, 37, 45, 69n5, 78, 95, 142, 156, 186, 187, 193
Sweet, Ossian, 203–4

Taney, Roger B., 16, 17n2, 104, 121, 122, 162, 168, 203, 204, 222
Tennessee, xxviii
Tennyson, Alfred Lord, 77
Tertullian (Quintus Septimius Florens Tertullianus), 152n27
Thirteenth Amendment, xix, 41, 44, 46, 47, 53, 77, 94, 96, 104, 106, 110, 121, 122, 123, 149, 150, 168, 169, 185, 221
Thompson, John Edward West, 64
Thornbrough, Emma Lou, xv
Tilden, Samuel J., 66
Toombs, Robert A., 156, 223
Tourgée, Albion W., 160, 163n6
Touissaint L'Ouverture, 45, 71
Trotter, James Monroe, 194
Trotter, William Monroe, 194
Truth, Sojourner, 77
Tucker, Joseph Louis, 9, 13n2
Turner, Henry McNeal, xxxi, 241, 246n8, 264, 266, 271
Turner, James Milton, 194
Turner, Nat, xxv, 28, 70n8, 116, 136, 137, 149, 209–11
Tuskegee Institute, 85, 90, 173
Tyler, Ralph Waldo, 187, 188

UNIA. *See* Universal Negro Improvement Association
Universal Negro Improvement Association (UNIA), xxx, xxxi, xxxii, 201, 202

Vesey, Denmark, 28, 70n7, 116
Virginia, 108

Waite, Morrison R., 21
Walters, Alexander, xxviii, 187, 188
Ward, Samuel Ringgold, 29
Waring, Everett J., 249
Washington, Booker T., xv, xx, xxiii, xxvi, 85, 92, 165–67, 172, 178n4, 183n6, 184, 187, 188, 189, 190n1, 192–93, 196–97, 197n3, 253; relationship with T. Thomas Fortune xxiii–xxiv, xxviii, xxix–xxxx, 192–93, 196–97
Webster, Daniel, 33, 34, 55, 78, 146, 222, 253
Wells, Ida B. *See* Wells-Barnett, Ida B.
Wells-Barnett, Ida B. (Ida B. Wells), xv; anti-lynching activities of, xxviii, 155, 157n3, 158–59, 162n1, 226, 229n22, 246n10
White, George H., xviii
Williams v. Mississippi, xxviii
Wise, John Sargent, 37, 52, 59, 61, 65, 68

New Perspectives on the History of the South

Edited by John David Smith

"In the Country of the Enemy": The Civil War Reports of a Massachusetts Corporal, edited by William C. Harris (1999)

The Wild East: A Biography of the Great Smoky Mountains, by Margaret L. Brown (2000; first paperback edition, 2001)

Crime, Sexual Violence, and Clemency: Florida's Pardon Board and Penal System in the Progressive Era, by Vivien M. L. Miller (2000)

The New South's New Frontier: A Social History of Economic Development in Southwestern North Carolina, by Stephen Wallace Taylor (2001)

Redefining the Color Line: Black Activism in Little Rock, Arkansas, 1940–1970, by John A. Kirk (2002)

The Southern Dream of a Caribbean Empire, 1854–1861, by Robert E. May (2002)

Forging a Common Bond: Labor and Environmental Activism during the BASF Lockout, by Timothy J. Minchin (2003)

Dixie's Daughters: The United Daughters of the Confederacy and the Preservation of Confederate Culture, by Karen L. Cox (2003)

The Other War of 1812: The Patriot War and the American Invasion of Spanish East Florida, by James G. Cusick (2003)

"Lives Full of Struggle and Triumph": Southern Women, Their Institutions and Their Communities, edited by Bruce L. Clayton and John A. Salmond (2003)

German-Speaking Officers in the United States Colored Troops, 1863–1867, by Martin W. Öfele (2004)

Southern Struggles: The Southern Labor Movement and the Civil Rights Struggle, by John A. Salmond (2004)

Radio and the Struggle for Civil Rights in the South, by Brian Ward (2004, first paperback edition, 2006)

Luther P. Jackson and a Life for Civil Rights, by Michael Dennis (2004)

Southern Ladies, New Women: Race, Region, and Clubwomen in South Carolina, 1890–1930, by Joan Marie Johnson (2004)

Fighting Against the Odds: A History of Southern Labor Since World War II, by Timothy J. Minchin (2005, first paperback edition, 2006)

"Don't Sleep With Stevens!": The J. P. Stevens Campaign and the Struggle to Organize the South, 1963–1980, by Timothy J. Minchin (2005)

"The Ticket to Freedom:" The NAACP and the Struggle for Black Political Integration, by Manfred Berg (2005, first paperback edition, 2007)

"War Governor of the South": North Carolina's Zeb Vance in the Confederacy, by Joe A. Mobley (2005)

Planters' Progress: Modernizing Confederate Georgia, by Chad Morgan (2005)

The Officers of the CSS Shenandoah, by Angus Curry (2006)

The Rosenwald Schools of the American South, by Mary S. Hoffschwelle (2006)
Honor in Command: The Civil War Memoir of Lt. Freeman Sparks Bowley, 30th United States Colored Infantry, edited by Keith P. Wilson (2006)
A Black Congressman in the Age of Jim Crow: South Carolina's George Washington Murray, by John F. Marszalek (2006)
The Spirit and the Shotgun: Armed Resistance and the Struggle for Civil Rights, by Simon Wendt (2007)
Making a New South: Race, Leadership, and Community after the Civil War, edited by Paul A. Cimbala and Barton C. Shaw (2007)
From Rights to Economics: The Ongoing Struggle for Black Equality in the U.S. South, by Timothy J. Minchin (2008)
Slavery on Trial: Race, Class, and Criminal Justice in Antebellum Richmond, Virginia, by James M. Campbell (2008)
Welfare and Charity in the Antebellum South, by Timothy James Lockley (2008)
T. Thomas Fortune, the Afro-American Agitator: A Collection of Writings, 1880–1928, by Shawn Leigh Alexander (2008)
Francis Butler Simkins: A Life, by James S. Humphreys (2008)
Counterfeit Gentlemen: Manhood and Humor in the Old South, John Mayfield (2009)
The Southern Mind under Union Rule: The Diary of James Rumley, Beaufort, North Carolina, 1862-1865, Edited by Judkin Browning (2009)
The Quarters and the Fields: Slave Families in the Non-Cotton South, by Damian Alan Pargas (2010)
The Door of Hope: Republican Presidents and the First Southern Strategy, 1877-1933, by Edward O. Frantz (forthcoming)

www.ingramcontent.com/pod-product-compliance
Lightning Source LLC
Chambersburg PA
CBHW020941230426

43666CB00005B/120